Europe Unfolding

Blackwell Classic Histories of Europe

This series comprises new editions of seminal histories of Europe. Written by the leading scholars of their generation, the books represent both major works of historical analysis and interpretation and clear, authoritative overviews of the major periods of European history. All the volumes have been revised for inclusion in the series and include updated material to aid further study. *Blackwell Classic Histories of Europe* provides a forum in which these key works can continue to be enjoyed by scholars, students and general readers alike.

Published

Europe Hierarchy and Revolt: 1320–1480
Second Edition
George Holmes

Renaissance Europe: 1480–1520
Second Edition
John Hale

Reformation Europe: 1517–1559
Second Edition
G. R. Elton

Europe Divided: 1559–1598
Second Edition
J. H. Elliott

Europe Unfolding: 1648–1688
Second Edition
John Stoye

Revolutionary Europe: 1783–1815
Second Edition
George Rudé

Europe Reshaped: 1848–1878
Second Edition
J. A. S. Grenville

Europe Transformed: 1878–1919
Second Edition
Norman Stone

Forthcoming

Europe in Crisis: 1598–1648
Second Edition
Geoffrey Parker

Europe: Privilege and Protest 1730–1798
Second Edition
Olwen Hufton

EUROPE UNFOLDING
1648–1688

Second Edition

John Stoye

BLACKWELL
Publishers

Copyright © John Stoye 1969, 2000

The right of John Stoye to be identified as author of this work has been asserted in accordance with the Copyright, Designs and Patents Act 1988.

First published by Fontana in 1969
Second edition published by Blackwell Publishers Ltd 2000

2 4 6 8 10 9 7 5 3 1

Blackwell Publishers Ltd
108 Cowley Road
Oxford OX4 1JF
UK

Blackwell Publishers Inc.
350 Main Street
Malden, Massachusetts 02148
USA

British Library Cataloguing in Publication Data

A CIP catalogue record for this book is available from the British Library.

Library of Congress Cataloging-in-Publication Data

Stoye, John, 1917-
    Europe unfolding, 1648–1688/John Stoye.—2nd ed.
       p. cm. — (Blackwell classic histories of Europe)
    Includes bibliographical references and index.
    ISBN 0–631–22270–7 (alk. paper)—ISBN 0–631–21387–2 (pbk. : alk. paper)
       1. Europe—History—1648–1715. I. Title. II. Series.

D273.S78 2000
940.2'52–dc21

                                                                                    00-031020

ISBN   0 631 22270 7
       0 631 21387 2 (pbk)

Typeset in 10.5 on 12pt Sabon
by Kolam Information Services Pvt. Ltd, Pondicherry, India
Printed in Great Britain by TJ International, Padstow, Cornwall

This book is printed on acid-free paper

Contents

Maps

Preface to the First Edition

'*The learned* Grotius *tells us* in p. 34 of his Epistles, *that the* Athenians *in their* High Court *forbad all Introductory* Prefaces *and* Addresses, *because they hated Affected Ornaments, and what was not* to purpose *in their Discourses. We are as willing to follow 'em as possible.*' So begins a book entitled 'The Young Students-Library', published in 1692. I too would follow their example after thanking the kind friends, relatives, colleagues and editors (at Oxford, Cambridge and London) who have helped me in the writing of these pages. Here is a fairly short study covering an enormous area and a large number of subjects, but I have deliberately tried not to impose a rigid structure on the material. My wish is rather to show the character of Europe revealing itself bit by bit during a period of forty years. This was a landscape in which millions had to grope for a living, with a great many men anxious to do their work well. I am left with an abiding sense of size, diversity and riches, set in a framework of great hardship. It is easy to say, but important, that the world is neither simple nor small.

JWS
May 1969

Preface to the Second Edition

Nor, I imagine, would the Athenians of the learned Grotius have cared much for the idea of a second preface. All the same, let me express my great thanks for the survival of this work through so many years, and for the happy chance to correct certain errors, erase a little here and there, and rewrite some passages especially in chapters 2, 8 and 10; while adding many modern titles to the bibliography at the end for Further Reading. In this I was fortunate enough to have had much good advice from Laurence Brockliss, Peter Noll, David Parratt, Andrew Robinson and Tim Watson. I remain also deeply grateful to Richard Ollard, once of Fontana-Collins, for piloting the original work through the press, and to Helen Rappaport and the staff of Blackwells for their labours with the revised version. One other word, dear Athenians: this book gives an account of a short period in the history of Europe. In describing it, I could be no more than a momentary spectator of the longer-term changes which so much engage historians nowadays.

JWS
March, 2000

A New Stability at the Centre

Setting the Scene

Shortly before 1648 Dutch ships encircled Australia for the first time. Russians had reached the Pacific coast of Siberia. Frenchmen were sailing the Great Lakes of North America. A splendid new map of the world, showing recent discoveries, was presented by an Amsterdam publisher to diplomats in the German town of Münster, just when they were on the point of ending the Thirty Years War. It seems therefore that Europe has pressed its initiative far enough, by 1648, to compel historians to relate seriously the history of one continent to that of all the others.

This they must do, but with a good deal of caution. The Spanish empire in America sent less bullion to Spain in the second half of the seventeenth century, and took fewer immigrants, than in the second half of the sixteenth. Emigration from one part of Europe to another mattered a great deal more. The Dutch and English East India Companies, though wealthy and expanding, contributed less to the economic activity of these two peoples than did their European trades. Consideration for the colonies of America slowly had greater influence on general European politics, but such powerful statesmen as Louis XIV and William III knew and cared little about them. The brightest intellects realised that fresh data on a highly developed civilisation like the Chinese, or on primitive communities, were significantly disruptive in the fields of religious and philosophical study; but they seem isolated figures in a society where a conservative clergy, Catholic, Protestant and Orthodox, still dominated the literate. The peoples of Europe were normally parochial in outlook and their major interests were confined to Europe, in spite of brave earlier efforts at reconnaissance into a wider world. They had fully enough to think about.

During the single year of 1648 there was news of serious riots in Moscow. Class war broke out in the Ukraine between Polish lords and Ukrainian subjects. Mutinous Janissaries slaughtered the sultan in Istanbul. Uproar in Paris forced what looked like profound constitutional changes from the queen-regent and Cardinal Mazarin, while a few months later Charles I of England was condemned by a revolutionary tribunal and executed. On the other hand, Spanish troops and ships crushed insurrection at Naples. In the elective monarchy of Poland childless Wladislaw IV had died in May 1648, but the Diet appeared to favour the hereditary principle by choosing his brother John Casimir as the new king in November. All these events disclosed the multiple tensions in Europe. Some people came to believe in a universal spirit of insubordination, resulting from an infection which spread from place to place. Yet whatever they thought about this, and whatever historians may decide were the underlying elements of such unrest at so many points, probably the most important news in 1648 was of three great peace treaties. Taken together, these ended the 'eighty years war' between the Dutch and the king of Spain, the 'thirty years war' of Germany and Bohemia, and the war of the emperor with the allied kings of Sweden and France, and the friends of both parties. The Franco-Spanish struggle continued but the Westphalian settlement, the work of a whole congress of diplomats at Münster and Osnabrück, altered the general framework in Europe. It gave to the central regions of the continent a new stability which ultimately counted for more than the dangerous tremors elsewhere. This was one reason why what followed proved to be a half-century of rivalry between states, rather than of social or intellectual upheaval. In a good many respects, we might say, it was a period of history without change.

Here, then, centrally placed, the Empire would be the great shock absorber inside Europe. Its populations lacked the coordinated strength to press either east or west, until after 1683 they found momentum enough to drive into Ottoman Hungary. They lacked the thrust, and therefore the opportunity, to compete with western traders and governments, Dutch, English and French, in the struggle for commercial empire overseas. And they failed to generate the intellectual fever which had earlier set moving the Protestant reformation, not only in Germany but also farther afield. After 1648 the chances of sweeping change looked much stronger in eastern Europe: opposing forces and creeds, Islamic and Orthodox as well as Protestant and Catholic, would be pushing forward or pushed back, over very wide areas. So, if we consider the stable centre first, it seems appropriate to consider the eastern peoples next, before turning to that oceanic edge of Europe which western writers are perhaps too quick to see as the focus of the world worth knowing. In place of a historical view which lays most emphasis on lands washed by the Atlantic and western Mediterranean – with their extension in settlements on south and then north America – the hub of Europe is really found in the old Holy Roman empire, with spokes radiating out to the Baltic and the Carpathians, to Istanbul and Kiev, as well as to Paris, London and Madrid.

There is also another choice to be made, between the forces of change and forces resisting it. In the thought or habits of the intelligent and prosperous few, many novelties certainly appear in the west between 1650 and 1700. Imagine the scene in their houses: men have taken to wearing enormous wigs on their heads while they sit at their 'bureau' (of a new design) to write at. They have a clock in the room which tells the time far more accurately than the older timepieces. They have discarded the old chests which opened at the top, in favour of chests-of-drawers. They have more gate-legged and folding tables, more caned or upholstered chairs, more lacquered cabinets brought from the Far East which their own craftsmen imitate with growing skill. They drink coffee and chocolate and tea, and consume ever more sugar and tobacco. Sitting at their tables or bureaux, these bewigged gentlemen wrote verse in rhymed couplets to the neglect of other forms of poetry, and also a much simpler and tidier prose than their fathers. As to the content of what they wrote, they were increasingly less convinced that the ancient world produced better artists and scientists than the 'moderns', and with all deference to revealed Christianity were more aware of the mathematical element in the physical universe. Yet always they formed a tiny minority by comparison with the peasants, herdsmen, foresters, village craftsmen and village clergy, small townsmen and menial servants who had to make a living in that enormous landscape set between the Atlantic and the Urals. This majority sensed vividly enough good and bad luck, but not change in the life of one generation by contrast with another generation which came immediately before or afterwards. Theirs was not a universe of theological or mathematical principles but simply an existence dominated by varying harvests and the erratic though perpetual visitation of epidemics. In the bad years their largely unaltered methods of husbandry and their compound of old cures and spells were equally useless. Of human agencies, they were most keenly aware of the local landlord and the more distant lord who was king or prince, who together required labour services and rents and taxes, and – with their opponents – led the troops which entered or providentially by passed a particular tract of country. Kings and lords, also, appointed and replaced the clergy, and the clergy looked after marriages and burials, and gave the parish a simple account of First and Last Things. Under such conditions it is possible to get closer to the population as a whole if we regard the political surface tremors over a large area, rather than look too narrowly at the minority which may have been pioneering ideas, arts or inventions for the following generation. In this period it is more important to build up a relatively static view of the scene while the years pass by than to search for the origins of future change.

The Holy Roman Empire in 1648

The signature of the Westphalian treaties was only a stage in the process of pacifying the Empire. Fighting ended at once east of the Rhine, but Spain and Lorraine had been kept out of the final bargaining at Münster so that west of the river Spanish, French and the duke of Lorraine's forces continued in action. Above all, the duke's tattered mercenaries raided far and wide for supplies. They helped to reduce Franche Comté and parts of Champagne to ashes during the next few years, at the same time causing alarm on the other side of the Rhine. They were responsible for the first efforts made after 1648 by nervous princes to group together for mutual defence; alliances of this type remained a commonplace of German politics after 1648, foreshadowing the famous League of the Rhine in 1658 and many later agreements. The difficulty was always to fix the cash payments and number of troops due from the member states. Alliances were therefore often based on the old Imperial 'Circles', groups of states accustomed to a periodic assembly of princes or envoys, and to the use of Imperial tax schedules. This archaic framework made business curiously intricate, with politicians conferring constantly in many modest courts or towns, and their agenda multiplying all the time in an atmosphere thick with protocol. It led to endless and futile shadow-boxing as well as to serious friction. German historians of the nineteenth century spluttered with patriotic indignation as they wound through these mazes. Their successors tend to analyse with greater sympathy the attempt at a working federation of sovereign states.

In the treaties of 1648 a number of constitutional questions were deliberately left for the next meeting of the Imperial Diet to settle. Such omissions point to the underlying strength of Emperor Ferdinand III's position in spite of his defeats during the war. France and the more radical German princes had wanted a clause which debarred an emperor from securing the election of a successor during his own lifetime: in the past, they knew, the Habsburg family had often kept the Imperial crown because the reigning emperor himself arranged and supervised the election of a 'king of the Romans' (who automatically succeeded as emperor in due course). If the emperor died before his succession was settled, the Habsburg candidates would be much less well placed to follow him. The radicals saw here a chance of snapping the bond between the Habsburgs and the

Empire, a crucial issue in European politics between 1500 and 1800. They linked with it the 'Capitulations', a constitutional charter which every new emperor had to sign. They wanted to insert in the treaties a revised charter, designed to prune Imperial authority still further. Ferdinand got his way; these matters were left over for the Diet. Some 'princes' also tried at Münster to challenge the varied prerogatives of the 'electors'. Why should they alone elect the king of the Romans or emperor? Why should their standing committee of envoys, at Regensburg, settle business which concerned other rulers of the Empire? In posing such awkward questions the reforming party convinced the electors of the interest which they shared with the emperor himself. That alliance was indeed a fundamental, in spite of lesser points of disagreement. It explains why the structure of the Empire was altered so little in 1648, and altered so slowly afterwards. One significant novelty had been accepted at Westphalia: the creation of a new seat in the College of Electors for Karl Ludwig, eldest surviving son of the Elector Palatine who lost the battle of the White Hill in 1620. He returned from exile in England, thanks to Dutch and Swedish pressure, in order to govern from the ruined castle of Heidelberg his inheritance along the Rhine and Neckar; but his father's victorious opponent, Maximilian of Bavaria, kept the Upper Palatinate (adjoining Bohemia) and the senior electoral title which had belonged to Karl Ludwig's ancestors. The new creation, and the seniority of electors, were both topics intensely debated at the time.

In 1652 Ferdinand summoned the Diet. When he opened it in June 1653, in that historic city hall of Regensburg which had already seen so many Diets come and go, he confronted an assembly of the greatest antiquity. He was flanked by seven electors or their deputies: the three Protestant rulers of Saxony, Brandenburg, the Palatinate, and the four Catholics of Bavaria, Mainz, Cologne and Trier. At the lower end of the hall, facing Ferdinand, were representatives from the Imperial Cities. A clause in the Westphalian treaties had vaguely promised them more power, the right to a vote which would have to be taken notice of before the other Colleges presented a resolution of the Diet to the emperor, but this was not yet confirmed. Between the electors and the humble burgher deputies sat the princes. About seventy were present, much the largest and most varied element in the whole Diet. Like the Electors' College, the College of Princes had both lay and ecclesiastical members. It contained powerful rulers such as the queen of Sweden and the rulers of the Brunswick duchies, together with the totally insignificant spokesmen for miscellaneous groups of Imperial Counts. A new element was formed by princes recently awarded their titles by the emperor. They were nearly all Austrians, and some possessed no territorial dignity in the Empire.

Quarrelling on the point was certain, once the Diet got down to business. A number of politicians in Regensburg were determined not to allow majorities to bind minorities, so that Ferdinand's ability to create new votes in this way looked highly controversial.

The Estates of the Empire, then, were intact. In consequence the old divisions of rank were maintained in German society. Lords and their ladies came from all parts of the country to the Diet, and the galas they attended gave many a chance to insist on their status. Problems of precedence in the privileged orders of society, like religion, were master passions of the age. Precedence was the gauge of value and reputation.

Political manoeuvring soon showed the strength of the conservatives. The Diet's opening had been delayed, partly because Ferdinand invited the electors to meet him in Prague beforehand in order to commit them to choose his elder son, also Ferdinand, as king of the Romans. France, much weaker than in 1648, was powerless to intervene; the four Catholic electors were friendly. Saxony, as ever, remained loyal to the Habsburgs. The Elector Palatine was satisfied by a flattering welcome after the dusty years of exile. Above all, Ferdinand won over Frederick William of Brandenburg by supporting him against Sweden. He declined to recognise formally the queen of Sweden's recent title to her new possessions in the Empire, or to admit her envoys to the forthcoming Diet, until the Swedish government agreed to withdraw from areas in Pomerania claimed by Brandenburg. Christina's ministers ultimately gave way, and the electors promised to choose Ferdinand IV as king of the Romans. The election took place in Augsburg, the coronation in Regensburg, and only then the Habsburg officials allowed the Diet to begin. Those reformers who had wanted to delay the choice of the next emperor until after Ferdinand III's death, and to redraft the capitulations before electing him, were defeated.

The course of the Diet was also to favour those who wanted no change. The Westphalian treaties had stipulated that there should be legal and judicial reforms. The Diet made proposals designed to improve the judicial work of the Imperial tribunals; but they were never carried out. The justifiable hope of the Imperial Cities that they would be given an effective vote in the Diet's proceedings was soon crushed. Those princes who wanted to attack the privileges and pre-eminence of the electors were also disappointed after much debate. On the question of taxation it was the turn of the Habsburg government to be repulsed by the weight of opposition. This refused to concede that a majority vote for the levy of Imperial taxes could bind the minority which opposed it.

The treaties of 1648 had decided that a majority in the Diet – or in the College of Electors – could not bind a minority in matters of religion. They asserted in plain terms the sovereign rights of all German rulers. And the Diet of 1653 now strangled the slender chance of creating an efficient tax system for the Empire as a whole. The constitution therefore barred the proper exercise of a sovereign authority either by the emperor or by the Diet itself. On the other hand, the rulers great and small had finally won their freedom. They were to venerate the Holy Roman empire of the German nation because this made an Imperial autocracy unlikely; and autocracy was the nightmare which had loomed so large in their thoughts since Emperor Ferdinand II's victories in the 1620s and 1630s. It still swayed their political judgment for thirty years after 1648. But political theorists who exposed the absurdity of the Empire's constitution, and the many pamphleteers who lamented German military impotence, wasted their breath. Certainly, the risks of foreign intervention became greater because the Empire lacked a central government except on paper, but this was the worthwhile price of liberty. There is a profound historical issue here. The destruction of liberties within the German states, as princes subdued local assemblies of privileged orders, was indeed a victory for that general drift towards absolutism which has often been taken as the theme *par excellence* of the century. But in some respects this movement was very restricted. It was counterbalanced by the preservation of provincial or princely or municipal liberties within federal constitutions in an immense area of central Europe, which includes the Empire, the Swiss Cantons, the United Provinces and Poland.

Ferdinand III's successful stroke in pushing through the coronation of his son Ferdinand was soon undone. Ferdinand IV died in December 1654. At that date the Habsburg government did not dare to propose the election of the emperor's younger son, Leopold. Circumstances were now much less favourable.

Zealots and Statesmen

The settlement of 1555 had broken with the Empire's medieval past by conferring on Lutheran states a lawful authority formerly enjoyed by Catholic rulers alone; but, by the so-called 'ecclesiastical reservation', it did not allow them to continue annexing church lands. According to the Protestants, Catholic rulers were likewise debarred from harassing Estates in their dominions which had already turned to Lutheranism; this was a Protestant view of the so-called 'Ferdinandian declaration', an undertaking given by Emperor Ferdinand I. Other creeds, whether Calvinist or sectarian, secured no legal recognition whatever. But in the course of a century two great electoral families, of Brandenburg and the Palatinate, and some other princes, embraced the teaching of Calvin. The limitations imposed on rulers in 1555 to act as they wished, in secularising church lands or in disciplining Estates who failed to conform with their own religious practice, had all been torn to shreds. Between 1620 and 1640, Catholics and Protestants were each presented at one moment or another with an intoxicating prospect of future gains, gains then snatched from their grasp by the misfortunes of war. After 1640 only the small but active group of zealots on both sides failed to see that a new compromise was needed for the sake of peace. The chance of reaching an agreement dawned when the French and Swedish governments, having won at Münster and Osnabrück vital concessions of territory in the Empire, declined to listen to the zealots; the papal nuncio in Münster (later to become Pope Alexander VII) was affronted by Cardinal Mazarin's attitude, and Protestant exiles from Bohemia were no less bitter about the callous Swedes. But most important of all, the court of Vienna had by then chosen a realistic line of policy which rejected the more militant Catholic demands for Germany.

In 1648 the Habsburg ministers insisted, and the Protestants agreed, that Ferdinand III's authority should remain intact in the hereditary Habsburg lands. No concessions protecting the Protestant in Germany were to limit Ferdinand III's right to impose Catholic uniformity in Bohemia, Moravia and the Austrian duchies. On the other hand, he sacrificed Catholic interests by allowing Protestant states – Sweden, Brandenburg, Mecklenburg and the dukes of Brunswick – 'satisfaction' in north Germany. He assented to the secularisation of many bishoprics and other foundations for this purpose, giving up for good the principle of 'ecclesiastical reservation'. The practical result of these mutual concessions was to safeguard a Habsburg and Catholic sphere of predominance in central Europe, but to give Protestantism absolute security in a wide belt of territory stretching inland from the Baltic and North Sea casts. The one was in any case buttressed by Catholic Bavaria, the other by Saxony, always the citadel of orthodox Lutheranism. After a tremendous amount of bargaining – influenced, of course, by the battles and sieges still in progress – the parties reached a further agreement. It was of cardinal importance. They declared that the conditions existing on 1 January 1624 should be the criterion for adjudicating all local disputes between the confessions over property, the use of church buildings, the degree of tolerance extended to minorities and so on. In places where dissenters could not claim that they enjoyed any legal rights in 1624 the ruler was still entitled to enforce public conformity; but the treaty required him to offer either a limited toleration or, if he preferred to expel dissenters, to give them reasonable time to dispose of lands and goods.

The effect of this choice of 1624 as standard was marked in several areas. For example, Lutheranism revived in Württemberg under the restored authority of Duke Eberhart III. The secularising here of church lands, lost by the Catholics during the Reformation but won back again after 1627 and in 1648 lost for ever, was a landmark in south German history. The choice of 1624, and not of 1618 or 1630, also shows that this new religious agreement was a compromise, struck willy-nilly by the protagonists after a painful assessment of each other's strength and willingness to risk a total breakdown in the haggle for peace. Statesmen had at last overpowered the clerical idealists, and their calculations devised a settlement sound enough to resist the most dangerous threats to it after 1648. The Catholic church later brought off some striking *coups* by winning over individual rulers such as Duke John Frederick of Hanover and even Elector Augustus I of Saxony; but the Westphalian treaties deprived them of any right to enforce a new creed on their subjects. Similarly, the Lutherans had tried to get the negotiators to turn down the Calvinist rulers' demand that their confession should be placed on an equal footing with Catholicism and Lutheranism. They failed, but many cases occurred in the next few decades of Calvinist worshippers harassed by Lutheran clergy. Yet this friction never caused a major dispute. There were so many towns (above all, the Imperial Cities) and countrysides where the opposing denominations coexisted, so many instances of Estates and their rulers differing confessionally, while the distance was often so short which a man had to travel to reach a community professing the faith of his choice, that conditions inside the Empire were at least in this respect more civilised than they had been during the war.

It was, of course, an authoritarian solution as well as a compromise. After 1648 a large number of 'church ordinances' were issued or reissued all over Germany. These show that in Lutheran, Calvinist and Catholic states alike lay officials assisted the clergy in enforcing attendance at services and the punctual taking of communion. State and church in close alliance dealt everywhere with the backsliding of those who belonged to the state–church; the clergy preached obedience to the government, and were themselves protected from popular criticism. Instead, they wrangled with each other, unyielding in acrimony.

The protest of Pope Innocent X against the treaties of Westphalia in his open letter *De Zelo*, drafted at the end of 1648 but published in 1651, betrayed indignation and sorrow. All the same, the structure of the Catholic church continued to fit snugly into a conservatively ordered German society after the war. Episcopal sees were still given, only too often, to Habsburg and Wittelsbach princes as well as to the best noble families of the Rhineland. A large number of richly

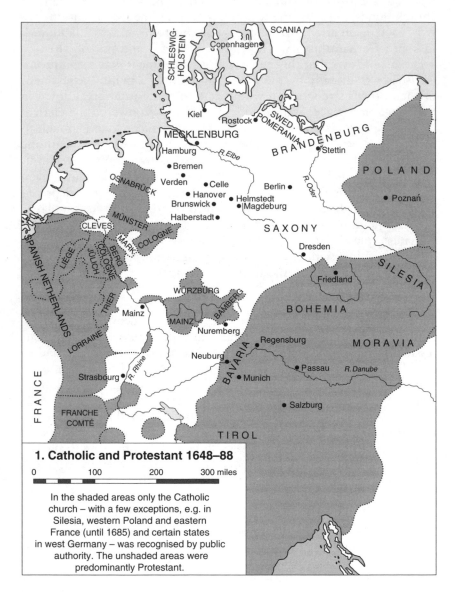

1. Catholic and Protestant 1648–88

0   100   200   300 miles

In the shaded areas only the Catholic
church – with a few exceptions, e.g. in
Silesia, western Poland and eastern
France (until 1685) and certain states
in west Germany – was recognised by public
authority. The unshaded areas were
predominantly Protestant.

Map 1

endowed cathedral chapters remained intact, and in these a great many stalls were always assigned to men of birth, who had to give proof of their untainted descent; and the chapters elected the bishops. Protestant gentry in the north took a similar interest in the few old foundations where the state left an endowment intact, but they were much less well placed than their Catholic contemporaries whose families tapped the revenues of cathedrals, monasteries and nunneries in Cologne, Liège, Strasbourg, Mainz, Würzburg, Bamberg, Eichstätt and elsewhere. At an infinitely humbler level, large numbers of poor vicars-choral and altar-servants laboured in these Catholic churches over which the noble chapters presided; they corresponded to the unprivileged, and they came from unprivileged households, in the world outside. A body of energetic and educated priests held their own between these groupings, and some of them entered the chapters. Lutheran society was rather differently constituted. If our historical atlases show a multitude of lines vainly attempting to demarcate the frontiers of seventeeth-century German principalities, a more important cultural frontier separated the Catholics of the Empire from Lutherans and Calvinists. In Protestant society the clergy were predominantly the sons of clergy, reinforced by the sons of burghers, while nobles played a much smaller part in church affairs. It was particularly the families of respectable Lutheran townsmen which produced cadets who commonly chose beetween state service and the ministry; the prestige of the latter was often highly regarded. In all the Protestant churches of northern Europe, in southwest Germany and Protestant Switzerland, clans or dynasties of clergy and the close alliance of pastors with townsmen were distinctive features of contemporary society, whereas in the Catholic lands noblemen tended to dominate the hierarchy.

Lutheran preachers and university professors still held a central position in the intellectual controversies of Europe. Profoundly convinced that they were the repository of the true faith, for which they thanked their founder Martin Luther, they feared to betray the Divine trust if they faltered in their duty of opposing either Roman or Calvinist error. From one point of view they may strike us as stony conservatives, intolerant of change. They made no fresh converts in Europe, did not care for missionary enterprise overseas (until the very end of the century), and apparently made few concessions to the ethos of commercial enterprise, although Lutheran Hamburg was one of the most vigorous trading centres of the entire continent. From another, they continued tirelessly to resist mistaken novelties by writing, preaching and teaching. Their researches into Reformation history were solid. Their outpouring of religious poetry, and the development of Lutheran church services thanks to new advances in organ building and organ playing, enshrined incomparable values for civilised mankind. From their congregations would come Pufendorf and Leibniz, and later Bach and Handel. Moreover, their own controversies revealed a certain vigour. At one extreme George Calixtus of the university of Helmstedt (near Brunswick) had argued in favour of 'syncretism' down to his death in 1656. He distinguished between circumstantials and fundamentals in religion, and his followers continued to hold that the opposing Christian creeds stood on common ground. They supported the movement for a union of the churches which an impressive handful of men, like John Durie the Scotsman, Rojas y Spinola the Catholic of Spanish descent from Gelderland, and Leibniz, believed to be the one possible solvent of Europe's heartbreaking confessional discord. But stalwarts at the universities of Wittenberg and Jena bitterly resisted such surrenders to error, taking their stand on the old Lutheran formularies. At Rostock University an outspoken preacher, Theodore Grossgebauer, published some fascinating sermons and pamphlets in the 1650s which echo that concern for social problems felt by the English sectaries of his day. His was an approach to radical principles which outraged the orthodox. If there were no major impulses stirring in the world of Lutheranism – before the new devotional movement of Pietism emerged around 1680 – it was still very much alive.

The Economy of Central Europe

Neither in 1648 nor in 1653 did the assembled politicians deal with economic problems. Older Imperial laws on currency, guilds and tolls remained unaltered. All the economic disadvantages of political fragmentation were quietly accepted. It is not easy to judge how important this failure was under seventeenth century conditions. The United Provinces flourished, in spite of municipal and provincial fiscal barriers of every kind. The French monarchy, for all its authority, was never able to get rid of these internal obstacles to the movement of goods; Colbert kept and used the guilds, without ridding them of their defects. Certainly, no one in 1653 had the knowledge or vision to argue that future prosperity in the Empire, like future peace, depended on measures agreed in common. Some German thinkers of the next generation began to consider the idea, but what a modern writer calls 'Imperial mercantilism' never grew proper roots. Freer trade within larger areas might have helped, but the real problems of the time were different. No happy accident, like the discovery of new mines in central Europe two centuries earlier, brought easy riches and spare capital to the south German cities. There was little chance of sharing with the western states more than a small part of the profits of overseas trade. The inland areas, often damaged and depopulated, had to generate fresh wealth unaided. Reconstruction was slow, piece-meal, and depended on varied local conditions, individual effort and old ideas; no large-scale bureaucracy wielded the power to accelerate or disturb the process by experimenting with novel remedies.

During the war years northwest Germany had escaped serious losses because the prosperous Dutch offered a market for surplus goods and labour. Seasonal employment in the United Provinces allowed many Germans to return home to their families with money saved. Hamburg, Bremen to a lesser extent, and even Emden, continued to supply the hinterland with overseas goods. In Cologne and Frankfurt experience also showed that the warring armies preferred business to continue, in order to provide them with supplies of corn, cattle, horses and armaments. Dealers were certainly squeezed by a system of licences, imposed at strategic points on the trade routes, but the economy of the Lower Rhineland was fairly buoyant. Unfortunately, when the fighting ended the general position of the Imperial Cities did not improve, and may have pos-itively declined. The territorial princes, anxious for revenue, were less ready than before to agree to the burghers' demands that trade should be 'free'. Instead, they never hesitated to restrict the movement of commodities by raising the transit tolls. It was after 1648 that the multiplication of these charges really began to choke the commerce of Germany's river systems. Towns on the Rhine and Oder suffered most, but the Swedes – from their base in the former archiepiscopal lands of Bremen – and the duke of Oldenburg combined to strangle the trade of Bremen itself from their points of vantage on the lower Weser. Ham-burg was confronted by jealous Brunswick interest upstream on the Elbe, and by the king of Denmark downstream; but the city's magni-ficent fortifications, very large population (which rose steadily during the war and for twenty years afterwards) and outstandingly vigorous conduct of trade, helped to safeguard it against these powerful enem-ies for the time being. All the same, there is a striking contrast between the ascendancy of Dutch cities in the Dutch provinces and this failure of the greater German cities to do more than maintain themselves within the Empire.

The main impact of the war was felt farther south and east. Popula-tion declined by a half in the Rhenish Palatinate and the lowland parts of Württemberg, in western Brandenburg, Mecklenburg and Pomer-ania. Losses were hardly less severe in western Saxony, Alsace, and in scattered areas of Franconia and Thuringia. A broad band of territory stretching right across the Empire from southwest to northeast was the major casualty. Deserted villages or houses, and derelict farmland, were the visible consequences of a period during which mortality had gone up so sharply because country folk fled for safety to the walled towns, where fearful overcrowding caused fearful epidemics.

After 1648, in certain cases before it, reconstruction slowly began. Karl Ludwig in the Palatinate set about refounding the city of Mannheim, and assiduously encouraged immigration by promising tolerance in religion, offering tax-free years to the settler, and getting new houses built. In Württemberg and Baden the problem of universal indebtedness was tackled by publicly authorising the repudiation of certain types of old debt. Brandenburg officials were soon to attempt detailed surveys in order to discover where resettlement was most urgently needed. But the real interest of these post-war years lies less in state policies than in a spontaneous population movement. Historians now draw a vivid picture of emigration from the poorer Alpine countrysides of Upper Austria, Styria and Switzerland, due as much to the agrarian misery as to religious intolerance, into under-populated places in south, central and west Germany. For example, peasant families from near Linz were making their way up the Danube valley to Regensburg. From this centre numbers of them have been identified going on to the much devastated and depopulated area west of Nuremberg. And not only did they come to rest in territory ruled by Protestant princes like the margrave of Ansbach. In this curiously fragmented countryside the city of Nuremberg possessed properties within the dominion of the sternly Catholic duke of Pfalz-Neuburg. His officials were embarrassed to find Austrian Protestants settled and settling in his duchy during the 1650s. Somewhat hesitatingly, they decided to let them stay. These Austrians also found employment on the lands of Catholic ecclesiastical foundations. The majority of Swiss emigrants went to Alsace and the Palatinate. Czechs and Germans from Bohemia continued to cross the frontier into neighbouring Saxony; in most cases, like the Protestant inhabitants of Wallenstein's former principality of Friedland in north Bohemia, they simply moved over the hills to live in a quiet country not far from their old homes. A fair number of Holsteiners fanned southwards, although more of them preferred to try their luck in the parts round Hamburg than in Mecklenburg and Brandenburg. A few Mennonites from Holland ventured up the Rhine. To all this must be added an internal movement which is more difficult to trace. Volumes of repressive legislation testify that many people, especially young and unattached persons, shifted restlessly from one landlord to another, as well as from region to region. Dismissed soldiers wanted a livelihood.

Governments were more effective in Lower Saxony and Westphalia than elsewhere. They ordered local officials to insist that deserted peasant holdings which had been taken over by privileged landlords, who were harder to tax, should be restored to the peasants. They set about enlarging other holdings to their original extent: in such cases the peasant had been compelled in bad times to dispose of parcels of land to meet debts or to pay taxes. They wanted to give that section of the community which paid the principal direct tax to the ruler sufficient resources to do so, and greater security. The old land law of this region favoured the tenant, the fighting had done less damage and caused fewer losses in manpower than farther south or east, but some good rulers could claim credit for what the jargon of their time (as well as ours) called the 'reintegration' of a substantial peasantry between the rivers Weser and Elbe.

Eastwards economic conditions varied, but almost everywhere the political influence of landlords was greater than in west Germany. During the war labour in Saxony had been scarce so that wage rates were high. A run of good harvests immediately afterwards brought down food prices to such an extent that the landlords suffered. Their interest was to persuade Elector John George I and his government to bring in legislation binding the peasant and his family firmly to hereditary holdings. They wanted wage rates for landless men fixed at the lowest possible level. Their tenants and indeed all the poorer classes desired to remain free, either to bargain for better pay or to emigrate to the towns; and the towns welcomed this additional labour. Social bitterness in the countryside, and wrangling between nobility and municipalities, were both intense. In 1651 the elector published an important Labour Ordinance. It entitled lords to pre-empt the service of their peasant, and of his sons and daughters, and also fixed wages at very low rates. Under John George II, who succeeded his father in 1656 and later described himself as 'the Nobleman's Friend', a new decree in 1661 confirmed the victory of the landlords. They fastened on the unprivileged an economic sub-jection which lasted until the nineteenth century. Wittenberg Univer-sity protested in vain at this denial of man's natural liberty. On the other hand, the population of Saxony recovered its war losses, many derelict lands bloomed again, Leipzig as a trading centre seems to have taken business from both Nuremberg and Frankfurt-on-the-Oder between 1650 and 1700, while at least in some of the smaller Saxon principalities the administration was of high quality.

The labour laws of the John Georges were echoed throughout central and Baltic Europe. Frederick William of Brandenburg spoke the same language in his general ordinances of 1644, 1645 and 1651. At the slightest sign that peasants were seeking to organise, whether to defend themselves against Swedish troops or their own lords – as in the district of Prignitz in 1645, 1646, 1648, 1650 and 1656 – he repulsed them brusquely. Already in 1645 the Estates in Mecklenburg and Pomerania had issued similar ordinances, which were repeated by the Swedish government for its half of Pomerania at a later date. All these laws – the most austere, but among the most important memorials of the society which enacted them – are characteristic of a political community in which the dual control of ruler and privileged Estates holds down the rural masses in subjection, while spasmodic-ally peasants singly or in groups evade and defy the law. In every case they forbade workers to remove from their domicile without the consent of their lords, and gave the lords a prior claim on the labour of their subjects' children. This second restriction cut deeply into the notion of personal freedom, and always tended to make subjection hereditary. It was increasingly applied to the 'Bauern', the large class which had earlier preserved a proprietary right in their holdings although they owed rents and services to a landlord. The 'Bauern' now came closer in status to the smaller class of real subjects or serfs; and they had less and less in common with the still smaller minority of really free peasant proprietors. There were also many cases in which the indebtedness of tenants to lords led, in one respect or another, to a decline in status.

Ordered society came much closer to collapse in the north-east than in Saxony. A symptom was the fall in population beyond the Elbe, commonly mounting to a loss of 50 per cent by comparison with the pre-war years. The Altmark of Brandenburg lies just west of the Elbe. The decline in this district increased progressively from west to east, rising from 15 to 20 per cent to nearly 60 per cent in the stretch nearest the river. The most cautious figures for many other parts of Brandenburg, Mecklenburg and Pomerania are as bad or worse. Such losses were naturally reflected in empty peasant hold-ings, lower revenues for the lords and lower taxes for the ruler. Indebtedness at all levels of society was universal, although indi-vidual officers and officials had funds to spare. 'The peasant is dead with all his family, the house is in ruins, the fields are waste,' were the eternally repeated phrases in inventories of the time; and the fact that there had been little fighting in this part of the country since 1640 makes population figures for the years 1648–52 the more depressing. It was an emptier landscape than in 1600, starved of every kind of asset but above all of manpower.

This overriding factor explains the labour laws: workers were so precious as rent-and tax-payers, as field- or house-servants, that they and their children had to be tied to a domicile as firmly as possible. It was not in the least a matter of ejecting peasants from their lands in order to enlarge the domain farms, a development common enough in both earlier and later periods. It was the no less brutal process of binding them fast to lordships. A landowner, trying to reconstruct his hard-hit property, recognised that a settled peasantry – equipped, if at all possible, with its own ploughing teams and employees – remained a precious element in the economy on which he himself depended for a revenue. He wanted peasants, and the signs are that after 1648 he restored peasant holdings if he could. On certain manors in both east and west Mecklenburg the number of such holdings crept gradually back to the number existing in 1600 or 1630. In others, probably a majority, it is clear that the total area farmed in 1700 was larger than in 1660, not so large as in 1630, and that the lord's share of the diminished total had increased. Any advance was bound to be slow. The small neighbouring towns required little surplus agricultural produce. Less could be exported. The indebtedness was pervasive, and Swedish demands for compensation in 1648–50 carried away a good deal of what spare capital there was. An impoverished gentry dealt with impoverished countrymen. Vacant holdings were therefore often loosely attached to home farms, and the poor either took over smaller plots of ground than had been worked by a more prosperous peasantry in the past, or became landless labourers solely employed by the lord. It was the impoverishment which first led to a decline in the peasant's status rather than the other way round. But certainly legislation endorsed the decline. It treated benevolently the lords' claim on land and labour, and harshly the former rights attached to their peasants' tenure. It built up a legal framework in which a scarcity of labour did not help the labourer.

All this affected princes with sovereign titles no less than private lords who enjoyed rights of jurisdiction. In essence both shared authority, and shared territory, in which most of the labouring population were subjects of one or the other. But for everyone, rich and poor, the long years of war had meant 'extraordinary' taxes in addition to ordinary rents, 'contributions' which in their minds chiefly distinguished 'war' from 'peace'. In and after 1648 it was a common assumption – and a pious hope – that rulers in peacetime would be satisfied with the revenue of their hereditary demesne, and the miscellaneous tolls and dues which belonged to their prerogative. The prince's superior private wealth was reckoned the financial basis of administration, bearing the costs of government. He therefore suffered directly from dismal economic conditions, the shortage of labour, good ground gone to waste, timber spoilt and livestock lost. The chronic shortage of his personal revenue was one of the most important, most urgent problems of the day.

The difficulties were no doubt economic, and also administrative. Regional variations make any simple statement risky, but the main local unit of the larger patrimonies in north Germany was the *Amt*, run by a 'director' and a 'corn inspector' presiding over a bevy of humbler officials; they were entitled to a salary and allowances in kind. The land under the *Amt's* jurisdiction was divided into ground held by the ruler's peasants, and the farms worked directly by employees, but the farms also relied on compulsory labour by the peasants. These had to render payments in kind as well, so that the ordinary revenue of the *Amt* took the form of crops and stock and timber, coming partly from farms and partly from the peasant holdings. The officials deducted expenses for repairs and wages, despatched corn to the ruler's households, honoured his 'assignations' (instructions to pay) which reached them from from time to time, and disposed of surplus commodities if they could at a local market. Furthermore, as the example of Brandenburg shows, no central organism supervised the scattered *Ämter*; the senior officials tended to be members of the local nobility. Rudimentary auditing could not check the value of an endless sequence of payments in kind, rendered to or by these men. No inducements were offered them to increase the revenues in their charge. Accurate estimates of acreage, numbers of tenants and stock, were lacking. Worst of all, the elector had been forced to borrow heavily for many years, and this involved mortgaging and alienating parts of the demesne in every one of his territories from the Rhine to the Vistula. During the winter of 1651–2 a committee of advisers proposed a new and strictly controlled policy of leasing out his lands for limited periods of years. They also wished to convert transactions in kind into transactions in coin: they believed this to be the key to more efficient accounting. The experiments were tried, but soon petered out. They barely tinkered with the bread-and-butter problem which beset society and government.

Lacking sufficient rents, or alienating the demense which produced them – in order to raise credits and settle old debts – a state had to tax. Lacking sufficient taxes, direct and indirect, a state had to extend its demesne and increase the revenue from rents of one type or another. The alternatives were posed almost everywhere in Europe; if England and France with their more advanced economies chose one, Charles X and Charles XI of Sweden would lay much greater emphasis on the other.[1] The choice depended partly on the character of the constitution. In some German principalities taxation would be maintained, and then increased after 1648, because there was no longer any difficulty about dictating either to the territorial nobility or to the unprivileged. The ruler's inherited authority was unquestioned. In others, the issue still turned on the future course of events at home and abroad.

Autocracies and Estates

The most complete autocrat in central Europe before 1618 had been Maximilian I of Bavaria. He could not give his son Ferdinand Maria, who reigned from 1651 until 1679, more than a fraction of his own

1   See below, pp. 115, 251–4; for a similar problem in Piedmont, p. 135–6.

force of character, but he bequeathed a patrimony in which the lay nobility was tamed, and increasingly wealthy ecclesiastical foundations depended on the ruler and supported him. The universities of Ingolstadt and Dillingen supplied the administration with competent jurists, and although the permanent 'Estates Committee' sometimes queried government tax demands it was not much more than a body of office-holders responsible for collecting certain taxes, and managing most of the government debt. The occasional full meetings of the Estates were talkative but impotent. When Maximilian died, his widow took over as Regent for some years. Her only real difficulties were with her daughter-in-law who patronised Italian artists, musicians and adventurers with great extravagance; but in this period court splendour was normally an acceptable emblem of the ruler's unfettered supremacy. Ferdinand Maria, in spite of his lethargy, from time to time announced bluntly enough the theory of government that God had entrusted him with a total responsibility: neither the Imperial Diet nor his peoples had rights in Bavaria which entitled them to limit his prerogative. His family also held another of the electorates. From 1650 until 1688 Max Henry, cousin to Ferdinand Maria, reigned as the archbishop elector of Cologne. In retrospect, it seems astonishing that a man in this position who spent his whole life unwilling to play the part of either a priest or a statesman, and became obsessed by alchemy and the collection of precious stones, should not have caused resentment. He was immovable.

There was also no difficulty in the Lutheran Brunswick lands around the three courts of Wolfenbüttel, Celle and Hanover. The patrimony was split repeatedly, to satisfy the claims of four brothers who moved in kaleidoscopic fashion from one apanage to another. But each asserted himself. The townsmen of Hanover had been powerless to stop Christian Ludwig taxing them, bringing in troops, building fortifications or annexing municipal property in order to enlarge his palace – all to their detriment. Ernest Augustus, greatest of the family, proved the harsh founder of modern Hanover, but he, and his brothers George William and John Frederick (who turned Catholic), were so secure in the enjoyment of their hereditary rights that they could afford to spend long periods in the Italy they all loved with such passion. Augustus their cousin, creator of a marvellous library at Wolfenbüttel, ruled his subjects like the rigid schoolmaster he was. The Estates in these duchies were submissive and co-operative. They mediated anxiously to stop private quarrels in the ruling family from getting out of hand. They played their part in officering Brunswick regiments. They accepted the autocratic administration in which they took some of, but not all, the pickings. For these princes followed the general practice of employing both natives and 'foreigners', men both of noble and of non-noble birth; with the non-nobles sometimes ultimately winning a title. In the 1650s the Brunswick rulers were sending out on diplomatic missions their chancellors, lawyers who came from a burgher background; a noble named von Winterstädt who rose from the post of a garrison commander to the highest political offices; and Thomas Grote (1594–1657), employed during his career by many princes, son of a non-noble in Celle – whose own son Otto (1620–87) would spend his life in the Hanoverian service, ending with the dignity of a *Freiherr* of the Empire. Throughout Germany, indeed, place-hunters moved restlessly about with no particular loyalties to honour. Servants of one ruler assiduously took bribes from another. A miscellany of sovereign courts may have reduced the country to political and economic impotence, but helped to create enough posts to appease the hunger of the literate classes for a livelihood. It made for social stability.

At the same time, not far off, there were two important corridors of almost perpetual disturbance in the structure of European politics for the next fifty years. One was a coastal strip running east-west all the way from Riga, through Schleswig-Holstein, as far as the Netherlands. The second ran south from the Netherlands to Switzerland. At vital points, within or close to these corridors, the territorial claims of various princes conflicted while authority was still shared between the prince and the local Estates. Here the whole future of government, its character at home and its foreign relations, remained an open question.

A crucial decision at Westphalia concerned Pomerania, along the Baltic coast: Sweden was allowed to keep the better part of it. The emperor and France both decided that this was a price worth paying for Swedish willingness to accept a general settlement. The Dutch refused to back the elector of Brandenburg's claim, and his recent marriage with a daughter of Frederick Henry, prince of Orange, did not help him. His interest in the west Baltic ports as a springboard for overseas trade has probably been exaggerated by historians, but with angry reluctance he insisted on compensation elsewhere. He was given Minden in the Weser valley; Halberstadt; and a promise that on the death of the reigning 'administrator' the lands of the old Magdeburg archbishopric would also fall to him. Such gains notably increased Frederick William's influence in northwest Germany. They were useful stepping-stones linking Berlin with the Rhenish duchies of his original inheritance. When Sweden finally offered him a portion of Pomerania, he could feel that his defiance of the great powers had been justified. This success owed nothing to the force of arms, very little to his councillors (whom he overruled), and almost everything to his obstinacy. By contrast, in Magdeburg the 'administrator' was a Saxon prince, and it might have been expected that the elector of Saxony would not lightly let the reversion fall to Brandenburg; but the inertia of the Dresden court in international politics was an almost constant feature of the next thirty years.

Frederick William's difficulties were almost greater in the Rhineland. Here, he and the duke of Pfalz-Neuburg by no means accepted a solution of earlier disputes which had allotted to one the duchies of Cleves and Mark, and to the other Berg and Jülich. Each still hoped to dispossess his rival. The elector, with the Dutch, supported the Protestants in the duke's territory. The duke encouraged Catholics still resident in the elector's duchies, counting on help from other Catholic states. This was entangled with a constitutional problem. The elector, determined to oppose the duke by force of arms if necessary, had first to assert effective authority in Cleves and Mark. He raised troops, installed garrisons and requested the local Estates to pay the cost by raising fresh taxes. He cultivated the friendship of Frederick Henry, captain-general of the Dutch army. The Estates resisted his tax demands, and looked for help from interests in Holland opposed to the Orange party. Their special envoy at the Hague was a splendid propagandist, who argued that the Estates in Cleves and the seven United Provinces should stand together for liberty against the autocratic instincts of Hohenzollern and Orange princes, now threateningly allied by the elector's marriage. The townsmen of Wesel and Emmerich in Cleves had interests in common with Dutch traders, while some Cleves gentry were landowners in the Dutch provinces. They disliked an assertive Hohenzollern ruler whose other dominions were remote. At least in their eyes, Pomerania was not worth the bones of a single Rhinelander.

The elector's surrender to the Estates of Cleves in an agreement named the Recess of October 1649 looks pretty well complete. In 1650 Prince William II's death inaugurated a long period of Orange weakness in the Netherlands, while Mazarin's régime collapsed in France in the following year. The Recess therefore belongs to a phase in this part of Europe in which the opponents of royal or princely power had the upper hand. In 1651 the elector went to war with Pfalz-Neuburg. It was a short burst of midsummer madness and he had to accept the emperor's mediation. The Cleves-Jülich question smouldered on, but there was no combustion.

At the same time, in Brandenburg itself a different debate ended peaceably. The elector summoned a full meeting of the Estates to Berlin and a celebrated constitutional document, the Charter of July 1653, was the result of its proceedings. This has been variously interpreted as the elector's victory over the nobility, a victory for the nobility because they pruned severely his demand to tax them, or a compromise which gave the elector effective power as a sovereign but left landowners in full control of the countryside. Indeed, their claim to collect from their subjects the direct taxes required by the elector, to exercise jurisdiction and to insist on compulsory labour, were all confirmed in the seventy-two complicated clauses of the Charter.

It was much more of a compromise than a victory for either party, because nobody intended to press to extremes. The angry tension which disturbed Paris and London at this period, the interaction of mobs with court factions and army officers, were missing in Berlin. An important group of Hohenzollern councillors themselves belonged to the foremost landowning families of Brandenburg; Hempo von Knesebeck, for example, the gentry's most vigorous champion, and Thomas von Knesebeck the elector's spokesman, were brothers. The actors here simply haggled, and always believed in the probability of a bargain, though no one denied that taxation was a fundamental problem. The elector assumed that the dangers of his position after 1648 justified costly armaments. But for the Estates a transcendent need to reduce taxes, and their constitutional right to discuss them, were infinitely more important. It was they, as much as he, who suffered from a failure to improve the finances of his domain. He had to fall back on more direct taxes, and his need increased their grievances. Unauthorised assemblies of gentry in 1650 and 1651 clearly signalled danger, and Frederick William therefore agreed to this full meeting of the Estates. He first pitched his terms high, asking for a vote to authorise taxation for five years. The Estates responded with a full catalogue of grievances and of rights enshrined in earlier charters which they wished to have confirmed. He gradually wore down his critics by repeated prorogations, until a short final debate in June and July 1653 led to agreement.

He was promised a sum of money spread over seven years, sufficient to maintain a force of 1800 men. He set up a military treasury, to which the Estates' administration in the country districts had to transmit the sums collected from their subjects. This was perceptibly less burdensome than what had been taken – sometimes by 'execution' or distraint – between 1648 and 1652. More important the Diet's tranquil close and the Charter itself show that, even where the Estates had preserved their rights much more fully than in Bavaria or Brunswick, the cleavage of interest between them and the ruler was not necessarily dangerous. It was bridged over by a working partnership, by the sufficiently close ties between the Estates and a prince's circle of advisers. The next two decades would see the ending of this dualism in the Hohenzollern lands. During another prolonged round of warfare in northern Europe, Frederick William acquired the military resources which permanently increased his power, even in peacetime. The political significance of the Estates' assemblies in Brandenburg, Cleves and Mark, and his duchy of East Prussia, gradually withered away after 1660. His judgment, and not their consent, fixed the level of taxation although landlord resistance confined his new consumption taxes (or 'excises') to the towns. Such a change could perhaps have been foreseen in 1653, but only the retrospection of historians has given it an air of inevitability. In any case, the more important point is that war itself, and unremitting rivalry between states great and small, were never disruptive enough to upheave the main pillars of the Westphalian settlement in Germany. The fervid and restless Empire which confronted the Emperor Charles V in 1519 had been left far behind.

2

The Crises of Eastern Europe

Revolution in the Ukraine

While central Europe slowly recovered some stability, signs of weakness multiplied farther east. Poland came close to dissolution after 1648, and the Ottoman empire was paralysed by a long series of urban and rural revolts. The temporary decay of these two governments contributed as much as anything else to warfare which overshadowed half a continent, and in turn led to the decadence of broad areas between the lower Danube and the Baltic for at least a century. These conditions gave Peter I's Muscovy a chance to rise to the stature of a great European power and, less directly, helped Vienna to build an extended Danubian empire.

At first sight, the huge confederation of Poland and Lithuania had prospered during the reign of Wladislaw IV (1632–48). The Russians failed to recapture Smolensk. The Swedes were compelled to make concessions in order to have a truce between the two states renewed in 1635. What looked like the last great Cossack rebellion in the Ukraine was suppressed in 1638. Polish officers controlled the remnant of 'registered' Cossack militia serving the Polish government as frontier guards, and a new fortress at Kodak far down the Dnieper kept watch on outlaw Cossack communities surviving in that area. Other fortified points were built on both sides of the river. Polish lordships spread out over the Ukraine, and appeared to strengthen their grip on the subject peasantry. Large estates already existed farther west, in Volhynia and Podolia. From here some labour was moved eastwards to colonise new lands. Other people moved east or south in order to escape subjection; but if they settled they also tended to join the labouring class, either on new estates or the older properties of Ukrainian lords and gentry. One must visualise a man like Jerome Wiśnowiecki (1612–51) brought up in the Orthodox faith, an educated traveller to Italy and the Netherlands in his

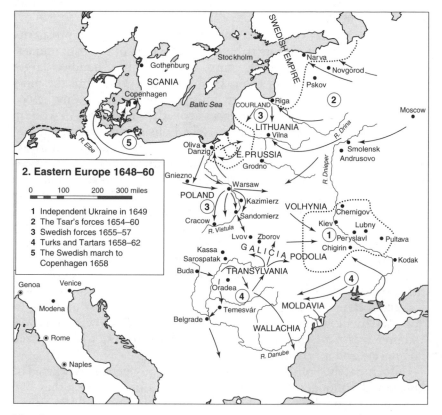

2. Eastern Europe 1648–60

0   100   200   300 miles

1 Independent Ukraine in 1649
2 The Tsar's forces 1654–60
3 Swedish forces 1655–57
4 Turks and Tartars 1658–62
5 The Swedish march to
   Copenhagen 1658

Gothenburg

Stockholm

SCANIA

Copenhagen

Baltic Sea

SWEDISH EMPIRE

Narva

Novgorod

Pskov

Riga

COURLAND

③

R. Drina

Moscow

LITHUANIA

Vilna

②

R. Elbe

⑤

Oliva
Danzig

E. PRUSSIA

Grodno

Smolensk
Andrusovo

R. Dnieper

Gniezno

Warsaw

POLAND

③

Kazimierz

Sandomierz

VOLHYNIA

Chernigov

Cracow

R. Vistula

Lvov   Zborov

Kiev

Peryslavl

Lubny

①

Pultava

Chigirin

Kassa

Sarospatak

G A L I C I A

PODOLIA

Kodak

Buda

TRANSYLVANIA

Oradea   ④

Temesvár

MOLDAVIA

④

Genoa   Venice

Modena

Rome

Belgrade

WALLACHIA

Naples

R. Danube

Map 2

youth, announcing his conversion to Rome in 1632, taking part in wars against the Russians and Tartars, but above all building up his tremendous properties. On the left bank of the Dnieper he had something like a principality of his own, with his private army of retainers and his chancery. He organised his economy by means of a strict enforcement of labour service. He built and endowed Catholic churches. He married an heiress from a family with similar assets. He fought and litigated against both relatives and neighbours. His capital township was Lubny, not far from Pultava; but he had other possessions in Volynia.

This spectacular colonial expansion was matched by the prosperity of the Vistula valley and its tributaries. The port of Danzig, unquestionably the greatest trading centre on the Baltic, handled larger grain exports in the years 1633–49 than at any time until the nineteenth century, mostly to western Europe. The German wars helped to make the city prosperous; refugees arrived, as elsewhere in western Poland, and new building went up.[1] The Polish landlord interest had pressed hard for the pacifications with Sweden in 1629 and 1635, and in the Diet restrained the king's intermittent proposals for warfare. The growing of surplus corn, the storage of it in such buildings as the handsome brick siloes at Kazimierz – on the Vistula, half-way between Cracow and Warsaw – the shipping of it downstream, deals with the Danzigers, further deals with the Dutch who transported it to the west: this was the main credit item in the Polish economy. Riga, under Swedish sovereignty, came second to Danzig, and handled the grain and timber shipped down the river Dvina and its tributaries by the great magnates of Lithuania. Notable among them was the Calvinist branch of the Radziwill family. Janusz and Boguslaw Radziwill were as strongly Calvinist as Wiśnowiecki in the Ukraine was Catholic; and they too had fortresses, widely spread dominions and a private sense of sovereignty.

Unfortunately, Polish government was already getting weaker. The king could no longer dismiss high provincial officials, once they had been appointed. He could not appoint any such office-holders, lay or clerical, who were not noble. The landed aristocracies were never sufficiently counter-balanced by an alliance between king and church, or between the king and members of less privileged classes. The national Diets, held every two years by the law of the constitution and meeting alternately in Warsaw for Poland and in Grodno for Lithuania, were still sometimes swayed by a personal appeal from the

1 In this halcyon period a wealthy brewer here began constructing and using enormous telescopes – of greater focal length than hitherto – to study the moon. The *Selenographia* of Hevelius, published in 1647, is the first complete lunar atlas. The frontispiece of the book includes a charming view of the walls and towers of Danzig.

ruler; but delegates from the many local Diets to the national assemblies increasingly voiced an extreme assertion of provincial rights. Above all, they would refer a demand for taxes back to the provinces which had declined, deliberately, to give them authority to accept financial sacrifices in their name. It was therefore impossible for the crown to develop a new tax system replacing the revenue of lands or dues which had fallen, almost everywhere, into the hands of dignitaries from the dominant lordly families. The particularism of Polish Prussia, the western areas (Great Poland) with their focus at Poznań, Little Poland which looked to Cracow, or of Lithuania vis-à-vis Poland, tended to make this vast country a federation of smaller aristocratic Estates. A time was at hand when foreign observers in Warsaw and Danzig would be gloomily assessing the magnitude of threats to Poland from outside, from Muscovy or Sweden or the sultan, while native politicians remained preoccupied by the duty of each locality to defend its interests against the king and other provinces. Most Poles still regarded their elected king as essential to the well-being of all, and their constitution as a marvellous heritage, intricate but effective, protecting both liberty and order. On the other hand, the bias for freedom inevitably cut deeply even into the fabric of local unity. An assumption of the sacred rights of every noble citizen too often paralysed provincial Diets as well as those of Warsaw and Grodno. It had become a powerful habit of mind which hindered common action.

Many faiths co-existed in Poland, and the Catholic revival had gone to work with relative gentleness. A weak central government ruled out the chances of enforcing uniformity. Great men could be tolerant or intolerant on their estates, to Catholics, Lutherans, Calvinists, Unitarians or Jews, as they wished. But the crucial religious problem of eastern Europe was the future of large Orthodox populations in Lithuania and the Ukraine, extending as far west as Vilna and Lvov. Here were people who would identify the Roman church with their landlord, a landlord who spoke a different language from theirs. They hated him, and his church, and his numerous Jewish leaseholders and innkeepers. These Orthodox, also, through their own clergy, were open to the influence of a religious revival then radiating strongly from a number of centres: from the Orthodox 'brotherhoods' at Kiev, Lvov, Vilna and elsewhere, the schools they founded, and (from 1647) the new 'Collegium' of Kiev. King Wladislaw and his predecessor had recognised the independent status of an Orthodox hierarchy; the Cossack officers on both sides of the Dnieper happily supported them. But religious tension was also likely where Orthodox folk worshipped under the authority of Orthodox bishops–who recognised the primacy of Rome. These Uniate clergy, though often in dispute with their Polish Catholic brethren, were scorned by the true Orthodox. In general, here was a world of religious agitation compounding the antagonism between landlord and peasant, or between settlers and those on the move.

In 1646, eight years after the Polish government put Cossack regiments under its direct control, Wladislaw turned again to one of his bigger dreams, a coalition of Christian powers against the sultan. This involved the plan of an attack on Ottoman garrisons and settlements along the Black Sea. The Polish Diet was opposed, and rejected the scheme; but a group of Cossack officers had already been invited to Warsaw to discuss it. They returned home disappointed and furious. One of them, Bogdan Chmielnicki, then decamped and fled 200 miles down the Dnieper to the *sich* (or settlement),[2] the main centre of independent Cossacks in the Dnieper basin. Assembling a motley but numerous host of supporters, speedily developing his talent as a political leader, Chmielnicki next ventured on a dash still further south to confer with the Tartar Khan. He won some assurance of Tartar co-operation, and quickly returned to lead his Cossacks against the Polish force sent to restore order. By the end of May 1648, shortly after Wladislaw's death, Chmielnicki – chosen as hetman (or leader) by his colleagues – had won several encounters.

A rebellious clique of officers soon found, to the increasing bewilderment of some of them, that they were touching off revolution on a far grander scale. Instability along the frontier – with groups of Cossacks and Tartars switching erratically from mutual raiding to short-lived partnerships which their Polish and Turkish overlords intermittently encouraged and then vetoed – this was familiar enough to all concerned. What now followed in the Ukraine transformed the normal patterns of indiscipline. Chmielnicki's headquarters, down the river from Kiev, became the headquarters of an insurrectionary government.

The grievances of Cossack officers (such as Chmielnicki himself) were overshadowed in 1648 by an extraordinary uprising which spread rapidly from one district to another on both sides of the Dnieper. By June a new folk-hero, Krivonos 'the one-eyed', was active in Podolia. Wiśnowiecki retreated from Lubny to the west; his forces tried to terrorise as they moved, which at once led to counter-violence. The unprivileged, the subjects, the Ukrainians, the Orthodox, were rising against their Catholic Polish masters. They swarmed to join Chmielnicki's army. They all wanted to stop being peasants who paid tribute, in order to become Cossack soldiers who paid nothing, and to reverse the process by which Poles had step by

2   This was situated close to the first of the famous series of rapids, stretching 70 miles downstream, which obstructed transport along the river for centuries.

step reduced the number of 'registered' or authorised Cossack troops while colonisation and settlement increased the population of labouring subjects. Chmielnicki, canny by instinct, appreciative of the dangers, increasingly ambitious as power thrust itself upon him, tried to harness this popular movement. He needed the maximum support, while keeping his forces within manageable limits of size, and checking a flight from the land which threatened famine with anarchy. He also understood that his future depended on the whole constellation of eastern Europe, and during the summer of 1648 first got into touch with rulers of the Carpathian principalities, Moldavia and Transylvania, and even with Moscow and Istanbul. At length, after this period of preparation, he marched west in August. His remarkable expedition swept through the Ukraine and Galicia, won a big battle, besieged Lvov, extorted from the city a large ransom and then turned north. He was now 400 miles from the middle Dnieper and only 150 from Warsaw, where the Diet had met to choose a new king, but drew back for the winter to Kiev. Great lunges forward and back again, by Cossack (and Tartar) horsemen in the rapid course of a single campaigning season, are characteristic of warfare in eastern Europe at this date. Their nomadic military tradition survived almost intact through most of the century.

This Ukrainian revolution of 1648 was one of the greatest events of the age, with momentous consequences. Chmielnicki first presented a threat to the Poles. Tartars and the Russians intervened, then the Swedes, then the Transylvanians; the constitution and economy of the great Polish and Lithuanian confederation were both dealt blows from which they never fully recovered. The power of the Moscow government, and on a smaller scale the elector of Brandenburg's, gained proportionately. Some contemporaries forsaw 'a total subversion of the state' in Poland. Even here in Danzig, wrote one man in June 1648, we are not safe from so mobile an enemy; there are no fortified places between us and them; they are peasantries, set against the nobles; they kill nobles, priests and Jews without mercy; and they stir up other peasants and townsmen against their lords, so that many are forced into rebellion against their wishes. Worse, this coincided with the interregnum, and another observer wrote from Warsaw in September that members of the Diet seemed to idle their time away in country houses outside the city. He believed that they would be completely defenceless if the enemy bands managed to reach them. But these fears for the immediate future were exaggerated. Little evidence has yet been collected to show that the revolutionary peasant movement spread westward with any serious effect beyond the boundaries of Volhynia and Podolia; nor did it spread into Muscovy. The Polish constitution in fact stood up well to the crisis, and the Diet wasted little time in choosing John Casimir

(Wladislaw's brother) in preference to other candidates. He at once arranged to marry his predecessor's widow, Marie Louise Gonzaga-Nevers, who had brought with her a French dowry, French followers and the French style of courtly life to Warsaw in 1646, and who prepared the way for that close tie of the Poles with Louis XIV's diplomatic system later in the century, a new feature in international politics.

The new king turned to face Chmielnicki, who declared to Polish commissioners sent to negotiate with him: 'I am a small and insignificant man but by the will of God I have become the independent ruler of Rus.'[3] It was true. For a very short period he had successfully welded together the most varied elements, outlaw communities far down the Dnieper, the intractable circle of his brother officers, and the Ukrainian peasants, towns and clergy. After a triumphant Christmas at Kiev where Orthodox clergy did their best to expound to him his duty to defend the Orthodox interest, he refused to settle with John Casimir's envoys. Neither Chmielnicki nor his followers were willing to return to that subordination which the Poles regarded as both lawful and essential. The Ukrainian army again moved west to Podolia and again defeated the Polish forces. The truce of Zborov, which followed, allowed the number of 'registered' Cossacks to rise to the very high figure of 40,000, dissolved the Uniate church, and gave independent authority to Hetman Chmielnicki in the provinces of Kiev, Braslav and Chernigov. These terms, and also the controversial points which they omit, are very illuminating. It was intolerable to the Polish interest that the Cossacks should keep so large a force of privileged soldiery; but it was intolerable to the Ukrainians that they should not all universally enjoy the rights of registered Cossacks. They wanted to get rid of the Polish lords from a very wide area, but the treaty seemed to have left Polish authority intact in all but three provinces. On the other hand, for the Catholic bishops the Uniate church was a useful instrument which enabled them to control many Orthodox clergy and populations; they resented this surrender to the independent Orthodox of Kiev, a round lost in the ecclesiastic struggle for power. But a pacification of sorts lasted until the Poles had collected their strength again. Heavy fighting in the summer of 1651 culminated in a Polish victory, partly because the hetman was deserted by the Tartars, who were veering to the side of John Casimir. In a new agreement, arranged after the Poles had advanced to the Dnieper again, the registered Cossack host was cut down to 20,000, and Chmielnicki gave up two provinces. It was a

3   This is the concluding sentence from a speech summarised by the Polish commissioners who heard it. M. Hrushevsky, *History of the Ukraine* (New Haven, 1941), p. 284.

signal to him that he must find allies. It was a signal to militants of the Ukrainian world that their leaders wanted to sell out to the Poles; the Cossack commanders, after all, were masters not men. It was a signal to some Poles and to politicians farther west, as well as to Moscow, that John Casimir had strengthened his position.

Chmielnicki's diplomacy had earlier been aimed chiefly at the smaller states on the edge of the Ottoman empire. He secured a marriage between his son and a daughter of the prince of Moldavia. He kept in touch with George II Rákóczi of Transylvania, who longed to intervene in either Poland or Moldavia. Janusz Radziwill in Lithuania, married to another daughter of the Moldavian ruler, entered the picture. All these men groped for a new alignment of forces with an uncertain, erratic touch. But even more uncertain and much more important was the attitude of the tsar's government in Moscow.

Muscovy: The Code of 1649

There were signs of tension in Muscovy around 1648, but under conditions hardly paralleled in other parts of Europe. His subjects accepted the view that the tsar enjoyed an over riding authority. He could do as he wished with his empire: the land, and all its inhabitants formed his own *votchiny* or personal property. But his power to make and to co-ordinate the laws was only dimly understood. He was a governor rather than a legislator, so that the autocracy was in practice exercised by some forty offices in Moscow, where their functions overlapped and conflicted in a bewildering fashion. Each office tended to develop its own set of precedents, which in any case remained unpublished. The old general codes of law were obsolete in many particulars. If violence abounded in the provinces, litigation in the capital demanded a vicious compound of chicanery and corruption. A positive decision in one office was liable to be reversed by proceedings in another. Very few men could be certain where they stood in matters of tax or grants of land, in suits over fugitive peasants or in commercial disputes. Uncertainty in the law, combined with the centralised character of government, intensified many grievances. Clarification and reform were both badly needed.

Although the tsar's authority had been strengthened since the Time of Troubles came to a close, after the election of Michael Romanov in 1613, many 'middling sort' of servicemen obliged to serve him were always restive. They lived for the most part off grants of land assigned for their maintenance, the *pomestiya* tenures which bound them to obey instructions from the court. Above all, they had to play a full part in the defence of the empire, fighting Poles on the western frontiers and Tartars who continually raided an immense band of partially settled territory south of Moscow. The assembly in the capital of *pomestiya*-holders before a campaigning season opened was a familiar occasion; having come also to do business with government offices (like the *pomestiya* office), they were then able to discuss together their common grievances. They grumbled because state taxes had increased markedly in the last ten years. They grumbled because their grants of land were often smaller than their entitlement; and crop yields, worse in some years than others, were always very low. In consequence they had to drive their peasants hard in order to collect the necessary foodstuffs and taxes; and as a further consequence peasant families continually decamped from the central provinces round Moscow to the emptier and more fertile lands east and south. Almost worse, powerful interests like the 'strong men' favoured by the tsar, and the tsar's relatives, and the larger monasteries, met the need for more labour by tempting peasants on other people's lands to move out and settle on their own estates. They sometimes used influence at Moscow to gain the upper hand in bargains which resulted in the authorised transfer, or 'export', of peasants from the villages of humble servicemen to their own. At the same time they were offering artisans handsome terms to migrate to townships or suburbs under their direct control. This robbed old-established towns of an important minority of tax-payers.

The complaints of *pomestiya*-holders and townsmen had been expressed on many occasions when the tsar summoned a *zemsky sobor*: an assembly of notables, including representatives from the provinces. Despite their rivalries both the lesser and the greater land-holders wanted a stronger right to discipline the peasantry, and the government stood to gain by satisfying them. Soldiers could not fight for the tsar if they received too little in rents and labour services. Taxes lost their value if tax-payers were always running away. While this fundamental matter was intermittently discussed, popular griev-ances came abruptly to the fore. The feeling of plain men in Moscow, that administration had fallen into the hands of a corrupt ring of courtiers and officials since young Tsar Alexei succeeded his father Tsar Michael in 1645, increased in vehemence. His marriage to Maria Miloslavsky in January 1648, followed at once by a marriage between Maria's sister and his chief adviser Morozov, seemed to prove everyone's worst suspicions. Ivan Miloslavsky, her brother, was another swift and extraordinarily successful parvenu. It may be that a rival group in the Kremlin encouraged agitators outside, but in any case Morozov's attempted reforms met with mounting disap-proval. His new scheme for raising a tax on salt was soon withdrawn but other tax increases, coupled with reduced pay for many state servants, fanned the discontent. There was trouble over common grazing lands outside the city (now taken over by a few rich individuals) and Russian merchants were incensed by Morozov's favour to privileged foreign importers; they had protested in vain. On the first two days of June 1648 crowds went into action outside and then inside the Kremlin, and for a moment terrorised Alexei himself. Then fires broke out in the city; three senior officials were seized by the mob and slaughtered. Morozov fled. Luckily for the Tsar it seems that most of the guards, the *streltsy*, were loyal and with their help order in Moscow was soon restored. But the popular movement spread, especially in the countryside and towns north of the city, and consequently numbers of the threatened servicemen and townsmen hurried into Moscow. Their leaders pressed the court for what they judged the only workable response to the whole tangle of their grievances: they wanted an 'assembly of the land' of the customary kind, the *zemsky sobor* of spokesmen for the Tsar's subjects. This body would join with the Tsar's ministers in revising the laws, and produce a new Code of Law. Alexei's advisers set up a 'commission' to satisfy this demand. In September a sobor duly assembled. The government, commission and sobor settled down to hard and hurried labour – the haste was indeed a feature of their work – so that the completed document (a roll 900 feet long and containing over 800 clauses) was ready early in 1649. It was a most important step towards a settlement of Muscovy after the turmoil.

Although this Code restated the law and determined legal procedure over a very wide field, the most famous of its enactments deal with a crux of the age, the restless movement of peasant families. They sum up and tighten all the older laws on this topic. Before 1649, there were still limits set to the period during which a lord could take legal proceedings to recover a fugitive; in future, his claim would never lapse. Before 1649 only the head of a peasant household, a man whose name was entered in the census returns, could be lawfully proceeded against for desertion. Now the entire family, including sons and nephews, were forbidden to leave their original place of work. Before 1649 it was not clear how far the tsar's edicts infringed the freedom of humbler men who occupied less than a complete peasant holding; henceforth these were included in the veto on unauthorised departure. Such regulations in due course cemented the alliance between an autocratic government and the class of its servant-landlords. They created a fiscal system which produced more revenues for the tsar by tying subjects firmly to lords and by counting and taxing the peasant households on each estate; but for the moment, discipline in the countrysides and money in the tsar's coffers were both lacking. These difficulties help to account for the slow, cautious stages by which

Muscovy entered the struggle for mastery in White Russia, Lithuania and the Ukraine.

The Tsar's authority therefore survived in this difficult phase; and the convulsion had been decidedly less than the terrible early years of the century, Russia's real Time of Troubles. Significantly, in 1653 a full assembly of the *zemsky sobor* was summoned for the last time. Thereafter the court must have felt less need to take the pulse of the country.

Foreign Intervention in Poland

Alexei's advisers naturally wanted to make use of the Polish–Ukrainian upheaval in 1648 but were too preoccupied to do so. A mission sent to Warsaw in 1650 simply aired grievances while Muscovy settled down again. In 1651 the Metropolitan of Novgorod came to Moscow: this amazingly ambitious man, Nikon, had great influence with the Tsar and welcomed the idea of a Holy War, whether against Protestant Swedes or the Romanist Poles; and Alexei soon made him the Patriarch of Moscow, The meeting of a *zemsky sobor* meanwhile sang a different song, discussing the idea of war but protesting against fresh taxation. Another distraction was a Moscow fire in 1652, one of the worst recorded, which led to the expulsion of foreigners (who were said to live in tax-exempt houses) from the city, to be confined to a new settlement outside. But when the Poles defeated the Cossacks and their forces reappeared on the Dnieper left bank, the Russians grew correspondingly alarmed. Chmielnicki, who risked being ground to dust between the two millstones of a Polish army and Tartar raiders, skilfully insinuated that he would have to appeal for aid to the sultan by recognising Ottoman suzerainty in the Ukraine lands. Early in 1653 the Moscow government, having decided to intervene in Poland, decided also accept the hetman's alternative offer of an alliance with the tsar.

A famous bargain resulted, 'the treaty of Peryslavl' of 1654. Ukrainian and Russian historians have spilled quarts of ink in trying to measure its significance. In this modest town east of the Dnieper, Hetman Chmielnicki and all the Cossack army were reluctantly compelled to accept in perpetuity and without qualification the authority of the tsar over them. This was an initial act of submission, insisted on by Alexei's envoy, and in accordance with the normal Russian theory of the relationship between ruler and subjects. Only then, in conversation but not in writing, the envoy gave an assurance that the tsar would respect Cossack liberties. Some months later, in Moscow, most of his promises were set out in a document which the tsar accepted; so that the whole transaction resembled a treaty, but it depended on the hetman's first unconditional submission at Pery-slavl. Alexei contented himself with the general claim to sovereignty, leaving nearly all the liberties of the Cossacks intact. They could elect their hetman, subject to the tsar's confirmation, and the hetman retained real authority. He continued to command the army of 60,000 registered men, and he could still negotiate with foreign courts, although he promised to inform Moscow of what took place. The Cossacks kept their special rights and privileges, and their own tribunals. In return the civilian interest in the Ukraine was sacrificed. The tsar obtained authority to receive taxes from the towns, and to dispose of lands formerly held by the Polish nobility – although nothing was said of the forcible annexation of such properties by many determined individuals, both soldiers and peasants, since the rebellion of 1648. He also won control of the church and its lands, after undertaking to respect the existing posses-sion of churches and monasteries. The question of the Moscow patriarch's jurisdiction over the metropolitan of Kiev was left untouched. Finally, tsar and hetman agreed to act together against Poland. For both, this was the immediate point, and neither could foresee that the details of their bargain would affect long-term devel-opments in south Russia.

The Russians' advance to Smolensk began in April 1654. They took it in October and crossed the watershed from the upper Dnieper to the Dvina, where the prospect of their descent downstream directly concerned another of the greater European powers. The Swedish government was drawn into the eastern crisis.

When the Ukraine revolted and Wladislaw died, in 1648, a view was argued in Berlin and Stockholm that Elector Frederick William and Queen Christina should take advantage of Polish difficulties. Both held their hand, and the Poles weathered this first burst of the storm. By 1654 almost everybody believed that radical changes were unavoidable. Alexei had asserted his sovereign right to a vast area which the Poles considered a part of their own 'Res Publica', and had promised to protect a rebel – Chmielnicki – against the king of Poland. He was therefore committed to war. Victory for the tsar would alter the whole balance of power, and increase the pressure which he could put on the Tartars, Poland, the Swedish Baltic pro-vinces, the independent duchy of Courland and even East Prussia. As a Hohenzollern minister advised Frederick William, the capture of Riga by the Russians would be 'hell' for the elector. It would be worse than that for the Swedish crown and for the Swedish magnate families which had laid hands so profitably on Estonia, Livonia and Ingria. Moreover, reports from Moscow made it clear that the Rus-sians' animus against the Poles could very easily be turned against Sweden. If they longed to recapture Smolensk, Ordyn-Nashchokin, the able governor of Pskov, would have given priority to an advance towards the Baltic. If Archbishop Nikon relished the prospect of war against the Catholics, there had also been serious brushes between zealous Lutheran pastors in Estonia and some of the Orthodox inhabitants; friction which has been called a miniature *Kulturkampf*. On a grander scale, the entire design of a safe and docile empire for Stockholm in the east Baltic was threatened.

In June 1654 Christina abdicated and Charles X succeeded her. The mainspring of his famous invasion of Poland in 1655 was a conviction that Swedish imperial interests required him to intervene, to share in remodelling the structure of eastern Europe when far-reaching changes were judged certain after the fall of Smolensk. The theory that he wanted to solve his acute financial problem at home, by shifting his troops across the Baltic, seems incorrect. The number of men maintained in Sweden at that date was very small. The cost of mobilisation alarmed his advisers. His own desire to carry out drastic fiscal reforms was thwarted by his decision to fight. Nor does Charles's temperament fully explain the crowded military history of his reign; his earlier career reveals a very moderate, restrained statesman and commander. He was less of a militant than either Gustav Adolf or Charles XII. But with every month that passed in the second half of 1654 it became harder to overlook the news reaching him from many points across the Baltic. His chancellor, Eric Oxenstierna, fresh from the governorship of Estonia, was quick to brief and to warn him. Two other difficulties had to be carefully weighed. The first was Denmark, the old adversary; but King Frederick III played his hand at this period quietly enough. The other was the state of the Empire, but feuding with Brandenburg over Pomerania now ended and the Habsburg interest weakened when the king of the Romans died in 1654. In fact, Sweden's interests in central Europe seemed safe at a point of time when danger threatened farther east.

The most interesting element in the preliminaries to Charles X's attack on the Poles was the least important: Protestant radicalism. The treaty of 1648, which appeared to betray the Protestant cause in Austria and Bohemia, horrified exiles in Germany, Poland and Hungary. Their despair chimed with the prophesies of a few influential visionaries who foresaw the year 1655 as a time of upheaval and salvation. They dreamt of a Second Coming, the monarchy of Christ, and of a new hero arising to scatter the servants of Satan. The single ruling family affected by these ideas were the Rákóczis of Transylvania where a sprinkling of the Calvinist ministers were true sectaries. Sigismund, younger brother of Prince George II Rákóczi, patronised a circle of extremists of whom the most widely known was Dravik (or 'Dravidius'). The visions of Dravik convinced one very great man of their truth. Amos Comenius of the Moravian Brethren, the progressive teacher, the tireless traveller to Hungary, Sweden, Holland and England, whose correspondence flowed back and forth between these countries, used his famous Academy at Lezno in Poland – a refuge to the Moravians offered by the Leszczyński family – as a post office for the Protestant interest in east Europe. At the end of 1654 Rákóczi sent an envoy to London and Stockholm, who first of all called on Comenius. Swedish envoys bound for Transylvania and Istanbul would shortly do the same. Dravik was certain, and Comenius agreed, that the extraordinary event of Charles X's accession verified Biblical and his own prophecies. It revealed God's will. The sword was poised, ready to do His work in the world. The avenging hero was at hand. But Charles himself treated such messengers from the Protestant south with the utmost caution. The stricter Lutherans in Sweden, then recovering their grip after a short period of shy experiment, looked harshly on everything to do with the sectaries. The new war indeed proved fatal to the Protestants of Poland.

The Swedish king, by the end of 1654, could try either to ally with the Poles against the Russians, or to take what he wanted from Poland in order to anticipate the Russians. He fixed as his price for an alliance the surrender of Polish claims to sovereignty over Courland and Polish Prussia. It was too much to ask of John Casimir, while the Swedes broke off the discussions in April 1655. Any more delay would upset their time-table for large-scale military operations in that year. Next year, it seemed to them, might be too late. The defensive desire to anticipate the Russians (and Brandenburg) was now overshadowed by the simpler motive to win dominance in Poland.

Charles planned a double advance: from Pomerania through Brandenburg to western Poland, and from Riga southwards with a smaller force. From this decision sprang his emphatic triumphs of 1655. He entered Poznań, then Warsaw, then Cracow, while John Casimir fell back. The case for consolidating first of all along the lower Vistula was stronger than Charles realised, but a short sharp drive upstream appeared to him not too dangerous an entanglement. Placing garrisons in Cracow and Sandomierz, he then returned north. Many Polish commanders, after their defeat or even before, recognised his authority. The other Swedish army started from Riga even before the king left Stettin. It swept over the duchy of Courland with great harshness. It occupied Polish territory which the Russians were approaching by slower stages. It took an important fortress on the Dvina which the Russians had tried, but failed, to capture. Tsar Alexei entered Vilna, and accordingly the Lithuanian Grand Hetman Janusz Radziwill accepted Charles as his feudal superior. Chmielnicki's Cossacks were also setting foot in the southern sectors of this vast tract, and the Russians grew deeply suspicious of them.

The warfare of 1655 suggested to the Cossack leader that he, like Radziwill, had an interest in common with the Swedes. At the same time Charles drove John Casimir before him out of Poland to a refuge in Habsburg Silesia, and forced the elector of Brandenburg to sign a treaty at Königsberg (January 1656). This converted East Prussia into a fief of the Swedish crown, and gave the Swedes privileged access to the Prussian ports of Memel and Pillau, plus half their revenues. Combined with Radziwill's undertaking for Lithuania, and with Charles's new grip on the Vistula below Warsaw, the Königsberg treaty unveils a new and larger Swedish sphere of influence in the making. It seemed to bring nearer to fulfilment than ever before the old Swedish dream of an effective *dominium maris Baltici*.

Unfortunately, the very depth of his penetration inland involved Charles in a commitment which it was very difficult to limit. A Swedish force in Cracow weighed like an incubus on the Habsburg emperor who feared for his sovereignty in Hungary and Silesia, where Protestants hoped for better times as a second Gustav Adolf approached the frontier. Vienna therefore worked for an alliance with John Casimir and, if possible, Frederick William. The growth of Swedish power roused another, deeply interested, government to intervene. The Dutch were by no means ready to let Sweden compete seriously for the greatest prize of all in the Baltic, their own commercial dominance, which depended for a substantial part of its profits on freedom of access to Danzig in Polish Prussia. And for every Polish commander who surrendered in 1655 to the Swedish troops' superior striking power, another fought back in 1656. Charles hurried inland a second time, but the potent mixture of patriotic and Catholic hatred for an oppressive Protestant invader, fanned by appeals from the clergy, helped to push back the Swedes. Charles found it prudent to offer Brandenburg four Polish provinces – to be held as fiefs of the Swedish crown. A combined force of Swedes and Brandenburgers fought a celebrated engagement outside Warsaw in July 1656 against John Casimir, who had returned from Silesia, but their victory did not break the general deadlock. A Dutch fleet entered the Baltic to prevent Danzig falling to Sweden, and John Casimir himself entered the city. While the Poles descended the Vistula again, the Russians attacked the Swedish Baltic lands. They besieged Riga (without success) and raided into Ingria and Finland far to the north. Far to the south the Swedes in turn sought help from Chmielnicki and George Rákóczi of Transylvania. Swedish envoys travelled enormous distances in the course of 1656 back and forth across the Carpathians, in order to coax these two suspicious rulers (and also the Tartar Khan in the Crimea) to join Sweden in a combined assault on Poland. They offered a partition of conquered territory between the victors.

Early in 1657 George of Transylvania crossed into Poland. Cossacks but not the Tartars, joined him. For a third time Charles X himself moved up the Vistula to join the Transylvanians when news arrived which altered the whole situation in Europe. He learnt of a full-scale assault by Denmark on Sweden. Leaving his allies completely in the lurch, he withdrew at once with speedy efficiency towards Pomerania. Rákóczi reached Warsaw, but the fiasco of his own tragic retreat soon began. Bewildered, starved of supplies, deserted by the Cossacks and the Swedes, hammered both by Poles and Tartars, his force disintegrated. He had to pay an immense indemnity before reaching home. In the course of a few weeks the pressure on Poland from outside had been eased. It was not to be repeated in anything like such a menacing form until the Turkish invasions of the 1670s. At the close of 1657 there were still Swedish troops on the lower Vistula and in Cracow, but the terms of the treaty of Oliva in 1660 did not transfer an inch of Polish territory to the government in Stockholm. In 1658 the Russo-Polish campaigning began again, but in a decade of desultory and destructive warfare the tsar's troops always remained a long way behind the line of their westward advance in 1655. The truce of Andrusovo in 1667 confirmed all Polish losses in the Ukraine east of the Dnieper, and of Smolensk and its territory. A Muscovite garrison would continue to hold Kiev. What had not occurred, and was no longer a possibility, was the partition of John Casimir's kingdom predicted so often in earlier years.

The Survival of Poland

The impact of these wars in Poland itself was nevertheless profoundly important. General signs of decay are plain enough. The density of the population decreased. A heavy fall in the birthrate in the decades 1650–60 and 1670–80 (the latter coinciding with the Turkish wars) was not offset by recoveries after 1660 or 1680. At the same time, the mints began to issue a flood of copper and debased silver coins. In the resulting dislocation of wages and prices the rise in wages lagged noticeably behind rising prices, so that the home market's capacity to stimulate fresh activity dwindled to vanishing point. Past prosperity had in any case been due largely to the export of surplus grain down the Vistula. International conditions favouring this trade now came to an end (see below, p. 106). Almost worse, Charles X's campaigns were based on a repeated use of the easy route up and down the Vistula. His opponents followed in his wake. Quartering and requisitioning, as well as the destructive activity of many small parties of raiders, did terrible damage in this central region. Afterwards, with the foreign demand for Polish grain less than it had been, with Polish towns too few and too small to provide a healthy market for country produce, any real incentive to make good the losses was missing. Danzig continued to export more rye and wheat than any other Baltic port, but low returns from toll stations on the Vistula not far below Warsaw suggest that agriculture in Prussia, nearer the coast, recovered more completely than ever proved possible in central Poland.

To judge from the archive of two of the largest property owners in the entire country, the archbishop and chapter of Gniezno, when the area of land under cultivation declined there was no consequent reduction in forced labour service for the unprivileged. On the contrary, in bad times the lord wanted labour more cheaply than before, while peasant holdings were commonly the worst hit by war and depression. The result seems to have been an increase in the numbers of a landless rural proletariat. Chronic indebtedness was normal. Poor men got into debt because they could not pay dues or taxes, because they lost goods and animals, because crops failed so that they had to borrow to buy seed for the next sowing. In some instances they made bequests to a church on the security of their possessions; if they could not pay what they had promised, the clergy foreclosed. In the best years of peace the tremendous legal and economic privileges of noblemen on one hand, and the low yield of crops on the other, always accentuated the hardness of life. In war, rival forces pillaged the countryside, manpower disappeared and the forest edged back over what had been tillage or pasture. Humbler members of the privileged gentry were also in difficulties. The customary division of an inheritance between heirs often led to a fatal disintegration of the family economy, so that there was a noticeable difference between villages in the possession of a single lord and villages divided into the diminutive holdings of several small gentry. Alternatively, loans were raised to satisfy those with claims on such a property, and high interest soon accumulated with the debt.

Not everyone suffered in such a society. The less prosperous noble who could not survive on his own fields sometimes entered a great man's service as the *podstarosta* who ran an estate, assisted by overseers. Or he joined the band of noble retainers who followed a magnate in war and attended him at the national assemblies. There also remained noble families of medium standing who formed the backbone of many provincial Diets. Other provinces were dominated by more powerful families who built up great patrimonies by inheritance, good marriages, the chance elimination of too many heirs, and by the acquisition of offices allowing them to take over former crown lands. John Sobieski was a splendidly representative magnate from the southeast. His mother's grandparents had all belonged to military and landowning families in a part of Poland exposed to Tartar or Turkish raids, where both the risks and profits were high. His father was a respected statesman. His elder brother died in a skirmish with the Tartars in 1652, so that John inherited wealth and position. By marrying a Frenchwoman who was a widow with claims on the vast estate of her first husband, a Zamoyski, his assets were multiplied. He had also behind him a Jesuit education, a tour of western Europe, attendance on an embassy to Istanbul, and experience in the wars. He could hope to play a part at court, manoeuvring on equal terms with the leading families of south and west Poland or the overpowering grandees of Lithuania.

Earlier in the century the country as a whole, and wealthy enlightened lords in particular, gained by the arrival of immigrants or refugees. Dutchmen drained marshes in the Vistula delta. Lutherans and Moravian Brethren hastened after 1620 from the lands of the Bohemian crown into west and southwest Poland. Their communities in the town of Lezno flourished under the patronage of the Leszczyński family, even though Boguslaw Leszczyński was converted to Rome in 1642. Their churches in the diocese of Poznań were numerous. But long before 1648 the Catholic interest became less tolerant as it grew stronger. The Catholic bishops were the best-organised party in the Polish political system. Legislation inspired by them was already modifying older edicts allowing toleration, when the Swedish war immeasurably intensified the Catholic element in Polish patriotic feeling. Polish and immigrant Protestants were accused of helping the enemy, and identified with him by popular feeling. John Casimir's resurgence in 1657 led to the destruction of many Protestant churches by fanaticised troops and peasants. Refugees had to move back to Silesia or into Germany again, and after 1655 Poland ceased to benefit by immigration from the west. It has been calculated that only twenty-five Protestant communities out of an earlier total of 200 in south Poland survived the Cossack and Swedish wars. In Poznań things were better. Some Lutheran churches were destroyed while harsh episcopal visitations caused trouble, but Protestant craft guilds in the towns survived and tough-minded pastors and lecturers maintained the characteristic institutions of Lutheran church life.

The Diet had proved single-minded enough about religious matters to order the expulsion of Unitarians from the country, and in 1668 threatened with the death penalty Catholic converts to Protestantism. On the far more important problem of constitutional reform it failed to agree. Polish setbacks during the long crisis, admittedly, roused a party of reformers in 1658–61 to examine the national assembly's procedural defects. Above all, they feared the threat to orderly business posed by the doctrine – which came to symbolise a cult of lawful liberty after it was enforced for the first time in 1652 – that the adverse vote of a single deputy (the so-called *liberum veto*) dissolved a meeting of the Diet. A scheme drafted by the chancellors of Poland and Lithuania planned to alter the system of voting so that a two-thirds majority on a secret ballot could bind the minority. The royal right to veto bills passed in this way was heavily qualified. Diets were to meet annually for six weeks. Neither court nor nobility were enthusiastic, and between them they buried what has been called the most significant plan for reform in Poland before the days of Stanislas-Augustus in the eighteenth century. The much simpler alternative of strengthening the royal authority by electing the king's successor in John Casimir's lifetime, in order to avoid the familiar drawbacks of an interregnum, stood even less chance of winning enough support. It ran counter to a clause in earlier coronation charters, rightly regarded by the Poles as an indispensable safeguard of the liberties they prized. In their view, an election *vivente rege* inevitably paved the direct road to autocracy; if future rulers – unlike John Casimir – had a son, it would lead to hereditary monarchy. Worse still, the French queen of John Casimir championed a French candidate for the succession, so that the Poles suspected the evils of foreign domination. They pushed the logic of their objections still further. Many refused point-blank to co-operate in the king's attempt of 1663 to recover the Ukraine because they feared to strengthen his government; and indeed the court hoped that victory on the frontier would help it to overcome opposition and to nominate the king's successor. These calculations were soon respectable commonplaces in Polish politics, and during the next thirty years military and foreign affairs increasingly became mere counters in the struggle of factions at home. When John Casimir returned empty-handed from the Ukraine George Lubomirski, grand-marshall of the Polish crown, organised a conspiracy. He was denounced and dismissed. His estates were confiscated. He fled over the Silesian border, and raised a force of mercenaries. He then returned to Poland, waged war on the king and defeated him. The court had to agree to drop an election of John Casimir's successor *vivente rege*. All this, in the eyes of constitutionalists, was 'lawful insurrection', a permissible defence of the privileges claimed by Lubomirski for himself and other Polish noblemen.

Such a concept of aristocratic liberties, which ran to extremes and endangered the state, of course had powerful echoes elsewhere. Magyar nobles were soon to appeal to the Sultan and to Louis XIV for aid against their Habsburg ruler. The Dutch republicans, although they did not rebel, made use of Cromwell and Louis in maintaining their interest against the house of Orange. A handful of English noblemen begged a foreign prince in 1688 to intervene with a powerful fleet and army against their legitimate but dangerous ruler.

In the Empire, constitutional reform and the pre-election of a successor to the reigning emperor had already met with the same intense opposition which confronted John Casimir and, later, John Sobieski. This attitude of mind remained one of the two strongest impulses in contemporary politics. The second impulse, in reaction, strove to crush the first by an extension of state authority.

Across the Carpathians the difficulties of the greatest contemporary autocracy were no less clearly displayed.

Revolts in the Ottoman Empire

Unquestionably the focus of the Ottoman Empire was Istanbul. An enormous population, perhaps 700,000 people, surrounded the headquarters of government. Here the communications by land through the Balkans and through Anatolia, or by water from the Mediterranean and Black Sea, were joined together, bringing to the city supplies of all kinds from territory near and far. From Istanbul commanders and administrators were sent to their posts as widely separated as Buda and Bagdad, Cairo, the Morea and Trebizond. Coming the other way would be units of Spahis, or cavalry servicemen, summoned from the lands assigned them, mostly in Anatolia. The Janisseries, or infantrymen, were recruited more commonly from the Balkan provinces, or in Istanbul itself. The Ottoman government, for a few exceptional years after 1640, appeared adequately in control of this vast empire, and of the great city. An admirable grand vezir had followed an oustanding ruler, Sultan Murad IV (1625–40).

Yet by 1648 and 1649 there were manifold signs of weakness. From 1644 Sultan Ibrahim I, deservedly entitled 'the Mad', disordered everything by holding sway through the officers of his household, rather than accepting guidance from those charged to command the various bodies of troops or administer the tax-system. He disregarded his grand vezirs, the council of vezirs, and the senior men of law and learning. He was luxury-loving and exorbitant. His Greek mother and other women in the elaborate household, though often intriguing against him, enjoyed excessive influence. At the same time he agreed to begin a new war for Crete, against Venice in 1645, which soon required a great increase of numbers in the armed forces, and taxes to pay for them; and neither in Istanbul nor Crete were the men punctually or fully paid. Essential military equipment, including ships and munitions, was in dangerously short supply. Financial crises soon followed, one after another, while Venetian flotillas stood close to the Dardanelles for months at a time, and Venetian commanders won victories in Dalmatia. In Anatolia meanwhile, bands of outlaws and troops commanded by rebellious provincial officeholders often roamed unchecked over wide tracts of country. Then at last, in August 1648, a number of the highest dignitaries in and outside the court combined, momentarily. The Janissaries of the capital, led by their Aga, were brought into the palace to depose and imprison the irresponsible Sultan. They found a successor in the person of his seven-year old son, Mehmet; the first flicker of opposition to this led a week later to the killing of Ibrahim. There were precedents for this coup, the theologians and lawyers had little difficulty in reconciling it with Islamic law. No issue of political principle seems to have been posed in the Ottoman world, as it was in England five months later. But Mehmed IV's minority, like Ibrahim's misgovernment, aggravated all the ordinary problems of court management in Istanbul. One upheaval led inevitably to the next in the following eight years; thirteen grand vezirs were appointed; they ruled for a few months or less, then to be dismissed or exiled or executed. Anarchy in the sultan's palace was intensified by the struggle for power between his grandmother and his mother, in which the so-called 'black' and 'white' elements of the household played a leading part.

The revolution of August was followed by further trouble in October. Money taken from Ibrahim's private hoard and from his proscribed favourites satisfied the janissaries, but other bodies of men in the court and capital – the Spahis, and the 'Pages' (cadets grouped in the different schools of the sultan's palaces) – felt aggrieved by the less generous treatment accorded them. The Pages were not promoted in accordance with the old rules determining their advancement on a change of rulers. Uproar ended after janissaries crushed the desperate resistance of both Pages and Spahis in the centre of the city: but friction between various sections of the Ottoman army remained a major weakness in the empire even when more effective grand vezirs asserted themselves after 1656. It made the double task of checking rebellion in Anatolia and Syria, and of pressing on with the war against Venice, so much the more difficult. The rebels, inspired partly by a strong contemporary upsurge of sectarian religious passion, advanced right across Anatolia to the shores of the Bosphorus by July 1649; and the same sects had a following among the Janissaries of the capital. The government, vulnerable and therefore conciliatory, on this occasion skilfully patched up a settlement.

The problem here was inevitably in part one of finance. Three-quarters of each year's expenditure was needed for military purposes. Annual revenue also amounted to three-quarters, or a little less, of the total expenditure so that the deficit had to be met by confiscation, loans, the increased sale of offices and manipulation of the currency. In 1650–1 Grand Vezir Melek Ahmed tried to impose new taxes and debased the new coinage struck, while calling up its nominal value. This measure soon wafted the fever of remonstrance from enemies in the palace to the barracks and bazaars. Unluckily, at the time penalties were also being imposed on sectarian preachers, who defended the people's taste for wine and tobacco, and this made things worse. A rising of Istanbul traders led to Melek Ahmed's fall in August 1651. Repeatedly the same causes were producing the same consequences. Weaker statesmen could not maintain themselves in office. The stronger, who attempted reform, met with the fiercer opposition.

In 1653 another grand vezir who insisted on financial retrenchment was succeeded by a useless old gentleman of ninety, and he in turn by a more forceful character who fell foul of Murad, the powerful captain-admiral. Murad had no difficulty in toppling his enemy. Mutinous troops soon brought the sultan to sanction a new round of executions; but Murad, now grand vezir, simply reaped the whirlwind. All sorts of discontented persons were flocking into the capital from Anatolia. Unorthodox dervishes roused popular passion against orthodox teachers and preachers, troops were now rebellious by force of habit, and there seemed no fiscal alternative to the minting of those debased coins which enraged the Istanbul tradesmen as well as the troops; the same restlessness could be observed in many lesser but still important cities elsewhere. Order was breaking down on a much wider scale in the Ottoman empire than at the time of Sultan Ibrahim's death in 1648. But disintegration reached its climax at the capital in March 1656 with the action of the soldiery, many of them recently returned from Crete and unpaid. They assembled in the Hippodrome, and rejected the smooth offers of messengers sent from the palace to which they then advanced. Formalities which in theory controlled the presenting of a petition from troops to the 'Divan' of councillors, with the sultan sitting concealed behind an embrasure, gave place to outright terrorism. The ruler surrendered councillors and servants to mob-violence. A new grand vezir was replaced by yet another within the space of a few hours. Two months passed before 'the lords of the Hippodrome' were brought under control. Two months later still, the Venetians won an important battle outside the Dardanelles, and followed this up by taking the islands of Tenedos and Lemnos. The blood-bath at the capital, the shock of more alarming naval defeats than any since Lepanto, and enemy blockading which sent up prices again, ushered in a new order. A consensus of persons in the Imperial palace, including the sultan's mother, seems to have agreed to give the widest possible powers to a prospective grand vezir who demanded them as a condition of taking office, the experienced Albanian statesman, Mehmed Köprülü. He represented the view, more widespread than a few years earlier, that the terror of authority deserved support against the spread of anarchy.

Mehmed Köprülü

For the previous eight years the upheavals of Poland and the Ukraine had drawn in Sweden, Muscovy, Brandenburg and impinged on the principalities of Transylvania, Wallachia and Moldavia. Over these forerunners of modern Romania as well as the khanate of Crimea, the sultan claimed suzerainty. Yet the Istanbul government, trapped by its own crisis, had been too weak to play an active role, so that the rulers enjoyed unaccustomed freedom of action. A notable episode in mid-seventeenth-century Europe was this feverish phase of Carpathian politics, which would end after Mustafa Köprülü's intervention in 1657. He restored Ottoman dominance in this northern rim of the empire, itself a counterpart to the equally troubled Ottoman border in eastern Anatolia and northern Syria.

Prince Basil 'the Wolf' of Moldavia and Prince Matthew Basarab of Wallachia the two Danubian principalities had already held power for many years (since 1634 and 1632 respectively). In different ways they were virtuoso performers. Basil copied Byzantine precedents in the organisation of his court and government, while storing away much wealth. Matthew impressed contemporaries as a warlike prince, who kept both his aristocratic boyar militia and his force of mercenaries fully employed. Both endowed the Orthodox clergy richly, while they were persistent rivals. On the other hand, across the Carpathians was prince George Rakoczi II of Transylvania, an ambitious but raw young man, the fortunate heir of landed wealth in Habsburg Hungary as well as in his own domain, where his father had increased his princely authority at the expense of the Estates. When Wladislaw IV died in 1648, George at once dreamt of winning election as the next king of Poland. The Poles' choice of John Casimir disappointed him.

The long, uncertain frontier between Moldavia and Poland made Basil's position a delicate one from the moment the Cossacks drove westwards. He oscillated dangerously between a stance of friendship or hostility towards the Cossack hetman, who stood between his lands and the Tartar raiders, and fought for Orthodoxy against the Catholics.

Yet Chmielnicki was a difficult neighbour, in 1650 encouraging Tartar raids into Moldavia, and in 1652 sending offers of alliance to Istanbul on condition that a part of Moldavia was handed over to the Cossacks. At the same time he pressed for the marriage of his son Timothy with one of Basil's daughters. The wedding took place in

May 1652. Momentarily the Cossack, Tartar and Moldavian rulers formed a combined interest, arousing the antipathy of the Poles on one flank and of Transylvania and Wallachia on the other. In 1653 a welter of palace-revolutions, sieges and raids brought Basil's reign to an end. Chmielnicki was robbed of an ally and his flimsy diplomatic system fell to pieces. Basil's successor looked to George of Transylvania for support.

The Ottoman government was an almost passive spectator of this change. Cossack ships from the Dnieper marauded intermittently as far as the Bosphorus, and at the same time Chmielnicki himself vainly invited the sultan's ministers to protect the Ukraine against aggressors. The weakness of Istanbul strengthened the hand of Moscow. The Cossacks turned to the tsar for help, and the Ukraine fell within the Russian sphere of influence after the treaty of Peryslavl.

When Matthew of Wallachia died in 1654 his courtiers and soldiers settled the succession and the Ottoman court took little part. Prince Constantine Sherban began his rule by trying to get rid of some costly and disorderly mercenary troops. They rebelled, and George of Transylvania then offered to bring his own forces to help. A resounding victory in July 1655 put Constantine back in power but gave George ascendancy on both sides of the Carpathians. It turned the Turks decisively against him just before Mehmed Köprülü appeared on the scene; and western envoys at the sultan's court were soon reporting that the Tartars had been ordered to bring fire and sword into the principalities. At the same time Swedish envoys arrived to invite George to join in a fresh attack on Poland. They appealed to the common cause of Protestantism, and offered a noble slice of Polish territory. His decision to join them coincided with Köprülü's rise to supremacy at Istanbul. He took his army northwards early in 1657 and was defeated. His losses in Poland deprived him of the power to defend Transylvania, or to preserve his influence in the other Carpathian courts, against a devastating onslaught from the south.

He and the two other princes now confronted the government which claimed authority over them all. Mehmed Köprülü may have been determined to assert his authority in the court, capital, and throughout the empire. But he realised that a reorganisation of the Carpathian frontier deserved the highest priority of all. This no doubt correct, very important decision lamentably extended to neighbouring areas the warfare long since weighing on the Ukraine and Poland. It accentuated the decadence in eastern Europe after 1648 which is one of the brute facts of the period.

Before 1657 ended the Estates of Transylvania prudently chose a new prince, while the grand vezir himself appointed new rulers for

Moldavia and Wallachia – one an Albanian and the other a Greek. The Tartars, many of them wheeling back from Poland, carried out a series of frightening raids into all three countries, while Turks pushed up to the edge of the Carpathians from their citadels on the lower Danube. The deposed rulers withdrew to Transylvania or Hungary, preparing to fight again, while hundreds of miles to the south the grand vezir at Adrianople assembled his main army to deal with them. The governor of Buda in Ottoman Hungary also mobilised. In 1658, 1660, 1661 and 1662 one or more of these separate forces was employed to besiege fortresses, burn towns, take up captives and overcome any opposition they met. A map of their itineraries[4] – comparable with the itineraries of Charles X and his forces in Poland – reveals graphically the repeated punishment inflicted on many districts. But the opposition was by no means slight. George Rákóczi could at first rely on manpower and rents raised on his own lands in the north. If the Habsburg government held back nervously, some Magyar families from Habsburg Hungary joined him. Above all, he relied on various interests in Transylvania itself, where the war accentuated social discord. Humble men with little to lose wanted to resist the Turks, accusing timorous property owners as appeasers who seemed too willing to raise extra taxes in order to meet the sultan's demand for a higher annual tribute than in the past. In the old Saxon towns the unprivileged clashed with burghers, and in certain country sides peasantry flocked to Rákóczi's banners while their landlords in the Estates wanted a settlement with the Turks; but other gentry also supported the leader whom they continued to regard as their lawful ruler. Twice in 1657 and in September 1658, the Estates named a new prince who satisfied the Turk; and twice, in January 1658 and September 1659, they acknowledged George again. He died of wounds in 1660 after the governor of Buda had completely defeated him; but the Transylvanians showed loyalty to another patriot, John Kemény, having deposed the Ottoman puppet; and another twelve months passed before he too died in battle, and resistance came to an end. The Turks fastened a new prince on the country, Michael Apafi, insisted on the punctual payment of tribute, and kept the great military strongpoint of Nagyvárad[5] which gave them direct control over a strip of territory stretching north from their old base at Temesvár to an area wedged between Transylvania and Habsburg Upper Hungary. The pressure they could henceforward exert on the Transylvanians was irresistible.

4   See map 2, p. 25 above.
5   *Grosswardein* to the Habsburg statesmen in Vienna, *Nagyvárad* to the Magyars, *Oradea Mare* in Romania at the present time. Temesvár is likewise Timişoara today.

In 1658 Köprülü was summoned back to Adrianople to deal with mounting unrest in Anatolia, while his nominee in Wallachia soon played him false, joined forces with the enemy in Transylvania, and helped to eject the other puppet from Moldavia. Again the Tartars were summoned, and pulverised their opponents. From 1661 signs multiplied that the Ottoman government was at last strengthening its grip on this side of the Carpathians. Kaleidoscopic changes continued in the two courts, but mattered less. Bucharest, on instructions from the grand vezir, now became the permanent residence of the prince of Wallachia. The political and financial influence of the Greeks, and the military dominance of the Turks, tamed the survivors of older native families in court politics. It is not easy to discover what changes occurred lower down the social scale, but in Transylvania the general impoverishment due to war and taxation seems to have been responsible for infiltration by Romanian-speaking groups into areas where Saxons, Szeklers and Magyars had formerly been much more numerous. In some ways, the rise of the Romanians proved the greater toughness of a pastoral economy under harsh conditions than of town-life or agriculture. The Saxon towns decayed, but shepherds survived. Flocks and herds continued to move backwards and forwards seasonally between the plains and the hills. They were the chief source of wealth for noble proprietors who rarely saw them; the sheep sold well in the markets of Istanbul.

Mehmed Köprülü died in 1661, after five years of rule. He had deliberately turned aside to deal with the major problems of the sultan's northern frontier, but combined this with a resolute attack on the political instability nearer home, while he at least held the Venetians in check. Superficially, and it is still very difficult to scratch far below the surface, he does not appear to have restored order in the government by measures different from those used by his predecessors. There were executions, confiscations, the dismissal of unreliable officials to distant posts; the grand vezir was careful to make certain, before he took any particularly drastic action, that he had secured the loyalty of the janissary commanders and he no doubt joined the use of outright terrorism with the ability to choose new men and good men. But two points stand out. One is that the sultan himself now proved old enough and firm enough to give unwavering support to the grand vezir; he had suffered too much in the crisis in the spring in 1656, learning a lesson he did not forget. From that time forward he took his court to Adrianople, rarely visiting the capital, with the fortunate and perhaps unforeseen consequence that dissatisfied elements in the populace of Istanbul, and trouble-makers among his household troops or servants, could no longer combine. Secondly, the finances improved. Compulsory loans guaranteed wages. Expenditure was reduced by combining thoroughly the schedules of those to whom wages were due, and cutting them down. Fief-holders had to pay for the reissue of the diplomas which assigned them their property. Tribute from the principalities went up enormously, in the case of Transylvania almost threefold. In 1660–1 the official budget was balanced, and very probably army pay was not in arrears between 1660 and 1680. The Köprülüs had no economic programme such as Colbert visualised; but they believed in good housekeeping.

In 1657, by observing a stricter time-table than usual in the Istanbul wharfs, the captain-general took a new fleet into the Aegean before the Venetians were ready. Ships from Barbary and Egypt were coming to join him. But one defeat at sea followed another before Köprülü thoroughly purged the command, the crews, the janissaries involved, and recaptured the islands of Tenedos and Lemnos. Two years later he greatly improved the fortification guarding the Dardanelles. This finally checked the Venetians and the Cretan war degenerated into a stalemate which suited the Turks perfectly while they dealt with their Carpathian problem. It was the converse of that predicament facing the Swedish king, which forced him to withdraw from Poland in order to fight the Danes.

For a long period, therefore, the cumulative result of trouble in widely scattered areas had been to make a general recovery unlikely in the eastern half of the continent. Two great empires, Polish and Turkish, sometimes seemed on the point of dissolution. Then, rather mysteriously, and shortly after treaties of peace were also signed in west and northern Europe (1659–60), everything tended to simmer down again after an immense wastage of human energy.

This upheaval had inevitably produced its flow of refugees. When the Cossacks rose in the Ukraine they assaulted not only the Poles but also the Jews, whom they hated as bailiffs on Polish estates, tax and tithe farmers, publicans or money-lenders. Important Jewish communities in Podolia and Volhynia were blotted out. Many Jews were taken captive by Tartars who shipped them across the Black Sea to Istanbul for sale in the slave market. Others escaped to the Danubian principalities, or fled west, to be joined by those who suffered in Lithuania when the Russians entered Vilna. Polish resistance to the Swedes after 1655 was accompanied by a second wave of anti-semitism. A sizeable emigration into north Germany, the Rhineland and Holland followed.[6] Old Jewish communities, as at Istanbul and Smyrna, responded to the call on their goodwill. They paid for the redemption of captives, helped the refugees, and organised an appeal

[6] A parallel movement of Unitarians from Poland to Transylvania, Silesia and Holland began in 1658, after the Diet's decree against them (see above, p. 41). But the fruitful period of Unitarian influence from eastern Europe on the west – particularly affecting the sectaries in Holland and England – was already over.

for more funds from the Jews in Venice, Leghorn and Amsterdam. This dispersion was not only a significant result of the warfare in Poland. It made a profound impression on thoughtful rabbis and students of the faith, bringing to the surface of their minds a conviction that such an ordeal was the sign that God intended a change for His people, which could be none other than the coming of the Messiah. Nathan 'of Hanover', in his work on *The Great Abyss* published at Venice in 1653, was one refugee whose account of the tragedy in Poland is strongly tinged with Messianic premonitions of this greatest of all conceivable revolutions in human history. Elements in the Jewish communities at Salonika and Smyrna were just as deeply troubled, and in 1665 the extraordinary person emerged who proclaimed himself the Messiah. Sabbatai Zevi, born in Smyrna, raised a ferment among his fellow-Jews throughout Europe and Asia Minor. His career, and the origin of his ideas, show how closely linked were the causes of tension in an area stretching from the Baltic to the Aegean. As we shall see, at the same time some Jews also left Spain and Portugal to look for refuge elsewhere. But they, moving inwards from the western edge of the continent, traversed a political landscape with far more sharply defined and strongly defended historic boundaries – separating one state from another – than were visible on either side of the Carpathians in those disastrous years.

3

The Eclipse of France

Mazarin's Mistake

In spite of this difference, around the year 1650 it is possible to fit a
working model of eastern Europe fairly neatly on to the west. Poland
matches France, Brandenburg the United Provinces, Sweden England
and Muscovy Spain. Encircled, France has become a theatre of civil
war and foreign intervention like Poland, while its strength decreases.
This deceptive similarity persisted for a few years during the Fronde
but in fact the long-term trend after 1648 discloses the rising power
of France, centrally situated, and to a greater or less extent dominating the surrounding countries. The decay of Poland continued, long
after a reviving Bourbon government had checked the apparent disintegration of France. By contemporary standards the kingdom administered by Cardinal Richelieu was a highly centralised state of great
size. Other autocracies existed, but they were smaller. Other large
empires existed, but they were loosely federated under a hereditary
or elected ruler. Any crisis in France, in this phase of its history, was a
crisis at the centre of power. Once such a crisis had been resolved or
headed off, popular grievances and social tensions mattered very
little.

For the French monarchy, the Westphalian treaties richly rewarded
intervention in the Thirty Years War and five years of diplomacy at
Münster. The terms for a settlement originally drafted by Richelieu
were for the most part adopted by Mazarin. He insisted on, and
received, the emperor's formal acknowledgment that the king of
France's century-old right to 'protect' the bishoprics of Metz, Toul
and Verdun should be converted into full sovereignty. Richelieu's new
Parlement in Metz now possessed authority to enforce Louis XIV's
claims on all the ancient dependencies of the three bishoprics, and
French lawyers were well aware that important parcels of such
territory stretched right through the duchy of Lorraine and far

down the Moselle valley. Other clauses in the Münster treaty transferred from the Habsburgs to the king of France many properties, and also an overriding sovereignty, in Alsace on the left bank of the Rhine. On the right bank of the river France received the citadels of Philippsburg and Breisach. These were the more valuable, because the emperor and his allies undertook never to fortify any points on the territory which bordered the Rhine between the two strongholds.

But French successes in 1648 were all overshadowed by Mazarin's fundamental miscalculation during the same year. It seems clear that he realised too late that the internal condition of France imperatively required relief from the burdens, especially the tax burden, of the long war. The instructions to his diplomats became a shade less rigid in August and he took the opportunity to make peace with the emperor. He had failed to come to terms with Spain because he confidently expected to squeeze further concessions from Madrid. The Spaniards made their separate peace with the Dutch. French power to put pressure on Spain was reduced by this diplomatic defeat and already the stresses inside France, previously magnified but controlled by the ferocious discipline of Richelieu before 1642, were getting out of hand. Arising from many special grievances a general exasperation had come to the boil.

There is a decidedly freakish element in Mazarin's rise to power which partly accounts for the agitations of the 'Fronde'. Richelieu, who had him made a cardinal and with whose encouragement he became a French subject, originally intended to employ this first-class papal diplomat of Sicilian origin as an expert on Italian affairs. Louis XIII, before he died, signified that Mazarin should be a member of the Council of Regency; Louis XIV was then five years old. The queen-mother, Anne of Austria, was strong enough to have the terms of her husband's will set aside. Having secured full authority as Regent, against his intentions, she proceeded to govern with the advice of the cardinal: her relationship with him was based on real affection and unbounded respect for his judgment. Military and diplomatic successes consolidated his influence. It was in this period that he brought over from Italy the first consignment of his numerous nephews and nieces, set up his headquarters at the Palais-Royal where the queen lived, and accumulated a fortune which he spent on building, the collection of works of art and fine books. His wealth and name dominated that part of Paris which lay between the Palais-Royal and the north wall of the city. He, like Richelieu, had gradually become a 'first' minister; yet his position did not depend on the favour of a ruling monarch, but on the much more fragile props of the queen-mother and the slick management of court politics during a minority. Many Frenchmen held strongly that dominance by a single minister was only permissible if a fully responsible king sanctioned it. During a minority, they felt, it was a dangerous breach of the proper conventions of government. When a child reigned who could not shoulder the supreme authority, his ministers were inevitably more liable to criticism than those of an adult ruler. When the regent preferred to rely on one man, a foreign cardinal, opposition to such a first minister was bound to swell. Royal princes, ambitious statesmen – like Chavigny and Châteauneuf, expelled from office by Richelieu, patiently or impatiently waiting for an opportunity to climb back to power – and, to some extent, everybody with a grievance who could express their grievances blamed Mazarin. Unlike Anne of Austria, a Spanish infanta, they did not believe that this Italian favourite was indispensable. They believed it the less when the government floundered. Right through the Fronde opposition rallied to the call for the dismissal of Anne's chosen minister. Her personal choice was in fact a prime cause of the political uproar.

Another was the rising prestige of the great family interest of the Condés. King Henry IV's father and Henry I Prince of Condé were brothers. For many years the next prince was heir presumptive to the throne. In turn his son, although docile under Richelieu, never ceased to increase and consolidate his wealth. The next of the line soon unfurled his own colours. The glory of victory at Rocroi in 1643 was, above all, Condé glory. The father died in 1646. Governorships in Berry, Bourbonnais and Champagne, vast inherited properties, the highest military command and the title of 'First Prince of the Blood' combined to give the young man colossal influence. His sister was the duchess of Longueville, her husband the greatest nobleman in Normandy. His brother Conti enjoyed large ecclesiastical revenues and the privileges of a high-ranking nobleman in the church. By comparison Louis XIV's uncle, Gaston Duke of Orleans, with his title of 'Lieutenant-General of the Realm', was an ineffective figure who failed to be as important as he might have been. For some years Condé was loyal to the queen-mother but few failed to see that the unexpected dominance of Mazarin, and the Condé interest, would never be easy to harmonise in the difficult course of a minority.

The Two Monarchies of France

Historians have recently learnt to draw a detailed picture of the repeated popular risings which broke out in the countrysides of western France from 1630 onwards, with less frequent but very serious disturbances in Normandy, Languedoc and Provence. Moreover, very large numbers of people were constantly on the move, and many came to the towns where they added to the dangerously unstable elements in urban society. In Paris, the population increased with alarming speed, filling up the area inside the walls and over-flowing into new suburbs. Rather surprisingly, rural disturbances of this type died down for the ten years after 1645. But the government's fiscal pressure, unbearably severe since Richelieu's time, increasingly affected the stronger as well as the humbler elements of society. The administration first squeezed one interest, then another, until the strain became universal. In addition to the *taille*, rising consumption taxes added to rising prices hit the poor, fresh taxation on houses in Paris enraged property owners (and led to an increase in rents), while the creation and sale of new offices diminished the value of existing offices because the profits had to be shared; the taxation of office-holders, by various methods, also increased. D'Emeri, the *surinten-dant des finances*, believed that royal credit depended above all on the small groups of financiers and tax farmers who could actually advance ready money to the various royal treasuries on the security of taxes. Therefore more taxes were raised to satisfy them; but this meant an increasingly heavy attack on the pockets of privileged persons who themselves claimed to belong to the governing authority in France.

As the internal state of the country grew worse the Paris Parlement protested more loudly. Peers and princes were entitled to sit in this assembly, but it was normally directed by the highest legal office-holders in the land. They were often men of great wealth and learning, with an intellectual tradition based on the idea that their Parlement was a sovereign court in permanent session and therefore superior in status even to the Estates-General, which only met at the king's bidding. In their view the five tribunals of Parlement functioning in the Palais, that ancient centre of Capetian admin-istration in the heart of Paris, were integral parts of the royal govern-ment which neither the royal ministers nor indeed anyone else had a right to disregard. Parlement registered and enforced the royal edicts; the provincial Parlements of Rouen, Rennes, Bordeaux, Toulouse, Aix and Dijon also registered and enforced them. This procedure required a scrutiny of what the government proposed. No one dis-puted the king's power to call a special session – the *lit de justice* – in the Grand' Chambre of the Palais, for the purpose of enforcing his sovereign will that what he wished to enact could not be tampered with, but many lawyers believed that Parlement had a right of respectful remonstrance. Bolder spirits held that it was entitled to examine and 'verify' edicts after a *lit de justice* had taken place. Richelieu, of course, bullied Parlements and pruned their powers; he exiled and imprisoned those who objected too candidly. Mazarin was milder in his methods, but he and the queen-mother were determined to hand down intact to Louis XIV, when the royal minority ended with his thirteenth birthday, the authoritarian legacy of Louis XIII and Richelieu. Accordingly, some Frenchmen were now convinced that the use of a sovereign's power to arrest, imprison, exile or execute, without regard for what they considered the proper process of law, was in fact a growing abuse of power.

This agitation, increasingly intense during the early years of Louis's minority, had its roots deep in the history of France. To understand what happened in the second half of the century, we must visualise two kinds of monarchy in 1648 within a single kingdom, in intimate contact with each other but more or less distinguishable. In one, what remained of the crown's demense co-existed with a large cluster of lordships or seigneuries held by noble families of varying eminence, and with provincial governorships held by the greater nobility. Lordships were transmitted by inheritance and marriage; although in the gift of the crown, governorships were also often handed down from one generation to another of the same family. This *noblesse d'epée*, the *gentilhommes*, men who in theory all had to serve the king with their sword – a duty which was the right of their ancient lineage – regarded themselves as an 'order' distinct from civilians, from both the humbler lawyers and administrators, and from the *noblesse de robe* who held the highest legal offices. But a great many civilians resembled the gentry of the sword in one fundamental respect: they also enjoyed a hereditary status which they expected the crown to recognise. Theirs was an interest, no less than the interest of holders of fiefs and lordships, which helped to constitute the monarchy. They assumed that the king's sovereignty (at least outside the royal household) co-existed with that of his 'sovereign courts' – like the Parlement, the Cour des Aides, the Chambres des Comptes and Grand Conseil in Paris, and their counterparts in the more distant provinces. These, and many inferior branches of the administration all over the country were staffed by officials whose posts had a proprietary quality recognised by the crown. Such offices had their price, like land or houses. The combined value, for example, set in 1665 on certain revenue offices held by the 'treasurers of France' and their subordinates was some 38,000,000 *livres*, or 17 per cent of the value of all the offices in the kingdom. They could be bought and sold. Such offices, since the early seventeenth century, could also be transmitted to heirs by paying an annual tax on them, the *paulette*. Whatever the friction between a military nobility based on the land, and office-holders (who themselves acquired an enormous amount of the best landed property), or between nobility of the robe and the lesser functionaries in small provincial towns, all formed part of a constitution in which the king, working within a legal framework of greater or less antiquity, acknowledged the rights of these privileged classes. The church similarly owed obedience to the king, but enjoyed a status the essential privileges of which he could not touch.

The other type of monarchy within the French government came increasingly to the fore under Cardinal Richelieu. It emphasised the overriding supremacy or sovereignty of the king throughout the realm, working through his chancellor, ministers, secretaries of state, councillors, masters of requests and the intendants sent out to deal with special problems on the frontiers or in the provinces. It cut into the semi-independent jurisdiction of lordships, frowning on the old power of greater lords to raise troops of gentry and peasants, and on the loyalty of these to their lords when this conflicted with the duty of subjection to the king. It tried to insist that noblemen paid the *taille* on part of their property, together with an oppressive equivalent in cash for their old obligation to do military service. In some areas, as in Béarn and Metz, it used new Parlements to assert royal authority; preferring in others to curtail the independence of old provincial Parlements and Estates, as in Normandy and Dauphiné, or at least manoeuvring to pit one against another, as in Brittany. Ministers and intendants were given extraordinary powers to enforce the royal will, brushing aside the ancient tribunals and bureaux. Edicts, which had to be verified by Parlements, were being replaced by proclamations published simply at the king's will and pleasure. Litigation was 'evoked' (or revoked) from the proper court and determined by councillors and masters-of-request appointed by the chancellor to settle it. The administration of the *taille* was taken from the long-established 'treasurers of France' by the intendants, who from 1643 began to farm it out to contractors and on occasion assisted them with troops or police. To the protesting peasant population the extension of this system of collection, already employed to bring in the duties on salt and wine, was a monstrous innovation. The older financial office-holders, robbed of authority and profit, regarded it with the same mistrust.

The friction between the two forms of monarchy was normally limited, and concealed, by close personal connections which still joined sovereign courts like the Paris Parlement and the Grand Conseil to the royal household or the chancellor's staff. The *procureur-général* and the *avocat-général*, for example, were specifically royal spokesmen in the Parlement. And the intendants were as a rule selected from the masters-of-requests, who had bought their places and played a part in parliamentary proceedings; in later life some returned to occupy parliamentary office. Other masters-of-requests, without becoming intendants, inherited or purchased at an earlier stage of their careers places in the Paris Parlement or a similar court, which opposed the excesses of autocratic government. Again, if many in the *noblesse de robe* hated the tribe of financiers and tax farmers, others married the daughters of these wealthy and successful men. From a common point of departure, in fact, those seeking a career might travel in different directions. One master-of-requests became an intendant, well paid, but with only a temporary commission, and learnt to wield special powers to serve the authoritarian interests of the crown. Another became an office-holder who respected a constitutional theory that historic 'sovereign' bodies were truly sovereign, except when restrained by the personal and visible exercise of a monarchy's personal authority. Many played both parts in the course of their working lives. The friction between two concepts of government was unmistakable. The same personnel, to a considerable extent, served both. The chances of a working compromise between them remained high.

The dominant classes, however divided, were also held together by a common interest *vis-à-vis* the great mass of the population. They were literate, and in varying degrees they all enjoyed some kind of legal privilege. The majority were illiterate or unlettered, and subject to the full rigour of arbitrary jurisdiction and taxation. Although all estimates for French government finance at this date must be cautiously treated, it looks as if about one-half of the annual gross revenue in 1649 was swallowed up by the payment of interest on debts and the cost of collecting the taxes. These two items are not properly distinguishable because the income of many office-holders concerned with tax administration was the equivalent of interest paid on the capital which they advanced to acquire such offices, and to exploit them. The 'rentes' handled by the Hôtel de Ville in Paris were in the same way taken mainly from the *taille* and other taxes, and paid out as interest to those who invested their savings on this security. Other office-holders and other types of government creditor had also to be satisfied, as far as possible, from current revenue. In addition, the scale of war expenditure meant that the annual deficits were huge. Further borrowing was essential, involving the alienation of still more revenue, and its anticipation for years ahead. A steady decline in royal credit pushed up the rate of interest to a ruinous height which again increased the debt. The details may be confusing, but it is at least clear that taxes paid by the masses provided a common pasture for the court and for every kind of royal servant or royal creditor. If the intendant could not insist on the payment of taxes by hard-pressed peasants, the tax farmer was ruined; if the tax farmer was ruined, he could not transmit the due amounts of *taille*, *gabelle* or the *aides* to those responsible for paying what was due to the *rentier* or office-holder. In 1648 the government of Mazarin and

Anne of Austria tried various methods of watering down or repudiating its old debt to a wide range of creditors, and of forcing them to incur new ones: the case for a reform of the administration accordingly looked very strong to those threatened. But the widespread breakdown of a settled administration during the next few years hurt them even more and they preferred thereafter to obey an unreformed autocracy.

By July 1648 the office-holders' opposition to the Regency's latest fiscal proposals had led them to defy the government. They boldly formed a combined assembly of Parlement and the other sovereign courts in Paris, and produced a programme of reform. Imprisonment without trial, fresh taxation or the creation of new offices without consent of Parlement, and the appointment of intendants (except in frontier provinces), were declared illegal. The *rentes* were to be paid more punctually. The *taille* proposed for 1649 was cut sharply, d'Emeri was dismissed, and a special tribunal appointed to bring fraudulent financiers to justice. These points were included in a Declaration signed by Anne on 22 October 1648, and more or less confirmed in March 1649. At least on paper the monarchy had been stripped of those very powers which both Richelieu and Mazarin judged essential for good government. In substance if not in theory, there had been a compact or treaty between ruler and subjects. Yet the Paris Parlement's claim to act as the guardian of limited monarchy in France, enforced momentarily, amounted to very little. It simply became one factor among many others in a short period of total instability. Then the king's government revived and at once insisted that the Paris Parlement should concern itself only with litigation, not with matters of state. A royal Declaration of 22 October 1652 forbade it to meddle in politics or finance. The assembly ventured, with a last flicker of obstinancy in 1655, to start discussing some recent fiscal decrees: the young Louis XIV on this occasion entered the Palais in his hunting costume, vetoed any further debate, and said to those present (in so many words) that he, and not they, constituted the state in France. 'L'état, c'est moi.' The most important legacies of the movement were probably two. Just as the king had learnt personally to detest the Parlements, just as no one expressed greater hatred and contempt for them than the young Colbert who had entered Mazarin's service in 1650, a bias of this kind no doubt coloured the minds of a whole generation of efficient intendants and other public servants in the next generation. On the other hand, among certain lawyers an attitude of reserve towards the rigours of autocracy survived. This came to the surface during Nicholas Fouquet's famous trial in 1661–4, and then submerged again until the end of the reign.

The Nobles, the Populace and the Provinces

The profound disturbance of the years 1648–52 did not stem merely from the grievances of office-holders. Between the drafting of the reforms in July 1648, and their full acceptance by the Regent in October, the government prepared counter-measures. In protest, a popular rising broke out in central Paris on 25 August and ended with the government's complete rebuff. In December Mazarin and Condé – who was then his ally – again laid their plans, removed the court from the capital and assembled troops to enforce a blockade and crush the opposition. During an unsuccessful siege of six weeks the Parisians stood by their leaders in the Parlement, who defied the court before negotiating with it. The Regent had to confirm her surrenders of 1648 by signing the treaty of Reuil in March 1649. Rioting in the streets also played a part in the manoeuvres which enabled Mazarin to arrest and imprison Condé, Conti and Long-ueville in January 1650; and when Mazarin was driven out of Paris in February 1651, so that Condé returned in triumph. But Condé failed to keep his hold on the court, and soon left it in order to organise rebellion. His campaigning brought him to Paris in June 1652, when popular elements were again feverish and militant. This was their last effort and their last chance. The police and good discipline of Paris were afterwards one of Colbert's great preoccupations. He was right but historians have not yet fully explained why the 'popular' risings in Paris occurred at precisely this period. For example, it is possible to show that from 1645 the normal cost of rye and wheat began to rise in the Paris markets. There, and in some other parts of France, grain was often in terrifyingly short supply between 1648 and 1653–4. This coincided with and was partly responsible for an acute economic depression. Wages and rents fell, unemployment and mortality increased. Early in 1648 the number of listed bankrupticies increased in Paris. Against such a background the threat of still higher taxation naturally caused profound alarm. On the other hand conditions are not uniformly bad during a bad period, and the worst harvests occurred in 1647, 1649 and 1651. They did not occur, as might be expected, in 1648 and 1652. On the whole, it is easier to show that political instability and civil war intensified economic hardships during the Fronde than that economic hardship was responsible for popular unrest in Paris.

Rumour, propaganda, and hero-worship or popular hatred: each of these could be a stimulus. The genesis of the rising in August 1648 is plain. A threat of coercion by royal troops crystallised with the arrest of the *parlementaire* Broussel – a white-haired patriarch who had earlier made himself conspicuous by opposing decrees for new taxes. At once the whole population of the Île de la Cité – on which the Palais stood, and where trade was closely connected with the staff and clients of its tribunals and other 'sovereign courts' – rose in protest. It was a demonstration by both bourgeois and people, collaborating in a spontaneous resistance to authority. Neither the court nor the timid dignitaries of the Hôtel de Ville could stop the assembling of armed citizens or the erection of barricades across the streets. On this occasion, Broussel was the hero to be rescued at all costs. But the solidarity soon came under heavy pressure. The burghers were speedily alarmed by the spectacle of violence which upset business and excused damage to property. Their fears were confirmed during the siege of 1649, and from this date onwards the ancient organisation of their guards was to be normally employed in trying to control more lawless elements. They wanted the enforcement of the royal authority, after their first and only defiance of it. The people, or 'populace', did not draw back in this way. They continued to focus loyalty on such favourites as Broussel and the duke of Beaufort, and hatred on other familiar figures; above all on Mazarin, but intermittently on Condé or the president of the Parlement, Mathieu Molé, whose conservative constitutionalism was quite incomprehensible to simple folk. Nor were they without allies. The outstanding feature of this period in French history is the interlocking of aristocratic and parliamentary opposition to the court with popular unrest in Paris. After the crowds had risen in 1648, alert politicians soon moved in to exploit and encourage it. The greatest of these manipulators was de Retz, the coadjutor and successor-designate of his uncle, the archbishop of Paris. This extraordinary man, strategically placed at Notre-Dame, tuned the pulpits when he wished, inspired a voluminous pamphlet literature and brought the people into politics for a few hectic years. Judged from the palace of Versailles a generation afterwards, it was an unforgivable crime.

De Retz was of course a nobleman. It was the aristocratic opposition, and aristocratic faction, which did most to intensify the disturbance in Paris by encouraging Parlement and citizens to resist Mazarin, and to spread disturbance over the kingdom by linking it with previously existing centres of friction in the provinces. When Mazarin and Condé decided to repudiate the constitutional Declaration at the end of 1648, and to bring an army against Paris, de Retz and others promised to help the Parlement. When the court then left the city, some noblemen stayed behind. They were quickly joined by others. Condé's brother Conti, his sister the duchess of Longueville, the dukes of Longueville, Beaufort, Elbœuf, Bouillon, Rochefoucauld jostled together in uneasy alliance. They were volatile, quick to turn on friends or to come to terms with a rival in order to crush a third party. Theirs was a kaleidoscopic school of politics, the art of using faction brought to a high point of finish. Like their women – the duchesses of Longueville, Chevreuse, Nemours and others – they never thought seriously about theories of government, but made a reality of that world of the imagination which, as playgoers and romance readers, they already inhabited. The heroes of Corneille or such romances as the *Grand Cyrus* (dedicated to the duchess of Longueville in 1649) were often engaged in mortal strife with a tyrant or an innocent ruler's oppressive minister, and whipped up the passions of the crowd against authority. The heroines urged on their men to desperate stratagems. It was now possible, at last, to play an active part in the theatricals of a more exciting stage.

The grievances, influence and attitude of particular noblemen were varied. The Vendôme family, for example, had been deprived by Richelieu of the title and emoluments of the admiralty and the governorship of Brittany. One of the Vendômes, the duke of Beaufort, a very unimpressive grandson of Henri Quatre, now emerged as an idol of the Paris crowds. Members of the Guise family also suffered under Richelieu; one of them, Elbœuf, soon sided with the Parlement in 1649. It was not forgotten that his forefathers allied with radicals in Paris sixty years earlier. Protestant magnates were equally involved. Richelieu had confiscated from the duke of Bouillon his principality of Sedan, close to the Luxembourg frontier, and the duke meant to recover it. In 1649, as a rebel in Paris, he hoped for help from his brother Turenne – whose name comes from a family stronghold in the upper Dordogne – at this date a victorious general in Germany, with troops ready for action elsewhere since the signature of peace at Münster. But Bouillon had other cards to play elsewhere. The old duke de la Trémouille, his father-in-law, might be expected to raise a force of Protestant gentry in the Dordogne region. The duke of Saint-Simon governor of Blaye, and the duke of Rochefoucauld governor of Poitou, both Catholics, had similar grievances against the royal minister. Powerful people of this type reckoned on the aid and sympathy of much more numerous groups. Mazarin's announcement in January of an Estates-General, summoned to meet at Orleans in March, was a counterbid to pacify the provincial gentry[1], but it stood little chance of softening their profound resentment against a court which, they felt, had treated them too harshly for too long while favouring a new generation of upstart officials.

To rouse influential men in these western areas also threatened to complicate the task of maintaining royal control in Bordeaux. Here

---

1   The local assemblies which met to prepare for this meeting were suspended, on royal instructions, in September 1649.

the troubles were probably more deep-seated than in Paris. The dukes of Épernon, of the greatest noble family in Guienne, had been governors of the city since 1622. Many members of the Bordeaux Parlement, rich men allied with the provincial treasurers, proprietors of the best rural properties and vineyards, detested them. The municipality, divided between merchants and lesser lawyers, and in opposition to the high nobility of the robe, tended to obey the governors. The humbler masters of trades, and the artisans, were always hard to restrain; many must have taken part in the very serious rising of 1635. In 1648 Épernon caused an uproar among the populace by permitting exports of grain from districts which normally supplied Bordeaux. He began to repair the castle of Château-Trompette, overlooking the city, and fortified Libourne near by. Troops withdrawn from the front in Catalonia were quartered in Guienne. News from Paris caused the greatest excitement, adding venom to all the local causes of discord. Senior members of the Parlement took the lead in opposition to Épernon. They were supported, as on earlier occasions and as in Paris, by the poorest classes. The municipality at first dithered, trying not to take sides, but then joined with the Parlement in defying the governor's authority.

In Normandy the alignments were different. The duke of Longueville, the governor, had been passed over in the competition for a number of attractive posts, both in Normandy and at court. In the province of his ancestral power, therefore, the governor now linked a strong aristocratic interest with the Parlement at Rouen, which was at daggers drawn with Richelieu and Mazarin for many years. These ministers had insisted on the device known as the *semestre*, creating by sale of office new councillorships in the Parlement and then dividing the whole body of councillors into two halves, which each functioned for six months at a time. The tactic raised funds for the government, placed 'new' office-holders by the side of the 'old', and made it more difficult for the latter to resist the registration of royal financial edicts. The Palais at Rouen, profoundly irritated, welcomed the alliance of Longueville; they both defied the court, which in 1649 found itself seriously weakened by this insubordination in an area uncomfortably close to Paris. In any case, the taxes had been so harsh in Normandy during the previous ten years that Anne of Austria – who in 1647 carefully avoided Rouen on a journey from Dieppe to Paris – could not rely on popular sympathy. Plain men hated the intendants far more than they hated the higher nobility. The imminent collapse of all royal authority in Normandy helped to persuade Mazarin to have Condé, Conti and Longueville arrested in January 1650.

Conditions in Provence were at first somewhat like those in Guienne and Bordeaux, but later followed the Norman pattern.

The governor, the prince of Alais, was a grandson of King Charles IX. Backed by the court, he had been at odds with the Parlement at Aix; the creation and sale of new offices, and the institution of the *semestre*, both caused him trouble. This quarrel was patched up at the end of 1648, renewed in January 1649, patched up again, but the intermittent violence of 'la guerre du semestre' only came to a close in August. Parties were formed both in Aix and Marseilles, and the hot-tempered municipal politics of the two towns merged into the struggle between governor and Parlement. The provincial nobility was also divided. The general challenge to authority in France certainly added to the unrest here and gave local discords a chance to break out with greater bitterness than before, but did not apparently alter their character. In the confusion one significant point became clearer: Alais' kinship and sympathy with Condé. As the rift between Condé and Mazarin grew wider at court, late in 1649, it looked as if Alais in Provence would take his cue from Condé.

In other parts of the country the old political issues did not necessarily become more serious as the news of trouble in Paris or Bordeaux filtered through. Bouillon and his allies in fact failed to push Poitou or Limousin into rebellion; the Protestants were quiet. In Brittany the traditional antagonism of Estates and Parlement, although it was no longer kept under control by firm central government, did not lead to civil warfare until 1651. But in eastern France what has been called the 'guerre de ravage' afflicted one region after another. From 1636 onwards enemy partisans had been raiding from Franche-Comté into Burgundy and Bresse; they continued to do so intermittently until 1658. In 1649 the royal troops could not maintain themselves except by ruthless quartering and requisitioning in Champagne and Picardie. Mercenaries brought back from Germany inflicted immense hardship on the rural population. The forces employed by Condé to blockade Paris did more damage to the surrounding countryside than to the city itself. Angélique Arnauld, abbess of the famous monastery of Port-Royal des Champs, 25 miles southwest of Paris has left a frightening account of the devastation caused by troops in her neighbourhood.[2] The inhabitants were robbed of their food – 'if they have half as much bread as they need, they are reckoned lucky' – and of their horses. They brought foodstuffs and furniture, and piled them up in the chapel of the monastery, considering this the best refuge available. At the same time, the stoppage of easy communications between Paris and the provinces was a grave blow to business everywhere. The very poor harvest of 1649 made bad times worse.

---

2 A. Feillet, *La misère au temps de la Fronde* (ed. 1886), pp. 127–8.

The Fracture of Government

The next phase was dominated by the rivalry between Mazarin and Condé. Their uneasy alliance had broken down in the course of 1649. Condé, reunited with the other members of his family, became so powerful that early in October Mazarin formally agreed not to make any important official appointments in future, nor even to arrange marriages for his nieces and nephews, without the prince's consent. A very unsubtle politician, Condé insulted the queen-regent, alarmed the king's uncle Orleans, and by his pretensions alienated some important but mercurial leaders of the real *frondeur* nobility, like the duchess of Chevreuse and de Retz himself. These accordingly combined with Mazarin. Condé, Conti and Longueville were arrested (18 January 1650). Mazarin had his chance to recover control of affairs. He failed; and he failed because the divisive elements in society had become so strong during the recent upheavals that a government which lacked the stiffening and prestiage of a king's personal authority proved too weak to repress them. Mazarin's tactical errors were now dwarfed by the general weakness of a minority.

The court tried to assert itself in 1650 by various methods. The first was by showing the flag and the king's person in the provinces. Condé's supporters, after his arrest, had fled from Paris and looked for help elsewhere. The court followed them. Its itineraries tell their own story: an expedition to Normandy in February; another, with considerable forces, to Burgundy where the hereditary influence of the Condé family was strong, in March and April; most important of all, the court and its troops traversed western France in July and August to subdue the points of restlessness and disloyalty, above all to tackle the problem of Bordeaux. Louis entered this city on 5 October. Mazarin intended to go on to Provence but his long absence had left him exposed to dangerous manoeuvres in Paris, so the court returned to Fontainebleau in November. Such itineraries from one part of the kingdom to another would have struck a medieval ruler as familiar practice.

The government also struggled to keep the administration going. The chancellor Pierre Séguier, who had been appointed by Richelieu in 1635 and remained almost continuously in office until he died in 1678; Michel Le Tellier, an untiring bureaucratic genius and secretary of state for war since 1642; Hugues de Lionne, the able director of French diplomacy under Mazarin's guidance – these men were still at their posts. The appointment of Nicholas Fouquet as *procureur-général* in the Paris Parlement gave the court a loyal and skilful spokesman where one was most needed. The Council of State, the *conseil d'en haut*, had survived, and Louis XIV is said to have attended it for the first time in his long career on 7 September 1649 at the age of eleven. One of the most important central institutions in later administrative history, the *conseil des depêches*, responsible for government in the provinces, emerges at about this time. In the provinces the sweeping abolition of the intendants had robbed the court of its most effective officials. But Mazarin and the regent never intended to honour their word, and the chancellor soon began to send masters-of-requests to different parts of the country to supervise the conduct of business in the king's interest. They caused a great deal of alarm to those who recognised a wolf in sheep's clothing, and there is no further trace of them in 1651 and 1652. The masters-of-requests were back at this kind of work by September 1653, and it was only a question of time before they found themselves entitled intendants as before, and enjoying similar extraordinary powers.

The arrest of Condé at first looked like the act of strong government, determined to enforce its supremacy in the state. The sequel showed, on the contrary, how strong were those elements in France which still acted as a brake on the royal authority. 'Madame,' a conservative lawyer is reported to have said to Anne of Austria in January 1650, 'what have you done? These are children of the Royal House.' They were indeed the greatest in the land, detained in prison without trial. Such a breach of the laws confirmed in 1648 worried even the most cautious leaders of the Paris Parlement. While they feared any repetition of the revolutionary proceedings of 1648–9, they regarded Condé's imprisonment from this constitutional point of view and it led them back to the idea that the queen-mother's reliance on Mazarin was the greatest danger of all. Churchmen were equally alarmed. They took a particular interest in the arrest of Conti, one of their own number, and a startling attack of this kind on the lawful privilege of the church likewise appeared to them a fundamental issue. It was, of course, also a pretext for opposition; and they soon refused to vote their customary 'free gift' to the crown. A movement demanding the summons of an Estates-General again gathered impetus. The Parlement opposed such a plan, but churchmen and noblemen in Paris favoured it. Just as important, a loyal Condé interest existed. The *Memoirs* of Pierre Lenet show movingly how a servant and client of the family took the news of the arrest: it was a dastardly, tyrannical act against the saviour of the state, the victor at Rocroi in 1643 and at Paris in 1649. The country must rise to throw out the scheming foreign cardinal! The household at Chantilly where the princess dowager and the princess and infant heir were living, where the splendid Condé court was maintained by a circle of noblemen, officers and ladies, believed implicitly that a great wrong had been perpetrated by the king's enemies. They decided to appeal to the Parlement in Paris against the arbitrary detention of a peer – with his own honorary seat in the Parlement – while the younger princess went to raise the country south and west. Berry and Bourbonnais, dominated by the castle of Montrond Saint-Amand, were Condé lands. Help from Rochefoucauld, Bouillon, Saint-Simon and others, was expected. The journey of the princess did not entirely justify these hopes; but she secured entry into Bordeaux. The humbler inhabitants welcomed her first, and then the Parlement and municipality. The Condé interest took firm root in the city.

By January 1651 the possible alignments, and indeed the whole pattern of events after each major crisis, had become sickeningly familiar to observers. When the balance of influence tipped too far in favour of Mazarin and the regent, certain court and territorial factions learnt to combine with the Parlement against them. They also managed to bring into play popular elements in Paris, while the provinces were too disturbed to help the court. This was the position in the first half of 1649, although Mazarin still enjoyed the advantage of Condé's loyalty. When Condé himself threatened to engross power at the end of 1649, Mazarin picked up support from various groups earlier opposed to him. But in January 1651 the same groups of *frondeur* noblemen, plus the Parlement and populace, were brought into action against the government. Mazarin counted on riding the storm by releasing Condé on conditions, but what followed soon showed how badly he misjudged. The Palais-Royal was under siege by the mob for a fortnight, with the king and queen-mother prisoners in all but name for a still longer period. Condé returned confidently to Paris. The cardinal fled to a refuge near Cologne. Momentarily the whole administration was weakened. Mazarin continued to advise Anne of Austria by correspondence, but her own influence reached its lowest point. Séguier, Le Tellier, Lionne and other ministers were denounced by the duke of Orleans (whose circle of courtiers and relatives pushed increasingly to the front), or by Condé. They were dismissed, but soon found their way back to office, the indispensable penmen of their age for any government in France. The parties of Orleans and Condé quickly fell out. But Condé's efforts to win a practical working dominance automatically set moving once more the fatal mechanism which at intervals linked one faction with another to build an alliance strong enough to crush the remaining faction, now deliberately isolated. And there were further lines of cleavage. The Paris Parlement still looked with suspicion at the suggested summons of an Estates-General. It also voted that in future all cardinals should be excluded from the royal government, irritating the clergy in general and in particular de Retz, who was bidding for the regent's help in securing him this very title of cardinal from the pope. He hoped to take Mazarin's place. De Retz in fact was swinging into action against Condé, whom the regent and the factions prepared to arrest a second time.

Condé was an intransigent blundering politician who failed to use his great influence to the best advantage. He could not reconcile himself to any loss of power; but power steadily slipped from his hands as he alienated potential aristocratic and ministerial support- ers, groups in the Paris Parlement, and ordinary citizens who feared the disorders of another rebellion. Both parties stood on the brink of violence for a few days in August 1651 – before they then gingerly drew back, preferring to see whether the forthcoming declaration of Louis XIV's majority would somehow resolve the crisis. The cere- monial which ended the minority in September, and with it the special powers of Anne as regent and Orleans as lieutenant-general, did nothing of the kind. A flat refusal was sent to Chantilly when Condé demanded a voice in any appointments to office made under the new régime; and he immediately hurried south to raise the country. Condé's temper, as much as his hereditary status, caused fearful misfortune during the next twelve months but there is some- thing to be said for the view that he was forced into rebellion.

Mazarin felt equally slighted. A royal declaration had been pub- lished, condemning him as a corrupt counsellor and forbidding him ever to re-enter France. He received secret assurances of the king's favour, it is true, but Condé and the cardinal each had reason to think that those nearest the crown now rejected them both. The later dominance of Mazarin, for which Condé was unintentionally respon- sible, would have astonished most observers in 1651.

The Struggle for Paris

The eclipse of the monarchy inside France and in Europe was glar- ingly exposed by Condé. Mazarin's Mediterranean policy had already collapsed. The last French outpost on the Tuscan coastline, as well as Tortosa in Spain, fell to the Castilians in 1650. Louis's commander in Catalonia sent his cavalry back to help the rebels in France, and Philip IV offered the prince men, money and ships. The ships would sail for the Gironde estuary. The troops would enter Champagne from the Netherlands. The duke of Nemours, who had joined Condé in his flight from Paris, prepared to bring to France a force of 8,000 German mercenaries put at his disposal by Philip's viceroy in Brussels. The very names of their colonels – Hohenlohe, Kinski and Fürstenberg – suggest that soldiery raised in the Thirty Years War were simply moving from one terrain to another. Nor was this all. The French court authorised the commanders of frontier towns to allow the duke of Lorraine to enter the country with his freebooters. His help was a more than doubtful quantity, his power to inflict harm on rural populations beyond dispute. For a limited time the France of 1651–2 resembled the Poland of 1655–8.

In many regions during the minority a conspicuous feature of French provincial life was the ability of territorial nobilities (and of members of certain Parlements) to raise troops of gentry and peasantry. Another was the great influence of the same nobility in such towns as Paris, Bordeaux, Orleans and Angers. They overawed municipal corporations, raised support from the urban populace, and in cases of necessity pitted one against the other. All the same, it gradually became clear that the support for Condé was too narrowly based to give him a real chance of success. His former ally, Longueville, refused to budge so that Normandy remained outside the struggle. Disorders in Brittany and Provence were too remote to affect it. He relied most on useful friends in such areas as Anjou, Poitou and Limousin, and on his hereditary influence in central France. Above all, he hoped to exploit the situation in Bordeaux, which he entered in September. The radicals here had organised themselves into an insurrectionary body known as the 'Ormée' (from the elm trees in a square where they first assembled to take joint decisions), they were in touch with the English revolutionaries so that a tinge of genuine Leveller doctrine affected their political thinking, they were strong enough to counteract the growing conservatism of burghers whom their views alarmed, and they now rallied to Condé. One of the groupings in the Bordeaux Parlement also backed him. But the city proved no more than a convenient base, and he was unable to hold down country beyond the Gironde or the Garonne. The arrival of Spanish ships in the estuary added to tension inside Bordeaux. While the king, court and royal army were based on Poitiers, Condé sympathisers managed to keep the Loire districts in a state of uproar, and Nemours joined them with his mercenaries. Weighing all the possibilities early in 1652, Condé himself decided to break out from the military stalemate round Bordeaux and to make a dash northwards. He joined his confederates not far from Orleans on 1 April, was successful in a brilliant miniature campaign, just failed to capture Louis in person and moved rapidly on to Paris, leaving his troops to follow him. It was a desperate move, with profound consequences for the history of Louis XIV's reign.

Feeling in the capital was feverish and divided. It is easy to see that many people feared that the arrival of Condé would lead automatically to hardship and bloodshed. The attitude of a majority in the Parlement and other sovereign courts, and of the 'bons bourgeois', was never in doubt. De Retz, now nominated a cardinal, feared the man whom he had done most to injure. But the duke of Orleans in

his palace, the Luxembourg, erratic as ever and no longer the lieutenant-general, was persuaded that the liberty of royal princes should be
upheld against a tyranny exercised in the royal name. In his en-
tourage were some effective agitators; and new pamphlets in circulation carried anti-royalist declamations to the point of republicanism.
Most important of all, there were some men in every walk of life
moved by hatred of Mazarin. Before the end of 1651 it became
known that the court, swayed by Anne of Austria, was again turning
to the cardinal while fighting the prince: but her tactic made it much
easier for Condé to win sympathy from those for whom this loathing
was the beginning and end of thought about politics. 'Vive le roi et
les princes et point de Mazarin' was their cry, momentarily substituted for the old and enduring popular plea of 'Vive le roi sans taille
et sans gabelle'.

Indeed, the cardinal soon bid high again. He raised a small army
by lavish offers to unemployed troops in the Rhineland. He secured a
private invitation to come to the court from Anne and Louis, and
then the French government's formal disavowal of the decree of
banishment. By the end of January 1652 he was in Poitiers with
useful reinforcements. He had also persuaded Turenne to come to
terms with the crown after years of antagonism, so that a first-class
general was available to match Condé. But his own return further
stiffened the opposition. For individual nobles, individual members
of Parlement and elements far lower in the social scale, it was an
intolerable provocation and justified resistance to the royal forces
sent against Condé. It even justified Condé's appeal for help to
Spanish commanders on the frontier and to the duke of Lorraine.

From April to June the battle for Paris raged. Outside the walls
armies under Turenne, Condé, and Lorraine cut intersecting paths of
destruction. A great asset to the inhabitants had been that a considerable part of their food normally came from the immediate neighbourhood, and many did not need corn reaching the city markets from
farther afield; both sources were now reduced to a trickle. The
Parlement and the Hôtel de Ville saw to the manning of the walls,
and refused to admit any of the combatant troops. Sections of the
populace grew increasingly restless. Condé's agents, with encouragement from Orleans' household in the Luxembourg, got them to
rabble anyone suspected of opposing the princes. The orderly transaction of business in the Palais came to an end, although a small
group of *parlementaires* – with that old fire-eater Broussel in the
van – warmly supported Condé. Hostility to Mazarin remained
the battle-cry and pretext for refusing to obey the court, but a
more primitive rejection of all authority rapidly got the upper
hand. Or so peaceable men felt, while the municipality tried vainly
to keep order. Early in July it summoned to the Hôtel de Ville an

extraordinary assembly of notables from every quarter of the city, in order to consider new measures for the protection of life and property.

At this point, the military struggle outside the walls came to a head. Turenne at last managed to mount an attack on Condé's troops around the suburb of St Antoine, close to the Bastille. They were forced back to the city gate. But pressure within the city to allow them a safe retreat mounted too. The authorities gave way to Condé, but not to Turenne. The exhausted soldiers of the rebel princes had at last entered Paris; and within two days Condé used them to coerce the deputies already summoned to the Hôtel de Ville. The massacre which followed, on 4 July 1652, was the climax and downfall of the Fronde. As much as any single event could do, it contributed to the future dominance of Louis XIV. The soldiers were posted round the building. The deputies arrived. Condé, no doubt unnerved by weariness after the battle, failed to judge the situation coolly. When the trend of debate in the assembly did not satisfy him, he gave his men their cue to do as they – and he – wished. There was a fusillade and a massacre, the municipal guards fought back, and finally the building was set on fire. It is not possible to say how many were asphyxiated or burnt alive; but the discredit of Condé and Orleans was soon complete. They could no longer control their troops. Their scheme to organise a provisional government under Orleans as lieutenant-general, a title conferred upon him by what remained of the Parlement in the Palais, broke down. Higher taxes were aimlessly decreed by this body. Prices were rising fast. The royal court summoned members of the Parlement – and the numbers who came increased rapidly – to meet in Pontoise, and made the gesture of arranging Mazarin's temporary dismissal. The bourgeoisie were encouraged to expel Orleans' nominees from the Hôtel de Ville, and to send a loyal deputation to the king. Condé's last hope, that the duke of Lorraine would come to the rescue, flickered and faded. The duke approached Paris once more and then preferred to withdraw. Condé accompanied him to Flanders, to serve the king of Spain. The government had triumphed at the vital point, in Paris itself.

Pacification in Guienne followed in July 1653 after a growing royalist movement finally proved strong enough to defeat the Ormée party in bitter fighting on the streets. The Spaniards left the Gironde estuary. Conti, the duchess of Longueville and the duke of Orleans remained in France but they were powerless. De Retz was imprisoned, before escaping to Rome. Mazarin returned from Champagne to hold power for the rest of his life.

It is sometimes felt that the intricate events of the Fronde are not worth the effort of describing them. Here was a series of rebellions which, if not just a dangerous game played by idle courtiers, were never connected with significant spiritual or intellectual ferment. No intelligent popular leaders appeared in Paris, and on balance the best French literature of protest at this date is poor enough by comparison with the best Leveller pamphlets in England. The conservative reaction which followed led government and society straight back to the suffocating discipline enforced earlier by Cardinal Richelieu, and intensified later by Colbert. A contrary view maintains that the Fronde was the significant climax of a long-term movement of resistance by the labouring classes against feudalism and absolutism. The *frondeurs* in 1648–52 were driven from behind by the masses, it is argued, and after the former were defeated the latter despairingly commenced a second cycle of peasant risings which occurred at intervals for another twenty years. Without doubt many of the provincial nobility, victims of heavy royal pressure since 1630 and of deteriorating economic conditions which increased prices and lowered rents (in certain areas), desperately wanted relief in 1648. For this reason they harped on the old traditional remedy, the summons of an Estates-General. The court seemed on the point of giving way to this demand in 1649 and again in 1651, so that France came close to much more severe modifications of Richelieu's absolute monarchy than were in fact conceded for a short time. The political upheaval was therefore not just a set of aristocratic tiffs, but a near miss at some sort of revolution, with a great deal depending on the personality of Condé. What seems indisputable is that the Fronde, and the economic and demographic recession which coincided with it,[3] had a predictable effect on later French history. Opposition was discredited, the royal authority was enhanced. For decades the propertied and intellectual classes as a whole preferred to serve the monarchy. Some took refuge in religious controversy which gave them an opportunity to defy authority without running the risk of causing real trouble; and for this reason the state always remained extraordinarily sensitive to the imagined dangers of Jansenist disobedience. But Louis XIV's ascendancy in France owed a great deal to the acceptance of autocracy, as well as to its enforcement, after a period of intense unrest coupled with unparalleled hardship. The habit of obedience grew. The instinct for protest withered. This was particularly true of Paris; and in the seventeenth century, if such cities as Paris, Istanbul, Moscow or London, centres of population and wealth in a thinly populated world, were docile, then government was safe.

The events of 1649, and still more of 1652, brought to the area round the capital the miseries already familiar farther east, where

---

3   It must be borne in mind that the economic and demographic disasters of France in the years 1691–6 were comparable in scale with those of 1648–53; but scarcely a dog barked. Political changes in the interval between the two periods were decisive.

French and other troops had been weighing on the countryside for many years, and also farther west in the chief areas of agrarian disturbance. Such men as St Vincent de Paul and Charles Maignart de Bernières, anxious to relieve suffering, collected money and supplies in Paris and organised their distribution in the worst-hit areas outside. By 1652 they realised that the problem was just as serious nearer home, and began to give more aid to the old and poor, the waifs and invalids, of the city's crowded parishes. But we must not over-draw this picture; life went on during the worst moments of the long crisis. Jean Racine, an orphan, lost his grandfather and guardian, who died in 1649. The grandmother took the boy to Port-Royal des Champs. Racine's first schooling under Jansenist masters therefore coincided with the Fronde; personal, not public, disaster moulded his early career. Again, in 1648 the Pascal family left Rouen and settled in Paris. For Blaise Pascal the next few years were a period of extreme intellectual tension. He continued with his scientific enquiries; his first religious experience was assimilated, if somewhat uneasily. Jacqueline, the sister, was more direct; she waited for her father to die, and then in 1652 entered Port-Royal as a novice. One detail is worth notice. Biographers have examined the financial transactions between Blaise and Jacqueline in the autumn of 1651 after their father's death. These show a French family of considerable property surviving the trouble in Paris with most of its assets intact. The sister transferred her inheritance to the brother, partly in the form of outstanding loans to individuals, partly in *rentes* on the Hôtel de Ville. She had to surrender these if she became a nun, receiving in return an annual income which her brother undertook to pay. This was a complex bargain, but lawyers and notaries went hither and thither on the business and finally satisfied their difficult clients – while the Fronde continued. People of this kind put security and property first. The catastrophic events of 1652, like the agitation three and four years earlier, helped to numb their political instincts for another century.

4

The Survival of Spain

Catalonia and Naples Recovered

The symptoms of Spanish decline were already clear to many observers by 1648 although these disorders in France served to mask them; but the survival of a great cluster of dominions under Habsburg rule is the really striking feature of this period. With the outbreak of widespread rebellious movements from 1640, it was by no means a foregone conclusion that the bulk of that huge empire would still present European statesmen with their chief problem fifty years later.

A famous text in Cardinal Mazarin's career is an instruction of January 1646 to his envoys, that they should offer to restore Catalonia in exchange for a surrender of the Spanish Netherlands to France. It has been relied upon to show that he was willing to sacrifice recent gains south of the Pyrenees in order to improve the vital and vulnerable defences east of Paris. The Catalans, after rising against Philip IV in 1640, had transferred their allegiance to the king of France. Louis XIII himself entered Perpignan in triumph. Rosas was taken in 1645, Lerida in 1648. French viceroys resided in Barcelona. It is assumed, all the same, that Mazarin regarded Catalonia as no more than a valuable pawn in the diplomatic game, available as a bargaining counter when negotiations for a settlement began. This view is surely mistaken. At the height of his success Mazarin planned a fundamental recasting of the state system in the Mediterranean world, with Bourbon power planted firmly south of the Alps and south of the Pyrenees. Spanish overlordship in Naples and Catalonia, Spanish garrisons in Tuscany, would both disappear. Philip's influence in Rome and Genoa would be severely pruned. Moreover, the substantial French military effort drew support from other developments making for expansion southwards. French emigration over the Pyrenees, both seasonal and permanent, which reached its climax early in the seventeenth century, had been concentrated on Catalonia.

Commercial ties between Marseilles and Barcelona were very close, with Marseilles using the bullion profits of this trade to pay for imports from the Levant; and although times were bad after 1640, French businessmen were reported to be gaining ground in Barcelona. Some Frenchmen also felt convinced that their king was properly asserting no more than his inalienable right to lordship in the Pyrenees and Catalonia. His was a claim to rule based on early charters and treaties which they regarded as flawless. The bishop of Conflans Pierre La Marca, the trusted permanent commissary from Paris in Barcelona, was the scholarly champion of this point of view; and his great folio, published many years later, the *Marca Hispanica*, contains the justification of Bourbon claims to sovereignty in ancient dependencies of the counts of Toulouse and kings of Navarre now inherited by the kings of France.

Already before 1648 the Madrid government tried hard to undo past mistakes in Catalonia, by guaranteeing the liberties of the old constitution which Olivares had seemed to threaten. It was helped by the growing unpopularity of the new administration which relied upon French support. The soldiery, as ever, alienated the rural population which in any case suffered from a run of poor harvests. The collapse of rebellion in Naples was followed by news of the growing paralysis inside France; both encouraged the Spaniards to press forward. When Mazarin imprisoned Condé in January 1650 he also ordered La Marca to arrest Marsin, an ally of Condé's who commanded the French forces in Catalonia. The Castilians began a slow but steady advance down the Ebro valley towards Barcelona. They brought the viceroy of Naples, Philip's natural son Don John, with a fleet from Naples and Palermo and with German troops from north Italy across the Mediterranean, to commence a blockade of the city late in 1651. The double effect of food shortage and epidemics was then at its most acute, while the French position in Catalonia suffered from the renewed crisis in France. The release of Condé led in turn to Marsin's release from his prison in Perpignan; he returned over the mountains to command the troops while La Marca had to withdraw in disgust. Finally Marsin himself went to help Condé in Bordeaux. Although the Spanish found it very difficult to assemble a sufficient army, and there were many delays, Barcelona finally fell in October 1652. Mazarin rightly saw this as a disaster of the first magnitude. Catalan rebels had to form an *émigré* government in Perpignan, while Don John began with reasonable success to tackle the multiple problems of administering the reconquered province. He won the support of the clergy, and the new authorities in Catalonia proved firm in their monetary policy, putting an end to the legal currency of a great mass of debased coinage. Conditions slowly improved in the later 1650s.

Mazarin by no means gave up the struggle. In each year from 1653 to 1656 the French asserted themselves in a limited way. From their base at Rosas and elsewhere along the old frontier they edged into Spanish territory along the Pyrenees. Only in 1657 were they content to hold the points already gained. In fact, the warfare of nearly twenty years dictated to the negotiators of 1658–9 the outlines of a settlement here: France could not keep its recent conquest of Catalonia; Spain could not keep its ancient hold on Roussillon. The proceedings of an expert commission set up by the peace treaty to trace out the new frontier in detail is full of interest. La Marca fought like a tiger to secure the maximum for Louis XIV on the basis of ancient right. He was not in the least conscious that the Pyrenees formed a 'natural' or a military frontier. But the upshot was to draw this frontier along the band of high ground, and to disregard the ancient cultural community of Roussillon and Catalonia. The French government soon introduced the *gabelle* into its new conquest, but the *conseil souverain* set up at Perpignan was partly staffed by *émigré* Catalans. The Spaniards were still hoping for an insurrection there in 1674, but against this must be set the apparent readiness with which people in Barcelona accepted the loss of Roussillon by the treaty of 1659. Their traditional dislike for, and rivalry with, the citizens of Perpignan had something to do with it. These Pyrenean clauses formed the most permanent part of the treaty of the Pyrenees.

The Catalan rebellion had presented a fundamental challenge to the government at Madrid, which cannot be said of the risings in Palermo or Naples in 1647–9. They frightened the Spaniards; but it was much more difficult for Mazarin to intervene effectively at either point, while the local challenge to Philip IV was in fact less serious.

The viceroys of Sicily and Naples simply lacked the force to restore order immediately in very large towns once the crowds got out of hand. In 1647 the grain shortage had become such in Sicily (in good years a land exporting corn) that the municipality of Palermo could no longer hold down the price of bread except by allowing a reduction in the size of loaves, at a time when famished persons were flocking in from the countryside. Riots broke out, and one man in particular – Giuseppe d'Alesio – pushed forward to lead those much humbler than himself. He was ambitious, while his education and instincts combined to fire his language with the ancient republican ideal of civic equality. The rich and the territorial nobility did indeed monopolise municipal government in Palermo, the conditions were awful, and he detonated the view of many on the streets that the rich and privileged exploited the common misery. Momentarily the viceroy had to give way, and d'Alesio acquired the office of 'syndic' of the city. Within a few weeks a new combination of forces, including the viceroy, the head of the Inquisition, many noblemen, many masters of guilds, and a section of the mob, had overturned and slaughtered him: so meagre was the support for d'Alesio on the basis of his programme for better government, lower taxes, cheaper bread and exclusion from the municipality of nobles who were not citizens of Palermo. In effect, the propertied classes rallied to the viceroy in whom they saw the guarantor of the internal peace and discipline which accorded with their interests. The short-lived upheaval of Palermo had echoes in rural districts, where there were signs of real tension between gentry and peasants, and also in such towns as Syracuse and Catania where heavy taxes on the silk trade appear to have been the main grievance. During the crisis Messina gave Madrid no qualms. The old antagonism of this city and Palermo was one useful buttress of the Spanish overlordship in Sicily.

Unrest in Naples was on a larger scale. The counterpart to d'Alesio here was not the famous fishermonger's boy Masaniello, killed nine days after leading the mob to protest against a new fruit-tax, and then given a marvellous funeral; the figure who became an ikon of popular revolution for decades ahead. Instead it was Giulio Genoino, who was in some respects the counterpart of the *parlementaire* in Paris, Broussel. A very old man, a radical sage, he believed that the people had been thrust out of their rightful place in the municipality and then oppressed by the rich, who bought titles of nobility and prospered by farming the taxes which increased the price of bread and fruit. He used the idols of the crowd to win office for himself, and visualised a new form of municipal government in which representatives of the people and of the old, legitimate, nobility joined forces for the common good. But in Naples a *frondeur* element, the readiness of individual noblemen to exploit the crisis, was much more noticeable than in Sicily; and, like the *frondeurs* of Paris they hoped for help from outside. After all, for over a century the traditional impulse of those few actively opposed to Spanish dominance in the kingdom had been to look to France. In addition the influential cardinal archbishop of Naples, Filomarino, was closely connected with the Francophile party in Italy. A man of modest origins in a position of great power, he seems to have disliked the nobility as well as the viceroy, and sympathised with the populace. He could, and did, play a devious part; if opportunity offered, he also was ready to accept French intervention.

Mazarin at this date worked for far-reaching changes in Italy. He pressed the duke of Modena to attack the Spaniards in Lombardy. Recovering from earlier setbacks in his dealings with Pope Innocent X, a formidable political opponent, he had built up the French interest in Rome again. He used his fleet in 1646 to capture useful harbours in Elba and Tuscany from their Spanish garrisons. Yet the French naval repulses of December 1647 and August 1648 were

decisive for the later history of south Italy. Before the first of these
dates reinforcements from Spain under Don John reached the Bay of
Naples. Friction between the viceroy's many enemies had already led
to Masaniello's violent death and the removal of Genoino, while new
popular leaders now reacted to increased Spanish pressure – from
Don John's ships and from a number of fortified points holding out
inside the city – by proclaiming a republic. A French pretender, the
duke of Guise (who came without Mazarin's permission), then
arrived from Rome; a month later the French fleet appeared. A
hard battle was fought, but the ships from which Mazarin expected
so much had to withdraw. While Don John guarded the approaches
by sea, the revolution in Naples collapsed. Mazarin prepared a
second expedition on a bigger scale and a fleet under Prince Thomas
of Savoy arrived off the city on 6 August – twenty days before the
arrest of Broussel in Paris (see p. 60 above). The attempt to land
troops at Salerno proved a fiasco, Spaniards and Neapolitans combining to drive them back to the boats. For the next ten years the
French naval force was a nullity in the Mediterranean and elsewhere.
This weakness helped the Spaniards to keep their empire together,
but how lucky they were! For if Naples had risen a few years later,
when the English and Dutch governments began sending powerful
squadrons into the Mediterranean, Philip IV would probably have
had to reckon with an opponent strong enough at sea to stop his own
troops and ships moving easily from one threatened point to another.

On land a very different set of circumstances favoured his government. Although there were *frondeur* noblemen in Naples, the privileged orders soon realised that they had everything to lose if the
revolution continued. Genoino first tried to focus popular feeling
against the nobility's and the tax farmers' stranglehold on the municipality. Cross-currents of opinion in the city weakened the force of
this grievance, but violence quickly spread to the provinces, where
class hatred was more articulate than anywhere else in Europe at the
time. Apparently some four-fifths of the total population of the kingdom of Naples (outside the capital city) were subject to the jurisdiction of lords who either owned or controlled by far the greatest part
of the land. Many townships once directly subject to the crown had
recently been alienated. The beneficiaries were often ecclesiastical
foundations, or families of Genoese extraction whose credits to the
crown had been cancelled by these grants of provincial revenue. They
had also married into, or purchased from, the older territorial
families. Estates were protected by the legal devices of entail and
primogeniture and, in the case of the church, by the safeguard of
mortmain. These conditions prevailed in Sicily and Sardinia as well
as in Naples, but here the bitterness seems to have concentrated on a
particular aspect of the land question. For centuries the privileged

orders and the unprivileged were at odds over the great issue of what was, what was not, communal ground, and what were the rights of each on this land. The citizens of many townships had the strongest conviction, sharpened by endless litigation, that their claims were based on old precedent; while piece by piece the lords annexed these lands to their own property. As taxation of the unprivileged increased during the Thirty Years War, the country grew poorer, and the necessity grew greater for both parties to make use of every scrap of ground which promised any economic advantage. When the signal of rebellion was raised in the city of Naples, war between the hench-men of absentee landlords and the rural population – normally limited to small-scale affrays or hearings in the courts – became public and widespread. Both the townships and countrysides of Calabria, Basilicata and Bari, and the far south around Lecce and Otranto, were deeply disturbed. Around Naples itself the consequences were obvious. The people rose against the lords, but the lords flocked loyally to the rescue of the Spanish viceroy. In spite of personal feuds they co-operated sufficiently to blockade the city by land, to cut off supplies badly needed by the friends of the duke of Guise or the popular leader Annese in the early months of 1648, and to reinforce the few Spanish troops at critical moments. When the Count Oñate arrived from Rome early in March, appointed by Philip as his new viceroy, the revolution was practically over. Mazarin's second expeditionary force arrived too late to find effective allies.

Historians continue to debate whether Oñate and his successors improved the lot of the unprivileged by harsh measures against individual nobles, or weakly accepted the practical dominance of the nobility in the state. In 1648, certainly, the royal government and the privileged orders as a whole recognised their great common interest in restoring internal peace on the old basis. The Spanish monarchy in Naples, as in Catalonia and the Netherlands, now warded off any dangerous aristocratic disaffection by declining to tamper with the existing constitutional framework. Ineffectiveness, and the lack of any decided reforming impulse, helped to leave it intact long after the crisis of the mid-century was over. And whatever the miseries of its provinces, of the Mezzogiorno, Naples remained the largest city on the shore of the Mediterranean and a great centre of civilised life. Alongside the populace and the rich lived various categories of literate tradesmen and well-educated professional men. Many lawyers maintained their traditional anticlericalism, defending lay interests against the pretensions of the church. Teachers in the university made the study of Descartes' work the basis of a critical outlook which did not spare conservative notions in philosophy and science. There were enlightened noblemen and good Jesuit schools and daring painters. Born in a house on the 'street of the booksellers' (or San Biagio dei Librai) in 1668, that great philosophical thinker of the next century, Giambattista Vico, benefited from this environment and from the education which it gave him. When a certain Sicilian lady named Scarlatti became the mistress of a senior official, in Naples in 1683, the appointment of her brother Alessandro Scarlatti as *maestro di capella* in the viceroy's chapel soon followed – it was an important event in the musical history of Europe.

Plague, Silver and Status

In one important respect the place of Naples in the Spanish empire did alter at this period. During the 1630s and 1640s the Council of Italy in Madrid had never ceased to demand from the viceroys money and men for use in Lombardy or the theatres of war north of the Alps. The Spaniards still appeared strong enough to counter all Mazarin's efforts after 1653 to reopen the fighting in Italy on any scale; they recovered the Tuscan ports. Their admirable viceroy in Milan helped the duke of Mantua to expel French troops from the famous fortress of Casale (in October 1652) which for over twenty years had been the main outpost of France in north Italy. Even the marriage of another niece to the duke of Modena in 1655 did not bring Mazarin any worthwhile military reward. But Neapolitan contributions to the Spanish cause now lagged sadly behind, while the great decimation of the city itself by plague in 1656 depleted both public and private revenue.

This disaster, which any administration of the day would have been powerless to check, was in fact only one phase in the cycle of epidemics which struck at Valencia and Seville (1647–8), Catalonia (1650–4), Sardinia (1652–6), Languedoc (1653) and Genoa (1656). A very high death-rate – afflicting a band of territory right round the coast from Italy to Spain[1] – was probably one of the worst blows struck at a Mediterranean economy which had already been in decline for thirty years. At the same time, and in this respect governmental weakness played a bigger part, nothing did more to hamper ordinary commerce than piracy and privateering. These reached their maximum intensity in the western Mediterranean shortly after 1650, when ships from Algiers and other African harbours were prodigiously active. The Balearic islands provided a refuge for some of the toughest freebooters. Provençal noblemen, while the French navy in which they formerly served fell to pieces, went in for privateering

---

[1] See a remarkable *Journal of the Plague Year: The Diary of the Barcelona Tanner Miguel Pazets 1651* (ed. J. S. Amelang, New York, 1991).

on their own account. Large Dutch or English ships could protect themselves, their convoy system was superior and foreign merchants in Leghorn and Naples profited accordingly, but native traders of these seas could not so easily drive a peaceful business. It was still the case that Genoa remained an important banking centre for the Spaniards, and that bullion found a way here via Cadiz and Seville. It is also true that the Genoese Republic tackled the aftermath of the plague in 1656 with extraordinary vigour. But the Mediterranean world as a whole no longer helped positively to support Philip IV's international empire.

More tentatively, the same may be said of Spanish America. Whereas in every decade between 1580 and 1630 at least 50 million *pesos* of bullion imports from Peru and Mexico had been registered at Seville, the amount dropped to 25.5 millions in 1641–50, and did not rise above 10.7 in 1651–60. During the final stages of the great war in Europe the amount of fresh treasure, and the share of this at the Spanish government's disposal, fell to a catastrophically low level. Its power to maintain troops and to find allies was much impaired. There is some evidence that American silver output began to increase again after 1660, the amounts of bullion reaching Spain were still judged a matter of the highest interest in European diplomatic correspondence of 1670 and 1680, and everyone remained convinced of the enormous commercial significance of Spanish American trade. In its economic aspect the decade 1651–60 in Italy, Spain, and Spanish America may therefore have been the worst of the century.

The declining profit of the overseas empire to the monarchy would have mattered less if Spain itself had been stronger. Olivares had tried, but failed, to make Portugal and the lands of the crown of Aragon (including Catalonia and Valencia) contribute more generously to his ambitious imperial policy in Europe. He did so because the lands of Castile, with three-quarters of both the total population and total area of Spain, were visibly a decaying asset. Like Olivares, modern historians distinguish sharply between Castile where the king's power to tax was much greater, and the neighbouring regions where ancient constitutions remained practically intact, restricting the royal government at every turn. They also tend to confine the worst symptoms of decadence, such as a severe shrinkage in population or the collapse of industry or a demoralising monetary policy, to Castile. Elsewhere in Spain they find the symptoms less serious, so that a recovery from the phase of greatest hardship or apathy came about more easily. It is also fair to assume that by the middle of the century the decline of Castile had already gone a long way while recovery in the peripheral lands had not begun. In Castile itself the old monarchy grew weaker and the aristocracy stronger. Life for the unprivileged was so harsh that men of any local influence tried to acquire the status of *hidalguía* or nobility. The crown vainly instructed its officials to resist them. The chanceries of Valladolid and Granada examined countless disputed applications, but too often gave way; the persons concerned were able to prove that they had lived 'like noblemen' for a long time past. The percentage of accredited noblemen in the population increased. Normally town-dwellers with town houses, they lived on the income of their rural property and on quit rents. They were qualified to hold civic office, because in many municipalities the crown had accepted the principle of the *mitad de officios* – viz. that a minority of noblemen could claim half the official posts available. At a higher level, within the orbit of the royal court, climbing the ladder of rank absorbed the energy of many ambitious persons. Convention allowed fairly easily the outright purchase of titles by a man whose quality as a *hidalgo* was unquestioned. Accordingly, the crown sold such titles for cash or services, and new counts and marquises proliferated. At the highest level of all, there were 41 grandees in 1627 and 113 in 1707. The change resulted from both the crown's policy and the subject's need, but the interplay of these altered in character around the middle of the century.

Before the fall of Olivares the multiplication of honours had the effect of binding powerful interests to the court. The great flocked to Madrid, became obsessed with competition for precedence and office, and were not tempted to build up a territorial influence in distant provinces which might have alarmed the central government. Olivares himself naturally had something else in mind; he looked for funds wherever he could find them. His financial pressure on the aristocracy was direct and menacing. He compelled its members to raise troops and to give or lend money, and in return he sold or gave advances in rank. For their part, noblemen were often simply trying to make ends meet as economic pressures increased. Families could not maintain themselves as rents fell in the country and prices rose, except by competing for the rewards which rank and official favour alone made available. This, for example, was the significance of the Military Orders of Santiago, Calatrava and Alcantara in Castile; they provided revenues for lucky members of the high nobility, while lesser mortals who secured the privilege of entry into the orders won by doing so a valuable confirmation of their status as noblemen. After Olivares fell from power in 1642 the pressure of an authoritarian government gradually relaxed. Luis de Haro, his successor as Philip's principal adviser, was a softer man. The tone of the government altered. Little by little those who had been bullied found themselves able to take advantage of the administration's weakness. Although the wars continued they sacrificed a smaller part of their own revenues than before. They went on scrambling for office and title, but got the better of the bargain. They paid for titles but won more than they lost in the process. They also won greater political influence, both in court and in the provinces. It seems probable that, except by entering the church, fewer able commoners and ex-commoners were now able to climb the ladder of preferment from the bottom, overtaking on the way those already privileged, than in the days of Phillip II. The door opened less easily to the university-trained jurist. By the time the war against France ended in 1659 and the minority of Carlos II began in 1665, a golden or at least silver age for the high Castilian aristocracy had already begun. Behind the façade of royal authority, elderly grandees hugged tightly their social and political supremacy.

A by-product of this was the collapse of another element in Olivares' policy, his attempt to employ and exploit the converted Jews still in Spain (and Portugal). When he fell from power, a new inquisitor-general fell into line with popular prejudice. Don Diego de Arze Reynoso's period of office (1645–65) was associated with *autos da fé* on the grand scale, with renewed vigour towards those suspected of Judaism, while the chanceries – whatever their gentleness towards other candidates – insisted that a lineage free from Jewish elements was required for preferment. If wealth could often buy an advance in status, it was therefore with the important exception of Jewish wealth. This reaction must have added to the numbers of crypto-Jews seeking to leave the Peninsula, and to the increasing size of Jewish communities elsewhere. An attempt was made, from Amsterdam in 1653, to secure permission for a synagogue to be built at Antwerp, but the papal nuncios in Brussels and Madrid intervened to crush the scheme. A petition to Cromwell was more successful and, just as important, Charles II and James II would show the same tolerance towards the growing Jewish community in London.

A general decrease in the population of central Spain outside Madrid, with a decline in agriculture and the industrial activity of many towns, was of course far advanced by this period. One novelty deserves emphasis, the effect of the war with rebel Portugal. The Portuguese had risen in 1640, and the Spaniards did not finally recognise their independence until 1668. The cost of the struggle on both sides was enormous, and the motives of the Madrid court seem to have been fundamentally dynastic: the Habsburg ruler, by right king of Portugal, was not prepared to accept the claim of the usurping house of Braganza in the person of John IV. Considerations of economic or military advantage mattered, but less than the assertion of sovereignty. For a number of years after 1648 the chances of a reconquest looked brighter. The Portuguese, in spite of intense diplomatic activity, failed to get the negotiators at Westphalia to listen to them. Mazarin was curiously uncooperative. The Dutch, by making peace with Spain in 1648, while they were themselves committed to the policy of taking colonies from Portugal, had given the Spaniards an opportunity to commit more of their energy to the business of beating the Portuguese. But few men, except soldiers on the spot, seriously examined the difficulties of warfare along the geographical barrier protecting Portugal on the landward side. Philip IV and his advisers were never able to overcome them. It was not for want of trying. They conscripted troops to descend the Minho and Tagus valleys, to advance from Badajoz to Elvas, and even to take the southerly route towards Beja. But in each case the chief sufferers were the Spanish populations on lands which marched with the frontier. Before long the Council of Finance in Madrid, usually a flint-like body, was exempting from taxes many places in this area, a remission explained by massive depopulation which occurred there during the long war. Large towns became small ones in the course of twenty-eight years, and villages disappeared. It is noticeable that such losses seem to have been much heavier in western than in eastern Andalusia, while Estremadura was completely ruined. Galicia in the north, which tended to have a large surplus population, suffered proportionately for several decades.

Portugal's Defence

Madrid's failure was the measure of Lisbon's success. The union of both monarchies between 1580 and 1640 had left the old Portuguese governing institutions largely intact, and King John IV's advisers showed real energy in using or adapting them. The Council of State, a Council of War, an Overseas Council, the Cortes and the municipality of Lisbon functioned together to defend the revolution. Moreover, the situation was so dangerous while Spain threatened the mother-country, and the Dutch attacked its overseas empire, that the new Portuguese government accepted the need to make real sacrifices. John IV, and the regency which took over after his death in 1656, finally took advantage of the political flux in Europe to collect sufficient aid from abroad to safeguard their independence. They wore the Spaniards down.

One example of their realism was the foundation in 1649 of the 'General Brazil Company'. The crown allowed the new trading company a monopoly of the export to Brazil in return for an undertaking to finance and organise a system of armed convoys across the Atlantic. New ships were badly needed to beat off Dutch commerce raiding, which had been devastatingly successful in 1648. Portugal was robbed of its most valuable asset in European markets, the sugar imports from Brazil. King John, in the act of founding the company, severely limited the Inquisition's authority to confiscate the property of crypto-Jews – the 'new Christians'; and the financial resources of this suspect interest largely paid for a naval armament which in 1650 checked the Dutch raiders, and helped towards the reconquest of Dutch-occupied Brazil in 1654. Such a policy was only carried through in spite of bitter clerical opposition in Lisbon, and could not be enforced for long. The Jews in Brazil were compelled to leave the country when the Portuguese chased out the Dutch. Some removed to the West Indies and to New Amsterdam – they were the founders of the great modern Jewish community in New York.

Meanwhile English ships were hired for the Portuguese armadas, and reviving English naval power under the Commonwealth made its weight felt at Lisbon. The two governments first came to terms in 1654, although the Anglo-Dutch war had already providentially eased the Dutch pressure on Brazil. This treaty allowed the English to trade freely in Portuguese colonies, and to repair and provision warships in Portuguese harbours. The tariff on English goods was fixed at a reasonably low level; and the rights of English Protestant traders were safeguarded. It foreshadowed the further agreements of 1660 and 1661, which gave Portugal an ally providing troops and ships for the war against Spain, while the price of Charles II's marriage to Catherine of Braganza included the promise of a large dowry, and the cession to England of Tangier and Bombay. The permanent intimacy of the two Atlantic states, with its important commercial and naval consequences, dates from these years.

Commotion in the Baltic between 1655 and 1660 also helped the Portuguese. It strengthened the hand of interests in Holland which always disliked the Dutch West India Company's expensive commitment to the war in Brazil, or felt that an undisturbed trade in salt from the Portuguese coast promised safer returns than the risks of colonial responsibility in America. An ultimatum to Lisbon in 1657, demanding the cession of Brazil and Angola, was really the last fling of a militant party in the United Provinces. Portugal resisted, a blockade of the Tagus by Admiral de Ruyter petered out, while the English obviously profited by snatching business from Dutch merchants and shippers. The two governments of Lisbon and the Hague settled down to a long and wrangling negotiation which ended in 1662, with Portugal left in full control of its old American and African colonies (except in Guinea). The United Provinces secured a very large indemnity and the right to trade with the Portuguese empire on the same favourable terms as the English. Freed from the Dutch war, though not for many years from the crippling indemnity, assisted by forces raised in England and at last by substantial French support, the Braganza monarchy was far better placed to deal with a final Spanish attempt to crush it.

Flanders: The Anglo-French Alliance

Philip, reciting his troubles in endless letters of lamentation to his remarkable private correspondent, the Carmelite nun Maria of Agreda, rarely omitted to refer to the problem of Flanders. He had proved strong enough to win back the control of Catalonia and Italy, he would succeed in confining Oliver Cromwell's programme of conquest in America to Jamaica, but he was unable to defend the Spanish Netherlands. His failure there ran through two distinct phases before the treaty of the Pyrenees in 1659. During the Fronde he recaptured some but not all the points recently lost, Ypres, Gravelines, Mardyck and Dunkirk, without intervening effectively in France itself. After the Fronde, he could not stop Mazarin from winning a powerful friend in the English Protector or counterbalance this new French alliance by securing help from anybody else. Finally, even after the peace of 1659, his diplomatic isolation was still too complete not to give the Portuguese a decisive advantage in their battle for survival. When Louis XIV again attacked the Spanish Netherlands in 1667, Madrid at long last came to terms with Lisbon.

The military establishment centred on Brussels had always been divided between one section paid by the local tax system, and another which depended on remittances from Spain. The loyalty of the Fleming and Walloon populations could never have stood the strain of an experiment in autocratic government designed to bring in higher taxes more quickly. The Habsburgs, as in the past, shared authority with the Estates of the different provinces. They respected aristocratic and ecclesiastical privilege, which incidentally suited the interest of numerous Spanish noblemen who had married into local territorial families. Nor were the towns of Flanders prosperous enough to bear the burden of heavier taxes. Some flourished before the outbreak of war with France in 1635, but the signs of falling textile production and of a falling population multiplied as the movement of armies took its toll, particularly in Artois and Hainault. The Spanish monthly contribution was in theory fixed at 200,000 crowns, but the arrears were by now colossal, with debt charges in proportion. The viceroy in Flanders between 1647 and 1656, the Austrian Archduke Leopold William, never ceased to remind Philip in his very frank reports that efficient campaigning and the failure to supply him with money were fundamentally incompatible. Madrid asked the impossible, and he was asking the impossible from Madrid. As a result, the troops were often uncontrollable. Assembled at one moment, they melted away in the next. Considerations of strategy were at the mercy of their daily need to look for supplies where these could be found. The viceroy had to defer to his unreliable ally, the duke of Lorraine. Finally, the Spaniards arrested the duke and shipped him off to honourable detention in Toledo. But their relations with Condé were almost as bad after he joined them in 1652, although his deserved prestige as a general compelled them to defer to his tantrums. Half Europe resounded with the news when he won a great victory outside Valenciennes in 1656, driving back French forces which threatened to capture the town.

Philip's attempt to take the initiative on the French frontier closest to Paris therefore proved useless. Most of the fighting was confined to the besieging and relieving of towns (and their citadels) in Artois and Hainault. Vauban, who began his career by service under Condé in 1651, later commented that the organisation and equipment used in the siege warfare of his youth were sadly inadequate. Commanders seem to have picked their objectives for each campaign almost at random, as if they merely wanted a terrain on which to practise the sport of a warrior nobility; and these noble officers always retired to Paris and Brussels when their troops went into winter quarters. But even during the fighting season the search for forage mattered as much as anything else. As James Duke of York, who fought in turn for the French and the Spaniards, said of his troops in 1655: 'when they came within sight of that part of the Country which had not been already forag'd, it was altogether impossible either for me or their particular officers to keep them in order any longer... I cannot forbear to mention the great order and justice which were observed amongst Foragers... whosoever gets first into a Barne, or on a Haymowe, no man offers to disturb him, or to seize on any thing, till he has provided for himself; so that First come first serv'd'.[2] But he forbore to mention the peasants of Ath in southern Flanders, whose fields these were, in describing this normal aspect of seventeenth-century military and civilian life.

The diplomatic struggle between Madrid, Paris and London finally proved decisive. With great promptness de Haro had seen the value of an alliance with the revolutionary government in England, but was never able to bid high enough. London might have been tempted by concessions in America, but these were not offered. Mazarin was in a stronger position if he chose to server the links which still joined the exiled Stuarts to the Bourbon monarchy, and to exploit England's concern for the Protestant interest. Gradually, the French gained the upper hand. They signed their first treaty with Cromwell in October 1655, and then attempted to come to terms with Spain. Mazarin sent

2 *Memoirs of James II* (ed. A. Lytton Sells, 1962), pp. 213–14.

his agent, Lionne, secretly to Madrid in 1656; the secrecy was at the French request, in order not to alarm Cromwell.

The two parties were never far from agreement on the territorial problems of Catalonia, Italy, Burgundy, Lorraine and the Netherlands. Leopold William, from Brussels, did his best to convince the Spanish king that peace must be made. In his view, further warfare involved certain losses. Madrid laid greater stress on protecting Condé's position in any treaty, partly as a matter of honour, partly in order to assure his safe return to a position of influence in the French court; news of his victory at Valenciennes stiffened their attitude. They also refused to consider a proposal for the marriage of Louis XIV with the Infanta Maria Teresa, heiress presumptive to the whole Spanish empire; it suggested to them both danger and disgrace. Meanwhile the Venetian ambassadors and the papal nuncios in Madrid and Paris were keen observers of Lionne's unsuccessful negotiation. They desperately wanted peace between the major Catholic states in order to bring them into an alliance to save Venice from the sultan. For years they had been offering to mediate between France and Spain, and always both de Haro and Mazarin choked them off with empty phrases. For these two, the Aegean was a distant sideshow. They had no bias against the Ottoman sultan nor the English regicides, nor any bias at all for the pope. They set territorial aggrandisement or loss in a dynastic framework. The whole transaction of 1656 – the motives of those involved and of those who desperately wished to be involved – mirrors fairly enough the priorities of this period in international politics.

The war continued. Lionne's failure preceded a new Anglo-French treaty, with Mazarin boldly deducing that he must pay the price of this failure, and on Cromwell's terms. He offered Dunkirk and Mardyck, if they were captured, in return for military assistance. At this point Emperor Ferdinand III died; the French and Spaniards both turned to stir the pot in Germany.

The Treaty of the Pyrenees

For a number of years neither had been strong enough to exploit effectively the politics of the Empire. A fearful blow was struck at the combined Habsburg family interest when Vienna insisted on making a separate peace in 1648, and thereafter Philip of Spain could do little more than cherish the dynastic connection by marrying Ferdinand's daughter, cautiously rejecting the Austrian demand for the Infanta Maria Teresa's betrothal to the emperor's son. The government of Vienna, in 1656, at last allowed some Austrian regiments to cross the Alps into Lombardy, but anxiety over Swedish designs in

Poland naturally pared down its willingness to help the Spaniards. For his part, Mazarin was too weak to hinder the election of Ferdinand IV as king of the Romans (pp. 6–7 above). The death of the emperor, before his surviving son Leopold had been chosen by the electors to succeed him, now gave the cardinal what looked like the chance of a lifetime to strengthen the whole French position in Europe. Just as Philip's interest required Leopold's succession to preserve what still remained of Habsburg influence in Germany, Mazarin wanted a rejection of this candidature. As he pointed out to the Germans, Leopold himself had a claim by inheritance on Spain and was a suitor for the Infanta's hand: they, as much as the French, had suffered from the fatal association of the Empire with Spain since the days of Charles V. He urged them to consider Louis XIV or the elector of Bavaria for the Imperial title. In fact, he delayed but could not prevent the election of Leopold as emperor (July 1658); to this extent the Habsburg interest was secured. On the other hand, the German rulers drew up a 'capitulation' which went further than earlier charters in limiting Leopold's authority. He was barred from taking action against France. This was an emphatic victory for Mazarin, who also took Louis XIV into the new League of the Rhine (August 1658). Many princes joined in, promising to pool their forces and to resist any attempt by the Spaniards to get troops from Germany into the Netherlands.

The Anglo-French alliance meanwhile settled the main issue. Turenne with the help of 7000 English troops completely defeated Condé and forced Dunkirk to surrender (14 and 24 June). It is true that Louis XIV himself, an eager spectator of the campaign, soon afterwards fell desperately ill of typhus, and this coincided with serious unrest inside France. Many Frenchmen feared a fresh convulsion, others felt aghast at the surrender of Dunkirk to Cromwell. Mazarin rode out these domestic storms, thanks to the king's recovery, while Turenne's autumn advance to the outskirts of Brussels marked a further stage in the destruction of Spanish imperial power.

Negotiations for peace, which began almost at once and ended with the treaty of the Pyrenees a year later, did not succeed merely because the Spaniards accepted that the combination of England and France was irresistible. Responsibility for the treaty, and its special character, belongs much more to Mazarin. The cardinal began to feel that his own strength was giving out. Louis's almost fatal illness made him realise that, if the king died, the heir-apparent (Philip of Orleans, Louis's brother) would find it extremely difficult to assert unquestioned authority for years to come. Louis himself posed another problem. Now aged twenty, his romance with Marie Mancini (December 1658 – June 1659) was being carried on in a way which suggested to the lady's uncle, Mazarin, that the king failed to appreciate the supreme political necessity for contracting a marriage which served the state. There are no hints that the strain of war on the finances or economy of France influenced the cardinal's judgment; other arguments convinced him of the need for a settlement, in order to round off his life-work and assure the future of the Bourbon monarchy. He had proposed, in 1656 and earlier, a pacification combined with a marriage treaty. A match between Louis and the elder Infanta now attracted him as the all-important symbol of peace with victory abroad, and of a settled kingdom at home. The fixing of frontier lines and the details of a commercial agreement were to test the endurance of the negotiators to breaking-point. Mazarin himself shared fully in the long haggle. But what mattered most to him at this stage of his career was the prestige of a peace-maker, bringing one era in France and Europe to an end, and inaugurating another before he quitted the scene.

Since 1646 (when his son Balthazar died) Philip IV dared not allow the betrothal of an infanta. Had he done so, there was a near-certainty that the Spanish empire would disintegrate after his death, with any son-in-law a prominent claimant for the lion's share.[4] The birth of Philip Prosper in 1657 (he died in 1661) appeared to safeguard the succession in Spain, so that de Haro decided to run the risk of the infante's early death and to concede what Mazarin now wanted: a victorious peace and a claim, of uncertain value, on the Spanish succession. Everyone realised that Maria Teresa would renounce, formally, her rights in the inheritance, and the French shrewdly tried to counter this by a clause in the final treaty which made renunciation dependent on the prompt payment of her dowry by Spain. The point proved of great technical importance in later controversy, but it was always overshadowed by two major truths. Philip's dynastic position was no longer so weak as it had been before 1657. Mazarin had won for the Bourbons a dynastic victory of considerable promise.

In November 1658 conversations began at Lyon. A truce and then a preliminary treaty of peace were signed in Paris by midsummer, and after a series of personal interviews between de Haro and Mazarin on 'the Island of Pheasants' in the river Bidassoa, the full treaty of the Pyrenees was completed by November 1659 in a document of 124 clauses. France won Roussillon and Cerdagne; nearly all Artois, together with Gravelines in Flanders, in the northeast; a few scattered places in Hainault, with the position strengthened by a veto on any Spanish fortification in the country between them; a point or two in the Spanish duchy of Luxembourg; and concessions which amounted to a real grip on Lorraine, which the duke accepted in 1661. Philip

4 See the dynastic tables, no. 2, p. 294 below.

retained everything else in the Netherlands and his authority was restored fully in Franche-Comté. He accepted the agreements of 1648 which scheduled the French gains in Alsace. Spanish predominance in Italy remained unaffected while the French interest in Savoy-Piedmont, unchallenged since 1642, was tacitly confirmed. The total exclusion of the pope from the whole negotiation prompted great bitterness in Rome. With respect to Portugal, the French disclaimed their interest in the House of Braganza; but the ink of these clauses was no sooner dry than they evaded them. A Portuguese envoy at Saint-Jean-de-Luz felt utterly crushed by his treatment, but he had no real need to be dismayed. Philip also won Condé a full pardon. Another prince, allied to Spain and a cousin of Louis XIV, took the trouble to travel hundreds of miles to the Bidassoa in order to influence de Haro and Mazarin; but neither was prepared to commit themselves to the apparently hopeless cause of Charles Stuart. The two ministers did not depart from this cautious standpoint until the moment was reached six months later when King Charles II came into his own again, luckily uninhibited by commitments to either France or Spain.

The match between Louis and the elder Infanta, the inspiration of the treaty, involved a second series of journeys to the Pyrenees for many dignitaries from Paris and Madrid before the marriage could be celebrated in the church of Saint-Jean-de-Luz on 9 June 1660. On the Spanish side, one very great man was deeply involved in the whole cumbersome business. Lodgings, transport and other arrangements which had to be made for the itinerary concerned an official bearing the title of *aposentador del Rey*, who was also the king's painter. Velázquez is a standing reminder of the mingled virtues and vices of the Spanish court. His many studies of Philip IV surpass the portraiture of any other monarch in European history since 1640. His marvellous 'Maids of Honour' (Las Meninas, of 1656) – with its rendering of dwarfs and obeisances, and the elaborate costume of princes in even informal moments – show that this sometimes grotesque manner of life could provide the opportunity for a cultural achievement of the highest quality. His indebtedness, when he died shortly after returning from San Sebastian, illustrates well the inability of the administration to pay its servants their wages. His genius, some may think, almost atones for the general decay of Castile in the later seventeenth century.

5

The Standstill of the North

The Government of the Dutch

Twelve years earlier, on 15 May 1648 a fine room in the Münster town hall had filled with notables for a solemn occasion: they ratified the peace between Philip of Spain and the United Provinces. They ended a whole phase of European history deeply moulded by the clash of a Mediterranean, Atlantic, Catholic empire against an alliance of Protestant municipalities adjoining the North Sea, a provincial nobility of the same region, and the princely Orange family. It is true that the Spaniards also held Franche-Comté, Luxembourg and the loyal Belgian provinces; while the Dutch, like the Spaniards, had an overseas empire and in addition world-wide trading interests. All the same, this had become the competition of one power drawing its resources from Italy, Spain and America, with another based on northern Europe. The Dutch triumphed in 1648, but their future would continue to depend on a framework stretching between the points of Danzig, Riga, Stockholm, Copenhagen and London.

A party for peace, led by statesmen in the province of Holland and in Holland by the municipality of Amsterdam, had pushed through the treaty. They profited from Prince Frederick Henry's fading grip on business before he died in 1647, and from his son's political inexperience, but with unconscious irony claimed to fear the prince of Orange's growing strength. William II was captain-general of the Dutch army, captain-general of the navy, and stadhouder – the highest civilian dignitary – in five of the seven provinces, with hereditary possessions scattered through the Netherlands. If the Dutch made further conquests in Flanders or Brabant, this might well add to his power and to the size of his patrimony – the territorial aspect of Orange politics, with both France and Spain rumoured to be offering members of the family lordships in the Spanish Netherlands, was not overlooked by critics. Nor were Orange dynastic sympathies.

William favoured his brothers-in-law, the young Charles Stuart's cause in England and the elector of Brandenburg in the Rhineland duchies (p. 21 above). The province of Holland, much the strongest of the seven, wanted peace kept with the English Commonwealth if possible, in order not to damage trade by maritime warfare. Their businessmen hoped to reduce military expenditure which diminished, by requiring heavy taxation, the assets which they could use more profitably in other ways; and they disliked the enormous growth of the state debt in recent years. Besides, particularly in Amsterdam, they gave a much higher priority to Baltic questions. In 1645, on their pressure, a fleet had been sent to keep the Danish Sound open during the war between Sweden and Denmark, a measure which they judged more important than Prince Frederick Henry's plan for an attack on Antwerp. In 1649, again on the initiative of Amsterdam, the permanent redemption of the Sound tolls was being negotiated with the Copenhagen government: a bold proposal, to compound for the dues paid by Dutch shippers with a large capital payment and a small yearly rental thereafter. Critics objected that this would mean taxing all the provinces, in order to raise the capital, for the future benefit of Amsterdam. Supporters of the scheme held, with Orange interests disagreeing violently, that the outlay was possible because expenditure on troops and for tresses at home could now be cut.

Certain dignitaries in the larger Dutch cities, those who cared to consider broader issues, not only suspected Orange policies abroad. For them, the execution thirty years earlier of Oldenbarneveldt and the exile of his colleagues, had provided martyrs; theirs was the cause of 'liberty'. Men who honoured this saw the rise of the house of Orange as a tendency towards autocracy in the state. A few saw the issue clearly enough to want what they believed to be a dangerous growth reversed with the accession of a new prince. Others simply opposed any further extension of Orange influence. In their eyes, the long war had magnified the authority of the captain-general and of the military chiefs who belonged to his staff, soldiers or courtiers for whom municipal patricians felt a certain suspicion. Many foreign elements existed in the Dutch army, which to a marked degree was an amalgam of soldiers of fortune from all the scattered regions of Protestant Europe, depending on the captain-general rather than on the Estates of the seven provinces. The latter, especially Holland with financial responsibility for more than half the military budget, paid the piper; but the princes of Orange often seemed to call the tune to which the foreign troops and companies danced. The problem of the army in Dutch politics in and after 1648 was as critical as the disbanding of the queen of Sweden's regiments in Germany, or the 'case of the army' in England after the first civil war ended in 1646. As in England, it raised the issue of sovereignty in the state. But the

army of the United Provinces was never a focus of political radicalism, focusing instead the traditions and ambitions of the house of
Orange. On the other hand the Estates of Holland, like the English
Parliament, spoke for civilian and tax-paying parts of the community, and looked more sympathetically at the case for powerful naval
armaments. It had a firmer grip on naval expenditure. Three out of
the five Colleges of Admiralty were based on Amsterdam, Rotterdam
and Hoorn in Holland, which had representatives sitting in the other
two, at Middelburg (for Zeeland) and Harlingen (for Friesland).

In July 1648, after the war with Spain ended, the States-General
was presented with a plan for a moderate reduction in the size of the
Dutch army. Holland demanded sharper measures. The province got
its way, and then began to cut into the pensions and pay of officers,
with the military interest very much on the defensive. Between the
autumn of 1649 and the summer of 1650 debate at the Hague grew
dangerously shrill. Friends of the court and army in the States-
General resisted a new proposal from the Holland deputies to reduce
the standing force still further, while Holland threatened to fix its
contribution without referring to the States-General at all. It also
broke the law and spirit of the Union, in the opinion of some, by
sending an envoy to London to express regret for pro-Stuart demonstrations at the Hague. Prince William decided on new tactics.

He was encouraged by Mazarin's successful stroke in Paris in
January 1650, the arrest of Condé. His friends convinced him that
the Hollanders were challenging his rightful authority. Quite clearly,
Holland did not intend to endorse his foreign policy or to allow the
States-General – sensitive to greater Orange influence in Zeeland and
the other provinces – to dictate the level of Dutch military expenditure. It remains difficult to determine which of the two points was
uppermost in the minds of those opposed to William, because one
impinged on the other. It is equally difficult to decide whether
William was more intent to join Mazarin in attacking the Spanish
Netherlands or to give help to Charles II against the Commonwealth.
Mutual suspicion reached a climax when the prince visited the towns
of Holland in turn, demanded their cooperation, and was coldly
received. Accordingly, in July 1650 he arrested at the Hague a
number of the leading Holland statesmen, among them Jacob de
Witt the Pensionary of Dordrecht, and prepared an armed assault
on Amsterdam. The municipality here, led by Cornelius Bicker, as
rich as he was energetic and public-spirited, repulsed the attackers.
Neither party could claim an outright victory. The arrested deputies,
imprisoned in the Loevestein fortress (where the followers of Oldenbarneveldt had been imprisoned many years before) were released,
but the prince's authority was hardly diminished by the gesture. A
compromise fixed the size of the army, while the right of the Estates

of Holland to take unilateral decisions on this question was not admitted by the States-General. The significant fact is that the tension gradually died down, as if men were afraid of it. Then, suddenly, William fell ill and died in November.

His death was the decisive event in Dutch history in the middle years of the century. It was of greater importance than the constitutional tug-of-war in 1648–50. An heir, Prince William III, was born a month afterwards. His mother Mary Stuart, his grandmother Amalia, and other members of the family, quarrelled ceaselessly, and this double misfortune of death and disunity gave the opposing interest a marvellous opportunity to seize power. The 'stadhouderless' government (1651–72) associated with the name of Jacob de Witt's uncommonly gifted son, John de Witt, owed some of its character to the recent quarrels of the province with William II. It owed far more to the accident of a minority. Indeed, in terms of seventeenth-century dynastic history this was just another minority, comparable in its effects with those of Mehmed IV, Louis XIV and of Christina and Charles XI of Sweden. An infant prince's authority was automatically weak during his youth but later, if he had any talent at all, automatically became stronger. In Spain Carlos II was too feeble to govern although he grew to manhood; William III proved too gifted not to govern. In England the forces of change under the stress of civil war were so exceptionally powerful that they challenged and overthrew an adult ruler. Dutch discontents rested on a shallower foundation. They had less to oppose.

Grotius, of Oldenbarneveldt's party, earlier gave publicity to a historical theory of 'the Batavian republic', with constitutional rights handed down from remote antiquity, but there were few signs of resolute republicanism in Dutch intellectual life. Ludlow, Milton and Harrington were much bolder, notions of immemorial right and the Norman yoke cut much deeper in England. Instead, the small group of 'regent' families in each Dutch city attended first and foremost to the business of keeping a firm hand on municipal government. It provided the town councillors, aldermen, burgomasters and usually the pensionary, the chief spokesman sent to the provincial Estates. Aldermen and burgomasters were elected at regular intervals, new life-members of the corporation were co-opted as senior members died off. All took the keenest interest in jobs, such as the appointment of directors of local chambers in the East and West India Companies, or of officers for the burgher militias. Rivalry was tempered by many 'contracts' between factions, and sometimes by an agreed 'rota' for the tenure of offices worked out for decades ahead. The working relationship of 'regents' with merchants or manufacturers varied from place to place. It was closer in Amsterdam than anywhere else, and probably less close in a majority of Dutch towns

in 1650 than in 1600. The class barrier which prevented mere burghers from rising to a command in the civilian guards, let alone
entering the corporation, seems to have been almost insurmountable;
but it was not a grievance with political repercussions. For one thing,
there were many posts in the middle or lower reaches of a municipal
administration which could be assigned to selected burghers, and
kept them quiet. As for the more prominent office-holders who
went as deputies to meetings of the provincial and general Estates,
they believed instinctively that the separate provinces had a right to
independence, and that defence of this right was the justification for
a Union of provinces. The towns of Holland also assumed that the
wealth of their province, contributing at least half the total federal
budget and shouldering much more than half the total debt, gave
them special responsibilities and a right to leadership. Appropriately,
the Estates of Holland and the States-General of the Union assembled
in the same building at the Hague. The governing circle which controlled affairs in a place like Dordrecht – of which the de Witt family
was an admirable representative – and the group of really rich men
who ran the municipality of Amsterdam – into which de Witt married a little later – therefore resented the apparent growth of the
Orange stadhouder's personal influence in Dutch politics under
Frederick Henry. Many opposed it. All considered themselves citizens, not subjects. But the lines of party division must not be drawn
with any sharpness, and most men were neutral. There was a strong
sense of loyalty to the house of Orange which did not dim easily,
even in those whose fathers had mourned for Oldenbarneveldt.
William II arbitrarily imprisoned leading statesmen in July 1650,
his own followers were passionate enough, but he in turn did not set
up a 'council of blood' in the manner of Alva. The foremost representative of Holland in 1648, Pensionary Adriaan Pauw, was the son of
Reinheer Pauw, one of Oldenbarneveldt's fiercest opponents.

The politicians whom William II had tried to crush turned the
tables in 1651. The Estates of Holland by-passed the States-General
in which the Orange interest was still strong, and invited the other
provinces to send new delegates to a special meeting at the Hague.
This is the so-called 'Great Assembly' of Dutch history. A few radicals hoped to secure a fresh constitutional settlement designed to
limit permanently the political strength of the Orange family. The
provincial delegations did not come to the Hague armed with authority to commit their own provinces to this, while the pensionary of the
Hollanders, venerable Jacob Cats the poet, never felt inclined to push
any issue to extremes. As a result, the most important decisions taken
were negative. Holland firmly announced that it did not intend to
elect the infant William III as its stadhouder, and persuaded the
Assembly not to elect a new captain-general or admiral-general.

These offices now lapsed. The right of other provinces to choose a new stadhouder for themselves could not be touched, but in four out of the six they were persuaded not to exercise it. In future, municipal oligarchies would co-opt their members and nominate to offices without deference or reference to the prince of Orange. Arbitration, in disputes between or within provinces, would be entrusted to loyal and impartial persons chosen from cities not involved: so much for the Orange stadhouders' old function as arbitrator. Each province would secure greater freedom to control individual regiments for which it raised the funds, and in choosing their officers up to the rank of colonel: so much for the old powers of the Orange captain-general. Finally, but most important, this massed gathering of Dutch statesmen paid homage to the logic of what was called 'true freedom', if not to the dictates of common sense, by omitting to alter the constitution of the States-General. The decisions of a majority of the provinces could still not override a dissentient province. War could not be declared, nor peace treaties accepted, without the unanimous approval of the seven provinces. The hereditary co-ordinating authority of the princes of Orange had been suspended, and a victory won against the modest trend towards this form of a more rigorous government. True freedom was thereby guaranteed; but the art of politics in the Netherlands, more than ever before, would in future require perpetual bargaining between individual provinces and cities. The Great Assembly at the Hague in 1651 had instincts very much in common with the Imperial Diet of Regensburg in 1653 and the Polish Diets of the next few years.

The Dutch, led by the province of Holland, soon showed that they could make this settlement work. The first Anglo-Dutch war began. The strength of the English fleet caused serious losses, and a public clamour broke out to give special powers to William Frederick, stadhouder of Groningen and Friesland, to act as deputy captain-general and admiral-general for the infant William. But a handful of efficient men sprang into action, co-ordinated the work of various colleges of admiralty or other administrative commissions, and of the Estates of provinces. New fleets were made ready for sea. John de Witt first came to the fore as an able deputy for the pensionary of Holland, and then obtained the office for himself. The government recovered its balance, and ultimately arranged a negotiation with Cromwell. The terms of peace, surprisingly, reinforced the Great Assembly's work. Cromwell – to defend himself against the Stuarts and their Orange cousins – demanded an assurance that the Orange family should not in future exercise authority in the United Provinces. The diplomacy was intricate, but he acquiesced when the province of Holland undertook never to appoint a member of the family as stadhouder, and never to authorise the States-General to appoint one as captain-general. Although de Witt and his admirable envoy in London, van Beverning, agreed to this with apparent reluctance, their own point of view accorded with Cromwell's. The new régime still depended on the youth of Prince William and the brawling of the Orange family, but the Act of Seclusion of May 1654, pushed through a secret session of the Estates of Holland, provided an extra safeguard for the future. Linking the governments of England and Holland it was the republican version of a dynastic marriage.

When de Witt published a celebrated defence of the measure, the so-called *Deduction* of the Holland Estates, he laid down anew the basic political arguments in favour of 'true freedom'. In fact, Holland had strained this freedom to the limit by using its power to determine both foreign and domestic policy. In doing so, it trenched on the freedom of other provinces but stiffened the whole government of the Union. With some amendments the system, presided over by John de Witt, lasted until 1672. The prince grew up, and Holland gave way inch by inch. In 1670 an 'act of harmony' reserved the offices of captain and admiral-general for William when he reached the age of twenty-two – although nomination as a stadhouder in any province would disqualify him. Early in 1672 the date fixed by the act was put forward by eight months[1]; the emergency of a war with both England and France visibly approached. War itself gave him back the old title of a stadhouder in five of the provinces. Before that, an intricate debate over these problems had been passionate enough, although on the whole the parties manoeuvred in order to compromise. After that, there was still no equivalent in Dutch provinces to the remoulding of borough charters and the purging of municipal oligarchies, attempted by every English ruler from Cromwell to James II. William was authorised to intervene in the towns, in 1672, but the changes in membership of their governing bodies were – on balance – slight. In this vital respect, 'true freedom' had been preserved. It was in 1688 that the major transformation occurred. The original Anglo-Dutch agreement to deny William III his political birthright was turned upside down, and he ruled in both countries.

Dutch Art and Commerce

Dutch internal affairs may look parochial, but their constitution defended standards of civilised life higher than anywhere else at this time. Enthusiasm for war, etched deep in the traditional code

---

[1] It was John de Witt himself who did not live to see William's twenty-second birthday. He was murdered on 20 August 1672, shortly after resigning his office.

of values honoured by princely courts in most parts of Europe, was here confronted by positive civilian values. The struggle to expand a great trading empire all over the world was rough and tough enough, but in a Dutch town hall the burgomasters meanwhile conferred in their chamber. In the nearby rooms officials administered justice, adjudicated in bankruptcy, registered proposed marriages, and kept an eye on municipal finance, waterways, streets, churches and orphanages or poor-houses. In their city dwellings more people had more good food, good textiles and good furniture than could easily be found in other lands. Nor did wealth simply accumulate, thanks partly to efficient local government. Making every allowance for the influence on them of older Flemish masters and of contemporary Italian styles of art, the Dutch did have a new vision of the world. Great masters taught them to look freshly at the setting of daily life. In the home, there were fruits and flowers heaped on the table, or the particular pleasure in watching someone read a letter or take a music lesson or drink from a fine translucent glass. Outside there were the qualities of light in the sky over a flattish landscape to study, the charm of boats laden with men and cattle crossing wide stretches of river, with church towers and windmills and ships in the distance. In a very restricted area, the Rhine delta, people practised or patronised a special artistic activity utterly beyond the capacity of their neighbours in Germany, or across the sea in East Anglia.

All this probably reached its zenith around the middle of the century but development still continued. The greatest of Dutch landscape painters, Jacob Ruysdael, had yet to show how to combine the dominance of one *motif*, a single tree-trunk or the water of a stream, with a broader treatment of everything round it. New fashions in portraiture arose, with an increasing preference for artists who could give their subjects the aristocratic airs of a sitter to Van Dyck; they corresponded with the tendency for members of the patrician class to buy country estates, to which titles were attached. In the same way burgomaster Cornelis de Graeff, who inspired the design and decoration of an immense new city hall for Amsterdam, begun in 1648 and opened in 1655 – today a monument of the most powerful single city in Europe at that date – brought to this municipal undertaking an enthusiasm for classical architecture based on recent Italian and French models.[2] Also in Amsterdam, Rembrandt observed and laboured ceaselessly. Nowhere else would it have been so easy for him to keep in touch with the Mennonites, whose particular Christian belief coloured his own view of the Gospel story; or to study so minutely the physiognomy and dress of the Jews who lived mainly in

2 See the fascinating K. Fremantle, *The Baroque Town Hall of Amsterdam* (Utrecht, 1959). This building is now the Royal Palace.

a part of the town close to his house. His dead wife Saskia had been a wealthy woman, but as he moved towards more subtle and less popular styles he overspent. A partial bankruptcy in 1656 led to the sale of many treasured possessions, of which the schedule lists exotic objects brought to Amsterdam from all the corners of the known world, including America, Persia and the Far East – an oblique reminder from an unexpected quarter that the Dutch had built up a commerce of amazing diversity on which their prosperity depended.

By 1648 the dominant features of this immensely active economy were long since fixed. Favoured by access to a large hinterland, shipbuilders and shippers managed to make a confederation of cities at the mouth of the Rhine and Meuse, in the strip between the Zuider Zee and North Sea, and on the islands of Zeeland, into something like a universal market-place. Here sellers and purchasers of a wide spread of commodities had the best chance of doing business on favourable terms. Accordingly, technical expertise in finance and insurance kept pace with expansion and stimulated it. If one takes a business like the Amsterdam firm of Daniel and Mathew Lestenon, dealing for decades in silk and salt, with trading interests in France, Spain, Italy and the Levant, with a stake in insurance and bank-ing, with an employee of the calibre of Jan Phoonsen, who argued authoritatively for technical reforms in procedure at the Bank of Amsterdam – in which, by 1661, 2,100 separate accounts were kept – a picture emerges of wealth handled with sophistication not equal-led in other countries. Moreover, because there were so many cities there could be no absolute monopoly. Delft competed vigorously with Rotterdam, Rotterdam and Hoorn and Dordrecht eagerly snapped up business from Amsterdam if opportunity offered. At Zaandam, a small place, shipbuilding forged ahead in the second half of the century in spite of fierce opposition from its privileged neighbour, Amsterdam. The towns of Zeeland were often at daggers drawn with those of Holland. The general constitution of the country was just sufficiently well-knit to restrain the excesses of rivalry, but not too centralised to put the economy in a strait-jacket for the benefit of sectional interests. Meanwhile the marine ventured all over the world, not only to carry exports out and imports back but also to profit from the carrying trade of different areas. The East India Company, from its base at Batavia in Java, dominated the internal commerce of the eastern seas in spite of some competition from English and local shippers. The West India Company, and smaller interloping concerns, handled trade in American and African waters. In the Mediterranean the Dutch carried goods between Istan-bul and Alexandria, between Smyrna and Marseilles, and from one Italian port to another. They sold and leased ships to Venetians and

Genoese. A common complaint in England and France was that successful competition with the Dutch first depended on the purchase of Dutch ships.

Linked with the marine were the fisheries, particularly for herring in the North Sea and whale in the Arctic. The herring industry involved countless partnerships, large and small, but it was strictly supervised by a board known as the 'Great Fishery', with deputies from Rotterdam, Delft, Schiedam, Enkhuizen and Brill, partly in order to exclude interlopers from Amsterdam and elsewhere, partly in order to maintain standards in salting and barrelling the fish. The salt was a vital import, brought from Biscay, Portugal and Spain. Salted fish was in turn exported almost everywhere. Possibly, the importance of this trade used to be overstated by historians; it is certain that a decline from earlier levels of activity, both in the herring and whale fisheries, only set in after 1700. Again, Leiden has been described as 'the largest industrial concentration' in Europe in the middle of the century. Its textile production was remarkable, even though English competition increased and intermittently threatened to ruin it. Prohibitions on the export of raw wool from England did even more damage. But after 1648 increasing quantities of wool were brought from Spain, and new dyeing techniques successfully introduced. Leiden reached the peak of its output shortly before 1670; this then began to fall, but in 1700 was still appreciably higher than in 1630.

Diversity gave the Dutch economy staying power. If one branch of business decayed, another took its place. Brewing flourished less in 1700 than in 1600, but Dutch shipbuilding was more vigorous in 1700 than in 1650. Similarly, during the third quarter of the century the West India Company went downhill. But the East India Company compensated for this disappointing record in the Atlantic. The name of Jan Maetsuycker, governor-general in Batavia from 1655 to 1673, an empire-builder ranking with Coen before him and Warren Hastings later, must always be associated with the steady expansion and consolidation of the Company in this period. The directors at Amsterdam, in 1651, themselves decided on a forward policy. In 1652 an expedition under van Riebeek took possession of the southern tip of Africa in order to safe guard communications with the east. In 1655 another expedition, this time from Java, made possible the siege of Colombo in Ceylon, which fell in May 1656. By the end of 1657 the Dutch occupied almost all the rich cinnamon-bearing lands once held by the Portuguese in the island. Five years later they had secured a number of points on the south India coasts. Rycloff van Goens, who administered Ceylon before he succeeded Maetsuycker at Batavia, dreamt of making Colombo a second Dutch capital in the east. Less spectacular was a bid for more commerce in

Siam and Cambodia. Although the ruler of Siam resented a growing Dutch monopoly of traffic in this region, English traders failed to help him, and he had to wait until the French intervened after 1680.

Yet the biggest contribution to Dutch urban prosperity was made by Baltic commerce with its many ramifications. As Danish officials year after year imposed their king's tariff at the Sound, noting down in their registers innumerable details about ships and cargoes, they left posterity proof enough of the long domination by the Dutch of Baltic commerce.

The bulk commodities which mattered most to many thousands of people in Europe were the corn of Poland, Prussia and Swedish Baltic provinces with a market in the west, and the salt of France and Portugal which was indispensable east of the Sound. The Baltic also provided a good market for textiles, fish and wine. The exports of Sweden and Finland, consisting of iron, copper, pitch and tar, were required mainly by the maritime states and Germany. It is possible to establish with reasonable confidence, from the Danish records, what proportion of most of these cargoes were carried through the Sound in Dutch ships.[3] Their share can be tabulated as follows:

	Rye	Salt	Iron	Cloth	Herrings	Rhenish wine
	%	%	%	%	%	%
1640–9	70	80	37	52	82	77
1650–7	66	67	34	42	72	91
1661–70	83	74	56	55	81	95
1671–80	82	50	32	54	64	90
1681–90	83	74	26	64	76	92

100% = the total bulk of each commodity carried by all shipping through the Sound in ten-yearly periods: except during the war 1658–60.

These percentages show that by the mid-century Dutchmen had built up a mastery of the Baltic carrying trade, which was then generally maintained; that it was adversely affected by warfare in the North Sea and Baltic, as in 1652–60 and in 1672–8, but revived again when peace returned; and that only the transport of Swedish iron escaped it, to fall definitely with the passage of these decades into other hands.

There were, of course, outworks of this northern trading system. The Dutch had a large interest in Norwegian timber and Silesian linens, some of which began their long journey to a profitable market

3 *Tijdschrift voor Geschiedenis*, 41 (1926), pp. 150–5; 71 (1958), pp. 188–205. For a full discussion of the reliability of these statistics, see P. Jeannin, 'Les Comptes du Sund', in *Revue Historique*, 231 (1964), pp. 55–102, 307–40.

in west Africa by shipment down the Oder to Stettin. They also supplied Muscovy with armaments, and played the largest part in exploiting the iron deposits and constructing the forges south of Moscow. But apart from direct traffic with Bergen in Norway and Gothenburg in Sweden, Baltic business all tended to merge into the cargoes of three principal 'fleets' which sailed annually from Holland in peace-time – in the spring, summer and autumn – with vessels bound for Danzig, Königsberg, Riga, Reval and Stockholm. They carried Dutch fish and cloth, French and German wine, French and Portuguese salt. Larger and cheaper to run than ships built anywhere else, they were for the most part not going east in ballast like many of their rivals; when the French writer Jean Eon published in 1647 his *Commerce Honorable*, appealing to his countrymen to put more energy and money into business, deploring the success of the Dutch in taking the profits of wine export from French traders, he went far to account for the same Dutch success in a very different part of Europe. Moreover, a part of the return cargoes from the Baltic had to be paid for by the export of money; but the very large Dutch trade with Spain, which increased after 1648 and benefited further from the Anglo-Spanish war of 1655–60, helped to bring precious metal to Amsterdam. Arrived at the Baltic ports, Dutchmen conducted business on such a scale that their demand was locally regarded as vital in determining prices, above all corn prices. The returns were brought through the Sound before winter began, and in the following year the cycle started anew.

All this makes it understandable that the Dutch government should listen so sensitively to every tremor in Baltic politics. The Danish and Swedish kings had to be checked in order to maintain a stable balance of power in which no state could dominate either the Sound or the ports. It was desirable to angle for concessions at the Sound which did not apply to other nationals, and to stop others from winning a similar advantage. It was necessary to be able to play off the bids and prices of dealers in Danzig against Königsberg, and of both against Riga. It was essential to keep trade moving in spite of Swedish, Polish or Danish military manoeuvres. Unfortunately, the upheaval caused by Charles X threatened the Dutch at every point, and they finally intervened in the northern crisis as principals. The rescue of Danzig by a Dutch fleet in 1656 (see above, p. 38) was only the first overt move taken to defend the Dutch commercial interest. De Witt might be somewhat cautious, other countrymen of his were more aggressive. They shared the same concern, illustrating in different ways the popular belief that this trade – above all, the traffic in corn – was a 'mother-trade', the base of prosperity in many branches of commerce. Ultimately, in 1660, they got the Baltic settlement they wanted.

Such an achievement was not an unqualified triumph. Indeed, it is possible that Amsterdam business circles struggled all the harder to defend themselves precisely because the general terms of trade became less favourable after the middle of the century. To judge from the number of ships reaching Amsterdam, and the revenue from import and export duties levied there, commercial activity reached a peak in the years 1648–51 which remained unsurpassed until the very end of the century. Even in peacetime – in 1660–4 and 1667–72 – business was less exuberant than it had been, while war at once involved heavy slumps. Between 1648 and 1651 Amsterdam certainly cashed in on an enormous demand for Baltic grain in western Europe, due to catastrophic harvests. After that, with the exceptional period of dearth over, historians are agreed that for thirty years – for causes which are still hard to uncover – the market was decidedly less buoyant than it had been. This was not because the difference in price between eastern and western grain was smaller than in the past, nor because technical improvements in tillage and new types of crop reduced the need for imports. These changes occur later. But the total demand was smaller, and there is better evidence – at present – that the former tendency of the population to rise in Holland, Belgium, Italy, France and Spain was now reversed in some areas, halted in others, and elsewhere at least slowed down. It would be an error to overstate the decrease in shipments of Baltic corn westwards in the second half of the century: the calculation has been made that an annual average of 68,500 *lasts* of corn was carried through the Sound in 1600–49, 55,800 in 1650–99 and only 31,800 in 1700–49; and within the fifty-year period after 1650 scholars are now less inclined than they used to be to accentuate the extent of the decline before 1680 or of the recovery afterwards. They have flattened out the curves on their graphs, leaving the United Provinces with a level of prosperity higher than their neighbours, but no longer continuing to move ahead of them. What the Dutch importer and exporter had to do was to struggle in order to stand still, or to prevent his profits dropping too sharply. He defended a somewhat contracting trade, while against the same unfavourable background competitors in England and France sought to build up their own mercantile prosperity. De Witt and Colbert both confronted the same deeper problem.

The Dutch government's responsibility was to limit the possible political dangers threatening Dutch trade abroad, and to encourage effective administration at home. From this point of view, the province of Holland's management of its public debt appears very impressive. When the first Anglo-Dutch war ended, a series of conversions was arranged without destroying confidence. Creditors were offered the alternative of repayment or the continuation of their loans at a lower rate of interest. This saving, plus reduced military expenditure, allowed the authorities to set up a sinking fund in order to redeem further portions of the debt in future years. Holland persuaded the States-General to follow its example in dealing with the very much smaller federal debt, while interest rates in the country were lowered generally. In 1659 some anomalies in the law dealing with coinage were removed. No other state in Europe came near to this standard of public finance. The main defect in the United Provinces was a high level of consumption taxes, which impoverished the labouring population. However, on the backs of the poor the number of people who prospered in the provinces of Holland, Zeeland and Utrecht must still have been large by comparison with the number reaching similar standards of living in France or Germany – or indeed in the inland provinces of Overijssel and Drenthe, and Groningen, where the well-to-do were probably just as few as in northwest Germany. A traveller moving east from the Dutch coast towards the Empire crossed an economic boundary long before he reached the official frontier.

Another qualification to be made about the United Provinces in 1648 or in 1672 is almost more important, and more difficult to assess. The Dutch were a nation of both immigrants and emigrants. They were free to go where they liked, with their capital and skills. At first, when they settled overseas they benefited themselves, and possibly their relatives at home; but finally some ceased to be Dutchmen, and the countries of their adoption gained as much as they did. The English were helped to drain fenland, the Norwegians and Swedes and Russians to work their iron mines, in each case by improved methods. Of three Marselis brothers – a family originally from the southern Netherlands – one acted as the king of Denmark's agent in Holland, prospered greatly, and bought a country property near Haarlem; another built himself a fine house in the Dutch style at Oslo; the third became a Danish nobleman. Dutchmen were often moving spirits in new trading companies whether at Stockholm, Bordeaux or Genoa. Dutchmen fired the zeal and promoted the overseas ventures of such mercantilist-minded rulers as Jacob of Courland (who reigned 1642–82) and, later, Frederick William of Brandenburg. Frans Caron, after a long career in the Dutch East India Company,[4] and van Robais the textile manufacturer, were to be tempted by Colbert to serve Louis XIV. Ultimately, foreigners learnt by the Dutch example and became more effective rivals, although the Dutch were also drawing in their own stream of talented refugees, notably Flemings, Jews and Huguenots. The

4 For a glimpse of him farther afield, see F. Caron and J. Schouten, *A true description of the mighty kingdoms of Japan and Siam*, ed. C. R. Boxer (1935).

Swedes and Danes were finally checked in 1660, but England and France proved more serious rivals. Their governments, no less deliberately than those of Copenhagen and Stockholm, set out to curtail the economic supremacy of the United Provinces. It was to be a drawn battle, with the honours about even. Perhaps that double change of names on the map of seventeenth-century America is appropriate: New Sweden was annexed to New Netherlands in 1655, but the English conquest of 1664 merged both into settlements depending on New York.

The Swedish Empire; the Siege of Copenhagen

The Swedes, too, triumphed in 1648. They prudently gave up earlier, more ambitious plans for remodelling the Empire under Swedish domination. They contented themselves with a hefty indemnity to 'satisfy' their army, and with strategic anchorages on the German coastline – western Pomerania, ports in Mecklenburg, the duke of Holstein-Gottorp's firm friendship, and a strip between the rivers Elbe and Weser. In 1645 they had already won Halland on the Swedish side of the Kattegat, and some of the islands commanding the approach by sea to Stockholm and the Gulf of Finland, from the defeated king of Denmark.

As in the United Provinces, the toning down of more militant demands had been the work of a party anxious for a settlement. Within this party, some circles simply and sensibly preferred peace to war, welcomed it, and hoped for greater opportunities to acquire the veneers and standards of the best western society. Queen Christina was among them. Like a leading courtier of hers, Magnus Gabriel De la Gardie, who had recently returned from a sumptuous stay in Paris, she wanted the amenities of noble living. She wanted art and learning as well, an academy of scholars with its rules laid down by no less a person than Descartes, a finer palace in Stockholm, a library, a theatre and much else besides. Aristocratic families wished to build more new houses in and around the capital or in provinces both north and south of the Baltic. A young engineer also, Eric Dahlberg, went off to Italy to sketch and study classical architecture when the fighting ended. He would return to take part in future wars, to design fortifications in many places during a long life, and to produce drawings for a book which illustrates more vividly than any other the ascent of his country to the allegedly higher reaches of European culture: in his *Sweden Ancient and Modern* a reader may contrast its new and occasionally splendid palaces in Dutch Palladian style with the surviving work of the poor old Goths.

At a different level, the Stockholm government continued to be strongly mercantilist in its interests, visualising state policies and state control as the obvious instruments of economic progress. It now aimed to diminish the dependence of Swedish commerce on Dutch shipping. A new 'navigation act' of 1645 applied differential tariffs (in the ratio of 3:2:1) to foreign vessels calling in Swedish ports, to ordinary Swedish ships, and to Swedish ships which could be used for naval purposes. This discrimination against the Dutch continued until Charles XI reluctantly toned it down in 1679. Likewise, the government took advantage of victorious treaties with Denmark in 1645 and 1658 to press for and secure the complete abolition of tolls on Swedish ships and goods passing through the Sound. At home, it vigorously supervised foreign trade, and one result was the concentration of business at Stockholm. Three-quarters of all Swedish exports and imports passed through the city, partly because the famous copper-mine at Falun and the chief iron deposits were not far distant, partly because all other harbours in the Gulf of Bothnia – which could have handled the valuable exports of Finnish tar – were forbidden to engage in foreign trade. Everything had to go first to the staple port of Stockholm. The area of the city steadily increased, building and rebuilding always continued, and its population increased to 50,000 by 1670.

A bigger port than Stockholm, and the other main commercial centre of the empire, was Riga. It drew in trade from a hinterland which included parts of Poland, Courland and Muscovy. But the confused interplay of economic interests in this region was reflected by official policy. Gustav Adolf and Christian had alienated much crown-land in Latvia and Estonia to Swedish magnates; these profited, while the government overspent its local revenues in maintaining large garrisons to guard against threats from Muscovy or Poland. The burghers of Riga held on to most of their ancient franchises, including their staple right, although foreign merchants and the land-owners would have preferred to deal directly with one another. The government which granted particular favours to Stockholm disapproved of Riga's claim to the same sort of monopoly, because it strongly desired to encourage transit trade with Muscovy through the Swedish Baltic provinces. When Russian merchants persuaded Tsar Alexei in 1649 to cancel English trading privileges, Sweden tried hard to advertise in Moscow the commercial merits of a route between east and west which avoided the detour up to Archangel. Stockholm officials showed fresh interest in the Ingrian ports, Narva and Nyen (on the site of the future St Petersburg), which were closer to Novgorod and Moscow than Reval or Riga. They reduced the royal transit dues and were less restrictionist than local interests would have liked. Around 1650 hopes of a much extended Russian

trade fluttered in the Stockholm air but the immediate returns provided a disappointment. War with the tsar in 1655 soon disrupted
foreign business in the east Baltic. Real expansion, above all for
Narva, began thirty years later.

The institution entrusted with the details of this policy was the
Kommerscollegium, a body of councillors reorganised in 1651 with
the backing of Eric Oxenstierna, their president between 1652 and
1656. An interesting plan for two regional committees of the college
in the Baltic and German provinces was mooted, then dropped. In
some respects it wielded greater power than the counterparts (the
Council of Trade and Navigation, the *conseil de commerce*, *Kom-
merzkollegia*), which statesmen in England, France and Germany
coaxed into activity at this period, all with a concern to stimulate
commerce and industry. Through the Swedish college the government
appointed officials as town burgomasters, and enforced a rigid distinction between 'staple' towns and those restricted to retail trading.
It also supervised the Swedish Africa Company, started in 1649 with
a fort in Guinea, and the company which maintained a struggling
colony on the banks of the river Delaware. But the Swedes still
depended on Dutch capital and shipping in these overseas ventures,
and the loss of New Sweden in 1655 was a blow struck at one set of
Dutchmen by another as much as a defeat for the Swedish government. Schemes for long-distance trading, including the development
of an overland commerce through Muscovy to Asia, promised more
than they could perform. In this century Scandinavia played a mini-
mal role in the 'expansion of Europe'.

Much more important, the Baltic warfare of 1655–60 gave Sweden
its last chance to secure economic dominance in northern Europe,
but the upshot was a balance of the powers which restored and
confirmed the old Dutch supremacy. When a group of officers and
secretaries pushed Frederick III of Denmark into declaring war in
1657, with Charles X apparently embroiled deep in Poland (see
above, p. 38), they hoped for Dutch support. Conrad van Beuningen,
ambassador in Copenhagen, encouraged the Danes to take the
plunge. Prompted from Amsterdam, he was more militant than his
instructions from de Witt authorised. And, once they attacked –
along the immense frontier between Norway and Sweden, in Holstein, and across the Elbe into the Swedish Bremen lands – Cromwell
in London was scarcely less concerned. In this large and highly
sensitive area, tremors moved quickly right across the Baltic and
the North Sea; the interlocking of interests was far more complete
than in the Mediterranean, where the western powers could stand
aloof from the long war for Crete.

With a marvellous turn of speed, aided by peculiar weather conditions which permitted troops to cross the frozen sea from one

Danish island to another, Charles X brought his army from Poland via Pomerania to the gates of Copenhagen inside six months.[5] Success on this scale clarified his new war aims, effective domination of the Sound and full sovereignty over territory north of it. He secured both in the terms arranged at Roskilde (February 1658). This peace was extraordinarily brief. It became clear that not even Sweden under Charles X, let alone any other Baltic or German state, had the power to defy Dutch maritime strength so long as the ancient clash of interests between Denmark and Sweden continued. The naval resources and skill of the Baltic peoples lagged so far behind that of the Dutch (or of the English) that a local military supremacy on land could not offset the disadvantage at sea. The freezing winter of 1657–8 had momentarily given the Swedish army an advantage; normal conditions returned with the spring, and with them the ability of the Dutch navy to intervene in Baltic politics. The treaty of Roskilde had cancelled the alliance between Denmark and the United Provinces. It aimed to close the Baltic to any Dutch fleet which might in future attempt the sort of operation carried out in 1656 when Admiral de Witte appeared at Danzig and saved the city. It foreshadowed a control of the Sound not less burdensome to Dutch commerce than the measures of the Danish king before 1645, and promised to give Sweden a chance of manipulating port dues in Baltic harbours without having to defer to Dutch interests. Van Beuningen lost no time and spared no pains at Copenhagen in wrecking the peace. On the other hand, Charles's success was so considerable that he now wanted more than the letter of the Roskilde treaty allowed him. The Danes, in the further bargaining which was to precede a ratification of the treaty, wanted to give away less. Encouraged by van Beuningen, they found the original terms intolerable. In July 1658 Charles's troops were still in Denmark. While the debate continued, he abruptly proceeded to blockade the Danish capital by land and sea.

The most significant event in Europe, in 1658, was the response of the Copenhagen citizens to an appeal from their ruler. Threatened for the second time within twelve months, they promised Frederick to stand a siege; the loyalty of some leading citizens was braced by the idea that a Swedish victory would spell the cancellation of their extensive loans and credits to the Danish crown. Patriotic feeling buoyed up the resistance, the king was roused from his usual lethargy, and the city proved resilient enough to hold out until Dutch naval intervention began to tilt the scales against Sweden. A confused mesh of blockade, counter-blockade and attempted mediation by the United Provinces, England and France, persisted for months but the result was that Denmark (with Norway) continued as an independent power in Europe. These populations, under their ruler, were not to be subjected to dictation from Stockholm. The treaty of Roskilde was not replaced by something more draconic. Many of the uncertainties cleared away when Charles X suddenly fell ill and died in February 1660. The regency which took his place in Stockholm opted for peace both in Poland and Denmark.

Treaties signed at Oliva, near Danzig, completed the settlement. The cession of Scania to Sweden, and the final withdrawal of Swedish forces from Denmark, meant that neither would occupy a dominant position athwart the Sound. The Danes lost what had once been theirs. The Swedes lost the chance of controlling one of the keys of Europe, and of building a new Vasa empire south of the Baltic with a grip on Danzig and other Prussian ports. But the agreements also confirmed the Swedish title to their possessions in Germany. A recent alliance of Brandenburg, the emperor and Poland, to dislodge Sweden from Pomerania during the Danish war, had fought in vain. The compromises no doubt disappointed all the signatory powers. Given the general exhaustion, they were not intolerable to any; while Dutch ships once again threaded a way through the Sound to resume business. Their owners, certainly, had most reason to be satisfied. By comparison with the Anglo-Dutch wars of the fifties, sixties and seventies, which tended to shift the commercial balance in favour of the English challenger, the Baltic campaigns on land and sea ended with a standstill favouring the Dutch.

Rents and Taxes in the Baltic Lands

This struggle for commercial power overlaid a more deep-seated general problem, the dependence of governments in northern Europe on landed income. It absorbed human energy, and attracted rival loyalties, just as the rift between Orange and the province of Holland absorbed or attracted them in the United Provinces.

Swedish and Danish kings had always raised revenues from royal lands scattered over an enormous area, where most taxes and dues could only be paid in kind. It was easy enough to pay a servant by assigning him the right to collect such dues, but to use them to finance an army, to build a large fortress at a distant point, or even to acquire necessities and luxuries for the ruler's household, was still in this period a matter of the utmost difficulty. Money revenues only amounted to a part of his assets, while revenue in kind tended to be unmanageable and both came in too slowly. Royal properties were handed over to nobles and officials, who had to account for all or part of the proceeds, but the mechanism of control was so flimsy that over long periods land – with taxes, rents and the subjects who paid them – was liable to slip from the ruler's hands into those of his more powerful subjects. At the same time, wealthy native and foreign merchants advanced money, and were repaid in goods. In the Danish empire a particularly strong group of businessmen at Copenhagen not only offered cash to the crown. They used the corn with which they were repaid in order to exchange it profitably for Norwegian iron, and then they used the iron for further deals with the court. The next stage, here and in Sweden, was the raising of loans on the security of agricultural and mineral revenues. As government expenditure and royal debts mounted during the Thirty Years War, it proved difficult to recover control of the original sources of revenue. The most acquisitive noblemen and office-holders added crown lands to what they already held privately, and some merchants became landowners who in due course founded territorial families. Creditors could hardly protect themselves in any other way, while a government which repaid money debts with broad stretches of not very profitable land was striking a shrewd bargain. Every transaction of this kind depended on its detailed terms.

The conversion of kind into cash was accordingly a basic problem. The Danes hoped to get round the difficulty by screwing maximum returns from the Sound tolls, but defeat in the wars of 1643–5 and 1657–9 put paid to this. In Sweden Axel Oxenstierna, the great chancellor of Gustav Adolf and Christina, dreamt of solving the problem by expanding similar sources of cash revenue: from tariffs, port dues in all the Baltic harbours under Swedish control, and from consumption taxes. He hoped that urban development at home, and the encouragement of Swedish commerce by a policy of discrimination against the Dutch, would help to modernise the economy. With respect to the crown's older types of revenue, his views seem to have altered as time went by. At first he disliked, but could not evade, the necessity of alienating royal lands and taxes in order to reduce debts or to secure fresh funds: Christina's minority was characterised by her sale of both 'crown land' on which the tax-paying peasantry lacked security of tenure – and 'tax land'. The peasants of the latter were true proprietors, but of course tax-payers, and sales in this case meant that the crown surrendered its claim on the tax while a formerly free peasantry was liable to become dependents and tenants of the purchaser. Oxenstierna gradually made a virtue of the government's necessity. With all the instincts of a great landed proprietor he believed that private lords were the instruments best suited to build up the prosperity of rural society. On alienated crown land, exploited by intelligent owners, he hoped that the population would in due course pay much more to the crown with the rising cash yield of indirect taxation. Although the unprivileged orders – the burghers, clergy and peasants – were right in thinking that the alienation of crown revenues extended the fiscal privilege of a minority, Oxenstierna and his allies in theory accepted the principle that nobles must contribute a reasonable share of their wealth to the state.

This reasoned apology for disposing of the crown's old revenues to landlords, noblemen, office-holders, merchants or courtiers, was robbed of its plausibility by Queen Christina; and it is not clear that the chancellor protested with any firmness. The era of 'sales' was followed by another, that of 'donations', and during her reign the value of these seems to have equalled the combined total of all gifts and sales made under Gustav Adolf and during her minority, and of her own sales after 1642. As a result, two-thirds of the crown's territorial revenue had vanished by 1654 while the yield of new forms of money tax was far from filling the gap between expenditure and receipts. Oxenstierna's programme was premature, and reality emerged in the shape of increasing royal poverty amid a world of magnates, the families of Oxenstierna, Brahe and others, who held the highest offices and were strongly represented in the Council of State. The same pattern was repeated across the Baltic. In Estonia 45 per cent of the settled land was in the hands of Swedish magnate families, 12 per cent belonged to lesser noblemen of mixed origins who had seats in the assembly of the Nobles' Estate at Stockholm and 35 per cent still belonged to German gentry. In Pomerania, the so-called 'tablelands' of the former ruling prince had practically disappeared, 40 per cent of the alienations falling to the highest Swedish officers and officials, while much of the rest was equally divided between local nobility and burghers. The greatest beneficiary, when Bremen and Verden were annexed to the Swedish crown, was not the ruler but the governor-general: Hans Christopher Königsmarck, a German officer who made his fortune in the Vasa service. This brave new Swedish empire, in spite of its nobles' intrinsic loyalty to the dynasty, if looked at through a lens which distorts only slightly, has a good deal in common with the monarchy of Poland.

By 1650 there were clear signs that the whole position of the free peasant in Sweden, earlier one of the most secure in Europe, was in danger. By 1650, also, Christina had decided that she did not wish to marry, although the security of the state required this in order to settle the succession. From then on, for thirty years, the land question depended on the wishes, personality or maturity of the ruler.

Christina announced in 1649 that she could give no firm undertaking, but that if she married it would be to her cousin Prince Charles, the son of Gustav Adolf's sister[6]; and she persuaded both the Council of State and the Estates to bind themselves to choose

6   See the dynastic table, no. 7, p. 295 below.

Charles as her successor if she died childless. This strengthened the element of monarchy in the government. It adjusted the constitutional balance by making it more difficult for the Council and Estates, on Christina's death or abdication, to impose conditions before acknowledging a successor. Next year, she went further. The agitation of the peasants, clergy and burghers, when the harvest failed and the Estates were summoned, was intense. They demanded 'resumption': the crown must take back what the crown had surrendered to the nobles; this, not taxation by consent, was their programme of reform. The nobility feared upheaval but the queen encouraged the radicals, a tactic which helped her to extort from all parties a new declaration assigning the succession to Charles and his heirs – whether she married him or not. Then she turned sharply against those who attacked the nobles or demanded a resumption of alienated crown lands and taxes. She triumphed with ease. The opposition collapsed. Finally, this astonishing young woman organised for herself a coronation ceremony of the greatest splendour. Soon, perhaps already, she contemplated the double dream of abdication and conversion to Rome. For the moment, social disorder was smoothed over, monarchy within the constitution asserted and the succession clarified. On the other hand, magnates and favourites kept their gains.

Christina's abdication in 1654 was not only sensational. It was important, because Charles had already revealed his wish to reverse her attitude to the land question. He accepted the opposition programme of 1650. He rallied the unprivileged peasants, burghers and clergy – and also noblemen who by conviction and calculation preferred strong personal monarchy to aristocratic constitutionalism. The treasure in 1654, Herman Fleming, was a firm champion of resumption. He could see no other alternative to the government's chronic indebtedness. In 1655 the new king overrode critics in the Council of State by appealing to the Estates. These authorised a partial resumption, accepting Charles's demand for 25 per cent (in money) of the revenue from donations of land made since 1642. At this point the Polish war began, and disrupted the policy, but part of the praise or blame so often accorded to Charles XI for his sweeping measures after 1680 must be transferred to his father, who had taken the first critical steps along this path. War diverted Charles X and frustrated the commission – the *Reduktionskollegium* – which he appointed to carry out the resumption, but even the ever-rising tide of military expenditure did not tempt the king to allow further gifts and sales of lands (with trifling exceptions). He authorised mortgages, but these were far more strictly drawn than the easy grants of earlier years. Conservatives learnt to see resumption as a dangerous policy by which royal authority could be misused to strain the law and to cancel valid transfers of property.

The sudden death of Charles in 1660 put his four-year-old son on the throne. Discussions in the Estates, vehement but bloodless, showed that no one was prepared to attack the principle of personal monarchy. Clergy and burghers, and a few nobles like Fleming, stoutly proclaimed it the chief pillar of the state. In practice, the minority of Charles XI saved the day for aristocratic interests. They proceeded to rule through Magnus De la Gardie the new chancellor, the Council of State, and the senior nobles who sat in their splendid new *Riddarhus* at Stockholm when the Estates met. At first, a different treasurer tried to limit future expenditure and resisted, ineffectively, the further alienation of crown revenue. His colleagues gave him no help in trying to recover what had been lost. Later, the alienations continued and the richest families extended their tax exemptions. The government refrained from pressing for more taxes, though its poverty cut into the pay of officials, many of them modestly placed nobles who depended on their salaries; though, too, on any prudent estimate, more guns, forts, ships and men were needed to guard the empire overseas.

The surprising weakness of that empire after 1660 influenced European history for twenty years. High Swedish society seemed to have lost the zest or bias for war, and preferred political skirmishing at Stockholm, building and estate management. The tone was set by the queen mother, unskilled in affairs but artistic in her tastes, and by the chancellor. De la Gardie, while acting as chancellor of Uppsala university, revealed his views clearly enough. He wanted the sons of the clergy to be clergymen, and not to enter the state service. He disliked ambitious youths of peasant or burgher stock who tried to secure an academic training; they, equally, should stick to their fathers' place in life. In his view the sons of noblemen, educated privately or in exclusive academies, versed in modern languages and the ways of courts, were ordained to govern. And the sons of the greater noble families ranked high above the lesser, alone qualifying for entry into the Council of State if the existing members chose to nominate them. He considered hierarchy by inheritance the natural and necessary framework of society. Although strong factions among the councillors opposed him, while 'resumption' combined with a faith in strong personal monarchy never lacked able champions, the chancellor kept the strings of power in his hands; and kept the peace in northern Europe.

The English Deadlock

While Dutchmen and Swedes were becalmed by minorities which somewhat slackened the executive authority of their governments, it might be thought that revolutionary England would jolt the framework in northern Europe. The new régime, in certain fields, exhibited after 1649 an amazing weight and drive. There is no parallel in the seventeenth century, not even in Bohemia or the Ukraine, to the drastic redistribution of land and population in Ireland under Cromwell. The years of persistent Scottish pressure in English affairs, between 1639 and 1648, were revenged by an emphatic subjection of Scotland to England. The New Model army was followed by the creation of a new navy, of greater permanent importance, which challenged the Dutch, entered the Mediterranean in force, and enabled Cromwell to tilt decisively the balance of European power against the Spanish empire. At home, a radical ideological and social upheaval had been strong enough to overpower the many moderates in Westminster – 'presbyterian' or 'independent' – who manoeuvred helplessly to arrange a settlement during and after the civil war. To some extent it seized the men, like Cromwell himself, who seized the government. It produced radical constitutions, and radical patterns of ecclesiastical organisation. To those who would listen, John Milton or Samuel Hartlib believed, it promised a new dispensation and swift progress towards more of heaven upon earth. For others the Fifth Monarchy, of Christ himself, was verily at hand. Unfortunately for them, in spite of answering whispers from Bordeaux and even Hamburg, and rejoicing among scattered Protestants in eastern Europe, the response was slight. The 'English', by comparison with the 'French' or 'Russian' revolutions of a later age, was a parochial affair in the context of seventeenth-century Europe.

More important, in England itself what occurred tended to paralyse as much as to stimulate. The new order looked strong when the army purged or sifted the membership of successive parliaments with sovereign ease, or when measures were taken to assure the country's future control of its colonial empire. Soon the anchors dragged and the seams opened. After Oliver Cromwell's death, the attempt to fuse a popular revolutionary tradition – strongly represented in the middle and lower ranks of the army in 1659 – with some but not all the country's conservative elements, proved impossible. The paralysis which followed was unexpected but complete. Groping for a settlement the English turned again to the Stuart monarchy, but this restoration did no more than secure a truce, a breathing space in which to begin working towards a fresh solution of intractable problems. On one issue, religion, the Anglicans then forced on both the king and powerful minorities a concept of uniformity which in practice hived off 'dissent' from the church 'established', just as older laws penalised and isolated the Catholics. A fissure in the landscape of English society became permanent, with momentous consequences. On the other hand Charles II and his brother James belonged to Catholic Europe. Their mother Henrietta Maria, the old Catholic interest in Charles I's court, Catholic loyalty during the civil wars, the disproportionately large number of Catholic soldiers and courtiers from England, Ireland and Scotland forced into exile, their dependence for doles on the French and Spanish courts before 1660: all contributed something to the atmosphere of Whitehall after that date. The sacred principle of alliance between church and king was flawed from the start; the later Stuart rulers (before 1688) were not prepared to accept it, provoking and intensifying the spirit of opposition which made government more difficult. In any case, the English wanted security without oppression, they wanted a lighter government than in the days of Cromwell, less taxation and greater deference to the 'country' represented in parliament. By their enactments, and by their omissions, they secured these in 1660–1; but they had also concocted the elements for a long period of strain in which neither the king, nor a ministry, nor a parliament, nor the different interests outside, could feel other than frustrated. It was the equivalent of the situation posed by the minorities in the United Provinces and Sweden. The restoration or maintenance of ancient freedoms safeguarded many civilised values, but the risks of political disaster in a hostile world were correspondingly serious. In other parts of Europe the converse would soon be tried, an experiment with autocratic monarchy. The risks were different, but no less.

6

The Minor Experiments in Autocracy

Travellers' Tales

These were already the days of the educational 'tour' of Europe for young men of means. Travel, after schooling and before marriage, was thought important for those who did not want the long professional training in theology, medicine or law. Generally they omitted Spain, and the Muscovites took no part. Foreign visitors were rare in England, and seem to have passed rapidly through Switzerland unless they chose to reside in Geneva; but from England, Sweden, Lithuania and Poland on the periphery, youths came to visit France, Holland, Germany and Italy. They matriculated at universities without working for a degree. They joined the galas of strange courts and cities, stared at classical remains, learnt languages well or ill. And wherever they went it was their duty, as their tutors always told them, to note different constitutions, tribunals, methods of tax collection, currencies, and the forms of military and ecclesiastical organisation. They consigned a mass of detail on such topics to the diaries they were advised to keep. If they learnt anything, it was to take for granted the amazing variety of European manners, ways of thought and government. That was the essence of their experience on the *tour de France* or the *giro d'Italia*.

Equally, the historian finds that conditions in seventeenth-century Europe were above all determined by the constitutions of separate 'peoples' and 'lands'; and within each, smaller regions were often marked off from others by local liberties, loyalties and tenures. Every attempt to analyse state or provincial structures as if these conformed to certain standard models tends to obscure more than it explains. A diplomatic system, indeed, stitched the pieces together. Warfare, international trade and intellectual activity – like, for example, the copious literature of old and new guide-books which assisted our tourist and his tutor – overflowed nearly all frontiers. But their impact on most men was never more than part of the story; the other was the history of governments and provinces, each with a previous history which largely conditioned the next phase. It is accordingly hard to find any tendencies – towards absolutism, aristocratic rule, secularism, rationalism – which influenced developments in several places at approximately the same time. Local crises affected Europe more powerfully than 'European' trends or 'general' crises. Even the 'conjuncture' of the period depicted by economic historians – in which they see the combined adverse effects of a smaller flow of fresh bullion, lower real prices and a check to population increases, by contrast with the sixteenth and early seventeenth centuries – does not go far in explaining the economic fortunes of different regions within these forty years. Local, and short-term, conditions moulded them to a greater extent. Hereditary personal absolutism or hereditary oligarchy emerge erratically. Central administrations, whatever their constitutional basis, were getting stronger in some countries but in others got weaker. Only Admiral Nelson's way with a telescope can overlook this complexity. During the twenty years after 1650 there were important advances towards absolutism in France and Denmark, less important or less successful experiments of the same kind in Prussia, Hungary and even Piedmont. At the same time constitutional rule was restored in England, princely influence was restricted in the United Provinces and Sweden, governmental power decayed in Poland and Spain. In this wrestle with the facts, let us begin with the clearest example of a new autocracy.

Sovereignty in Denmark

Denmark appeared a stricken country when a phase of largely unsuccessful warfare ended with the treaties of Oliva in 1660. There was a grievous loss of territory across the Sound, surrendered to Stockholm. There were no funds to pay off troops, fresh revenue fell to a trickle, and the state debt mounted to a dizzy total. Worse, the 1650s saw Denmark weakened by contagion on a scale comparable with the epidemics in Spain and Italy. It seems that in Zealand and parts of Jutland the population decreased by 20 per cent in a decade, and did not recover these losses for over a century. War had simply speeded society on the path to ruin. Against this sombre background the Estates of noblemen, clergy and burghers, about 200 in all, met at Copenhagen on the royal summons in October 1660; and what followed showed that the balance of power in the country had altered fundamentally during the disasters. In 1648 when Frederick III's reign began, an alliance of his brothers-in-law – of whom one was Hannibal Sehested, viceroy of Norway – and of nobles in the Council of State had restricted the new ruler's powers before confirming his accession. At the same time they brushed aside clergy and burgher spokesmen who demanded reform, including the limitation of aristocratic fiscal privilege. Now, in 1660, although the king and his private advisers had been as responsible as anyone for the declaration of war against Sweden, the Council was universally blamed. The nobles whom it represented and defended were discredited, and much weaker than twelve years earlier. A party of burghers and clergy again demanded sweeping reforms, the siege of Copenhagen had stimulated a sharper sense of the court's common interest with the city, and the odds in favour of an alliance between court and radicals were greater. If the actual terms of such a bargain depended on personalities and events, it is significant that so unimpressive a ruler as Frederick succeeded in transforming the ancient Danish constitution. He never took the initiative, but with the tide running their way others took it for him.

The Council proposed a new tax on such necessities as bread, beer and meat, recognising at the same time the nobles' claim to exemption. At once the two unprivileged Estates countered with their programme of reform. They wanted to sell off royal lands to satisfy creditors. They spoke of converting what remained of the royal demense into peasant holdings, of ending villeinage and of imposing a national land tax based on a new assessment without regard to privilege. They hoped to give self-government to the different provinces, at the same time insisting that the Estates of the whole country should meet at regular intervals. The nobles and Council naturally objected, while their tactics did not lack subtlety. Offering certain concessions with respect to privilege, they sought to focus attention on the size of the army and the need to cut expenditure. It soon appeared that this bid for burgher support had some chance of success, but Frederick's advisers made a new move in the game by courting the friendship of Hans Nansen of Copenhagen who led the burghers, and Bishop Svane, the clergy's spokesman. After a few days of intensive secret discussion the reformers' original programme was side-tracked in favour of a simpler idea; a solution of the crisis, it was argued, depended on a formal declaration by all interests that the royal authority in the Danish empire was hereditary, not elective. Svane and Nansen persuaded their followers that the conferment of new powers on the ruler was needed to overcome those who had mismanaged affairs since Christian IV's death. They probably visualised, not the introduction of an absolute government, but a shift of emphasis in the constitution which would deprive the old Council of its aristocratic character, and the nobility of privileges which still threatened to block every attempt at reform. For somewhat similar reasons individual nobles and councillors – although it is relevant that the Council was not then at full strength, owing to the death of members and to absenteeism – felt that a concession of this kind would not necessarily harm their own future prospects.

The moving spirits behind the scene were at first the king's secretary Christopher Fagel, and other secretaries and army officers at court. But Hannibal Sehested returned home from a period of exile, and shrewdly gave them his full support. The burgher guards of Copenhagen were won over. And so, in the presence of troops and burghers who exerted the pressure of their enthusiasm, a ceremony took place on 18 October 1660 in which the three Estates recognised the king of Denmark's full hereditary authority. The consequences were remarkable. Representatives from the Estates and Council met to answer the critical question, what further modifications were required to bring the constitution into line with this new concept of authority in the state? They could not agree, except to a proposal that the decision should be left to the king. The idea of his sovereignty divided them least. He was to be judge and jury in his own cause. In effect, both the radical and the conservative interest collapsed together. The old Council vanished. The Estates never met again. Nansen and Svane effaced themselves before the rising stars of Sehested and Fagel. Frederick soon appointed new ministers. Among them were some of the old office-holders, but from that moment the dominant figure was Sehested, the new treasurer and possibly the greatest Danish statesman of the century. A document proclaiming the king's hereditary absolute power was circulated for signature by all the notable persons of the realm – it went from Denmark to Norway, Iceland and the Faröe Islands – in 1661 and 1662. No one jibbed at the formula, while the actual shaping of this new authoritarianism was Sehested's great achievement. His reforms were real enough, but they were not those which had figured in proposals of such men as Nansen and Svane.

He reorganised both the central and local administration. He introduced to Copenhagen government departments on the Swedish collegiate model: a new Council of State including non-noble elements like Nansen himself, appointed by the king; colleges of War and Admiralty; a supreme tribunal; and a treasury. In these, below the ministers, committees of bureaucrats were responsible for the conduct of business. In the provinces he converted the old 'fiefmen', with their private servants who had enforced order or collected dues, into mere officials assisted by secretaries. The secretaries were appointed by the court and instructed to keep an eye on their superiors. Equally, the king in future nominated officials in the towns.

Provincial independence, and municipal self-government, had gone for good. The treasurer wiped out the huge debt by forcing creditors to accept land in settlement of their claims. Between 1661 and 1664 most of the royal demense in Denmark, Norway and the duchies of Schleswig-Holstein disappeared. Considering the poor state of much of it, this was nearly always a compulsory settlement on terms which satisfied few of the beneficiaries. The monarchy had in effect declared a bankruptcy, but was no longer in debt.

Sehested's other main task was to tackle the enormous annual deficit. He reduced expenditure by getting rid of most of the troops. As for the revenue, it was essential to increase it. New taxes were needed to compensate for the loss of former crown lands and to give a better return. A fresh assessment was made of all property, noble and non-noble, forming the basis of a direct tax which may have been somewhat more equitable than the similar tax before 1660. Excises on the Dutch model were introduced at Copenhagen. The custom on imports and exports was raised. Gradually the treasurer brought his revenue more nearly into balance with expenditure in spite of a decline in the Sound tolls, now limited by concessions to the Swedes, Dutch and other foreign shippers. Sehested also realised that improved government finance depended in the long run on a more active economy, and did his best to encourage the bigger Copenhagen merchants. He welcomed the arrival of Jews from Holland or north Germany; and an official College of Commerce began work in 1668. If Danish conditions remained sluggish, he himself can hardly be blamed. Norway, where the timber trade expanded and the peasantry joined with richer men in buying up crown lands, was a much poorer country; but progress was more noticeable. Even so, Danish economic historians speak of a recovery in this decade which continued into the early years of the next.

Frederick III remained in the background. In his fine new library he enjoyed the conversation of Peter Schumacher the librarian, son of a Copenhagen wine merchant, who had spent many years of study in England, France and Spain. It was Schumacher who drafted the Danish 'Lex Regia', first published in 1709, a powerful theoretical statement of hereditary absolutism which emphasised the automatic transmission of sovereignty from one ruler to the next by means of a meticulously ordered precedence in the royal family. For practical political advice Frederick still relied on his secretary, Fagel. When Sehested finally fell from power, first Fagel and then Schumacher became the outstanding men of affairs in Denmark, owing everything to their talents and the autocracy they served. After Christian V's accession in 1670 Schumacher took the French title of 'secretary of state', while there are other indications that French administrative practice was taken as a model. More important, Christian announced the creation of new noble titles, counts and barons; Schumacher the wine merchant's son duly became Baron Griffenfeld. The tax exemptions of noble landlords were extended. A nobility, partly recruited from men of burgher origins, partly from German soldiers and officials, partly from old families of the country, again asserted itself in Denmark. The king remained an autocrat but – like Louis XIV – did not object to creating a new hereditary caste of privileged families.

Sovereignty in Prussia

At two other points in the Baltic region, the duchies of Holstein-Gottorp and East Prussia, an emphatic assertion of the prince's authority coincided with the changes in Denmark. In his treaty of peace with the Danes in 1660, the duke of Holstein's rights to his share of Schleswig and Holstein were recognised, and during the next decade he extended them to the detriment of the old privileged Estates. His chosen servants were jurists trained at the new university which he founded at Kiel; and he raised the money to reconstruct a large citadel to guard the Kiel estuary. His was a miniature autocracy. Connection by marriage with the Swedish royal family helped to maintain it, and to hold in check the ancient enemy at Copenhagen.

In the same way, treaties signed at Wehlau (1657) and Oliva (1660) gave the elector of Brandenburg an independent sovereignty over his duchy of East Prussia. This alteration proved an early instalment in the long process which both partitioned Poland and unified Prussia.

Since the fifteenth century the Estates of East Prussia had been able to defend their rights to a measure of self-government, which in practice depended on the division of lordship over them between the feudal overlord (the king of Poland) and the duke (now the elector of Brandenburg) who had to recognise Polish suzerainty. By 1650 the political structure of the duchy consisted of an overlord in Warsaw, a prince in distant Germany, a 'Little College' of administrators in Königsberg – all men of local Prussian families – and an assembly of Estates which met occasionally. The townsmen of the third Estate were always dominated by representatives from Königsberg, a city itself divided into three municipalities, each with a governing council of patricians, a tribunal, and a number of guilds and artisans' associations. It may seem odd to describe in one breath the Prussian Estates and the constitution of a single city, but Königsberg was perhaps the most stirring and vigorous place in the whole Baltic world. The university resounded with Lutheran controversy. The cultured patriciate, with its circle of poets headed by Simon

Dach to celebrate in rhyme innumerable births, betrothals, marriages and deaths in burgher families, enjoyed considerable wealth. And the city as a whole, although owning much rural property, defended a municipal interest against the landlord interest in the fields and forests outside. This cleavage robbed the duchy of real cohesion. Königsberg did not object to extra taxes on land; the lords acquiesced in the imposition of consumption taxes, which hit the towns harder. But both these interests, whatever the normal friction between them, desired a working independence. Königsberg aspired to the freedom enjoyed by its great rival, Danzig, in the Polish part of old Prussia. The gentry felt entitled to liberties which were no less than those claimed by nobleman under the Polish constitution to which they all belonged. The unprivileged had no place in these aristocratic concepts. The labour laws in Prussia were exceedingly harsh in their treatment of the subject masses. An important minority of formerly free peasants no longer had a voice in the assembly of Estates, while the alienation of the duke's demesne appears to have been so complete by this period that there could be no question of resumption, of recovering control of certain lands and peasantries, as in Sweden or Brandenburg itself. If Frederick William wanted revenue in East Prussia, he would have to be a sovereign demanding taxes rather than a landlord raising rents.

The emergency of war in 1655 naturally put a heavy strain on this constitution. The Estates voted extra taxation, a new military commissariat collected it. The Prussians hoped that both would disappear when campaigning mercifully moved to other areas. Instead, in 1657 they were shocked to learn of the elector's treaty with Poland, in which they had had no part although it dealt with the future of the duchy. By its terms the Polish king surrendered his old right to hear judicial appeals from East Prussia. The elector proceeded to set up his own court of appeal in Königsberg. In theory a claim to ultimate authority once reserved by Poland was now simply transferred to the Hohenzollern duke and his heirs; the Estates kept their rights. But the whole was bound to be more than the mere sum of its parts, and a clause in the treaty implied that old charters not in accord with the agreement could be abrogated. The elector soon appointed a governor with extensive powers, his cousin Boguslav Radziwill, and issued an edict for control of the local press.

A period of intense constitutional debate in East Prussia appeared to end on 18 October 1663, when the people solemnly swore allegiance to Frederick William as their sovereign ruler. This submission had not been held up by the landed interest. In 1661 a hint that the Prussians would appeal to the Poles – in spite of the treaty – forced Frederick William to call the Estates, but the gentry quickly came to terms. One leading personality in their discussions was Wallenrodt, a

Prussian gentleman, and from his youth a zealous servant of the ruler. He steadily steered his more provincially minded colleagues towards the elector's standpoint. The new sovereignty, he argued, should be accepted. The government was reducing the number of men under arms; the military commissariat would merge into the old civilian administration once more. Bargaining on constitutional niceties was irrelevant, and alarm unnecessary. It may be added that Wallenrodt, one of the greatest book collectors of his age in this part of Europe – rivalling even the governor, Radziwill – gave his splendid library to the Königsberg public in 1674. He made loyalty (or subservience) to the elector respectable. A majority in each of the three municipal councils of Königsberg also agreed to the new order. Then, as opposition seemed to die away, a new figure took up the lost cause of ancient liberties. Hieronymus Roth, sprung from a family of substantial burghers, and a president of one of the municipal tribunals, revelled in the talents of a popular orator who carried the crowds with him against more timid colleagues. He declaimed against the illegality of the 1657 treaty, and denounced a new charter of rights which the elector offered in return for the recognition of his sovereignty. It seems probable that he won support because the Königsbergers felt uneasily that they were the destined victims of any change. A new ducal fort had been built on the edge of the city. Its garrison already harassed the townsmen. New excises were to be feared, collected with the threat of force, and poor men would be the first to suffer. By July 1662 a radical confederation on a miniature scale had been mounted inside Königsberg, but in the autumn – to the relief of conservatives and most officials, who had long pleaded for such a move – Frederick William himself disembarked with 2000 men at the harbour of Pillau and entered the city. Roth, arrested and convicted of treason, was to spend many years in prison. In 1663 his countrymen made the gesture of submission which he implacably repudiated.

At first, they had reason to be satisfied. The elector trod gently in Prussia and the old form of government sufficed to maintain a standing force of about 3000 men. The governor was conciliatory. Taxes were discussed and voted, before they were collected. Then, when the horizon darkened again and the elector feared a new combination between Sweden and Poland to rob him of his duchy while he confronted Louis XIV in the Rhineland after 1672, the landed interest in Prussia found itself speaking with the voice of Roth, but speaking in vain. The government gradually and partially substituted an administration directed from Berlin for the older local organs of self-government. From 1673 taxation which the Estates had declined to sanction was collected by force. The standing army increased in size, and the bureaucracy of its commissariat took permanent root in the duchy which was now more nearly a province. The gentry's sullen resistance never undid the effects of that easy Hohenzollern triumph of the years 1657–63.

Frederick William always assumed that his powers were patrimonial. His responsibility to God for his subjects allowed him to judge whether any emergency justified the temporary suppression of their ordinary liberties. During the great war of 1655–60 and in the next few years he moved forward by gradual stages to give a new twist to this working premise, adopting new tactics without altering his ideas. The 'Political Testament' which he wrote for his son in 1668 remains intensely conservative in outlook. But the actual course of politics, he found, involved a perpetual military emergency. After 1660 the king of Poland did not honour the terms of the peace treaty. The Rhineland was unsettled. The Swedish government menaced Berlin from Pomerania, and he wanted Swedish Pomerania for himself. Accordingly, Frederick William took steps to retain a small army, a nucleus of seasoned men and officers in addition to his garrisons, ready in peace to anticipate the outbreak of war in any quarter. This justified heavier taxes, and an administration competent to collect them. Gradually a permanent army – the continuous history of some famous Hohenzollern regiments begins at this date – permanent taxes for the army, and a permanent commissariat, came into existence. Enemies or neighbours, often fearful of the elector, imitated his example in these matters; he had therefore once again to raise more men and more taxes, if necessary using the men to insist on the collection of taxes. Unconsciously, he came in the end to accept a notion of autocracy which in practice took little note of the subjects' interest or grievances. It also seemed to justify the state's overwhelming preoccupation with the prestige of military power, an element in Hohenzollern history until 1918.

Sovereignty in Hungary

In one respect the problems of Hungary, and of Denmark or Prussia, differed. There, the great question of religious reform and counter-reform was still open. Catholics confronted Protestants, and neither government nor subjects ever escaped for long from the grip of their clergy, of rival confessions which judged every issue domestic and international in terms of the struggle now a hundred years old. In response to this the Habsburg rulers, Ferdinand III and Leopold I, accepted the teaching of their clerical tutors that the restoration of Catholic uniformity was a fundamental of statecraft, the real solution of their difficulties, and meanwhile paid very little personal attention to fiscal and administrative questions. In Hungary they were mistaken on the main point, because it turned out that the Catholic revival and authoritarian government could not buttress each other as effectively as they had hoped. Their experiment broke down in the face of local opposition and external threats which combined against them.

From this angle Hungary mattered far more than Bohemia and Austria. The Protestant defeat of 1620 gave the Catholic interest every advantage in these lands, so that a mixture of compulsion and propaganda was enough to ensure the triumph of counter-reform by 1648. Henceforward, ecclesiastical politics in Bohemia generally concerned the Jesuits, and their Catholic opponents led by the archbishop of Prague, not the Catholics and the Protestants. But in Hungary the Protestant movement reached the climax of its power in 1647. The Diet at Pressburg then passed a law guaranteeing religious freedom, whatever a man's class or rank, and stipulating that churches and cemeteries which had been taken from Protestants in the immediate past should be handed back. This success owed much to the sheer weight of the Calvinist and Lutheran following in Hungary. It owed more to the princes of Transylvania, who had repeatedly intervened in their favour for many years past. The religious clauses in treaties between emperor and prince were often incorporated in the legislation of the Hungarian Diets at Pressburg, and the law of 1647 was George I Rákóczi's last great victory before his death. He dictated the settlement in Habsburg Hungary just when Sweden and the German Protestants decided to drop the cause of Protestant brethren in Habsburg Bohemia and Austria.

The situation was explosive because Protestant gains, reflected in the Diet's proceedings, were already matched by a recovery of the Catholic interest in certain circles. Two archbishops of Esztergom – Peter Pazmány and then George Lippay, who died in 1666 – were men of extraordinary zeal whose most important success was to reclaim for Catholicism many of the great landed families. Unlike the archbishops of Prague, they made the fullest possible use of Jesuit preaching and teaching; and from the Jesuit university of Nagyszombat (now Trnava[1]) the influence of the society radiated into all parts of the kingdom. Its educational standards seem gradually to have caught up with those set at an earlier period by the best Protestant academies. The enormous wealth of the archbishop, derived from lordships and tithes which had survived largely intact from the fifteenth century, was used to endow the new schools. The Catholic revival also learnt brilliantly to appeal to the unlettered, in Hungary as elsewhere; and educated priests took the trouble to learn Slovak. Once this Catholic movement got under way it profited from eager

1   See map 4, p. 232 below.

royal support. Habsburg kings of Hungary staffed the Hungarian treasury and chancery with Catholics. They could ensure that the number of Catholic bishops was kept up – even if their sees were deep in Turkish territory – so that Catholic voting power in the assembly of magnates in the Diets remained formidable: this, plus the conversion of a few more lay magnates helped to tilt the balance against the Protestant lords. Equally, some lesser Catholic church dignitaries still took part in the 'lower' assembly of the Diet, which at least reduced its anti-Catholic majority, represented by most deputies of the thirty-three Hungarian counties sent to Pressburg from the county assemblies. The choice of great officers of state, like the lord palatine and the chancellor, in any case depended more on the ruler than on the wishes of the Estates.

At the same time it is not possible to explain the course of politics in Hungary as a reflex of changing social conditions. These were practically static. From an early date great landed proprietors had been dominant in the triangle of country between the Turkish frontier, the Drava and Danube, with the archbishops of Esztergom and Kalocsa, and the families of Esterházy, Nádasdy, Draskovich preeminent among them. Grandees of this kind owned a smaller proportion of the high ground of Slovakia, but their share increased again in the upper Tisza valley. Here, the social tension was always acute. While the Rákóczi and Báthory familes ruled whole landscapes, many populous rural townships claimed a considerable measure of self-government in spite of their lords, and many minor gentry grimly held their own, decade after decade. Others served greater men as farmers, stewards and henchmen. The Reformation had made very little difference. The nobility who embraced Protestantism did not apparently annex episcopal or capitular lands, although in many cases they claimed the tithe due by their subjects. Their rights of ecclesiastical patronage had always been extensive, and they never considered surrendering them to Protestant clergy or congregations. At last, after 1600, a movement inspired by Magyar students who had visited England and Holland began to preach a type of 'congregationalism', asserting that churches and townships should choose their own ministers. They argued for lay membership in the presbyteries which – in the Protestant regions – were normally bodies of rather timorous churchmen subservient to local landowners or the prince of Transylvania. In the 1640s the radicals tried hard to win the favour of George I Rákóczi. When he died, his two sons George II and Sigismund split on this issue. The elder, in spite of his militant policies abroad, spurned the Puritans on his doorstep; the younger retreated from Transylvania to Sárospatak (in the Tisza valley), which for a few years remained the intellectual centre of advanced Protestantism in eastern Europe. As we have seen, Comenius came here and tried to carry the gospel of certain local visionaries to England, Sweden and Holland. But Sigismund and the leading Magyar teachers at Sárospatak were dead by 1660 and in that year their neighbouring stronghold, Nagyvárad (see p. 48 above), fell to the Turks. The whole episode was exceptional. The modern authority who tells us that Calvinism was 'an obedient lacquey of the feudal ruling class' in Hungary seems to be justified.[2]

The confessional struggle was therefore fought out within a social framework of remarkable fixity, but it became increasingly blurred by doubts and difficulties over another problem: the defence of Hungary in the face of a Turkish and Tartar assault on Transylvania. The grand vezir had revoked the Rákóczi title of prince, and declared forfeit the Rákóczi patrimony, of which a greater part lay in counties belonging to Habsburg Hungary. Nervously, the Vienna politicians hoped to avoid getting dragged into a war with the sultan. Tentatively, they wanted to strengthen a grip on regions once dominated by Rákóczi and self-governing assemblies of Protestant gentry. Gradually, they were impressed by the view of men like their military commander Montecuccoli, that the need to station an army in Hungary in order to defend it was an opportunity to crush every form of civil and ecclesiastical disobedience. Meanwhile, in the two Diets of 1659 and 1662 the expression of Protestant grievances grew stronger. In the first the deputies threatened to walk out, and in the second did so; but not before they had acclaimed Nicholas Zrínyi, a Catholic magnate who hungered for action against the Turks, speaking boldly against the government's confessional policy. From that moment the seeds of a new aristocratic opposition against the Habsburg court began to germinate. The Protestants lost the help of the Rákóczi dynasty on George II's death in 1660, but now courted the great Catholic lords who felt that Habsburg troops brought to Hungary to confront the Turks endangered the good old cause of ancient liberty.

The campaigning of 1661 and 1663–4 satisfied nobody. For Zrínyi and other Magyars (and Croats), Montecuccoli was over-cautious in facing the Turks but peremptory in overriding the patriots of Hungary. For Montecuccoli, Zrínyi seemed a rash unmethodical leader with undisciplined bands of retainers and volunteers, who failed to appreciate the true weight of the grand vezir's army. For the courts of Vienna and Adrianople the war had been something of an accident, due to faulty diplomacy. They much preferred the traditional stance (since 1606) of leaning back to back, leaving border forays in Hungary to border commanders, while reserving their strength for use

---

2   L. Makkai, 'The Hungarian Puritans and the English Revolution', *Acta Historica*, Budapest, V (1958), pp. 13–44.

farther west and farther east respectively. The grand vezir and Leopold's envoys soon agreed to a new twenty years' truce.

The Magyars, on the other hand, were incensed. This treaty of Vasvár confirmed a suspicion that Vienna wished to settle the problems of Hungary without consulting them. Acute resentment – fanned by damaging Turkish raids on Christian territory after the peace was signed – brought some Catholic nobles closer to the Protestant viewpoint. Habsburg pro-Catholic measures ceased to rally support for the crown. The zeal of the Jesuits pushed the Protestants into the arms of a powerful, rebellious aristocracy. Leopold declined to summon a new Diet, fearing open opposition. The next few years were dominated in Hungary by secret cabals which clumsily chewed over schemes for a grand patriotic uprising, the principal central European counterpart to the 'Fronde of the princes' in France twenty years earlier. Like Condé or the Polish magnates, like the Austrian and Bohemian Estates of an earlier generation, the Magyars felt justified in negotiating for help abroad. In their view, a separate Habsburg treaty with the Turks in which they had no voice, or the entry of 'foreign' troops into Hungary without their consent, were real breaches of the constitution. The greater Magyar lords and office-holders could legitimately approach their peers in other countries. They never accepted a notion of sovereignty which vested such a right solely in the king whom they had elected to govern in partnership with the Estates. They believed they shared with him an authority vested in the crown of St Stephen.

Wesselényi the lord palatine and Nádasdy the chancellor, affronted by Leopold's advisers, listened to offers which came principally from two sides. Nicholas Zrínyi was dead by the end of 1664, but his brother Peter succeeded him as lieutenant of Croatia, and Peter's brother-in-law Count Frangepán enjoyed great territorial influence in the same region. These lords of the south had their contacts with Venice, and with the French ambassador there. They toyed with the plan of offering the Hungarian crown to Louis XIV in return for aid, in order to end what they called a German despotism. Meanwhile the Protestant counties of the northeast, bitter against Catholic clergy who called on Habsburg military support to take over churches and schools, considered a new alliance with the prince of Transylvania, now an Ottoman puppet. They discussed the possible advantage to be gained by recognising Ottoman suzerainty: the sultan's officials tolerated Protestants and kept the Catholic clergy in check. This led to secret negotiations with the grand vezir, who preferred to send warning to Vienna. The plotting was careless. The plans leaked out. A point was reached when first one and then another of the patriots lost his nerve, and tried to come to terms with Vienna.

It was too late. A more resolute government had emerged with Leopold's new principal adviser, the Bohemian magnate Lobkowitz, and with the new Austrian chancellor, Johann Hocher. A lull in western Europe (before war broke out again in 1672) and the grand vezir's cordiality combined to give them a chance rare in Habsburg history: to concentrate on a domestic issue. They determined on strong measures which began with the arrest of the conspirators in March 1670. No Magyar was a member of the tribunal which sentenced Zrínyi, Nádasdy and Frangepán to death and confiscated their immense properties. The case against subjects guilty of treason seemed clear enough to Leopold's German, Bohemian or Italian servants. The equally valid case for Magyar constitutional rights was never heard at all. After a hopeless flurry of small-scale risings in the northeast the Habsburg attempt to impose autocracy in Hungary began.

A lieutenancy or *Gubernium*, and a German lieutenant-governor with complete authority, replaced the old office of the lord palatine. Instead of the Diet, a docile assembly of notables was summoned to Pressburg simply to ratify what Leopold demanded as sovereign. Extraordinary tribunals announced extraordinary judgments, which troops enforced. Lobkowitz, Montecuccoli – president of the Council of War in Vienna since 1668 – and Hocher, wanted to sweep away what they regarded as obsolete and divisive pleas of privilege, to insist on civil obedience and uniformity of worship, to collect taxes sufficient to maintain the foreign soldiers who defended the land and also policed it. The Hungarian episcopate agreed with them. The bishops saw no chance of suppressing the Protestant churches without altering the constitutional basis on which toleration had rested. They accepted an administration of major-generals in the spirit of Louis XIV. Their *dragonnades* anticipated his, and alarmed Protestant Europe. The militant Count Leopold Kollonich, Knight of Malta and Bishop of Wiener Neustadt was put in charge of Hungary's finances and played a leading part in the new government. The response of most of the lay magnates was equivocal. They had the patriotic satisfaction of replacing German Lutheran by Magyar Catholic officials in a number of towns. They detested Viennese justice and Viennese ordinances, but their zeal in driving Protestant ministers from churches and schools almost clinched the thesis that enforcement of religious uniformity rallied support for absolute monarchy. Others did not realise how quickly this would lead to a betrayal of constitutional right. The host of small Protestant gentry, naturally, championed liberty against the alliance of bishops and troops. Outforced, many took refuge in Calvinist Transylvania or Turkish Hungary, skirmishing back at intervals into their native land. The condition of Upper Hungary became anarchic after 1672, and soon had no parallel for savagery in Europe at the time. Habsburg commanders faced a violent but unorganised resistance to which political and religious passion, endemic social grievances and sheer banditry, all contributed. The effect of raiding from over the border and of reprisals was intensified by epidemics.

The insurgent captains long refused to co-operate with each other, but finally in August 1678 elected as their leader Imre Thököly (1656–1705), one of the Protestant nobles in exile. A more dangerous opposition in this area gradually emerged; the Habsburg garrisons barely survived. But it was not for this reason that the new régime was doomed, as Vienna at last recognised. The European situation had altered, and autocracy in Hungary could not be indefinitely combined with a policy of Habsburg resistance to mounting French pressure in Germany, while the Ottoman government under a new grand vezir threatened to give more help to Magyar rebels. Thököly, Kara Mustafa and Louis XIV: in spite of their mutual suspicion they each contributed to save the twin causes of Protestantism and aristocratic liberty in Hungary.

Leopold prepared to retrace his steps and summoned a regular Diet to meet him at Sopron in May 1681. At this gathering, twenty-seven out of sixty deputies from the counties and eighteen out of fifty-one from the towns were Protestant, but many Catholics also held out firmly for a revival of the old constitution. The *Gubernium* disappeared. Paul Esterházy was appointed to the office of lord palatine, a symbolic rebuttal of Leopold's recent claim to sovereignty in the state. The principle of no taxation without consent was affirmed, and safeguards against military oppression were offered. The ecclesiastical problem took months to solve. Thököly, who had refused to attend the Diet, begged the Protestant deputies to give nothing away. The papal nuncio – bearing in mind Pope Innocent XI's instruction that Christian union in the face of Islam justified leniency at this critical moment – managed to restrain the more excitable Catholics. News of the fall of Strasbourg to France came in opportunely, and the Dutch envoy to Vienna spoke up for the Protestant interest. Leopold and his councillors had to compromise, and drew up a carefully drafted confirmation of Protestant rights which both acknowledged and qualified them. The effect was to authorise Protestant worship and schools in towns and counties where they had survived, although Catholic clergy kept many of their gains since 1670. This Diet of Sopron in 1681 can very easily be overlooked, because it was soon afterwards overshadowed by years of warfare and the reconquest of Turkish Hungary. But if the autocratic experiment of the 1670s had merged without interruption into the reconquest, the Magyars would have found it even harder than they did to assert themselves. The rejection of absolute royal authority at Sopron was a valuable recent precedent when Vienna made a second bid for mastery in Hungary after 1688 – and when the Magyars rebelled again after 1700. As it was, one of the most important attempts since the Reformation to fashion a new régime based on Catholic uniformity and dynastic autocracy had proved a failure.

The Economy of Habsburg Lands

These Hungarian episodes have to be set against a dismal economic background. The Habsburg government appeared painfully sensitive to external forces because it was poor. It was poor because neither luck nor state policy had lately enriched the Habsburg lands. No fresh discoveries of precious or useful metals were made, as in earlier centuries. Iron in Austria and Styria, salt in the Tirol and Salzkammergut and northeast Hungary, mercury in Istria, and modest quantities of gold and silver from Slovakia, were still useful assets, but in this period none of them flourished sufficiently to bring real prosperity to the state or the community; there is a very clear contrast between Austrian mining and the contemporary history of Swedish iron or English coal. Even the handful of contractors, often of Italian or German origin, to whom some of the mines were farmed out did not compare in wealth with the capitalists of Nuremberg, let alone of Holland. The great Amsterdam firm of Deutz began to advance money to Leopold in 1668 on the security of Istrian and Slovakian mineral production, but its loans were modest enough. The native commercial or manufacturing interest counted for little. The burghers and municipalities of Vienna, Prague and Graz submitted meekly to Habsburg officialdom. Court expenditure stimulated business, raised rents and increased the population in Vienna. There, as at other provincial capitals, wealthy ecclesiastical foundations helped the building trades – churches and convents were built or rebuilt in large numbers after 1650, while few of the new palaces of noble families went up in Vienna before 1680 – but in the judgment of most foreign observers the towns of Austria and Hungary were poor places. (A Turkish traveller visiting Leopold's court in 1666, significantly took a much rosier view.) The guilds clung tightly to restrictive privileges because markets never expanded. Their craftsmanship was intensely conservative, and they did not dream of competing with foreign imports by imitating foreign technical skill. Silesia was the important exception to this stagnation; and flax, grown in a wide band along Bohemia's northern frontier, found many buyers who came from the larger German cities, particularly Leipzig.

Although individual 'projectors' bombarded the government with pet schemes for new forms of tax and new manufactures, Leopold retained a president of the Treasury who merely regarded his office as one of profit. Sinzendorf, between 1656 and 1680, was the devastatingly negative Habsburg counterpart to Colbert. His expertise was largely given to the task of alienating or mortgaging the regalities of the crown on favourable terms to suitable bidders; but he had no idea of any link between the economy as a whole and the finances of the state.

The most promising commercial venture of the period owed very little to Sinzendorf. After the Austro-Turkish treaty had been signed in 1664, a ceremonial embassy was sent from Vienna to Adrianople and it included one man, Lelio de Luca, who returned to preach the gospel of long-distance trade through the Balkans. He hoped to compete with Venice, which supplied Levantine goods to Austria, and with the Armenians and Serbs who traded through Ottoman Hungary. An 'Eastern Company' was founded. Its subscribers were mainly tax farmers and revenue officials, like de Luca himself. The Council of War disliked the project, the treasury was sympathetic, but not to the extent of investing government funds. In 1667 de Luca took the first cargoes of Silesian cloth and Austrian iron down the Danube. Depots were opened at Buda, Belgrade and Istanbul. More goods followed in 1668, when the first return consignment from the Levant also reached Vienna, including raw silk and cotton. It is easy to see that there were exciting possibilities in this new branch of commerce: an outlet for commodities from the Habsburg lands which by-passed the Venetians and other western traders; silk and cotton re-exports to manufacturers in Germany; and, possibly, new textile manufactures in Austria. In practice, little came of them. The company persevered, and did a fair though modest business until 1676, but growing friction with the Turks killed it. An effort had also been made to profit from the demand of Vienna and south Germany for the main export of the vast Hungarian plains, cattle. The same company was given a monopoly to supply the Viennese butchers, tanners, harness-makers and cobblers, but here again failed after a few successful years. This gallant but disappointing Habsburg imitation of the great trading companies in western Europe had been unable to overcome its problems. Some of the main promoters got into debt. The costs of overland transport in Ottoman territory proved too high. Neither the Magyar cattle owners and dealers, nor the Vienna butchers, welcomed a middleman. Finally the Eastern Company's privileges were not renewed, and it disappeared from the scene.

Piedmont

Unfold the map of Europe a little further, and consider one more example of a princely government groping for greater strength or wealth: the Piedmont of Charles Emmanuel II. It was a sad tract of country in 1650. Northwest Italy had recently suffered as much as anywhere from war and contagion. The conflict of France and Spain was entwined in that area with the struggle of Savoy princes against each other (1637–42). From an economic point of view recovery first of all presupposed peace, and peace was certainly kept for many years after 1659, but modern writers still find it hard to decide how much real improvement followed in the wake of this pacification or how far the government had already begun to lay a firm basis for the work of that iron reformer, Victor Amadeus II, who built up his autocracy and bureaucracy after 1700.

Indisputably Charles Emmanuel's chief minister, Giambattista Truchi – 'the little Colbert' – did good service during a lifetime of administrative activity. Truchi, a jurist by training, was first an auditor in the treasury or *Camera dei Conti* before the duke gave him wider powers, appointing him the general superintendent of finance in 1672. He was an outstanding figure in the modest personnel which staffed the Turin government. Some office-holders were noble by birth, but in the *Camera dei Conti* and the senate (or Parlement) a group of jurists, courtiers and business men profited personally in the duke's service. The most successful could expect to be ennobled by the ruler, and to join their families in marriage with older privileged families. The duke's insistence on his right to bestow nobility was one sign of the court's potential strength, at a time when most of his other claims to sovereignty proved difficult to enforce. All the assets of the plain and uplands of Piedmont, Savoy and Nice were divided between the duke, the nobles and church, and the 'communes' of the peasants; and it sometimes looked as if the shares of ruler and peasantry had been decreasing.

From 1653 onwards the government began to raise extra funds by publicly assigning certain taxes for the payment of the interest due. The subscriptions were the so-called *monti di fede*, and 60 per cent of the money was in fact provided by noblemen and churchmen. But they sank a much larger part of their savings elsewhere. They bought property from decaying families, small-holders and the duke. They lent to impoverished neighbouring communes, and such loans not only gave them a useful income: the indebted peasantry often had to surrender what remained of their common lands, or to accept the creditor's contention that his own land in the area of a township was exempt from the taxes for which that township had to answer to the duke's officials. The distinction between the nobility's feudal property, which was very slightly burdened with obsolete forms of tax, and 'allodial' property which bore the increasing weight of fresh taxation, was indeed crucial in Piedmont. The whole weight of the privileged interest lay behind the tendency to extend the area of their fiefs, while exemption from tax helped in turn to create the resources used for further loans to the ruler or the unprivileged, whether individuals or communes. Every effort was made to keep patrimonies intact, by legal settlements which either grouped the members of a single family into a loose association of partners, or relied on entails and primogeniture. The government heaped on the unprivileged higher direct taxes, but its need for money was so great that these too were often alienated to landowners, who exploited the claim to collect such taxes in order to increase their hold on the subject peasantry. Seigneurial rights of jurisdiction tightened this grip still further.

From a personal point of view, a man like Truchi benefited from such conditions. He carved for himself a fief from lands belonging to the municipality of Turin; inside the city his new palace was the last word in magnificence. But his general policy was an attempt to protect the duke's interest, anticipating the more effective autocracy of a later period. He improved, modestly, the rudimentary budgeting and book-keeping. He recovered fiefs when possible, and was careful to part with them again on rather stricter terms than in the past. As early as 1665 there are signs of his wish, and Charles Emmanuel's, to carry out a fresh survey of the whole country in order to discover how much allodial land had been improperly assimilated with feudal land. In 1670 he appointed commissioners to investigate the problem of communal debts. He enforced the payment of additional direct taxation by the peasants. He occasionally challenged the lords' seigneurial jurisdiction.

Meanwhile he cherished fervently schemes for promoting commerce. They gave pleasure to Charles Emmanuel, an extravagant man with a keen sense of the value of money, whose remarkable diaries show him interested in 'projects' of every kind. Truchi granted special privileges to foreigners who undertook to develop new techniques in the manufacture of textiles. He eagerly looked for profit from copper mining. On a bigger scale, he renewed the earlier attempts of the Turin government to exploit Piedmont's available points of entry to the Mediterranean, at Villafranca and Nice, and dreamt of an import-export centre ranking with Leghorn and Marseilles, which would enrich the whole country and the government with it. This involved making Villafranca a 'free port' to attract foreign shippers, and improving the difficult route over the Maritime Alps from the sea to Turin. The venture failed, but a commercial treaty with England, and the appointment of a Piedmontese consul at Lisbon in 1674, reveal the trend of Truchi's ideas. For similar reasons, both minister and ruler nurtured the traditional hatred of Turin for the Genoese Republic. Genoa had that commercial and financial character which went with a mastery of the coast. It dealt in money and goods while Piedmont seemed hopelessly landlocked and agricultural. It was to Truchi what the Dutch were to Colbert. While the French court prepared in 1670 and 1671 for the conquest of Holland, Charles Emmanuel planned his own assault on the Genoese. Taking advantage of a domestic upheaval in the city, this attack was launched in 1672, but the forces employed were by no means strong enough to crush a spirited defence along the appallingly difficult frontier which ran across the mountains. The duke had to desist, and he died in 1675.

His most permanent memorial was neither a record of conquest, nor his internal administration, but the architecture which he regarded as a prime responsibility of the virtuous prince. Piedmontese Baroque was partly his creation. When Turin had been enlarged, and architects such as Castellamonte or Guarini had built and rebuilt on the right scale, in the right style, churches and palaces: then, he assumed, the prince would have a stage on which to act his role appropriately. Charles Emmanuel's court galas, his lavish treatment of many mistresses, his faithful formal attendance at church, certainly owed much to Louis XIV's example; but a hint or two from the correspondence of the Piedmontese ambassador in Paris suggests that the French were themselves interested in what may be called the scenario at Turin. This was understandable. The governments of Copenhagen and Berlin had concentrated on purely political issues; Emperor Leopold – while delighting in costly entertainments which he could not afford – somehow lacked style as a patron. In Paris the king and ministers were not only determined to deal forcefully with a very wide range of governmental problems. They respected the duke of Piedmont's emphasis on the court as a spectacle, and indeed on a much grander scale visualised the court and monarchy of France as a spectacle for mankind.

7

The Major Experiment: France

Mazarin

From one angle the France of Louis XIV seems a compound of all its past history from the days of Saint Louis to Condé's rebellion. From another, it apparently owes a special debt to changes occurring within a very short space of time, between 1658 and 1661. When Mazarin had died and the king governed, the men of this period sensed the elements of a new order in court and country. Whether they were right is a question worth an answer.

Mazarin himself normally relied on personal finesse to damp down unrest. He hoped to control Bordeaux after 1653 by overtures to the amazingly unreliable governor of Brouage – a citadel farther down the Gironde – and made him a marshal of France. Military governors along the land frontier were treated with equal tenderness, whatever their past record. Conti was prudently married off to Mazarin's niece, Hortense Mancini.[1] An earlier Mancini marriage strengthened his influence in Brittany. It was alcove politics of high quality, important, but of limited interest. The cardinal also spent time and energy on perfecting the image of personal glory which he wished to enjoy and, after death, to leave with posterity. In zeal for wealth displayed with splendour he was among the last and greatest princes of the church. He invested his second fortune – speedily amassed since the Fronde – in more books, works of art, buildings and property, while by his will he endowed a foundation for educating scholars from Artois, Flanders, Roussillon and Pinerolo (in Piedmont) in order to

---

1   Conti was also the governor of Languedoc, enjoying a stupendous income from his official position, his supplementary royal pension, his abbeys and his lands. E. Le Roy Ladurie, *Les paysans de Languedoc* (1966), p. 485.

commemorate his conquests for France. This is at present the seat of the Académie Française, while his library helps to house the Bibliothèque Nationale. He was ably advised by his business manager Colbert. When the question of a purchase by Mazarin of the duke of Never's property of Nivernais came up in 1659, Colbert personally surveyed it with meticulous care and considered the high price finally agreed to be justified by the possibilities of the investment. These derived in part from the extent to which the duke had taken over royal authority in Nivernais by acting as the king's commissary. Mazarin or his heirs would enjoy almost sovereign power within its boundaries. The transaction seems somewhat remote from the spirit of Colbert's work a few years later. It entirely accorded with the cardinal's.

This private empire had previously depended on his intimacy with Anne of Austria. By now, much more turned on the temperament of Louis XIV. Aged sixteen he was crowned in Rheims cathedral on 7 July 1654 in a blaze of liturgical glory, and Mazarin started teaching the Lord's Anointed the business of government, introducing him to a sequence of councils in which minor matters were discussed. The young man was from the first profoundly awake to his unique status, emphasised by his tutors and the books they put before him, and by his tutors' memory of recent disorders; but he naturally preferred pleasure to chores. The cardinal had difficulty in convincing him that the ambition to be a great ruler depended on mastering the 'métier du roi', a phrase first used at about this date. The ageing minister observed with some alarm a maturing youth who failed to keep his amours distinct from serious politics. At this point the king grew up. He gave way to Mazarin, respected his relationship with the queen-mother, watched him falling ill and getting old. He determined to stand aside until the statesman died, and then to assert his right to real authority. It was not what many at court expected from the gadding young man, but he had learnt from a master to dissimulate with perfect control. Louis XIV's patient waiting on events before 1661 was his first outstanding display of a shrewd political instinct.

In any case an important and novel assertion of absolute royal authority, contrary to many ancient rights, was enforced in Provence immediately after the treaty of the Pyrenees. In spite of urgent appeals to intervene, Mazarin left the troubles of that area to simmer during the war, allowing them to reach a pitch of disorder early in 1659 no less intense than during the worst years of the Fronde. His local supporters were the duke of Mercœur, governor of the province and married to his niece Laura Martinozzi, and d'Oppède, president of the Aix Parlement, at a time when the municipality of Marseilles had fallen into the hands of noblemen determined to defend their liberties; their city still belonged in spirit to the old world of Italian patrician republics. The strongest party here was encouraged by the archbishop of Aix as well as by noblemen and office-holders in Provence who opposed the truculent d'Oppède. With peace secured, Mazarin at last took action. Louis XIV, having spent the winter of 1659–60 in Toulouse before going to meet his Spanish bride, led a powerful force across the Rhône and entered Marseilles in triumph. The walls were breached, the municipal constitution was revoked and a rigorous royal administration substituted. The old consuls were replaced by non-noble aldermen with restricted functions. The king appointed the new office-holders. The citadel of St Nicholas was planned, for a garrison to overawe the inhabitants. All the benefits of a more settled government were promised in Provence, to be paid for by greater subjection.

The Fiscal System

In his attitude towards the king Mazarin had inevitably considered the future, but he was himself satisfied by a restoration of the administrative and fiscal system of the pre-Fronde period. Such a negative approach to a critical problem was almost more significant. The 'ancien régime' took firmer root because no change was contemplated. Thereafter no one could tamper with it except in detail, not even Colbert. What was abolished at the Revolution was in essentials the work of Richelieu, preserved by Mazarin in 1653. In that year he chose two of his most loyal servants, Abel Servien and Nicholas Fouquet, to share the vacant office of the *surintendant des finances*. He toyed at first with the idea of repudiating on the grand scale old government liabilities to creditors, financiers and rentiers alike, but Fouquet soon persuaded him to rely on skilful management of the king's credit. By this Fouquet meant the old close collaboration in Paris of the *surintendant* with a small but influential circle of men, who were in a position to advance funds for immediate use in return for pledges of ultimate repayment with interest. There was here little idea of balancing expenditure against revenue. The administration simply worked on the short-term problem of collecting enough revenue to secure its credit with the fund-raisers – among whom were of course Mazarin, Fouquet and their clients. If the authority of the monarchy had been restored, so also was a financial system which was its chief weakness.

Fouquet, the relative and partner of some of the richest banking families of the capital, pleaded later with some justification that he saved the state in 1654 and again in 1658, when an absolute shortage of money appeared likely to cripple the government. He offered to maintain the flow of advances, and pacified important interests by offering to borrow on terms which were even more favourable to the creditor than those previously offered. He enriched himself in the process, as did Mazarin, but his own words show clearly how he carried the day in a small world of rich men. 'The expenses of the state would not have been met, for the most urgent needs and necessities, nor pay given to the troops...if I had not provided them; and I would not have been able to provide them if my wealth, my expenditure, my splendour of life and my liberality, together with the notice taken of my absolute reliability, had not given me credit'.[2] In fact, those who mattered most put their trust in the *surintendant* who created such an air of magnificent luxury in his new palace of Vaux-le-Vicomte, and who patronised so intelligently such men as La Fontaine and the painter Le Brun. The chronic poverty of governments and most of their subjects, the costly style of life in princely courts, and the fortunes made by politicians, were indeed of the essence of this period. Fouquet's apology gives an inkling of the mechanism behind such an unequal distribution of assets.

The *surintendant* was the highest financial dignitary in France: responsible to the king, he could not be called to account at the audits of the Chambre des Comptes. His powers included that of deciding which of the varied sources of royal revenue should be used to meet individual items of expenditure or liability; and auditors were never shown the detailed registers of certain parts of this expenditure, authorised by the issue of what were called 'ordonnances de comptants'. These were orders to pay, in which no reason for the payment was specified; nor were receipts asked for from the payee or his representative. The amounts disbursed under this heading increased colossally during the years immediately before the Fronde and among the reforms imposed by the Parlement in 1648 was a theoretically stringent limitation on the use of 'ordonnances de comptants'. In addition, when a treasurer had no money in the fund assigned by a superior official for the payment of a debt, and issued a bill instead, that bill was likely to become another abuse in the mechanism of receipt and payment. Who had power to reassign the bill to some better fund? Who had the influence to get that bill, very often after it had been sold by a despairing holder at a heavy discount, paid nearly in full? Why, those closest to the centre of power, with friends in the highest places round the cardinal and the *surintendant*.

There was an additional reason why the 'ordonnances de comptants' were so much used. The church, and indeed public opinion, remained strong enough to leave imprinted in the law a veto on

2 *Defenses de Mr Fouquet sur tous les points de son Procez* (1665), ii, p. 324.

usury, and accordingly a legal maximum on the rate of interest, usually 5 or $5\frac{1}{2}$ per cent. This became quite unrealistic in times of shortage, and when the government's credit sank very low. In consequence, if the state needed to borrow 1 million *livres* at 15 per cent, it issued receipts for the notional amount of 3 million, and 'ordonnances de comptants' for the payment of interest on this larger sum. The control was slack – too many persons had good reasons for allowing this to be the case – so that such notional claims to a fictitious capital could sometimes be converted into real claims for repayment from the treasury. Moreover, because the government's needs were so pressing it sanctioned increasingly heavy discounts on the sums borrowed, by the issue of so-called 'ordonnances de remise'. On occasion and in the right hands, these too could be extremely profitable.

In effect, the monarch's discretionary power had been vested in the *surintendant* and in his master, Mazarin, who used it to find finance which could not be raised by more normal methods, in order to carry on the government and enrich themselves. The normal methods were of course the varied forms of taxation, and the ordinary devices for anticipating a slow and laborious collection of taxes. In the case of the *taille*, money had to be found by innumerable poor men who often rendered payment to one another for private transactions in corn, wine and livestock; to find current coin for the village tax collector was a complication as well as a burden. But the state could not afford delay, and so the provincial 'receivers' and 'receivers-general' were linked together and to the main royal treasuries by contracts, which bound them to advance money to the king at agreed discounts; ultimately they were recouped by the tax-payers. In the same way, the indirect taxes were also farmed; and the king's officials would assign or earmark for particular creditors the yield of particular taxes in particular areas. If the farmer could not pay on demand, he issued bills to acknowledge his liability; but the central treasuries only received the balance of a farmer's annual payment after these assignations had been first deducted. It was a world in which men with property and liquid capital, often at great risk, profited from the state's extraordinary difficulty in raising revenue. The king's arbitrary power to tax was counterbalanced by his impotence to tax without relying on expensive credits, advances and discounts.

The system allowed handsome profits to a select circle at the top, and a decent return to more modest provincial operators, but much depended on the general buoyancy of the economy. Yields from the main crops had gone up again since the days of catastrophic shortage before 1652, so that under Fouquet the surplus available for taxes – as well as for the tithes of the church and for private rents – may have been just sufficient to meet the demand. When conditions in any region became intolerable, it was the collectors and farmers of the royal taxes who usually focused popular resentment. The campaign in Flanders which led to Turenne's victories in 1658, for example, coincided with serious unrest. Trouble along the Loire and in neighbouring Sologne then spread to Poitou, Anjou and Normandy. Here, gentry led the disaffected. Some wanted the Estates of Normandy summoned in accordance with an earlier royal promise, never kept. Another grievance was the attempt to tax men of substance who claimed to be noblemen, often without adequate proof of their status. Members of undoubted noble families joined them in secret and illegal assemblies. Such disorders at once hindered the flow of revenue to Paris and to the troops in the field, endangering further the government's credit but raising the stakes for those still able and bold enough to lend.

In this crisis and throughout the final stages of the war Fouquet kept the wheels of finance turning with extraordinary skill. Mazarin stood by him while he continued to borrow from his friends, assigning for their security the most reliable elements in the revenue. He also took care to satisfy Mazarin's own demands: for the cardinal invested heavily in the business of military contracts, and insisted that payment and repayment – taking into account generous discounts and lavish rates of interest – should be prompt in his case. But although Fouquet always deferred to Mazarin, who expressed occasional irritation but relied on him, in the background another voice now spoke up in much harsher tones.

Colbert, the cardinal's intendant while Fouquet was the king's *surintendant*, had gradually developed an itch for power which first made him the critic of a more highly placed rival, and then led him to think out what he believed to be an alternative and superior policy for the whole administration. Momentarily the two great financial empires of king and cardinal co-existed in uneasy partnership; he administered one of them on behalf of Mazarin, but feared to be the odd man out when Mazarin died. Meanwhile the cardinal's prosperity depended on getting the revenue authorities to assign him the best possible security for his loans and contracts, while he borrowed from others on reasonable terms because his credit was good. Colbert therefore had a direct interest in the efficient collection of taxes. When Mazarin took over the revenues of Montauban and Guienne in order to cover the costs (and more) of his contracts to supply the army with bread, Colbert learnt that the *taille* was often not paid because royal governors and persons of quality 'protected' rural communities, that assessment rolls were years out of date, and that the receivers secured an excessive discount from Paris. His correspondence during the risings of

1658, similarly, shows him convinced that efficient government and tax collection in the provinces would go far to eliminate the expensive borrowing from which too many financiers (including the *surintendant* himself) profited. For this reason he was interested in the appointment of intendants, recommending men – including a number of his own relatives – who accepted autocratic views whole-heartedly. He blamed slack intendants for the troubles in Normandy and Poitou.

His preoccupation with administrative business interlocked with another. From the time of the Fronde he never faltered in his bias against the Parlements, advising the strongest measures against them. He scorned an argument that royal authority should be 'counterbalanced' (his own word) by other authorities. He wanted to carry further the old policy of withdrawing from Parlements various classes of litigation in which the crown was involved. When the time came to deal with the arrested rebel leaders of 1658, he held that Parlements were not the appropriate tribunals: they were not reliable enough to judge and condemn in the manner required. Before long he turned this implacable bent of mind directly against the man whom he wished to replace.

Twice in 1659 he was rebuffed by Mazarin. Fouquet's colleague Abel Servien died, but the cardinal rejected the proposal that he himself should take over the *surintendant*'s office, which would have certainly given his personal adviser greater responsibility for government finance. A few months later Colbert tried again. He wanted Fouquet dismissed and arrested, and an extraordinary tribunal set up to recover from him and the whole tribe of his financiers their ill-gotten gains. There was no novelty about such a Chamber of Justice, which had been used to call *surintendants* to account in 1607, 1629 and 1635; but it is interesting to see how Colbert felt an equal antipathy for financiers and the ordinary process of law, whereas in 1648 members of the Paris Parlement had deeply mistrusted the alliance of the administration with its chosen ring of fund-raisers. There was an important change of alignment in the offing here. But Mazarin brushed Colbert aside for the second time. Fouquet remained as the sole *surintendant*, disturbed by what he had learnt of the intrigue against him, but still in full control of his great post. His reactions at this moment are no less interesting than Colbert's. Fearing dismissal and arrest, he considered from time to time a plan for mobilising his friends outside Paris, the governors of certain fortresses, the vice-admiral commanding royal ships in the Bay of Biscay, and other influential persons – who in fact signed professions of loyalty to Fouquet which still express the *frondeur* nobles' instinct that loyalty to the king was not the highest consideration. Mazarin consenting, Fouquet had also purchased the marquisate of Belle-Île, an island off the Biscay coast, which he hoped to turn into a fortified stronghold of his own. These ideas of self-protection, pondered over by the minister at intervals in 1657–9, were unfortunately committed to paper and formed the basis of the charge of treason later levelled against him at his trial.

Louis XIV in 1661

Against this background it is possible to judge the new personal monarchy which began during the night of 8/9 March 1661 when Mazarin died, and lasted until 1715, inaugurated by a famous double coup which set indelible marks on the rest of Louis's reign. First of the two blows was an emphatic formal pronouncement to the French court and the powers of Europe that the king himself intended to conduct his affairs, that in consequence all his ministers and officials were directly responsible to him. This might have been no more than a platitude about the nature of monarchy. What actually occurred took almost every observer by surprise. To the dismay of the queen-mother and other dignitaries, they were henceforward summoned no more to meetings of the councils of state. Louis invited only Le Tellier, Lionne and Fouquet to the most confidential of these, in which he presided over the transaction of business with the greatest diligence. The other councils were kept equally hard at work, the young ruler soon showing that he possessed personality and firmness enough to control the central organs of government. He had everything in his favour. The advantageous peace treaty with Spain and a Spanish marriage were really Mazarin's achievement, but the royal progress of the king and his queen from the Pyrenees to Paris was publicised in a way to endow Louis with the symbols of successful majesty. Conversely, the cardinal could be blamed for the oppressions of government while men looked for better things from the rising Sun, that ancient emblem of glory already annexed for the king by poets and decorators. But if he had lacked the determination to make his will felt by great and humble alike, the year 1661 would not have marked so clearly the beginning of a new era in France and Europe. Since 1630 the personal monarchy of the Bourbons was overshadowed by the practical dominance of the two 'first ministers', and weakened by a royal minority which led to the collapse of ordered government. Mazarin ultimately recovered his grip, but Louis now put an end to the whole system of control by an omnipotent deputy.

It was, of course, not much more than a change at the very highest level, a change of ruler rather than of government. The ministers, the judicial and financial administration, the conditions of life in cities and the countryside, were hardly affected. Those who had served Mazarin wished to serve Louis, looking back with horror at the dislocations of the Fronde and accepting without qualification the doctrine that unfettered monarchy was the only possible basis of good government. By this time, the most important *frondeurs* showed themselves equally loyal. Turenne, after his victories in 1658, was awarded the title of captain-general of the infantry; ten years later he would abjure the Protestant faith of his family. Above all, the royal pardon to Condé and his return to court conveniently symbolised the end of a schism. By appearing to repudiate his past he helped to discredit any future act of resistance to the crown. It was the most important gesture in a career which had affected the fortunes of France – not merely the court but also the population – at every turn for nearly twenty years.

In one important respect Louis continued where Mazarin left off, but quickly gave his policy a personal twist. Mazarin disliked the Company of the Holy Sacrament, a religious organisation which influenced public opinion on a wide front. This body (founded in 1630) survived the Fronde with a powerful headquarters in Paris and about fifty affiliated groups in the provinces. Funds were plentiful because the members gave generously. Its prime social concern was charity, but charity fused with a desire to raise morals and manners to the highest possible level of Catholic purity. It sometimes compelled royal officials, against their better judgment, to frown on masques, fairs and plays, and cases of blasphemy. It supported the law against duelling. It even took the law into its own hands, locking up loose women and unworthy priests in convents or private houses. As a result there had been popular demonstrations of protest in Bordeaux, Blois and Caen between 1658 and 1660. Ordinary people were annoyed by the Company's censorship of morals, and the government mistrusted an independent organisation ambitious enough, as in 1659, to adopt a plan for annual conferences with delegates to be sent from all parts of the country.

Nor did Mazarin forget the efforts made by St Vincent de Paul, a leader of the Company in earlier days, to discredit him with Anne of Austria. He still feared the same interest in 1658, and his energetic dislike of the 'cabale des dévots' was unconcealed at the end of his career. Alarmed, in the autumn of 1660 the officers of the Company in Paris began to take precautions, reducing the number of members who assembled at the regular weekly meetings, and ordering provincial groups to suspend correspondence with them. But on 14 December Mazarin secured a decree of the Parlement outlawing all such assemblies which met without the king's express permission to do so. Although the president of the Parlement, Lamoignon, was himself a member of the society and seems to have toned down the decree, the great days of the Company of the Holy Sacrament – at least in Paris – were over. As before, it managed charities, converted Huguenots, evangelised among the galley-slaves and saw to the catechising of the poor. It carried to a triumphant conclusion, after years of effort and with the queen-mother's help, the foundation of a Society for Foreign Missions in 1663 which from that day to this has laboured overseas, above all in Canada and Indo-China. But in France it now had to reckon with a stronger adversary even than Mazarin.

Louis XIV stood out emphatically against the 'dévot' interest. By his own conduct he exalted a different code of values. Nothing shocked Louis's mother more, and the whole circle of the devout at court, than their discovery in 1661 that marriage in no way tamed the king's passion for sexual adventure. His famous affair with Louise de la Vallière brought into existence the régime of the official mistress. The official world had to come to terms with it: Anne of Austria and Maria Teresa, Colbert and his wife who made arrangements for successive child-births, the Parlement which legitimised the royal bastards one by one, the king's confessors and the churchmen who preached before him. Bossuet, that rising young orator, encouraged by Anne of Austria, sympathetic to the Company of the Holy Sacrament, ventured to rebuke Louis publicly in his Lenten sermons of 1662. Soon he learnt to add the note of obsequiousness to his marvellous style, and accepted current realities in the court world where he was ambitious to shine with the king's favour. Between the eras of Mazarin's presumed secret marriage with Anne of Austria and of Louis XIV's own secret marriage with Mme de Maintenon lies the phase in which the king's ties with Mlle de la Vallière and Mme de Montespan, Mlle de Fontanges and others, set the tone. 'L'esprit du monde ne pouvait souffrir la Compagnie,' as a contemporary remarked later. Molière's *Tartuffe*, played first at the court in 1664, although it caused indignation in some circles, proved him right.

Fouquet and Colbert

Louis's other coup in 1661 was the arrest of Fouquet. Just before he died, Mazarin had recommended Colbert for the responsible post of 'intendant des finances' under the *surintendant*, and Colbert indeed might never have climbed higher; but the king's interest in listening to this relative stranger (in conversations for which there can be no recorded evidence) proved the sureness of his judgment. He was on the lookout for someone. In Colbert he picked the most remarkable of all his servants, and perhaps the most submissive.

For Mme de Motteville, noting the junketings of the court at Fontainebleau in that summer of 1661, what she called a 'golden age' had begun with the young king's complete control of his monarchy. She says nothing about the world outside, where one of the most serious depressions of the century descended on the country. The signs of harvest failure multiplied, corn prices soared, merchants reduced their orders for cloth, artisans got no employment and mortality increased. But it would be wrong to think that Colbert or Louis took this into consideration when the first turned once more to his long-standing assault on Fouquet, and the king held firm to his early resolve – he seems to have made up his mind on the matter by May – to get rid of the *surintendant* whom he had learnt to regard as too powerful, too rich, and sufficiently ambitious little by little to become Mazarin's successor as a 'premier ministre', once he himself slackened in attending to business. It would also be wrong to think that, on questions of financial or economic policy, there was a clear difference between Fouquet's measures since 1659 and most of what Colbert had in mind. Since peace was signed, the *surintendant* had increased the revenue from several indirect taxes by reassigning them to new farmers, recovered for the crown many alienated sources of income, written off useless claims for *taille* dating back to the years 1638–53, put a tax on Dutch ships using French ports, and shown interest in trading ventures overseas; his personal concern for the last item went back to the period before 1648. Finally, he reduced the total royal requirement for the *taille* of the whole country in 1661. But what attracted Colbert was power, and what attracted Louis XIV was Colbert's original proposal to Mazarin: the pulverising stroke of the *surintendant*'s arrest, to be followed by setting up a special tribunal to judge Fouquet and milk the great herd of government creditors. By this ruthless exercise of authority, by confiscation, by the repudiation or wholesale scaling down of debts, the royal finances would be strengthened. The king could then act with every prospect of success as his own *surintendant*, advised by a new council in which Colbert confidently hoped to play the leading role.

Fouquet was arrested at Nantes on 5 September. Louis masked his intentions until the very last moment, and took obvious pleasure in the theatrical assertion of power which he considered an essential element in statecraft. The office of *surintendant* was abolished, and a new council of finance began meeting on 15 September; Colbert was a member. Then, after an interval of two months during which many protests were made behind the scenes and rejected, Louis announced the creation of a Chamber of Justice to consider the finances of the kingdom and their management since 1635. It was to continue sitting until 1669. Its importance was immense. By setting up this tribunal to condemn Fouquet and scrutinise the claims of all who had advanced funds to the government during the last twenty-five years, Louis and Colbert made a bid to raise still higher the king's normal authority. They wanted to secure for him, permanently, the completeness of power which Richelieu had by delegation from Louis XIII during a long emergency. They rode roughshod over the premise that there were legitimate interests in France, other than the monarchy, which could use lawful methods to defend themselves against the monarch. With active resistance and constitutional protests already discredited during the Fronde, the whole duty of the literate classes to conform and to obey was now positively enforced.

The tribunal's proceedings stimulated the last gasp of serious lay criticism in France for many a day. The king and Colbert too glaringly lacked scruple in exploiting Fouquet's impounded papers while refusing to let him consult them. They first selected and then bullied the judges. Some judges and officials were therefore determined to follow the due order of legal proceedings, giving Fouquet a chance to argue his defence. Lamoignon presided until December 1662 and by no means satisfied Louis with his obvious lack of zeal for the royal interest; he was replaced by Séguier, the chancellor. Very skilful publicity by friends and relatives presented the case for Fouquet outside the court. Writers once maintained by this lavish patron were honourably slow to sell themselves to a higher and royal patron. Colbert meanwhile used the Chamber, as he always intended, not only to ruin Fouquet but also to attack the financiers and the holders of government *rentes*; financiers and rentiers accordingly felt a certain sympathy for his major victim. In the end, the total taken from individuals in liabilities cancelled and fines imposed may have amounted to a nominal 70 million *livres*. As for the *rentes*, Colbert's policy was no less draconic, but protest meetings at the Hôtel de Ville in March 1662, April 1663 and again in 1664, with members of the Parlement clearly sympathetic, led to something nearer a compromise. The government reduced an original total of around 28 million *livres* to 8 million. The actual annual amounts paid over to the holders were less than these figures suggest, before as well as after 1664, but the new policy was clearly designed to restore revenue to the king, and to permit lower direct taxation. It was certainly a blow at many propertied interests, some the savings of very modest families and charities.

The Chamber of Justice at last found Fouquet guilty on various counts, financial and political, and condemned him to banishment. This moderate verdict, after the prosecution had demanded death, and after the very persuasive pleading of the *parlementaire* Olivier d'Ormesson in mitigation, incensed Louis beyond measure. He implacably 'commuted' the sentence to perpetual imprisonment, and from 1664 until his death in 1680 solitary Fouquet in the fortress

of Pinerolo was a warning to those who served, or failed to serve, the
king. The ministers were henceforth subordinates to a degree that
Mazarin and the *surintendant* had never been. Here also was a
novelty, in degree if not in essence. In the long run, the political
significance of Colbert's rise to power in 1661 over-shadows his
administrative skills.

The New Scenario

This was also true from a different angle. Colbert, more than anyone
else, created the public image of Louis's majesty by setting the stage
for him. On I January 1664 he became *surintendant des bâtiments du
roi, arts et manufactures*. He had already begun to explore every
conceivable method for displaying the king's glory in stone and
decoration, in commemorative medals, in verse and festivities.
Mazarin's ideas on this topic were carried further and simplified,
because the cardinal inevitably linked his own prestige with the
king's. Louis now reigned and ruled alone. While common folk
were dying like flies in the spring of 1662 after a terrible winter of
dearth, Colbert organised the famous 'Carrousel' at the Louvre – a
tournament and equestrian ballet combined – which set a new standard of luxury and expense for courtly entertainment in Europe.[3] In
1663 he encouraged Jean Chapelain and Charles Perrault to start the
so-called 'little academy' which in due course flowered into the
Academy of Inscriptions and Literature: the members received pensions from the crown, and were directly instructed to find texts or
symbols depicting the greatness of Louis.[4] In architecture and décor
the political bias of Colbert's activity helped to create a new style, a
style fitted to express an unchallenged royal authority. Louis's superb
presence, his extraordinary hardiness in despising comfort, and his
total disregard for his subjects' capacity to bear too many taxes,
made him the perfect collaborator. No expense was spared, but at
the same time contemporaries began to echo the king in their desire
to get away from what were called 'filigranes' and 'bagatelles' –
useless ornament and unnecessary amenities. These were rejected
for a marble spaciousness in which, as Mme de Maintenon remarked
many years later, 'il faut périr en symétrie'.

Colbert had placed first on his list of priorities the adornment of
Paris as a worthy setting for the court and government. He wanted
an imposing Arc de Triomphe, for example, to mark the spot where

3   The Habsburgs took up the challenge with a similar entertainment in 1667, to
celebrate Leopold's marriage to *his* Infanta. It has been described as the most lavish
single festival in Viennese history.
4   For the foundation of the Academy of Science in Paris, see below, p. 180.

Louis and his queen ceremonially entered the city together in 1660. He visualised them residing in the grandest of European capitals, in the finest of European palaces, when a serious fire conveniently posed the whole question of repairing or rebuilding the Louvre. The suggestion was soon made to place Mazarin's new foundation for 'the four nations' (see above, p. 137) on the left bank of the Seine, opposite the royal palace; and to this day the confrontation across the river of that wing of the Louvre which Colbert built, with the façade and dome endowed by Mazarin survives as a triumph of urban planning. Soon Louis's personal preference for expansion in places outside the capital, at St Germain and Versailles, made itself felt. During the next few years, accordingly, a tremendous programme of construction was in full swing both in and outside Paris, before Versailles and other palaces were given priority over the Louvre. In order to supervise the large staff of interior decorators needed, Colbert concentrated many of the older workshops producing luxury articles in a single establishment, the Gobelins, and put Charles Le Brun in charge of them from 1662.

A critical phase in the struggle for a new style was fought out at the same time by Louis, Colbert and their advisers. Partly influenced by his long association with Mazarin, certainly pressed by such prominent Italians in Paris as Cardinal Francesco Barberini, Colbert wished to call the best Roman architects into consultation for work on the Louvre. The great Bernini was invited to Paris. Many designs were considered, and in 1667 a small committee tried to come to a final decision. Bernini's scheme appeared too radical to Louis, who did not wish to see the old accommodation swept completely away. The French experts, including some of the men who dominated architecture in France during the next twenty years, may have inspired this view; they certainly agreed with it. The plans ultimately adopted signified a defeat for the Italian influence so strong almost everywhere else in Europe. They were a victory for the French architectural profession – incorporated in one more new Academy in 1671, to dictate the canons of current design – under a ruler for whom building on the grand scale proved to be one of the master-passions, together with women and war. These passions, with Louis, were never mutually exclusive: the cost of the work at Versailles and at Clagny – destined for Mme de Montespan – during the war years after 1672, was staggering. It must be admitted that they were larger still after 1678.

A similar change had already occurred in another of the arts. A great Venetian musician returned like Bernini, empty-handed as he thought, from Paris to Italy. Invited by Mazarin to compose an opera to commemorate the treaty of 1659 and the marriage of 1660, Francesco Cavalli came to the French court with numerous other

Italian artists and technicians. At length, in February 1662, a magnificent new theatre in the Tuileries opened with the performance of Cavalli's *Ercole Amante* – but its acts were interespersed with a ballet entertainment, *Hercule Triomphant,* for which J. B. Lully composed the music and planned the dances; in these the king himself took his part, duly appearing as the 'Sun'. The ballet and its French verses stole the limelight from the opera. Lully, always a favourite with Louis, soon became undisputed master of the royal music, and Molière's brilliant collaborator. For twenty years a specifically Italian musical influence at the French court was reduced to a minimum

Behind the scenes Colbert continued as the supreme royal purveyor, at least in Louis's eyes. Colbert himself took a loftier view of his responsibilities.

The New Administration

The 'intendant des finances' who appears simply as a member of Louis XIV's new council of finance in September 1661 had composed the royal speech which opened the sessions of this body. Colbert became the chief adviser responsible for revenue and many branches of expenditure from this moment until he died in 1683, although the post of controller-general was not his until 1665. The title of *surintendant* disappeared for good, and a long line of controllers would vainly try to balance the monarchy's books until the Revolution. Colbert, however, bequeathed to French public finance and to the whole bureaucratic apparatus a bias in favour of rigour which was permanently valuable. It at least did something to hold in check the even stronger instinct to spend.

His chief complaint against Fouquet's management was precisely its wastefulness and confusion. He believed that, with his own orderly conduct of business, waste would disappear automatically. A government, and a monarch, who knew how much they had to spend, would not overspend. An official who had to render exact accounts was safe from corruption. A controller-general who had precise information about harvests, trades, shipping, bankruptcies, numbers of people in different districts and so on, would relate taxes to taxability and royal spending to taxes with all the greater effectiveness. At the very highest level, this attractive idea was doomed from the start. When one seeks to compare Louis XIV's power with his minister's, it is hard not to feel that all Colbert's devices for supervising both revenue and expenditure and for getting Louis to appreciate his intractable financial problems – the weekly council of finance presided over by the king, a monthly reading in council of the state of the accounts, an annual set of estimates for the forthcoming year, an annual review of actual revenue and expenditure for the previous twelve months, the neat little abstracts for the whole complex subject which he concocted 'for the pocket' of the king – all these simply filled an extravagant ruler with a sense of his unlimited capacity and right to spend. For in certain respects Louis was Fouquet on the throne.

Below this level, the gains were much clearer. The controller-general managed to obtain for himself a more accurate picture of the monarchy's finances and the country's economy than had been available before. In the process, he trained the men who learnt with him that administrative efficiency depended on an appreciation in detail of local conditions. At first, Colbert thought of intendants as officials with a temporary commission in the area to which they were sent for special reasons. Then, he seems to have reckoned that one intendant – with a commission to supervise the administration of several tax districts (or *généralités*) – would be sufficient. Next, he laid increasing emphasis on their duty to send to Paris detailed reports. A circular of 1664, requesting such reports, suggests that the intendants would be moved from time to time to new areas, in order to form a corps of officials who acquired a close working knowledge of the whole country. By 1666 he had modified and combined these ideas. He wanted one intendant for each *généralité*, reporting weekly to the controller-general. Regular correspondence, continuous and vigilant supervision from the centre, and stable administrative units, were new elements of strength for the royal government. Officials ought not to be office-holders with a proprietary right in their post, but men liable to dismissal or transfer; a more disciplined bureaucracy was in many ways Colbert's greatest achievement. In the later seventeenth century this élite of provincial administrators had no equivalent of comparable quality elsewhere in Europe. With its help he brought down the nominal totals of the *taille* imposed on France from 41 million *livres* in 1661 to around 34 million annually in 1669–71, while the real net income went up from 20 to 27 million. When the war after 1672 compelled him to raise his demand to 40 million again in 1675–7, this no doubt represented a far stiffer tax than the same nominal level of taxation in pre-Colbertian days. Louis XIV, it must always be remembered, was the richest man in Europe.

The other side of the coin gleamed less. Colbert lowered the *taille* as soon as the great war ended in 1678, but the net return had begun to drop more sharply still and does not seem to have risen above 24 million in 1680. In fact, administrative competence was to some extent offset by failure on the broader front. If the crown wanted too much, year in and year out, and if the rural economy also sagged – as in the 1680s – the rule of the intendants simply pressed too hard on the population.

Possibly another of Colbert's failures mitigated this. Society was divided into the large numbers who paid *taille*, and smaller numbers who did not. It was impoverishing to pay, and also ignoble. The *taille* meant subjection and imposed on the unprivileged the badge of subjection. Half-way up the social and economic ladder Colbert and his servants had to distinguish between those lawfully exempt from *taille*, and the 'faux nobles' and 'coqs de paroisse' who also managed to avoid payment. Exemption, whether legal or illegal, might well be the condition on which reasonable prosperity depended. In other cases, tax evasion prepared the way for a family's greater prosperity than in the past, and a higher status; in due course men who lived 'like noblemen' became noblemen. The government's attitude to this had been ambiguous. There were signs before 1648 that it was trying to unmask the 'false' noblemen. On the other hand, titles of nobility were occasionally put up for sale by the crown, while office-holding and the purchase of office conferred exemption from such burdens as the taille and billeting. Experts in heraldry openly went about the job of concocting plausible genealogies for those who employed them, in case royal officials wished to scrutinise their antecedents. It may well be that Colbert's efforts to stop people of means or local influence from slipping out of the assessment registers was on balance a failure. He was more successful than the government in Spain (see above, p. 82), but impeded without halting the process. He did not arrest the small but perceptible ascent of families from unprivileged to privileged status during this period.[5] Their benefit was the government's loss, while the fiscal pressure on those lower down the ladder of wealth proved unremitting.

Colbert also had to come to terms with both the office-holder and the owner of government *rentes*. His antipathy was only a by-product of the wrangle with Fouquet which led him willy-nilly to condemn what he judged excessive borrowing, and to preach the virtues of a budget with taxes balancing expenditure. He did not hesitate to return to Fouquet's methods when the war of 1672 dragged on. If his first decade of power had seen a brusque reduction in the amount paid to the rentier, and no further alienations, in the second these increased again. After the peace of 1678 the rentiers were far more gently handled than in 1661–4. By the end of Colbert's life, government *rentes* (paid mainly through the Hôtel de Ville in Paris) were firmly established and became the basis for fund-raising of this type in the following decades. The first controller-general would have shuddered at the gigantic total of the *rentes* alienated

---

5 At the same time, the exemption of noblemen from the *taille* was on balance more assured than before 1648. See P. Deyon, 'Rapport entre la noblesse française et la monarchie absolue', *Revue Historique*, 231 (1964), pp. 341–56.

after 1688, but he had sensibly compromised with yet another interest in the community.

The New Economic Policy

In the whole system, the question of consent to taxation hardly arose. The *pays d'état* enjoyed greater independence than the *pays d'election* but they were usually poorer, and in any case their privileges were those of noblemen and clergy only. What limited the power to tax was privilege, and also the ability of the subject to pay. That ability depended on economic conditions.

Colbert understood this, just as he understood that all his measures of reform interacted on each other. With a passion for detail, he still displayed an uncommon breadth of view. He thought of the state's financial management as a single problem, as well as a complex of many problems. He thought of the economy of France as a whole, dependent on but distinguishable from the prosperity of separate provinces and diverse interests; and he drew the conclusion that increases in government revenue and expenditure depended in turn on the prosperity of the economy. In a justly famous memorandum of 1670 he feared that the pressure of taxation was not allowing wealth to increase fast enough, and makes the point that – although royal expenditure soon restored to circulation the money collected by tax collectors – much of this expenditure in fact affected Paris and eight other *généralités*, so that the remaining *généralités* were being pumped dry. Anticipating war in future, he therefore wanted to reduce taxation and expenditure in order to leave intact stores of wealth for the crown to tap later on. He pinned most of his hopes for the future of the French economy on the revival of commerce and improvements in industry.

With respect to the first, a period of maximum activity on his part began in 1664 with the foundation of a new 'council of commerce'. He went to great lengths to engage the king's interest, and the draft of a speech which he made at its first meeting, in Louis's presence, marshalled all his favourite themes in outlining a comprehensive policy: on tolls, tariffs, trading companies, industrial undertakings, state aid and the improvement of commercial law. This involved, as he pointed out, earmarking some of Louis's present revenues for the sake of future gain, and taking up the king's valuable time with a disagreeable type of business. Louis allowed himself to be persuaded, and in September a public edict announced the foundation of the council, while letters to individual cities like Paris and Marseilles required their co-operation. Representatives from such places, chosen by the king, were to sit with other counsellors on this body. In practice, the initiatives of the next few years owed little to the council, nothing to Louis XIV, and almost everything to Colbert.

It did not take him long to appreciate the economic as well as the fiscal disadvantages of an anarchic tangle of tariffs imposed on the trader. The largest customs area in France, the 'five great farms', had a frontier cutting right across the country from west to east, for the most part at some distance south of the river Loire; it embraced most of the northern provinces with the exception of Artois, Flanders and Brittany. Elsewhere, people paid different tariffs, at different rates, to a number of different tax farmers. So he began in 1664 by rationalising the tariffs of the 'five great farms'. He stipulated for uniform dues on 580 distinct articles. It was an initial attack on the problem. His economic ideas, as distinct from his desire for a uniform administration, were merely hinted at in this measure. Import dues for the area were very slightly raised, and dues on goods leaving it slightly lowered. Rates on the export of certain raw materials were raised. In publishing these detailed changes, the king prefaced them with a grandiose justification for all his policies in previous years, from reductions in the *taille* to the maintenance of peace. An improved customs system, it was implied, came as another great instalment in a programme of reform.

In much the same spirit Colbert tried to get rid of obstacles to the freer movement of grain. He approved of the old tactic of permitting the export of corn after good harvests, or prohibiting it when the harvests were bad and corn prices too high. But because he was now better informed about the level of supplies in their *généralités* by the intendants, he could do this more discriminatingly than had been possible earlier. He rebuked the municipality of Bordeaux, when it tried to safeguard supplies and to keep prices down for the urban population by preventing its hinterlands from disposing of surplus grain elsewhere. For the government, collection of the *taille* depended on keeping grain prices up in periods of relative plenty, and for this reason Colbert wished to encourage the easy internal circulation of grain and, on occasion, its export overseas.

All the same, he remained convinced that royal revenue depended on the growth of industry and commerce: these, rather than agriculture,[6] could be stimulated by good government, which had the power and duty to supervise them. It was his assumption that bad or

6 The most positive of Colbert's measures for the peasants was his attempt to reduce the indebtedness of rural communities, and to recover for them their alienated communal lands. But his instructions of 1662 and 1667 were met by the successful resistance of propertied interests. (Cf. with the position in Naples and Piedmont, pp. 81, 134 above.) In this sphere Colbert was powerless to counteract the long-term decline of corn-prices, especially in the northern half of France, during his period of office – with its adverse consequences for both peasants and landlords.

excessive harvests were beyond the compass of human management, but that a languishing trade – as in the cloth centres of Rheims, Amiens and Beauvais for twenty years before 1660 – could be revived; and if revived, a prosperous trade positively enriched the state by sales abroad and by reducing foreign imports. He began to pay particular attention to the manufacture of textiles in 1666; his methods were simple and direct. He sent out agents to consult with guilds and municipalities, where they discussed on the spot existing regulations which laid down conditions of work, standards of workmanship and techniques of production. The officials then submitted to the minister and the council of commerce copies of the old regulation, together with changes they proposed. What he finally approved received royal sanction, and many new ordinances for different areas were issued in 1666 and 1667. A general regulation for the manufacture of woollens (and of cloth made of wool and linen mixed) was published in August 1669. Ordinances on dyeing appeared in 1669 and 1671, and in all about 200 such ordinances – local and general – for the supervision of industry were issued in Colbert's lifetime, mostly concerned with textiles. They formed the working basis of state supervision of industry in France for the next century. Much more elaborate instructions were drawn up after 1683, but it is arguable that they were therefore less useful. Colbert must not be blamed for the abuse of his policy.

To enforce it, he appointed inspectors or *commis des manufactures* in August 1669, while above them soon ranked a few senior inspectors. But Colbert also decreed that aldermen in the municipalities should deal with litigation arising out of the ordinances, and he was to be constantly exasperated by their unwillingness to enforce them with the rigour he required. Friction between royal officials and local interests over innumerable points of difficulty became a staple of economic life, and the balance of good and harm due to Colbert's initiative obviously varied from place to place. The degree of government interference in his day can easily be exaggerated. Inside the towns he never seriously intended to force all trades into the straitjacket of a tightly organised guild system, the *jurandes*, with a restricted membership and a local monopoly. Many occupations in many French towns remained open to all-comers, provided that they obeyed the ordinances regulating their calling. In other places the local pressure in favour of *jurandes* was itself very strong. Moreover, many crafts were practised in the countryside where supervision was generally less strict, and the guild system something of a rarity. Merchants distributed the materials for spinning, and to a lesser extent for weaving. Peasants added to their income by working for these dealers at lower rates than could be paid in towns, especially in the first half of the year before harvest-time. The terms of employment and standards of work both depended more on the state of business than on the government's claim to regulate them. In spite of fierce opposition from the towns, cottage industry seems to have increased during Louis's reign, while the monarchy can claim some credit for the high-quality goods produced in urban workshops later in the century.

All trades require supervision by the state, argued Colbert, but some require supervision and encouragement. The idea was a commonplace in this period, but he applied it on an astonishing scale. Initially, he extended the old policy of allowing special privileges to workshops employed by the court. In some cases these were, or became, the property of the crown, like the tapestry manufacture of the Gobelins. In others, he preferred to commission work from a privately owned concern, in order to encourage it to run the risk of producing fine wares for a very small market. He used both methods, or a compromise between them, for the manufacture of armaments. While his new naval arsenals had their own workshops, in Dauphiné a wealthy receiver-general of the *taille* tried to forge cannon and ships' anchors, with Colbert's encouragement. The Royal Company of Mines and Foundries in Languedoc, started in 1666, was a group of office-holders and financiers on whom he virtually imposed the task of exploiting local mineral resources in order to reduce lead and copper imports from abroad. In spite of the premiums which he offered, the concern failed miserably. In most of his ventures Colbert had to find the necessary capital by using royal funds and enlisting aid compulsorily from officials and merchants. Sometimes he requested provincial Estates and municipalities to contribute.[7] But at least for ten years – from 1664 until 1673 – he subsidised business directly and generously. Later, he still continued to offer monopolies, premiums and special advantages in securing labour, to those enterprises which he chose to honour with the title of *Manufactures Royales*. Privileges of this type, in his view, were temporary. They were designed to start up a new business or to revive an old one, until it was strong enough to stand the strain of open competition. His obstinate prodding kept the Languedoc draperies alive until at last, after 1690, they fulfilled his hopes of competing successfully with Dutch and English cloth in the Levant. He was just as generous and farsighted in the privileges which he gave to the small textile masters in the town of Sedan. Such measures enabled him to attract the foreign expertise in which he profoundly believed: German miners,

7 The most spectacular enterprise to which the state, the provincial Estates, and private funds all contributed, was the Languedoc Canal (completed in 1682). Here the initiative came from an individual, P. P. Riquet, 'homme de gabelle' and prosperous army contractor, but Colbert backed him to the hilt. See A. Maistre, *Le canal des deux mers... 1666–1810* (Toulouse 1968).

Dutch or Flemish weavers and dyers, Venetian glaziers and candle-
men, all had a good reception in France from the controller-general
and a poor one from competing domestic interests. He at least
proved that Louis XIV's monarchy had as much chance as other
régimes of attracting good-quality immigrants.

The fiscal calculation in these policies always remained potent in
Colbert's mind. He relied on the expansion of business to raise the
yield from indirect taxation (as distinct from *taille* on persons or
land), while he used better methods for collecting it. By a gradual
process, small and local tax farms had already been merging together
over a long period. Colbert now pressed for something more, and in
1668 negotiated another merger on a bigger scale. A gross return to
the crown of 43 million *livres* was promised annually. By 1683 he
had screwed this up to 66 million. Net yields always fell far below
gross figures but the united 'general' farm of a great variety of taxes,
leased out to powerful syndicates, was one of Colbert's principal
legacies to the tax structure of eighteenth-century France. It
depended, by comparison with the position in 1661, on an increase
in internal trading or on higher taxes affecting a wider range of
goods.

Some things he could not do. These tax farms were never replaced
by the direct administration of royal officials, on the model of
Danby's reforms in contemporary England. River navigation continued to be choked by private tolls, as in Germany. All the same,
on a more grandiose scale than anywhere else in Europe, Colbert
tried to stimulate trade and manufactures by state encouragement
and to tax the proceeds. Without being original in this respect, he set
a new example.

He applied the same devices to French overseas business. It was the
state's function to take the initiative, the subjects' duty to assist and
obey, and Monsieur Colbert's task peremptorily to associate the two.
Enlarging his countrymen's share in world trade by reducing imports
and increasing exports, getting these imports and exports carried in
French-built or at least French-owned ships, would build a surplus
and bring in bullion which enriched the monarch with the monarchy.
He therefore set out to restore the navy and marine, found new
companies for foreign trade, and enforce tariffs which encouraged
French commerce by hampering its rivals. The total achievement here
was patchy, scarred by many failures. Colbert's West and East India
Companies were both founded in 1664, his Northern Company
(designed to take from the Dutch French trade with the Baltic) in
1669. By 1678 the first and third had disappeared, while the second
was left with not much more than an old base in Madagascar and a
new settlement at Pondichery in India. The trade of Marseilles with
the Levant did not expand in Colbert's lifetime. The aggressive tariff

of 1667 was revoked to pay for peace with the Dutch, also in 1678. Yet the kernel may have been better than the shell. In the West Indies individual French traders and partnerships had followed in the wake of the state-financed company, and in due course superseded it. Higher duties on the import of foreign raw and refined sugar, the official encouragement given to the construction of refineries in France, were a stimulus to the planters in Martinique and Guadeloupe and to businessmen at home. In Canada, as in the West Indies, the government had first asserted the king's sovereign authority before transferring property and trading rights from an older company to the new one in 1664. A royal governor and an intendant arrived in Quebec. A royal regiment checked the Iroquois in 1666. For ten years Colbert handsomely subsidised emigrants and industries. This stiffening for the settlements above and below Quebec strengthened the link between the mother country and the missionaries and trappers, who were now fanning out to the headwaters of the Illinois and Mississippi. Such a desertion of a royal colony by its manpower was anathema to Colbert – but pointed the way overland to what later became Louisiana and New Orleans. At home, meanwhile, the great arsenals at Rochefort and Toulon showed that the king's navy was fast recovering from the dereliction of Mazarin's day. It stood ready to protect and extend French foreign trade – and, if opportunity offered, to menace foreign traders.

The New Army

France, under Colbert, had started to catch up with its European rivals overseas. France, under Louis XIV with Le Tellier and his son Louvois, had already surpassed the military power of its rivals in Europe.

Le Tellier, secretary for war, presided over a partial transformation of the French army; the crucial reforms were carried through between the treaty of the Pyrenees and Louis's next attack on the Spanish Netherlands. This army, in 1659, still remained one in which military office-holders great and small contracted to raise men for the crown. Apart from the regiments, the governors of provinces and cities and fortresses had their own 'free' companies. Royal princes had their own household troops. Two captain-generals, appointed for life, confirmed the nomination or promotion of all cavalry and infantry officers, in effect sharing the patronage with regimental colonels. Many Swiss, some Germans and a few Scottish regiments or troops were hired by agreements with cantons or officers who recruited the men. In the field, marshals and lieutenant-generals often declined to recognise any superior because the notion of seniority, calculated from the date of a commission, was understood but resisted. War with Spain had brought into existence a very large army, which professed loyalty to the crown but in fact formed that part of the social order least amenable to royal control. Its members took something from the king, with his power to find them money, and took more from the civilian population in either French or foreign territory. 'Intendants of war and justice' were sent to adjust the contacts of troops with civilians, but they too often depended on the goodwill of the troop commanders. Soldiers accepted as a matter of principle the crown's overriding authority, but they did so under conditions which allowed for an easy defence of their personal and professional interests.

This was Le Tellier's problem. He had to penetrate this intractable complex of military interests, and master it. The pacification of 1659 gave him his opportunity to enforce stricter royal and bureaucratic supervision over a smaller army. Nearly all the 'free' companies were disbanded, and Le Tellier quartered the king's regiments in the towns. It was an important step towards clipping the town governors of their independent commands. At the same time the crown, acting through Turenne who held the post of captain-general of the cavalry and in spite of the duke of Épernon, who was captain-general of the infantry, played a bigger part in the commissioning of regimental officers. After Épernon's death in July 1661 – shortly before the arrest of Fouquet – Louis announced a decision to take over his functions, which meant that the lieutenant-colonel of every infantry regiment was in future nominated by the crown. These lieutenant-colonels were normally effective commanders of their regiment; the colonel was an absentee proprietor. Le Tellier could not hope to get rid of the financial bargaining which determined appointments to the old commissioned ranks (like the captain's), and which set a market value on each. But he restricted venality in new ranks, like the lieutenant-colonel's or the major's. Gradually, the hierarchy in many regiments was altered sufficiently to give the king that working control over their organisation and discipline which he needed. For the same reason, Le Tellier tried to make sure that his commissaries supervised the whole business of paying the troops. In peacetime, and under Colbert, the treasurers-of-war received (and therefore advanced) funds with greater regularity. It was for Le Tellier's commissaries to see that the captains paid each man his due, and that deductions from pay by the company or regiment for purchases of clothing or medical supplies did not exceed what had been permitted by the secretary for war's carefully drafted regulations. Later, the bureaucracy itself made the deductions and handled the commissariat. In 1664 François Berthelot the financier secured his first contract to produce munitions on a national scale. The appointment of Colonel Martinet as inspector-general of infantry, in 1667, ushered in an age of increasingly standard drills, calibres and uniforms in some sections of Louis's armed force.

Le Tellier, no less than Colbert, was a great master of administrative detail. His work poses one broader issue. He helped to create a fixed military interest of a new kind in society, subordinate to the government, supervised at many points by civilian officials, but as harnessed to the profession of arms as the fief-holders or *condottieri* of earlier periods. Between 1659 and 1661 the government disbanded many regiments, and reduced the size and number of companies in many of the regiments which it kept; but a formidable army (estimates vary between 30,000 and 50,000 men and officers for 1661 and reach 90,000 for 1666), much the biggest in western Europe, remained as a permanent standing force costing between 15 and 20 million *livres* a year. Fouquet and Colbert and Louis XIV, alone among European statesmen, could raise such a sum at this period in peacetime. Almost more important, it was the nucleus of a much larger armament, because Le Tellier attached to the standing regiments many 'reformed' officers who had lost their companies or troops. These men lived on half-pay or less. Inevitably, they waited for the next war which would give them a chance of better pickings. Whenever the government authorised the raising of new regiments or added extra companies to old ones, new commissions for captains or lieutenants cost less to acquire than those to which a purchase price had already been attached. Whenever Louis XIV went to war in the following thirty years, the prospects of at least a livelihood in the army were momentarily improved. Meanwhile, the king's household troops were constantly expanded. They became the élite, open to men of wealth as well as of birth, overshadowing the provincial and proprietary regiments. For their members, the fortunes of war were a lottery which created vacancies and stepped up the prospects of promotion. The new hierarchy of ranks, insisted on by Le Tellier and Louvois, partially modified the precedence of social rank within the army. Rich and poor gentry alike shared in this powerful vested interest. France, as every contemporary observer noted, was a populous and military nation with a warrior nobility. Louis XIV may have admitted in his old age that he had loved war too much, but this very bias made him a ruler who took care of a professional army. He catered for it as well as for his own glory. The unprivileged tax-payers maintained it. The result was a partnership between the monarchy and certain segments of the social order in a long sequence of wars, which helped to give the ancien régime its resilience and toughness.

On balance, in France there had been a compromise between instincts for reform, and inertia. The king theoretically claimed dominion over the property and persons of all his subjects, while in practice his ministers wanted greater power for themselves under the king in order to govern more efficiently. The result was certainly stricter discipline – shown, for example, in the improved policing, cleaning and lighting of Paris after the first appointment of a *lieutenant de police* for the city in 1668, and by the new General Hospital of Paris, which from 1657 combined a number of old charities into one large organisation. Its function was to assist the helpless as competently as possible, and to intern able-bodied beggars and compel them to work. When the government extended these arrangements to other towns, the era of the workhouse really began in France. A permanent bureaucracy of a new type held the land in a firmer grip. At the same time, one failure was conspicuous: Colbert's attempt to reform and clarify the administration of justice. His Civil and Criminal Codes (1667–9, 1670) look impressive enough on paper, but they show how slight were the changes in procedure which he secured, while in spite of his efforts he could not draft them without taking expert advice from the conservative lawyers of Parlements whom he so despised.[8] But resistance to change in a conservative society owed a good deal to the ministers themselves. Under Louis XIV the king governed for thirty years by sharing out most of the responsibility between two great ministerial dynasties, the Le Telliers and Colberts. In their itch for wealth and preferment in church and state, in their desire to hand all this intact to the next generation of Le Telliers and Colberts, they defended the prejudices which in other contexts they opposed. Colbert, for one, died little less wealthy than Fouquet had been. His son Seignelay, like Le Tellier's son Louvois, inherited political power. Other sons or brothers of theirs, when very young men, became archbishops. Louis's ministers, by the standards of the age, governed well; but while they strengthened the state, their desire to transform it was at best partial.

8   Colbert's uncle, Colbert de Pussort, one of the most remarkable members of the family, had planned far more sweeping changes in this field.

8

The European Mind, 1640–70

The Issue of Jansenism

A similar conservatism was reflected in the world of learning, although some important shifts of emphasis occurred. For example, more teachers in western Europe were attracted by what they called 'positive' theology. Amid ceaseless controversy which encouraged it, this came to mean a study of the faith and practice of churchmen right through the centuries. A closer look at the past enabled Catholics to expose the inconsistency of Protestantism – the differences between what Luther taught shortly after 1517, and what the Lutherans now affirmed as unalterable truth. The Protestants found equally glaring contradictions between the practice of the early, medieval, and modern church of Rome. There were wrangles with this sort of bias long before 1650, but the appeal to history now became commonplace, a habit of mind working on the assumption that proofs of consistency in doctrine or government sounded the necessary note of revealed truth. Two of the century's most influential Catholic works summarise a whole argument by their titles: *The Permanence of the Church's Faith Concerning Communion* (1669–74) by Nicole, and *History of the Variations of the Protestant Churches* (1688) by Bossuet. Fortunately, there were great enterprises in historical scholarship of a less polemic kind. One, associated with the name of Jean Bolland and the Jesuit house at Antwerp, got under way with the publication of a first volume of their *Acta Sanctorum* in 1643. From that day to this the Bollandists have been editing documents bearing on the lives of Catholic saints. At almost the same moment French Benedictines organised a régime of research in the monastery of St Germain-des-Près – while this fashionable suburb of Louis XIV's capital grew rapidly round them – which produced work of very high quality during the next seventy years. The regular assembly of learned men at St Germain, no less than the new Observatory a mile away or the theatre of Racine, represents the civilisation of Paris in this period. It was a world deeply interested in antiquities – classical, Jewish and Christian – setting them all in the framework of a Creation less than 6000 years old.

That alliance between Nicole the Jansenist, and Bossuet, was significant for another reason. It appeared to show that the great quarrel between Jansenists and their Catholic critics had been settled, so that together they could swing into action against Protestant error. The impermanence of this truce in fact proved how profound were the issues in dispute before the 'peace of the church' in 1668.

The original Jansenist controversy was a debate about Christian doctrine. Attempts have been made to link it with the cleavage of interest in France between the servants of an autocratic monarchy and the older class of office-holders, who were being edged out of power by Richelieu and Mazarin. Jansenism, the argument runs, was a pessimistic creed of withdrawal from the world, attractive to men failing to maintain themselves. But too many individual examples show the contrary, that this creed began by persuading them to stand aside from secular affairs although power or profit were theirs for the asking.

It stemmed originally from the clergy in universities and other ecclesiastical foundations. Louvain in the Spanish Netherlands, sensitive to the challenge of Dutch Protestantism in its various forms, was no less important as a theological centre than Paris. Jansen, born in Utrecht, a Louvain professor and then bishop of Ypres, was one of a long line of post-Reformation Catholic scholars in that university who defended the rigid interpretation of St Augustine's teaching on salvation. They opposed others who argued in sympathy with the whole Tridentine reaction against Luther and Calvin, and who asserted that the Christian could earn salvation through his own efforts: his will, if directed aright, helped positively to procure the gift of God's grace. The more humanist approach meant assuming that the truths of the church were of a kind which ordinary people could accept without too harsh a suppression of ordinary instincts. It meant permitting the grant of absolution on easier terms than the stricter doctors allowed and, as a practical consequence, encouraging men to take the sacrament of communion frequently. Such views, particularly favoured by Jesuit teachers, harmonised with the needs of those who shouldered the main burden of Catholic missionary work in Europe and overseas.

In all these matters, a part of St Augustine's teaching could be interpreted to tend in the opposite direction. Augustine argued against any belittlement of God's power, and against any trust in the powers of man's conscious will. Adam, falling from his original state of felicity and grace, transmitted to every one of his descendants the radical vice of cupidity, the ineradicable love of self. Man could not help himself, unless God first worked through him with His own will, with that overriding power which the Augustinians writing in French were to define in their favourite formula: 'Grace efficace par elle-même.' For them, the rival notion of a grace which simply co-operated with the human will was an illusion powerless to transform the essential degradation of man and his environment. They were as absorbed by a concept of the Fall of Man as their contemporaries, John Milton in England (for whom Augustine was 'the most highly considered, oftenest quoted of the Fathers'), or the great Dutchman, the Catholic poet Vondel, whose *Lucifer* (1653) preceded *Paradise Lost* (1667).

Throughout Christian history the Roman church tried to hold the balance between these standpoints. Constantly it intervened in the disputes, inclining sometimes to one side, sometimes to the other. Both recognised the need for an ultimate judge, and Jansen explicitly accepted the pope's jurisdiction, unlike the Protestant disciples of Augustine. So did his contemporaries in France who shared most of his theological views, above all Cardinal Bérulle and Jean de Haur-anne, abbot of Saint-Cyran. Jansen himself died in 1638 and his great work, the *Augustinus*, was published immediately afterwards. Critics and champions went into action, and Urban VIII's bull *In Eminenti* responded by condemning both the book and the rival theses of the Louvain Jesuits.

Not far below the brilliant surface of Catholic revival in the Spanish Netherlands and France other discords gave trouble. The Jesuits and many new religious orders had gone to work in places where the secular clergy were slack or ineffective. Obedient to their superiors in Rome and elsewhere, they did not always recognise episcopal authority. They often antagonised it. Other reformers then began to stimulate bishops and parish priests to a zeal which matched that of Jesuits or Capucins or Cordeliers. Led by the tower-ing figure of Bérulle who founded the oratories of secular priests, by Saint-Cyran and by St Vincent de Paul, these men emphasised the sacred responsibilities and rights of bishops in the constitution of the church. The secular clergy accused some of the more militant orders and societies (and their lay friends) of trying to monopolise the congregations, goodwill and largesse of the faithful. Friction between them seemed incessant. It was an item on the agenda of every quinquennial assembly of the Gallican church, summoned by Louis XIII to give him financial aid. It caused local agitation in the Spanish Netherlands as in France. It meant that the ground was well prepared for the growth of clerical faction in many areas. The bishops had in any case good reason to try to protect what remained of their authority against the encroaching jurisdiction of pope and king.

Even if they had themselves been educated in Jesuit schools, they did not tend to look kindly on a privileged society which accepted without demur the infallibility of one and the sovereign rights of the other.

Bérulle and Saint-Cyran, defenders of the secular clergy, had been no less Augustinian in outlook than Jansen. Unlike him, they were also great spiritual directors, impressing the men and women who approached them with the fearful challenge of a religious life, which in their view must first operate by reducing the sinner to total humility of spirit. Saint-Cyran, partly through his friendship with the important *parlementaire* family of the Arnaulds, founded a new school of piety. He was the adviser of a reformed Cistercian nunnery, Port-Royal – which had been supported for many years by the Arnaulds – a body of nuns who moved from their old home outside Paris to the Faubourg St Jacques in 1628. One Arnauld paid for the new quarters. Another, Angélique, was the abbess. Others again were nuns. In due course more members of the same family formed the nucleus of that loose grouping known as the 'Messieurs' of Port-Royal. The Messieurs lived a secluded but intense religious life, residing in the grounds of the nunnery, either in the Faubourg St Jacques or at the deserted Port-Royal des Champs. The greatest of them was indisputably Antoine Arnauld, who linked the fortunes of this inconspicuous foundation with those of the whole Augustinian movement, and spent practically his entire career querying authority in church and state. In some respects he was the most influential Frenchman to oppose Louis XIV.

The issues raised by the Augustinians in France were complicated by the almost total failure of king and pope to act together. The friction between two such overlapping authorities was incessant. The Catholic League of sixteenth-century warfare, the return of the Jesuits to France, the active papal nuncios in Paris, had stimulated a contrary Gallican bias in many royal officials and Parlements. Richelieu held that Urban VIII's diplomacy favoured the Habsburgs unfairly, while Mazarin generated a personal animus against Urban's successors which cannot be explained entirely by political interest. Louis XIV inherited all these views and did not modify them until after 1688. It proved impossible to settle doctrinal disputes in France without invoking papal authority. It proved equally impossible for the pope to use his authority without trespassing on rights claimed by the king, the Parlements or even the bishops. Opponents of the French Augustinians were hampered by this feud throughout the century, but the case of the archbishopric of Paris typifies the whole difficulty in the 1650s. Mazarin had his inveterate opponent, de Retz, arrested in December 1652; but de Retz escaped. He was now a cardinal and, as coadjutor (see above, p. 61), had a firm legal claim to succeed the old archbishop, who died in 1654. Neither Rome nor the bishops were prepared to collaborate with the French government in deposing de Retz: the laws and liberties of the church would be threatened by such a measure. In consequence, until he himself agreed to relinquish the see in 1662, the orderly settlement of ecclesiastical problems in Paris was out of the question. It became so much the harder to enforce discipline, and to silence critics.

Although Saint-Cyran (who died in detention at Vincennes in 1641) disliked points of detail in Jansen's *Augustinus*, his followers in France came out strongly in defence of it. Battle was joined with the Jesuits. In 1643 Antoine Arnauld published his book on Frequent Communion, which does not argue against the practice of taking communion frequently but insists that the doctrinal wrong-headedness of the Jesuits and their friends led to a frivolous neglect of the Christian's duty to do penance, and to feel penitent, for his sins. It could be said, he found, that ladies of fashion went too quickly from the ball to the confessional, and from the confessional back to the ballroom. He stood for a rigorous theology in academic circles, and for a strict and special type of theology in the lay world. Writing in French, he appealed to a wider public than did the great Latin tome of the *Augustinus*, but both works became manifestoes for a movement which commanded growing sympathy and aroused growing hostility. A number of churchmen felt convinced that the 'friends of St Augustine' could be more accurately described as 'the sect of Jansenius', which resembled the followers of Calvin too closely and endangered orthodoxy. They did everything in their power to get Jansenist teaching condemned. In July 1649, after the close of the first Fronde, the syndic of the Sorbonne put before that notable body of theologians certain propositions – taken, as he said, from students' theses, but everyone appreciated their resemblance to the argument of Jansen – which were duly censured. The next round of civil commotion made it difficult to go further at the time, and the friends of St Augustine still gathered support. They took their cue from the Messieurs, above all from Antoine Arnauld, grouped round the foundation of Port-Royal.

This constituted a formidable interest. There were not only the nuns and the Messieurs, there were aristocratic patrons like the duke of Liancourt and Mme de Sablé, to be joined in due course by the duchess of Longueville and other disappointed *frondeurs* who turned to piety. Funds were plentiful. They financed the construction of new buildings for the monastery in the Faubourg St Jacques, where some of the patrons put up apartments for themselves, adjoining the nuns' quarters. They contributed to the organisation of charity by Maignart de Bernières (see above, p. 73), himself a Jansenist. Certain of the Messieurs set up as teachers, writing new text-books for a small number of pupils who came mostly from educated and wealthy homes. But to teach, in a seventeenth-century Catholic country, was to provoke automatically the Jesuits who ran the greatest schools and colleges.

Debate continued in the universities of Paris and Louvain, at assemblies of the Gallican church in 1650, 1655 and 1660, and in Rome, in order to get Jansenist ideas condemned or recognised. In 1653 Innocent X declared five propositions on Grace and Free Will heretical. Arnauld accepted that they were heretical because the pope condemned them, though claiming that they could not be found in Jansen's work. The Gallican assembly, and then Alexander VII, ruled that the condemned views were indeed Jansen's, but Cardinal Mazarin preferred to move very cautiously in the matter for another five years. In the last few months of his life he decided to enforce the official judgment, and in 1661 Louis ordered the bishops to see that all churchmen subscribed a Formulary repudiating both Jansen and the propositions, a step which bears comparison with the Act of Uniformity of the same year in England. In 1665 he repeated his summons, to which was added a threat to expel defaulters from their livings or foundations. The Formulary became a criterion, not only of orthodoxy but also of obedience to royal authority. Originally devised to restore order, it became a fearful irritant in French intellectual life.

Who in fact had authority? Papal bulls and nuncios provoked many sharp responses from the Paris Parlement, which held firmly that Rome must not encroach on the king's power in ecclesiastical affairs. A majority in the Gallican assemblies tried to co-operate with both pope and king, but individual bishops sympathised with the Jansenists and felt that their own responsibility ought not to be surrendered to Rome, Paris or to assemblies of this kind. The archbishop of Sens had published Innocent X's bull, for example, at the same time adding a pastoral instruction to his clergy which practically contradicted it. In 1664 four resolute bishops – of Alet, Pamiers, Angers (who was another member of the Arnauld family) and Beauvais – refused to publish the Formulary without qualifying it severely, and Louis failed to overawe them. Rome and Paris at last gave way when the four bishops began to attract increasing support from their brethren.

During the dispute one catchword, the distinction between Law and Fact, occurred continually. It sounds technical, but nothing else charged men's minds with such passionate excitement for at least a decade; old libraries are still laden with the weight of books on this controversy. Above all, it provoked the eighteen famous 'Letters written to a gentleman in the country from one of his friends'. Pascal was the literary genius who wrote the *Provincial Letters* when the

Sorbonne prepared to condemn Antoine Arnauld for believing that Jansen was not guilty of heresy, but a committee of the Messieurs supplied him with nearly all his arguments. Pascal's conversion was one of the sombre triumphs of the Port-Royal school of thought in its battle against humanism. In return, he gave the reading public a superb example of how to use what Gibbon in accurately described (in referring to these Letters) as 'the weapon of grave and temperate irony even in matters of ecclesiastical solemnity'. The debate, and Pascal's ferocious irony, were the more important for their influence on the predecessors of Voltaire and Gibbon.

Innocent X, in condemning propositions connected with the theme of Jansen's *Augustinus*, made it clear that the church accepted St Augustine's teaching. The Jansenists accordingly took refuge behind the distinction between law and fact. They claimed that the propositions could not be found *verbatim* or in substance in *Augustinus*. Jesuit writers, and many others, said that they were substantially there, and that this 'fact' could not be separated from the question of 'law' or doctrine. But for the Jansenists, the presence of the propositions in Jansen's writing was at the very least disputable, a matter of opinion. Even if they were related to some arguments in an immense folio of 1,000 pages, it was unreasonable to compel men to believe – as an article of faith – that the dead scholar would have interpreted them erroneously or heretically. After all, he was expounding St Augustine, that impeccable father of the church.

The protagonists were posing the fundamental problem of authority. The disciples of Port-Royal and Jansen, said their opponents, refused to obey the voice of the church and the orders of the king. Such defiance perverted the essential principle of orthodoxy; the whole notion of heresy disappeared if this disappeared. Calvin and Luther were blameless with Jansen. The church, retorted Arnauld and Pascal, had never in the past claimed and could not now claim an infallible voice in *all* matters. If it did, the consequences would be 'frightful', overturning 'the rule of tradition and consent in the church', and rendering all definitions of faith uncertain. This sounds extreme, and sounded to many an elaborate piece of self-deception, but it is arguable that the great achievement of 'the friends of St Augustine' in the seventeenth century was to safeguard a right of independent judgment within the Catholic church at a time when its intellectual vigour seems to have been decaying fast in many countries. The claim to infallibility had been carried to excessive lengths when the Formulary was imposed. In 1668 the king and the pope drew back. They allowed that 'respectful silence' on this trouble some fact of Jansen's heresy was sufficient, provided that the faithful undertook to condemn the erroneous propositions. Such was the gist of the truce for which Pope Clement IX can largely take the credit. It enabled the persecuted Messieurs such as Arnauld and Nicole (who had toned down the views of Arnauld) to come out of hiding. It made life gentler for those nuns of Port-Royal who refused to accept the Formulary. It allowed Catholic France to breathe again.

The *Provincial Letters*, having begun with a discussion of law and fact, had proceeded to a blistering attack on the abuses of Jesuit casuistry – 'and I am sure that you will detect easily enough in the relaxation of their moral standards the origin of their own doctrine on Grace'. Or, as Arnauld exclaimed: 'Leave Jansen out of it and listen to St Augustine, whom you cannot dare to treat as a heretic!'. These phrases come close to the heart of their thinking, and help to explain why the movement became so formidable. Augustine's notion of an irresistible grace which transformed man's otherwise powerless will, once taught by teachers themselves inspired by it, inspired the godly. They were convinced that rival teachers neglected Augustine; or, worse, perverted his thought with pernicious consequences for mankind. This was Arnauld's view when he wrote on frequent communion in 1643. It was his view, and Pascal's, in 1655. Nicole drove the same thought home in many elaborate studies later, on the moral doctrine of the Jesuits. The standpoint was deeply attractive. At one level, the secular priests of such cities as Paris and Rouen needed little convincing that Jesuits, Cordeliers and the like infiltrated into their parishes by offering piety on easy terms to the public. At another, good men hungered for the sense of righteousness. This the school of Saint-Cyran and Port-Royal promised them. Certainly, many French clergy sympathised with the aims of the Augustinian movement, and had subscribed to the Formulary with a mental reservation that Jansen's exposition remained valid. After 1668 they came out into the open. Port-Royal theology filtered into the newly founded seminaries for secular priests and into schools run by reformed religious orders. In the Benedictine 'Congregation of St Vannes' in Lorraine, for example, it has been shown that the teachers were deeply tinged with Jansenist influence, reaching this area by way of Louvain rather than Paris. When Innocent XI (1676–89) ultimately condemned a very large number of propositions taken from the work of the casuists, he conceded victory on at least one fundamental point to the men who had defied authority.

Muscovy: The Greeks and Old Believers

The early history of Jansenism in western Europe coincides strikingly with an acute crisis in the Orthodox church of Muscovy. Innovations here gave impetus to a similar significant movement of protest which survived as long as the Romanov dynasty.

In the sixteenth century two notions had captivated scholarly opinion in the Russian lands: one was that St Andrew long ago brought Christ's teaching directly to Muscovy, without any mediation by Greek missionaries; and the other that, after the Catholics' perversion of the Roman church of St Peter and Islam's seizure of Constantinople, Moscow itself was the single remaining citadel of Orthodoxy, indeed the 'Third Rome'. These views then faded and by the middle of the seventeenth century it was more commonly assumed that Muscovy was part of the universal Orthodox Church, presided over by the patriarchs of Constantinople/Istanbul, Antioch, Jerusalem, Alexandria and (since 1593) Moscow. The Slavonic liturgy and other texts of the Russian church either did not or ought not to differ significantly from those of the Greek church. It was realised that there might be differences, and between 1620 and 1650 a number of scholars set out to study the Orthodox texts and use the single Moscow printing press, in order to revise and then publish authentic copies for the use of clergy and teachers in Muscovy. After 1645 they were patronised by the young Tsar Alexei himself and his influential confessor. Teachers from Kiev and other Orthodox lands came to assist the native scholars and editors. The patriarchs of Jerusalem and Antioch, and a former patriarch of Istanbul, were welcome visitors in Moscow. Each of them spent some time there between 1649 and 1656, pleased to show precisely where Slavonic liturgy and worship deviated from what they thought were the proper formularies. New versions of the principal service-books were issued between 1650 and 1656. The most important intellectual development in eastern Europe, in the mid-seventeenth century was this attempt to alter, in certain respects, the understanding of Orthodoxy in Russia. It took place in the palace, cathedrals and monasteries of the Kremlin and a number of the larger monasteries elsewhere.

Another impulse attracted more popular attention. It concerned clergy and laity in the hundreds of churches and monasteries scattered across Muscovy. Among them moved a few reformers, men who passionately wanted a more devout manner in the conduct of church services, and in the behaviour of all those who came to worship. The familiar, ever sacred texts were to be recited at full length, not hurried through (as was common) by the device of several clergy chanting together different parts of the service. Sermons should be preached. Icons deserved veneration with the appropriate gestures. Noisy crowds of traders, drunkards and popular musicians, were to be kept at a decent distance from the churches. They were ascetic, puritan, conservative reformers and their attitude towards the patriarch and tsar who authorised change of any kind would be complex.

The extraordinary personality of Nikon, dominating the scene for a number of years, did much to determine what happened. A greatly gifted, forceful man who had been both a secular priest and a monk, who impressed Tsar Alexei deeply, he was appointed Archimandrite of the Novospassky monastery close to the Kremlin in 1646, Metropolitan of Novgorod in 1649, and in 1652 Patriarch of Moscow. His views have been the subject of the fiercest debate, but it seems clear that what he wanted above all was to assert the authority of his high office. The Patriarch Filarete (1623–36), father of the first Romanov Tsar, had already expanded its jurisdiction and increased its revenues. He used the title of 'Great Lord', just as the Tsar did. Once appointed, Nikon also considered himself in the light of a co-sovereign, whom Alexei naturally left in complete charge of state business in Moscow while he was himself absent for long periods, campaigning against the Poles and Swedes. Nikon also lost no opportunity of asserting the independence of the clergy against secular tribunals and tax-offices. He believed as fully in the forged 'Donation of Constantine' as any mediaeval pope. These ideas were his prime concern, and in principle they were defended by Patriarchs of Moscow to the end of the century, by Joachim (1674–90) and Adrian (1690–1700). In practice, this period witnessed the slow but steady decline of patriarchal influence, because neither Alexei nor his boyars nor his son Peter would acknowledge this extended clerical authority. The rulers drew away from and dominated the church.

Enjoying the fullness of power as Patriarch, Nikon believed that he could carry through every justifiable reform. He also believed that the Church of Muscovy should first examine, and then adopt, the criteria of Greek scholars and churchmen. At the beginning of Lent 1653 he began to enforce ceremonial changes in the Moscow churches. In each of the years 1654, 1655 and 1656 he summoned councils which authorised further changes. From the press flowed copies of the freshly edited version of the service-books. Gradually news of all this spread. Clergy and their following who wanted a revival of traditional piety became alarmed. They protested and resisted. The thought of new or alien usage seemed an assertion of evil, to be connected with the epidemic of the plague which in 1654 carried off thousands in Moscow and elsewhere. For many, this coincidence was simply cause and effect.

The immediate opposition was soon crushed. The most prominent of the conservative reformers, Ivan Neronov, came to terms with Nikon in 1657 and the greatest of them, Avvakum, had by then been sent to Siberia. But the patriarch showed himself so brutal and hasty that he stimulated a fanatical zeal in many who were unwilling to conform. A sense of disaffection began to seep into the population of scattered areas. Then, at a critical moment, his own difference with the tsar over the extent of patriarchal authority weakened the force of the whole administration. Alexei, as he grew older, became increasingly less willing to put up with an ecclesiastic who claimed to be another sovereign in his own right. In 1658 Nikon tried to overawe the tsar by a spectacular resignation of his office, and was taken at his word. The controversy dragged on until 1666, when a number of prominent Greek clergy who had been invited to Moscow collaborated with a council of Russian churchmen summoned by the tsar; they all agreed to the formal deposition of this turbulent priest. Although there had never been any real question, in official circles, of reversing the reforming policy in the church which Nikon himself had sponsored, such a long period of uncertainty made it far more difficult for the bishops and their assistants to deal with the conservatives. The council in 1665, before it deposed Nikon, solemnly anathematised those who refused to accept the new services. It was too late: the schismatics, or *raskolniki*, who preferred to call themselves Old Believers, had come to stay – until the twentieth century.

The points of difference between the Old Believers and the official church may seem to us trivial – whether to make the sign of the cross with two or three fingers, to sing the Hallelujah two or three times, to honour the 8-ended or the 4-ended cross, and to wear the beard or to shave it off – but the sense of antagonism was profound. It flowed from a fundamental refusal by individuals to recognise an authority which demanded of them an impossible surrender, the single path to salvation which the old practice of Holy Church provided. Salvation was a matter of eternal import. The primitive level of life on earth and the utter uncertainty of it, with death interposing for everyone at every turn of the road, made this easy for pious men to see. Moreover a very little contemporary learning took the argument a stage further. Rome had defaulted long ago. Constantinople was in the hands of the sultan. The tsar stood out as the one remaining Christian ruler, the Russian church as the one true church left. To alter Christian practice at this critical point of time was to hand over the world completely to Satan himself. For was it not written in the Book of Revelation: 'Here is wisdom. Let him that hath understanding count the number of the beast; for it is the number of a man; and his number is six hundred three-score and six'? Antichrist would reign from the year 1666, and at least from 1654 the enemies of Nikon were busy counting any signs which foretold the approach of this dreadful era. The *raskolniki* sometimes held that the tsar himself was Antichrist concealed: disguised, his reign had already begun. The most desperate among them drew the conclusion that only one course remained open to the Christian, 'to burn for Christ and the tradition of the Holy Fathers, in order to live eternally'. They immolated themselves by fire.

There were some extremist groups in Muscovy before prominent figures like Avvakum went into opposition, usually in remote hermitages and settlements. These swelled the resistance, made it all the more fanatical and encouraged the inevitable tendency to split into smaller sects. At the same time the government increasingly overshadowed the patriarch and bishops in the work of enforcing uniformity. The council of 1667 left the sentencing of heretics and schismatics to the tsar's tribunals, and fifteen years later his officers were ordered to track down all offenders of this type. That decision inaugurated the darkest phase of a pitiless persecution. Avvakum, for one, was burnt on Good Friday 1682. He had been sent in 1667 to a second exile, at Pusstozersk in northern Russia, and wrote there his extraordinary *Autobiography* and other works which were deviously carried by disciples across the country to stiffen the whole movement of resistance. The tradition of Old Believers gives as his last words before death: 'If ever you desert your castle it will perish, buried under the sand, and its end will be the end of the world.'

This was a revolution of religious despair, for which the nearest parallel at the time seems to have been the sporadic risings of extreme Calvinists in Scotland. It won most support in regions between the upper Volga and the Arctic, where there were fewer landlords and fewer serfs than farther south. The core of resistance to government was the ancient monastic stronghold of Solovetsky, on its island site in the White Sea; the monks held out from 1666 until January 1676. There were undoubtedly important groups of *raskolniki* in the town of Nijni Novgorod, and in the Don region, where official persecution was uncommonly severe in the years 1670–2. Even then, this type of opposition to government never merged with the far more general Cossack and peasant upheaval, which at the same moment spread east and north from the Don to the Volga. It only once joined hands with other malcontents, the occasion when Tsar Theodore's death in 1682 led to a rebellion of the guards in Moscow. The succession was hotly disputed, and some of the guards sympathised with the Old Believers who were facing the persecution which had led to Avvakum's martyrdom a few days earlier. One of their commanding officers, Khovansky, belonged to a small surviving circle of Old Believers in upper-class Moscow society. The soldiery ran riot. Khovansky tried to use them to press the Old Believer cause but a new government soon emerged and persecution continued under the guidance of that implacable policeman, patriarch Joachim of Moscow. The Russian Orthodox church had been reformed, it remained strongly entrenched, but its vitality was sapped during the boyhood of Peter the Great.

The New Sciences: Descartes

Such disputes, in eastern or western Europe, turned on ancient authority. Men quarrelled over St Augustine's teaching or the old Greek and old Muscovite texts and ceremonies. But during the generation after 1640 a small but growing number of people in the west became convinced that in certain fields the old standpoint was simply mistaken. It was judged inferior to their own intellectual achievement.

The most spectacular discussion implying this turned on a famous experiment by Torricelli, Galileo's successor in the post of 'philosopher' maintained by the grand duke of Tuscany. In Florence, in 1644, Torricelli produced mysteriously a vacant space at the upper end of a glass tube above a column of mercury after he had first completely filled the tube with mercury, and then set it up with the lower end – unstoppered – in a basin of mercury. Something similar was demonstrated a few years earlier to a group of churchmen in Rome and on both occasions there were individuals present who accepted the possibility of a vacuum in the tube – against the majority view on this question – and a further possibility that the surrounding atmosphere had weight which exerted pressure on the mercury in the basin – although scientists and philosophers commonly taught that air was weightless. Father Mersenne who had for many years organised a network of correspondence on scientific problems between scholars in France, Italy, England, Germany and Holland, saw Torricelli repeat his experiment in 1645. Returning to Paris, he tried but failed to carry it out for himself. Glass-works at Rouen came closer to Italian standards, and it was in Rouen that the Pascals, father and son and the circle round them, began to study the fascinating problems posed by Torricelli's experiment. Another Italian had produced the same phenomenon by a demonstration in Warsaw; but his printed accounts seem to have caused a greater stir outside Poland. In 1648 a group of men in London were excited by the hints given in letters from Mersenne, and performed the same experiment. The French were the most excited, and the man who combined a genius for rigorous thinking on the subject with a flair in giving it the maximum publicity was young Blaise Pascal. Between 1646 and 1648 he multiplied experiments which showed that, practically speaking, these 'Torricellian' tubes were empty at the top while the height of the mercury depended both on the weight and pressure of the atmosphere. The controversies continued at a time when political conditions deteriorated rapidly. In the stormy interval between Broussel's arrest and the siege of Paris by Condé and Mazarin, Pascal's brother-in-law Florian Perier made a famous ascent in

September 1648 of the Puy de Dôme, 3500 feet above the town of Clermont. He wished to compare the height of the mercury in a tube which he took up the mountain, with the height of mercury in a tube left under observation in the town during the same day. The result fully demonstrated to Pascal the agency of atmospheric pressure, and before the end of the year he printed Perier's precise record of what had been observed at Clermont. Within the next two years he completed his work (first published in 1663) on 'the equilibrium of fluids' and 'the weight of the mass of the air' which are the basis of modern hydrostatics and aerostatics. During the Fronde, from 1649 until March 1651 Perier at Clermont tried to keep detailed records of variations in the rise and fall of mercury in his tubes, and to persuade friends in Paris and Stockholm – of whom one was Descartes – to do likewise. Shortly afterwards, the duke of Tuscany sponsored a scheme of the same kind in order to compare the variations of air pressure in Florence and other Italian cities. In 1653 an English doctor copied the Puy de Dôme experiment by measurements taken at the town of Halifax in Yorkshire and on the top of Beacon Hill outside it. After the Royal Society was founded in 1660, experiments with the barometer – a name for the instrument had just come into use – continued until about 1664. By then this new concept of the atmosphere had become familiar and unexciting.

In editing Pascal's work for publication, Florian Perier pointed out that for a number of years the scientists in France knew of no method for creating a vacuum except by the experiment with mercury. Before 1648 Otto Guericke of Magdeburg was already using a pump in order to expel the air from wooden barrels and copper vessels. When the Imperial Diet met at Regensburg in 1654 he demonstrated publicly the extraordinary pressures which appeared to surround an evacuated copper sphere: teams of horses, pulling in opposite directions, failed to pull apart the two halves of Guericke's metal spheres. A book referring to Guericke's work, by a Jesuit professor at Würzburg, came to the attention of Robert Boyle at Oxford: he and Robert Hooke took the hint, greatly improved the mechanism of their pump, greatly enlarged the size of the vacuum with which they could experiment and by 1660 had published results. They would soon tabulate the inverse proportions of pressures and expansions, distinguish between the air's compressibility and elasticity. 'Boyle's Law' was announced in 1662. The air-pump took its place with the barometer in every laboratory.

Another device of these years altered the concept of time. Clocks were familiar enough in all the towns of Europe, faulty but indispensable, and shortly before he died Galileo had been using the equal swings of a pendulum to measure duration. Christian Huygens at the Hague, from his youth the friend of Descartes and Mersenne, began to wrestle with the notion of attaching a pendulum to clockwork – and hit on a solution in the last week of December 1656. Next year the first true pendulum clock was made at the Hague. Two months after Cromwell's death in 1658 an advertisement appeared in London for new clocks 'that go exact and keep equaller time'. Not very long afterwards a better type of escapement than Huygen's first device made this offer a promise. A craftsman like Thomas Tompion the clockmaker of London would in due course combine the quality of beautiful decorative work with mechanical precision in a new way. It is almost fair to say that the minute, and then the second, were discoveries of the two decades after 1650.

A more accurate measure of time was accompanied by a more accurate measurement of space, which revealed at one extreme the giant dimensions of the universe, and at the other things which on first acquaintance seemed infinitely small. Here again Huygens ranks among the pioneers. Combining a better theoretical understanding of the problems of focal length and spherical aberration, with strict attention to the practical business of grinding the lenses he required, he had produced a more effective telescope by 1655. Within ten years other essential refinements were added to this instrument of research. They included a micrometer which measured distance and diameters as these appeared at the focus of the object glass, and sextants or protractors which measured the angle at which a telescope was trained on particular objects – at moments of time recorded by the new pendulum clock. The findings could be compared with others made by a similar combination of instruments in other parts of the world. To put the change in broad terms, in 1650 a few wise men had a fair notion of the structure of the solar system, while in 1675 they had reasonably accurate measurements of its enormous size. As for the microscope, Robert Hooke gave wide publicity – in the copperplate engravings of his famous *Micrographia* in 1665 – to what could be achieved by combining a number of glasses in a 'compound' instrument. More often, in the immediate future, the extraordinary revelation of phenomena too small to be studied by the eye unaided depended on a simple combination of one lens, with a small aperture, and an adjustable holder for the specimen to be examined. To this was added a growing skill in dissection. A great debt was owed to a new generation of instrument-makers, in Leiden, London and Rome, who came rapidly to the fore. With their aid (and even without) the human body, animals, birds, fishes, insects and plants were all now more minutely inspected than ever before. Much reliable detail was accumulated. Scholars went avidly to work, while some of them could not neglect the impulse to speculate about the larger framework in which both the observer and what he observed appeared to be set.

The great reformulation of knowledge by Descartes in Holland had already been given stage by stage to the reading public: essays on optics, atmospheric phenomena and geometry, prefaced by the famous Discourse on Method, in 1637; six Meditations proving the existence of God, the immortality of the soul and the distinctness of soul and body, in 1642; the 'principles of philosophy' in 1644, which moved rapidly from metaphysics to a description of matter and motion in the physical universe, and embraced in their sweep not only the celestial bodies but also air, water, earth, fire and magnetism, constituents of the terrestrial globe. Finally, in 1649 he published a work on 'the passions of the soul'. Another enquiry, investigating the formation of the foetus, was not printed until 1663. The author claimed that he had, in a few precepts, grasped 'all the most general and important principles of human knowledge'. He never hesitated to apply them to many different branches of study.

It is very difficult to summarise fairly the immediate impact of Descartes on his age, but recent research has somewhat discredited the notion of a 'Cartesian revolution'. The intellectual vitality of the better European universities after 1600 was greater than used to be assumed, so that some of the chief academic disciplines were well accustomed to constant discussion and modification. The idea of a monolithic conservatism, entrenched in the Aristotelian 'doctrine of the schools', was dear to the malcontents and a handy bludgeon in controversy, but hardly accorded with the facts. On the other hand, the traditional element in much of Descartes's thought now seems no less obvious than its novelty. His Jesuit education, temperamental caution in the face of authority, disclaimers of any concern for politics, and zealous wooing of Catholic and Protestant churchmen before he allowed his work to be printed, likewise helped to soften or conceal the challenge of an argument which first withdrew all observed phenomena from the domain of theology, and then depicted them purely in terms of mathematical law or mechanical forces. Certain theologians were alarmed, and none more so than the Calvinist professor, Gisbert Voetius of Utrecht. Voetius waged unceasing war for many years against Cartesian theses offered for academic disputation in Dutch universities, but he used the accusation of 'Cartesian error' indiscriminatingly against any critic or rival. The Jansenist Arnauld (in the earlier part of his life), and certain leading Jesuits, approved of Descartes who in turn easily reconciled Catholic transubstantiation with his own opinions. In England, Hobbes exhibited many startling parallels with Descartes's account of the physical universe; but enemies of Hobbes rebutted his 'atheism' by borrowing from Cartesian metaphysics. At the same time, a few men went further. They revered the great Frenchman as their leader, the teacher to whom they owed a new vision of truth. Almost like Jansen, he acquired a party of devotees. Some fell away in due course, but the numbers increased after his death. Among such early Cartesians were Henry More in Christ's College, Cambridge, Spinoza as he broke away from the Jewish community in Amsterdam, and young Christian Huygens. After reading Descartes, says Huygens in so many words, everything made better sense.

The radicalism implicit in Cartesian doubt or the Cartesian doctrine of matter was also obscured by the very spread and expertise of his writing. Most of the discussion was too specialised to be of general interest. The opticians were not easily satisfied by his law of refraction. The mathematicians, led by Fermat in Toulouse and Roberval in Paris, disputed either his reasoning, or his claim to be the first with a demonstration – more and more such quarrels among scientists and mathematicians are one proof of the new intellectual climate – although without doubt Descartes's analytical geometry (and his introduction of algebraic symbols) remain for posterity among the greatest inventions of the century. The whole Cartesian doctrine of matter as 'closely packed', excluding any possibility of a vacuum, and of motion as circular, had to resist criticism from those who thought that they perceived a real vacuum in Torricelli's tubes or accepted Kepler's account of the elliptical orbit of planets. And the anatomists soon found fault with Descartes on many detailed points, above all in his account of the pineal gland, which he mistakenly believed to exist only in man – and which in his view alone linked the human body and soul.

In fact, René Descartes died in 1650, but Cartesianism really began to flourish after 1665. Before that date parts of his work in particular branches of science were under heavy attack. After it, his general intellectual approach reached a wider public. He helped to liberate the possible fields of scientific enquiry from theology, and extended them. He left revealed religion completely intact within a narrower field than before. He had also made some far-reaching suggestions which would be of interest for a long time to come. For him, matter extended indefinitely, just as material particles were infinitely divisible: therefore other worlds, and a 'plurality' of worlds, were conceivable. For him, animals were mere automata, while man alone had a soul: if other thinkers discarded the soul, they could then visualise man as another automaton, and develop new psychological theories to explain him. Finally the name of Descartes was thrown into the fashionable debate which pitted Moderns against Ancients in literature, art and science. The Moderns inevitably claimed for their party the great gladiator who had recently denied the merit of obsolete classical authors, and who advised the sensible man to put his trust in reasoned argument from sensible (and Cartesian) premises.

The 'experimental philosophy' of these years, which Descartes himself sometimes practised and sometimes appeared to reject, was normally the interest of men in close touch with the universities. The origins of the Royal Society in England have been disputed by scholars, but there is no reason to doubt the importance of a preliminary phase between 1649 and 1658 when a group of enthusiasts gathered at Oxford to perform 'inquisitive experiments' under the auspices of John Wilkins, Warden of Wadham College. Its members met frequently, drafted rules for the conduct of business, assembled apparatus, and toyed with the plan of cataloguing all books in the Bodleian Library which appeared relevant to their enquiries. The conditions for work of this kind must then have seemed more favourable in Oxford than in London, where some of the same men had been meeting to discuss scientific questions in the five years before 1649. Apart from several professors and heads of colleges, the gifted young pupil Christopher Wren and the equally gifted nobleman Robert Boyle were drawn into the circle. Boyle represents, even if he surpassed in genius, a very numerous element among the *virtuosi*: gentry or noblemen or courtiers, persons of leisure, who felt drawn to these new pastimes. Their liberality often kept the scientific gatherings going. Their influence, at least in England between 1660 and 1663, attracted the benevolent patronage of the crown. They may also have strengthened a less fortunate tendency to rest content with 'curiosities' and antiquarian lore which still figured largely in the annals of these societies for many decades to come. But what the English enthusiasts, whether academics or gentry, did appreciate was that experimental activity mercifully cut across the normal ideological divisions between Royalists, Covenanters and sectarians, just as it cut across the division between Catholic and Protestant on the Continent. Oxford became too much of an Anglican seminary again after 1660, and Oxford's loss was London's gain when Charles II conferred his charters (of 1662 and 1663) on the 'Royal Society of London for Promoting Natural Knowledge'.

The chequered history of groups and meetings which preceded the foundation of the *Académie des Sciences* in France, in 1666, has something in common with what occurred in England. Mersenne, who first brought scholars in Paris together for scientific discussion, died in 1648. No one replaced him immediately, while the Fronde made regular assemblies difficult. But two enlightened masters-of-requests advanced to the rescue. We hear of M. Le Pailleur, a good amateur mathematician – his library of 500 books was almost bare of theology but strong in both ancient and contemporary mathematical treatises – who held meetings at his house until he died in 1654. The other master-of-requests, M. de Montmor, had begun to do the same in 1653. He kept his scientific salon going for many years but lacked the thrust of Dr. John Wilkins. He was too easily satisfied by eloquent debate in matters where practical experiments were needed, although English and Dutch travellers admired what they saw and heard in his assembly. A few years later individual Frenchmen in their turn recognised that the foundation of the Royal Society, with its emphasis on regular experimental work, was a step forward worth copying. Colbert viewed the matter in terms of Louis XIV's prestige, but after some hesitation responded much more positively than any of Charles II's statesmen. He hived off a small number of mathematicians, astronomers, anatomists, with a chemist and a botanist, from the literary scholars whom the crown also patronised. He paid them, and provided facilities for an agreed programme of research. An illustrious group of French physicians soon began to publish studies 'to which the modern development of comparative anatomy may be directly traced'. The mathematicians and astronomers who had agitated so hard to win Colbert's support meanwhile persuaded him to construct an observatory. Built on the height of Montparnasse, this at first gave more pleasure to its architect than to the scientists, but under G. D. Cassini's direction quickly became an important centre of discussion. The need was also stressed for systematic checking and collection of data from different points on the globe – especially from a latitude closer to the equator than Paris. Colbert and Louis accordingly financed the first modern scientific expedition, in 1672, to Cayenne in French Guiana. Its results, combined with those of Cassini and Jean Picard from the Observatory, solved many problems – and posed others. But the use of state funds in this way, and the appointment of eminent foreigners like Huygens and Cassini as paid academicians who came to work in Paris, had no equivalent in England until Charles copied Louis to the extent of building a modest observatory at Greenwich.[1]

On the other hand the secretary of the London society, Henry Oldenburg from Bremen, began to publish its *Philosophical Transactions* in 1665. He was so successful in winning a European reputation for the Royal Society, that foreign researchers tended increasingly to send him their work for transmission to the wider world of learning. Such men as Malpighi at Bologna and Leeuwenhoeck in Delft wrote to London, not to Paris.

Soon after the new foundation founded by Colbert began its labours, the first of the new scientific academies which relied on princely patronage was dissolved. In Florence the experimentalists encouraged by the Medici family had been formally organised in

---

[1] Edmond Halley's journey to St Helena in 1677, to map the constellations of the southern hemisphere, was privately financed although a word from the king gave the young man a free passage in an East India Company ship.

1657. This *Accademia del Cimento* (the 'Experimental Society') carried out admirable work for a period of ten years, and then dispersed, so that by contrast the intellectual decay of the Tuscan court during Cosimo III's long reign (1670–1723) was all the more dismal. Italian contributions to scientific progress depended once again on the brilliance of individual professors in the old universities. No man in Europe would do better anatomical work than Malpighi at Bologna in the Papal States – or use more complex microscopes – and it was also in Bologna that Cassini made the name which persuaded Colbert to invite him to settle in Paris. But whatever the role of gifted personalities, the advancement of science now depended equally on group activity. Discoveries had to be checked by repeating the investigation elsewhere. Or a team had to work together, with one man using his instruments (as in a dissection), another drawing the diagrams and a third keeping the written record; assistants and witnesses were needed. Those who collaborated to publish the research done by a certain 'private college' of physicians in Amsterdam between 1664 and 1672, by another group at Copenhagen in 1673–80, or over a longer period by the German 'Academy of the Curiosities of Nature', like the more famous societies of London and Paris, had really hit on a new form of intellectual activity. This has to be balanced against a powerful impulse which in some important cases forced thinkers back from the moving frontiers of scientific enquiry. Pascal, the Dane Nicholas Steno who pioneered in several fields, and the Dutchman Jan Swammerdam who studied with conspicuous skill the anatomy and physiology of insects: all three turned away from their work after a decade, reproaching themselves for a labour too long misspent – and embraced once more the universe discerned by theologians. Each of these great men, in the last stage of his life, was much closer to the world of Bishop Jansen or Avvakum than had once seemed likely.

The World of Bernini

In spite of their continuing importance Italian men of science were still overshadowed by the tremendous vitality of Italian artists. After the long reign of Urban VIII Rome visibly displayed the effect of his powerful patronage. Bernini had already transformed the interior of St Peter's by building the great canopy or *baldacchino* under Michelangelo's dome. From 1656 he began to set in the apse the old relic of St Peter's chair, developing a design which grew ever more ambitious and imaginative as the work went on. An astonishing complex of marble, bronze, stucco and glass used the history and symbols of the Roman faith to convince believers that in this place, above all others, they were to perceive the link between heaven and earth, between the Father and His creation. At the same time the approach to the church was given its great curving colonnades, surmounted by an army of sculptured saints and martyrs. It was one of Bernini's achievements to impress on artists in many parts of the world for a long time to come his rendering and characterisation of these saints, martyrs and other persons. His drapery, his deeply hollowed eyes, his angels – or his dolphins and tritons, with the water playing over them in his famous Roman fountains – became part of an accepted stock of common images: even in remote Quebec, where in 1686 a bronze copy of Bernini's bust of Louis XIV was set up in the market-place. His extraordinary mastery of different arts, and blending of them together to achieve an effect of total harmony, intensified the impulse to create a new aesthetic framework within which churchmen or the members of a great man's household performed their duties. It was an ideal of public life not far removed from Milton's curious vision of the Nativity:

And all about the Courtly Stable,
Bright-harnest Angels sit in order serviceable.

Bernini was only the most gifted of many who found their way to Rome, profiting from the restless search of successive papal families for a prestige commemorated by artistic grandeur. His rival as an architect, Borromini, had a stronger influence on the next generation in Italy and elsewhere. His colleague, the painter Pietro da Cortona, inspired countless imitators to cover walls and ceilings in a manner that carried the eye insensibly from shapes designed by the architect to the work of the painter himself. The pillar of stone and the painted pillar now belonged together, inseparable and not always distinguishable. By a mastery of perspective and foreshortening, the vault or ceiling opened – it seemed – to depict the painted sky or heaven above.

Money became scarcer in Rome after 1650, but the economic decadence of Italy was slow to affect this movement before Innocent XI drew the conclusion which his austere character was bound to draw. He brought a remarkable era of papal patronage to a close.

Impoverishment no doubt spurred Italian painters to bid more eagerly for commissions from foreign princes and gentry on their travels, and to go abroad to look for work. But the most powerful alien influence in a vast area north of the Alps, including Austria, parts of Germany, Bohemia, western Hungary and Poland, had long been Italian. An important colony of Italian craftsmen worked in Prague since the reign of Emperor Rudolph; before 1620 they built for the Protestants what has been called 'the first Baroque building' in the city. Wallenstein commissioned the first of its palaces in this style and entrusted it to an Italian architect and fresco painters. Their dominance was still unchallenged when Count Czernin – who had earlier moved in a circle close to Bernini in Rome – asked Francesco Caratti in 1668 to design a palace in Prague which remains one of the finest monuments of the period in Europe. Through most of the century Italian engineer-architects, masons, carvers and stucco workers, particularly from Como and Bergamo, appear wherever new building is needed. When fire gutted the cathedral at Passau, in 1662, the bishop contracted with Carlo Lurago to rebuild the west front, nave and the whole interior in a modern style; and today the tourist can see both the stucco of seventeenth-century Italian masters inside the choir and its older Gothic exterior. They were also in Emperor Leopold's employ at Vienna, making stage sets and machinery for the court's theatricals or a new wing for his palace. They were in Munich and Vilna. They worked for the Esterházy family in Hungary, for the Lobkowitz in Bohemia (see pp. 130–1 above). Only France escaped their ascendancy. It was not until after 1680 that the Italians were rivalled by other architects of equal merit in Germany and Austria, where local craftsmen increasingly added new flavours to the great amount of work in hand for nobility and church. The Spaniards also at last began to build more freely, applying a wealth of novel surface ornament to façades, and indulging a passion for height marvellously expressed in new building at the ancient shrine of Santiago de Compostela.

There is another side to the Italian inspiration of this period. While Bernini in sculpture or Borromini in building moved boldly away from past practice, men of great talent were impressing on the European mind an image strictly based, as they thought, on ancient models. This was the landscape of the Roman Campagna. Painters studied the scenery round Rome, but then transformed it by the conventions which they adopted. These fixed the skyline, the siting of nearer and more distant groups of trees, with human figures in the foreground and a classical temple farther back or on one side. In such a setting, an almost Arcadian idyll became the world of Claude Lorraine. When Philip IV wanted pictures showing hermits in solitude for his new retreat outside Madrid, the 'Buen Retiro', it was to work of this type that he was advised to turn. A century later the English went further, and consciously tried to recreate in nature the art of Claude when they laid out their gardens anew. This vision of the painters must be paired with a different one, more public and fashionable in northern Europe under Louis XIV's influence. Here, formal gardens were designed to stretch from the esplanade and *parterres* in front of a palace as far as the eye could travel. Parallel avenues of sculptured urns and statues, pools and fountains – with carefully planned diagonals and cross-axes to diversify each prospect – were then closed by clipped hedges, by arbours and finally by the glades and shades of surrounding woodland. This was the world created by André Le Nôtre for Fouquet at Vaux-le-Vicomte, for Condé at Chantilly, for Colbert at Sceaux, and especially for Louis himself at Versailles. It modified the more dramatic Italian style of the century, in which formal alleys and watercourses were carved stepwise up the terraced hillsides; where visitors, or foreign travellers like John Evelyn, would climb to the top and look down with anticipated delight through the cypress trees at a villa far below them. But the echo of ancient Rome, emphasised by the garden statuary and the classical orders of every stone building in sight, was insistent in both styles. This note had to be struck. Nothing else would have satisfied the architects, princes or public, for whom some of the grandest of contemporary entertainments were staged in the open air, in the 'green theatres' of a garden like Versailles, with amateur dancers and masquers, professional actors and musicians all contributing.

From papal Bologna to papal Rome had come many a young artist to make his name. Music lovers of the later seventeenth century owed Bologna an equal debt. For there, in the austere old church of San Petronio and inspired by the Accademia Filarmonica (from 1664), was the greatest of contemporary schools for instrumental playing and composition. Two organs, a choir, a *concerto grosso* of strings and trumpets, together with a smaller group of soloists, were joined to accompany the services. The improved violins made in Cremona and Brescia soared to a mastery of the orchestra. Ultimately this school influenced many kinds of music, including performances in the new opera houses of Italian towns. A distinguished line of experts – among them Bernini – had not only given scene painting and stage machinery the facility to create a new world of make-believe, of fantasy constantly transformed; they had tackled the problem of producing entertainments which combined music, drama and spectacle in varying degrees. Banqueting halls and tennis courts adapted for the purpose, or the old unroofed theatres in London and Paris which took little account of acoustic and perspective problems, were no longer sufficient. The solution was to be a new building, clearly divided (by a proscenium arch and space for an orchestra) between the stage and the auditorium. This auditorium, generally of a horseshoe plan, contained tiers of boxes for those who owned them (and often rented them out), and a pit and galleries for the public which paid to enter. Baroque art is often said to be theatrical. The most novel Baroque contribution to civilised society was in fact this type of theatre and opera house. In these, passions too obviously corrosive in the world outside have ever since been resolved, or at least soothed away for a few hours. Even so, the harshness of the human condition, of politics and war, was not easily forgotten in the days of Innocent XI, Louvois and Titus Oates.

9

The Diplomacy and Warfare
of Louis XIV, 1660–80

The French Interest in Europe

A time-honoured view of Louis XIV's monarchy consists of soldiers
and diplomats combining under the king to fight wars and make
treaties which annexed fresh territory to France. It is accurate
enough. In twenty-five years after 1660 no other western ruler
could boast of expansion on this scale, while after 1688 twenty-five
years of defensive fighting proved that most of these French gains
were permanent. Artois, and parts of Flanders, Hainault, Luxembourg, Franche-Comté, Alsace and much of Lorraine were lost to
Spain and the Empire. New fortifications, and the largest standing
army in Europe, defended them. The state system of the west had
been altered in such a way that nothing short of an alliance of greater
and lesser states could achieve a balance of power with the French
monarchy; and, as every politician realised, alliances were terribly
difficult to hold together against an opponent whose resources could
in any case hardly be resisted in the field. The common awareness of
this was used time and again by French diplomats either to deter
states from joining forces against Louis, or to split partnerships
which they had failed to stop from forming at an earlier stage. To
the excellence of his military and diplomatic organisation Louis XIV
added one other advantage. His very large revenue, based on a big
population and many fertile provinces and his acknowledged right to
tax them, not only allowed him to maintain numerous troops and
ships. He could afford to subsidise foreign princes, and offer bribes
to foreign politicians who heeded his wishes.

Equally important, the assertion of royal authority in France after
the Fronde occurred when the rival Habsburg dynasty had lost the
power to use Austrian, Spanish or Italian resources – in any case

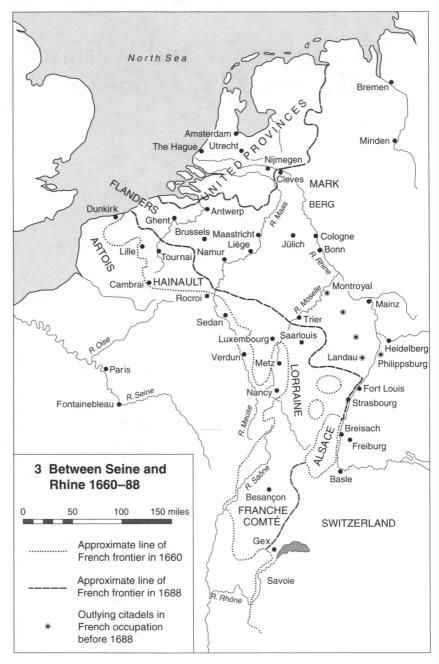

North Sea

Bremen

Minden

Amsterdam
The Hague
Utrecht
Nijmegen
Cleves
MARK
BERG

UNITED PROVINCES

FLANDERS
Dunkirk
Ghent
Antwerp
R. Maas
Cologne
Bonn
R. Rhine
Brussels
Maastricht
Jülich
ARTOIS
Lille
Tournai
Namur
Liège
Cambrai
HAINAULT
Rocroi
R. Moselle
Montroyal
Mainz
Sedan
Trier
R. Oise
Luxembourg
Saarlouis
Heidelberg
Verdun
Metz
Landau
Philippsburg
Paris
LORRAINE
Nancy
Fort Louis
R. Seine
Strasbourg
Fontainebleau
R. Meuse
Breisach
Freiburg
ALSACE
Basle

3 Between Seine and Rhine 1660–88

| 0 | 50 | 100 | 150 miles |

R. Saône
Besançon
FRANCHE
COMTÉ
SWITZERLAND

Gex

Savoie

R. Rhône

.... Approximate line of
French frontier in 1660

– – – – Approximate line of
French frontier in 1688

⊙ Outlying citadels in
French occupation
before 1688

Map 3

much diminished – to defend a vital belt of territory west of the Rhine valley, stretching from Switzerland to the North Sea. It is true that the southern Netherlands, Luxembourg and Franche-Comté remained subject to Philip IV. Alsace and most of Lorraine still belonged to the Empire. Yet each of these lands, just like a host of the lesser lordships on the left bank of the Rhine, was now practically defenceless. The Spanish viceroy in the Netherlands, with an army of considerable paper strength and many fortified towns under his command, would in future get little or no help from Spain. As for the German states, the fighting before 1648 left them with a well-founded prejudice against the Habsburgs, which helped to create the League of the Rhine in 1658. On one point the Rhinelanders were agreed: they would combine with each other, and with any other power, to bar the movement of Habsburg forces across Germany to the Netherlands. In 1657–9 and 1665–8 they were prepared to accept French conquests in Flanders. They were not prepared to let Leopold help in protecting this Spanish outpost. For similar reasons Lorraine and Franche-Comté were no better placed. Franz Lisola, a tireless Habsburg envoy, despairingly tried to alert governments by his diplomacy and public opinion by his pamphlets to the bogy of French domination over Europe. He could not save his native land of Franche-Comté from an inevitable fate. Louis invaded it in 1668, handed it back, conquered it again in 1674 and then kept it for good.

Another neighbouring area of great interest to the French government was Switzerland. The powerful local jealousies and loose federal organisation of the cantons offered Louis XIV a chance of using the same sort of diplomatic finesse which he practised farther north. During the past century French negotiators, battling against the Spanish viceroy in Milan who tried to do the same, had forged close links with individual families or parties in most of the cantons, both Protestant and Catholic. A new and elaborate bargain was worked out in the Franco-Swiss treaty of 1663, one of Lionne's most useful achievements. It has never won the fame of Louis's compacts with England in 1670, with Sweden in 1672, or with Brandenburg in 1679, but this alliance was in fact a cardinal element in the relations of Paris with the rest of Europe. For one thing, French diplomacy and French money – including sums paid in advance, sums owing but withheld until further deals were arranged, and pensions for selected persons – ensured that through the narrow corridor of Gex, between Spanish Franche-Comté and the duke of Piedmont's duchy of Savoy, Swiss volunteer troops continued to enter France in order to serve in Louis's army. If and when the cantonal authorities were obstructive, Louvois employed individual officers like the notorious Pierre Stouppa to recruit unofficially. The insistent need of the Swiss to win a livelihood abroad was partially satisfied by Louis XIV's own need for manpower. In the 1660s Spain still managed to raise Swiss troops, particularly from the Grisons. In the 1690s the Protestant cantons sent large contingents to fight under William of Orange. But between these two decades France scooped the Swiss pool, and 20,000 Swiss soldiers and their replacements fought for the king between 1672 and 1679.

The cantons helped Paris on a matter no less vital than recruitment. Lionne in 1665 evaded their demand that Louis XIV should guarantee the existing status of the Franche-Comté. The French always managed to stop the Swiss from taking any positive action to defend what could be arguably considered one of their vital interests, the existence of Franche-Comté as a useful buffer between themselves and France. The cantons never reacted here as the Dutch reacted to French expansion into the Spanish Netherlands.

Farther afield, France stood to gain from turmoil in two remote areas which distracted its Habsburg rival. Austria had to turn east to confront the problems of Hungary and Transylvania, the Spanish government obsessively refused to give way to 'rebel' Portugal. French diplomacy in the 1660s stoked both these fires, and at least in the case of Portugal Louis's ambassador at Madrid played a positive part in persuading the Spaniards not to compromise. The Anglo-Portuguese alliance owed much to French support. A general from the French army, Schomberg, directed the troops defending Lisbon.[1] Every government in Europe which toyed with the plan of an anti-French coalition, and a common defence of the Spanish Netherlands, had to reckon with the Spaniards' profound lack of concern for that region while they fought uselessly to recover Portugal. As to the Magyars and Turks, Louis's envoys encouraged their anti-Habsburg bias but this part of his diplomatic system was to be more fully developed at a later date. It already had the merit of alarming the Viennese. The difficulties over Portugal and Hungary neatly divided Spain and Austria. Madrid urged Vienna to make concessions to the Turks in order that troops might be freed for employment in western Europe. Vienna urged Madrid to negotiate with the Portuguese in order to free the Habsburg interest as a whole from what the Austrians regarded as a useless incubus. Relations between the two courts were very bad from 1658 until 1666, when the Spaniards at last carried out an old promise and sent the little Infanta Margareta to Vienna for her marriage with Leopold. Even after that, the French profited from the influence in Leopold's administration of statesmen who viewed the Spanish connection as a

---

1   This policy has a famous literary memorial in the pathetic 'Love-letters of a Portuguese Nun' (1st edn., Paris 1669). Their authorship is a puzzle, but they are addressed to a French officer recently in Portugal.

dangerous liability which should not be allowed to divert the emperor from his real duty: to attend to Hungary, and to make every effort to settle with Louis XIV for a partition of the Spanish empire when Carlos II died. The man at Vienna who had earlier staked his political future on the alliance with Spain, Prince Auersperg, joined this grouping in 1667. His motive was a personal one, but the impotence of the combined 'house of Austria' was patent to him at the time.

Above all, Louis XIV expected to profit from the commercial rivalry of England and Holland. Their antagonism outweighed every other motive which might have brought them together. He could accordingly manoeuvre with ease, but at first placed a higher value on the Franco-Dutch alliance (renewed in 1662) than on Anglo-French friendship. De Witt might be expected to play a bigger part than the English in settling in harmony with French wishes the future of the Spanish Netherlands, on which Louis and Lionne had their eyes fixed.

The Spanish Succession: Louis XIV

The historian Mignet, in 1835, suggested that 'the Spanish succession was the pivot on which the whole reign of Louis XIV turned'. More precisely, it was the crux of French foreign policy immediately before and after the death of Philip IV in September 1665, and again in the period before and after the death of Carlos II in November 1700, with a long interval in between. Few men doubted that Louis's marriage with Maria Teresa, only surviving child of Philip's first marriage, even allowing for her formal renunciation of the succession, gave France a powerful lever in Spain; but its weight depended on the survival or decease of Philip's sons by his second marriage.[2] Carlos II was born in November 1661, and thereafter we must accept that the politics of Europe turned to a curious extent on the steady physical decay of Philip IV and the health of a sickly child.

De Witt was willing to consider very far-reaching changes in the Netherlands in order to anticipate still bigger changes which might endanger Dutch security if Carlos died and Louis pressed his claims to the full. In 1663 he offered a partition, which would have drawn a new frontier between France and Holland along a line between Ostende and Maastricht, with everything south of it falling to France. Another proposal was a new independent republic, to be federated with the United Provinces but allied to France. It soon became clear that de Witt was seriously interested in plans of

2   See the dynastic tables, nos 2 and 3, pp. 295–6 below.

this sort only if Philip and Carlos both died. It was equally clear – perhaps he reckoned on the difficulty as a convenient bolt-hole – that many Dutch politicians disliked such proposals. They queried the legal basis of Maria Teresa's claim. They were not satisfied by Louis's argument that his wife's renunciation of that claim depended on a punctual payment of her dowry, and that Spain had defaulted; nor by Louis's other and more alarming thesis that no civil act (like the terms of his marriage contract) could destroy a natural right. When Carlos did not oblige the French by dying forthwith, Louis found himself forced back on a more limited and distinctly less plausible justification. 'Devolution' was the law of inheritance in certain parts of the Netherlands, by which property fell to the children of a first marriage and simply allowed the widowed parent temporary rights of occupation. Louis and Lionne now got their legal advisers to apply this to the case of Maria Teresa and Carlos: the queen of France was entitled to full and immediate possession of the Spanish Netherlands, or whatever part of it the French chose to claim, on the death of Philip IV. Carlos had no rights there against his half-sister and her children, even if he lived to succeed his father in the rest of the Spanish empire. De Witt quickly retorted that 'devolution' had never been applied to the succession of Burgundian princes, and negotiations on the problem faded out before the end of 1663. The Anglo-Dutch war began in 1664, and Louis did not deny that he was bound to assist de Witt.

When Philip died and the infant Carlos took his place in the autumn of 1665 the French publicly urged their claim by devolution. The formula sufficed to set in motion campaigning for which both the king and the military interest in France craved. It was a very weak substitute for the claim arising out of Louis's marriage if Carlos had died. In that case, the upheaval in Europe and the remodelling of boundaries would have been far more profound and much of his policy-making for many years was a substitute for the steps he would have taken to claim his wife's gigantic inheritance on the death of Carlos. What actually occurred may have benefited France, if not the French monarchy, by limiting the possibilities of aggrandisement. Without the blank cheque for which he had hoped, Louis learned to move cautiously in his dealings with foreign states in the first decade of his personal rule. He listened to Lionne who was extreme in his hatred of popes, but in other spheres combined a sense of purpose with an instinct for diplomatic finesse. He gave Colbert a chance.

The phase during which the king pressed Maria Teresa's claim by devolution on the Spanish Netherlands coincided with, and stimulated, his growing enthusiasm for the army. In 1658 Louis had paid his first visit to the Belgian theatre of war, and this turned out to set a precedent in a way which his long journey south in 1659–60 never did. In 1662 he visited Dunkirk. In 1665, when the death of Philip signalled action, he began to visualise a new role which he could play as the royal actor: the monarch who left his palaces in and around Paris in the spring, and made the easy trip northwards to review his forces camped in the Picardie plains, take part in military exercises, reward captains of the best companies, and inspect new fortifications in progress. One short step farther would take him on to Habsburg ground. It was a sign of his diplomatic prudence that he did not immediately enter the Netherlands after Philip's death. He had no wish to drive Spain into the arms of England, already at war with his own ally Holland. It was a sign of his new military bent that he not only sanctioned the raising of new cavalry regiments and added to the number of companies in foot-regiments at the close of 1665: he also inaugurated the great series of royal reviews in 1666. Some of these were held near Paris. The populace and court flocked out to see them. It was then that Louvois, the secretary for war's young son, came into closer contact with Louis, handled much of the detailed work of mobilisation and provoked Colbert's violent disapproval. The controller-general deplored the burden of such measures on the civilians of northern France – as large bodies of men crossed and recrossed the country to their different rendezvous. He disliked the extravagantly splendid equipment which the king demanded for these martial exercises.

It has often been said that an enemy on the Netherlands frontier, in the days of Richelieu and Mazarin, was dangerously close to Paris. The state's security required that the frontier should be pushed back. But this proximity suited Louis, who wanted a style of life enabling him both to dominate his court and capital, and appear as a soldier-king who led his forces across the border, took the credit for their victories and then came back to Paris before the campaigning season ended. The distances fitted the time-table. It is also said that Louis could hardly conceive of war except as a sequence of sieges, with such engineers as Vauban at hand to guarantee success. But in 1667 the Spaniards lacked an army to challenge the French in the field, and it was their weakness which tended to reduce war to the attack and defence of fortified places. Louis XIV's attitude owed more to the company he kept. In this period he saw much of Turenne, and decided to employ once again the military genius of Condé. These great representatives of a warlike aristocracy of princes could no longer deny, as they had done in the past, the association of rebellion and treason; but they still honoured a code of values which set the highest value of all on leadership amid the shock of war. Louis's notion of glory was partly shaped by these men. In due course he fused it with the attitude of Louvois, who laid far more stress on the size and discipline of an army – results of the zealous competence of civilian administrators like himself – than on the aura of command in generals whom he found so hard to control. Neither the king nor Turenne nor Louvois, to judge from their correspondence, regarded the labouring masses and the common soldier as more than pawns in the great game of Mars.

The War of 1667–8 and the Triple Alliance

Louis may have been disappointed by the treaty of Breda which ended the second Anglo-Dutch war in 1667, but his decision to attack the Spanish Netherlands did not depend on the uncertain relations of London and the Hague at this date. His forces were now ready and he wanted to use them. A full list of claims was sent off to Madrid, including Antwerp, Limburg, Malines, Gelderland – all far away to the north – Namur, Artois, Brabant, Cambrai, Hainault, a quarter of Luxembourg and a third of Franche-Comté: Louis demanded these, or an alternative equivalent, as his wife's right. Giving no time for an answer, he and Turenne, accompanied by Louvois and large forces, crossed into Belgium in September 1667.

A dozen places, big and small, had fallen by the end of the month. The whole area looked like a chess-board. Spain lost many pieces in different areas but kept outposts in country now dominated by the enemy. Meanwhile Louis planned a new move which Condé carried out in February 1668: the prince occupied Franche-Comté in force. Louis's exuberant temper at this period is best summed up in part of a letter which he wrote on 20 September 1667. 'I want everything got ready for the next campaign, to reach the goal I have in mind. I am trying to arrange affairs suitably, and will spare no pains. I ponder ideas which are by no means impracticable – they are marvellous!'[3] Turenne and Louvois looked forward with equal eagerness to great military activity in the following year, and Louvois seems to have hoped that in future the supply and pay of French troops could be found in Flanders by occupying enough of the country. This would meet Colbert's objections, and ease the strain of drawing back regiments to winter quarters in France.

During 1667 another French army had been posted in the area round Metz and Verdun to guard against the danger that Emperor Leopold would send troops across Germany to the Netherlands. Every opponent of France in Europe prayed for this. Every French envoy in foreign courts did what he could to encourage opposition to such a scheme. Gremonville at Vienna had the biggest part to play. Leopold, after much hesitation, while he watched the signs of growing

3 *Lettres et mémoires...de Turenne* (ed. Grimoard, 1732), i, 451.

disturbance in Hungary and made tentative bids for an anti-French alliance at the Hague, London, Berlin and Stockholm without ever committing himself to a firm offer, finally allowed his ministers to negotiate with Gremonville. A secret treaty of 20 January 1668 secured the emperor's consent to a settlement of Louis's dispute with Spain, although by it certain towns would be handed over to France. He undertook not to intervene in Belgium. As to the larger question of the Spanish succession if Carlos died childless: for the avoidance of future wars, the signatories declared, Louis should have as his share the Spanish Netherlands, Franche-Comté, Navarra (in Spain), the Philippines, the Spanish posts in Africa, Naples and Sicily. Everything else was assigned to Leopold. In effect, the Austrian government had agreed not to oppose the French during the existing crisis, and in the longer term to surrender its interest in the entire Netherlands and Franche-Comté. Louis's prospective gains were enormous, although he still had to gamble on Carlos's speedy death. Leopold, at least for the time being, could do nothing.

At the same moment (after Lord Chancellor Clarendon's fall from power), English politicians divided into those whose strongest bias remained anti-Dutch, and others who feared the growing power of France. Louis's new ambassador in London, the Protestant Ruvigny, clashed with Lisola, Leopold's envoy, who constantly went beyond his master's brief in working for an anti-French coalition. Ruvigny failed to restrain Charles II because he was not authorised to concede what the English ministers demanded – an offensive and defensive league against the Dutch, and a commercial treaty – so that Sir William Temple was instructed to conclude an offensive alliance with de Witt. De Witt wanted a settlement in Belgium, not an explosion; and he scaled down the offer. The alliance of 13 January 1668, subsequently called the Triple Alliance when Sweden joined in, confirmed the treaty of Breda. A public article bound the signatories, together with other friendly states, to compel Spain to settle for peace. A secret article bound the allied states to join Spain if France in turn refused the proposal, and in that case to restore by force the boundaries of Belgium set by the treaty of 1659. It was a threat to the Spaniards but did not conceal a warning to Louis XIV, who learnt of the secret clause almost immediately. De Witt had by now given up the notion of getting the French to renounce Maria Teresa's claim. He hoped instead for the broadly based guarantee of a new settlement in Belgium which gave Louis enough, but – from the Dutch standpoint – not too much. Certain other politicians took a different view of the alliance. Apart from the Englishmen Arlington and Temple, and also Lisola, the Dutchman van Beuningen who had lately returned from Paris was by now a relentless opponent of the French. Colbert's draconic new tariff of 1667, and the steady growth of Dunkirk as a fortified port, deeply alarmed commercial interests at Amsterdam which van Beuningen represented.

From the standpoint of Paris this crisis remains an enigma which historians have never unravelled convincingly. They point out that the secret agreement with Leopold gave Louis everything he wanted in this part of Europe if he held his hand for the time being. They note that the Anglo-Dutch alliance confronted France with a choice between making peace, on reasonable terms, and resisting a combination of powers which might join the Spaniards and collect support elsewhere; Lisbon was at length nearing agreement with Madrid, and Stockholm had veered away from Paris. Louis himself maintained, later on, that he preferred to be cautious and moderate at this stage. But the Austrian treaty was signed by the end of January, the Anglo-Dutch concert was announced at the same time, and French troops nevertheless triumphantly occupied Franche-Comté in February. Intensive preparations were made for a renewal of the fighting in Belgium. If there were sound arguments for peace, the fact remains that early in March 1668 few informed observers at the French court believed that the king would be content to forgo the prospect of another season's enjoyable warfare.

It seems that Louis, at the last minute, changed his mind by preferring the views of Colbert and Lionne to those of Turenne. One wanted to limit expenditure, the other to use weapons of diplomacy rather than of war, and a new Franco-Spanish treaty was signed at Aix-la-Chapelle, dated 2 May 1668. The French gave back Franche-Comté, knowing that they were strong enough to re-enter it whenever they wished. (They continued to demolish fortified places in this region, after the treaty, and before they marched out.) They kept their conquests in Belgium, of which Lille was incomparably the most important. For the next few years, nothing like a genuine frontier existed in this area. Outposts like Oudenarde and Tournai menaced Spanish Brussels and Ghent. A Spanish wedge of territory separated Dunkirk and Lille, while Cambrai and Saint-Omer also remained Spanish.

In retrospect, all this looks like an interim arrangement which foreshadows a fresh French advance. But untidy boundaries can last a long time if a sufficiently stable balance of power supports them, and Louis soon realised that he would make little further headway while Carlos lived, unless he managed to readjust in his favour the whole diplomatic system of western Europe. Possibly he made one of his greatest mistakes. The readjustment would not have been necessary if he had continued the war in 1668. The Anglo-Dutch alliance was far too fragile, the German states were far too disinterested in the Spanish Netherlands. By accepting the treaty of Aix-la-Chapelle he unintentionally encouraged the interests opposed to France. A foundation was laid for all the later alliances against the French monarchy, the notion of a necessary resistance to Louis was fostered. Van Beuningen, Temple and Lisola were, in their way, the forerunners of a movement. Lionne believed that he would have less difficulty in splitting the new and surprising Anglo-Dutch partnership, once peace was arranged, than if the fighting continued. However he found himself toiling long and hard before the scene was set to Louis's and his own satisfaction for the next major war over the Netherlands.

Lionne's Diplomacy

The king of France enjoyed one enormous advantage. The subordination of the court was complete; no foreign state could profit from the friction between ministers, or pit one French cabal against another. The possibility of treason or rebellion had vanished under so effective an autocrat. In England, the United Provinces and Sweden, signatories of the Triple Alliance, the domestic situation was utterly different. Constitutionalism meant party warfare, and involved party alignments abroad. It involved a perpetual curb on military expenditure. Troops and warships, and the use made of them, easily came to depend in part on foreign aid.

As early as August 1668 Lionne drafted instructions for a new French ambassador in London, Colbert de Croissy, whose mission was to break up the Anglo-Dutch connection and to edge Charles II into an alliance with France. He arrived in London when the restored Stuart régime had lost much popular support. Charles was all the more determined to assert his personal authority, in diplomacy and in domestic administration, even if he could not control Parliament. Partly for this reason, partly because Anglo-Dutch rivalry had as yet lost little of its earlier venom, partly because of Louis's offers of ready money, Charles committed himself in 1670 to the plan of a combined assault on the United Provinces. Both rulers undertook to leave intact the Spanish Netherlands. In February 1669 a new ambassador, Pomponne, also appeared at the Hague, with instructions very different from those of Colbert de Croissy. He was to listen to any offers from de Witt in case the continuing friction between English and Dutch, and the fears of de Witt that the Orange interest in Holland might plot with Charles II, compelled the Dutch government to sue to France for aid: but Pomponne was never to commit Louis to any form of compromise over the Spanish Netherlands. By the end of 1669 it became quite clear that no agreement on this, the critical problem, was possible.

French policy now assumed, as it had never done before, that the future expansion and prestige of the monarchy depended on defeating the Dutch. This proved a change of emphasis with ultimately profound consequences. The new antagonism would breathe fresh life into the struggle between Catholic and Protestant, and deprive the French Huguenots of an important practical safeguard of their position inside France. It would entwine a conflict between rival political ideals with the secular struggle between rival states or alliances. More immediately, Franco-Dutch commercial rivalry was sharpened by the growing friction. In spite of Colbert's conviction that the French economy ought to liberate itself from the incubus of Dutch dominance, the two countries had worked well together in the early stages of the Anglo-Dutch war of 1664–7. With Colbert's encouragement Dutch ships carried the French flag for protection against English attacks, and when Louis entered the fighting French salt and wine continued to reach foreign markets thanks to the Dutch. Only as the war of 1672 loomed closer did the controller-general visualise the economic advantages of a military victory. He hoped for terms of peace enabling his own trading companies to displace the Dutch East India Company in one part of the world, and other Dutch merchants elsewhere. He dreamt of the rival trading empire brought to its knees. But there are no signs that he determined French foreign policy after 1668, and he never ceased to grudge the tax burden which expanding military forces required. Commercial interest weighed more heavily on the Dutch side. Dunkirk in French hands was bad enough. If Antwerp went the same way, neither Amsterdam nor the towns of Zeeland could expect the French government to honour those clauses in the 1648 treaty between Spain and the United Netherlands which restricted the freedom of Belgian commerce.

As the chances of a friendly agreement faded after 1668, the Dutch had to rely on maintaining a balance of power favourable enough to deter Louis XIV. Van Beuningen, much more than de Witt, pinned his faith on the Triple Alliance. Very gradually, with a guarantee of the treaty of Aix-la-Chapelle as its focus, this partnership seemed to be getting stronger. Spain entered the bargaining. Sweden's demand for subsidies was at length satisfied, at least on paper. The respective forces which each signatory should put into the field in an emergency were fixed. One formal agreement was signed in May 1669, and another in January 1670. But the Dutch did not realise that the English court was secretly committing itself to an attack on Holland.

At the same time, Lionne and Louis met with great difficulties in Germany. The first signs of real unease at growing French power began to ripple through the Rhineland when the attack on Franche-

Comté in 1668 was followed by punitive forays against the duke of Lorraine in both 1669 and 1670. The elector of Mainz, effective architect of the League of 1658 which had leaned so heavily on France, began to look more sympathetically towards Vienna. Nervously he rebuilt the citadel at Mainz. He moved to the very edge of the French sphere of influence, while the elector of Trier moved with him. The Confederation of the Rhine was dead, so that Lionne had to go elsewhere. While Lisola and his friends – who knew nothing of Gremonville's secret compact – busily tried to bring Leopold into the Triple Alliance, the French countered by a successful offer to Bavaria: an agreement of December 1670 was to tie it to France for the next twelve years, anticipating the great Franco-Bavarian partnership of Marlborough's days. The ancient feud of Vienna and Munich could in any case never be stilled for long, and Louis XIV's ministers hoped to use Bavaria as a giant wedge thrust between Austria and the rest of the Empire. The elector's friendly neutrality proved immensely valuable to France.

Lionne worked still harder for an alliance of north German states, who might be willing in return for subsidies to attack the United Provinces. He needed to exploit the resentment caused by Dutch dominance in the whole area of the lower Rhine. He had to deprive de Witt of the troops which German states might be able to raise for him in return for Dutch pay. These arrogant burghers, it might be said, had never withdrawn their garrisons from towns and forts in the Brandenburg elector's duchy of Cleves. They too often encouraged municipalities such as the cities of Cologne, Münster and Brunswick, when neighbouring princes claimed sovereign rights over them. Dutch Protestantism, although a bond with Frederick William of Brandenburg – in spite of his other grievances – irritated and affronted the Catholic rulers of Münster, Cologne and Jülich. A military defeat of the Dutch would bring them territorial rewards on both sides of the Rhine. Lacing this brew with tempting financial offers, Franz von Fürstenberg – the elector of Cologne's minister who was the great factotum of the French in Germany – ranged widely from court to court. Fürstenberg, believing that the essential problem of statecraft in this part of Europe consisted in coming intelligently to terms with the rising power of France, belongs to an important group of men of different countries at this time, who were not French but served France. Count Peñeranda in Spain, Henry Jermyn Lord St Albans, and Count Morstejn in Poland all resembled him. Between 1668 and 1673 he gave of his best for the French interest.

At first the result was disappointing. Münster and Cologne were won over easily. It proved possible to arrange a preliminary treaty between France and Brandenburg, but all attempts to transform this into a positive alliance against the Dutch broke down, while the deviousness of various Brunswick brothers and cousins seemed in the end to leave the French government with only one friend among them, the Catholic convert, John Frederick duke of Hanover.

This was the position by the end of 1670. On the one hand, Louis's grip upon his recent conquests daily grew tighter. Intendants based on Lille and Dunkirk administered Flanders for him. A strong new citadel designed by Vauban was going up at Lille, to match the one already built in Dunkirk. Louvois had paid four visits since August 1668 to inspect the troops, and the fortifications in progress. Louis himself appeared in 1670, to see everything and to frighten the Dutch. (In the course of this trip his cousin Henrietta Stuart, duchess of Orleans, was sent to Dover to sign the first secret treaty with Charles II.) On the other hand, the diplomatic combination against the Dutch remained incomplete. When the king and his ministers came on one more round of inspection to Flanders in 1671, an important conference at Dunkirk decided that the assault on Holland would have to be put off for at least a year. It was judged necessary to woo one other major German power, until then left out of account: Sweden, the ruler of Bremen and Pomerania. Swedish forces, once placed ready for action at these points, would surely compel the Brandenburg elector and the Brunswick princes not to move with the Dutch against the French. The neutrality of these states, to be purchased on cheaper terms than their active military collaboration, was what was now required. Such an alteration in policy accorded with the wishes of Louvois, now gaining in influence. He wanted Louis's armament, under his auspices continually increasing in numbers and building up to a new pitch of efficiency, to take over the whole task of attacking the enemy. Fürstenberg's prime duty, instead of scurrying from one German court to another in the search for allies, was to control his own master, the ruler of both Cologne and Liège. The elector's lands would provide the direct route of approach and the convenient supply base, not for the troops of Louis's querulous German supporters but for his own superlative force.

Arnauld de Pomponne, till then ambassador at the Hague, was accordingly sent to Stockholm. (It was another stage in the rise to power of this gifted member of the great Jansenist family, and Louis appointed him secretary for foreign affairs after Lionne died in September 1671.) The negotiations with Sweden, among the most difficult in the whole series which preceded the war, ended with a Franco-Swedish treaty in April 1672. It is fascinating to see how the course of events gradually moved in favour of Louis. The party in Stockholm which had worked for the Triple Alliance lost ground because the promised Spanish subsidies were too slow in coming, and because the Dutch made no concessions to Sweden over their

Baltic commerce. The English government – thanks to French offers – was itself evidently withdrawing from the alliance and moving closer to France. Danish enthusiasm for a war of revenge against Sweden increased with the accession of Christian V in 1670; a circle of noisy swordsmen surrounded him. Emperor Leopold declined to listen to Swedish offers. At length the French appeared to get their way: the published treaty between Louis XIV and Charles XI bound Sweden to join forces with France if either were attacked and to defend the general settlements of 1648 and 1668. Secret articles, very complicated and contradictory after a long haggle, promised Sweden French subsidies, but still left the partnership loose enough to let Stockholm adopt the stance of a neutral, eager to mediate when war broke out. The treaty was therefore a bid to warn off the German powers from joining the Dutch, and completed the destruction of the Triple Alliance. It failed to convert Sweden into an active ally, willing to enter the fray. The new agreement was more significant than its terms suggested. As things turned out, Louis's alliance with England snapped after eighteen months of fighting, his alliance with Sweden grew stronger.

Louvois himself went to Cologne in December 1671 and completed the French deal with the elector. Four places in his territory were already assigned as supply depots for artillery and munitions and timber, some of them purchased in Amsterdam. The elector formally sanctioned the use of his lands by France and undertook to raise a force of 18,000 in return for subsidies. The bishop of Münster joined him in sharing the burden – and the payment. During the winter French forces began to make their way from Metz into the lands of Cologne. Large bodies of men assembled near Sedan and Charleroi, on the triangle of ground between the Meuse and its tributary Sambre which points north to Liège and the Dutch outpost of Maastricht. In February Louis XIV was shown a splendid summary account of the army at his disposal. There were 8000 household troops. There were fifty-eight regiments of infantry, some 86,000 men, and 25,000 cavalry. It was certainly the strongest single force in Europe since the days of Charles X and Cromwell. Its effective commanders bore the great names of Condé and Turenne; at fifty-one and sixty-one years of age they were highly experienced, but not too old. The king, unlike Emperor Leopold I who never showed his face on the field, unlike Dutch regents and burghers who hired their commanders to fight for them, was determined to wear the laurels of a soldier in the manner of his father and grandfather, warriors both.

He was challenging the wealthiest state in Europe. The United Provinces also enjoyed peculiar natural advantages in defence. We know far more about Louis's diplomacy than about the development of his military plans for an assault on the Dutch,[4] but apparently neither he nor his advisers understood the significance of the 'water-line', which could be flooded to protect the principal cities of Holland. Although the French ambassador at the Hague busily collected news items of every kind, there is no evidence that he was instructed to gather technical military intelligence. He failed to investigate in detail the lay-out of dykes and sluices along the waterline. By the standards of even thirty years later, French maps seem to have been very poor. England was no doubt a powerful ally, Cologne and Münster were useful, but Brandenburg was likely to be hostile and Sweden neutral. The risks which Louis ran seemed real enough, which adds a touch of genuine audacity to the remarkable enterprise of 1672.

The War of 1672–8

It is very difficult to give a summary account of the great war which lasted until 1679, much easier to explain why simplification is so difficult. From one angle this was a military exercise which got out of hand. From another, Louis XIV and those closest to him were always keener to engage in warfare than to fight with a precise object-ive in mind. The attack on Holland was a tantalising mixture of success and failure which soon offered the king an alternative possi-bility: gains in Germany. His advance towards the Rhineland scared many in the Empire, including the emperor, and these turned to sup-port the Dutch. When England withdrew from the struggle, it became necessary to involve Sweden actively on the French side. Fighting accordingly broke out in east Germany, so that Denmark took the opportunity to invade Scania. The operations against Holland had already overflowed into the Spanish Netherlands; and the intervention of Spain led France, now powerful at sea as well as on land, to assault other parts of the Habsburg empire, Catalonia and Sicily. The Dutch meanwhile struck at weaker French footholds in the West Indies and the Indian ocean.

This repercussion across the world impressed many contempor-aries, but Louis himself always thought first in terms of warfare across a broad band of territory between the Netherlands and Swit-zerland. The attack on Holland ushered in a phase when the French

4   A great deal must have depended on Turenne's previous experience: in 1665, the Spaniards having refused him entry into their territory, he found no difficulty in taking an expeditionary force down the Meuse valley to help the Dutch against the bishop of Münster, an ally of the English during the Anglo-Dutch War. In addition, the Estates of Liège had recently built the so-called 'New Road' from Liège to Sedan – in order to help traders to evade Spanish tolls in that area.

monarchy found itself step by step engaged on the permanent subjection of such regions as Alsace, Lorraine, Saarland and Franche-
Comté.

The Anglo-French onslaught of 1672 began in a spectacular fashion, but from the first the Dutch navy under de Ruyter and van
Ghent was strong enough to hold its own against the Anglo-French
fleet in a big battle off the Suffolk coast, and then – favoured by bad
weather – to defend the shoreline of Zeeland and Holland. By contrast the French forces moved effortlessly down both banks of the
Meuse, by-passing Maastricht. They entered the lands of Cologne,
pushed into Cleves, overwhelmed Dutch garrisons on the Rhine and
crossed it. The bishop of Münster broke into Overijsel and Friesland.
The French turned eastward and after an easy fording of another arm
of the river – which would be celebrated in prose and verse but by
none so splendidly as by tapestry workers of the Gobelins – poured
into Dutch territory. The Dutch seemed to be the victims of their own
errors and of bad luck. Their troops were split into a host of small
garrisons, while unusually dry weather had lowered the water-level
to such an extent that the French could ford where they wished.
Having reached Utrecht, Louis and his commanders misjudged the
situation. They too scattered their forces in widely spread garrisons,
or besieged places which did not matter. The Dutch had time to flood
a large area south of the Zuider Zee. Above all, having weakened his
striking power in this way, Louis demanded concessions so sweeping
when the Dutch tried to negotiate that they preferred to fight on. To
ask for a stunning indemnity and the surrender of territory on a
massive scale, together with liberty of public worship for Catholics,
was to pitch the price of peace too high. It was to strengthen and
unite the enemy, in spite of his deeply rooted provincialism. The king
returned to France, triumphant but empty-handed. Before the year
ended the new Dutch leader, William of Orange,[5] had even made a
bold southward dash to Charleroi which he failed to take.

Very speedily the fighting began on other fronts. Frederick William
of Brandenburg had joined the Dutch who also won a promise of
Spanish support. These moves impressed the court in Vienna, and
Leopold made a pact with Frederick William for a joint defence of
the Empire. An apparently formidable force of Brandenburgers and
Habsburg troops – who entered Germany from the western tip of
Bohemia – threatened the new French positions on the lower Rhine.
Turenne withdrew some regiments from Holland to counter them,
and went up the river as far as the Main. Early in 1673 he entered
Westphalia, and compelled Brandenburg to make a separate peace
with Louis in June.

5   For the change of government in the United Provinces, in 1672, see above, p. 98.

The French ministers may have taken this threat from the Empire more seriously than it deserved, but they never concentrated whole-heartedly on the destruction of Holland after the first few months of war. They did not rate it a paramount necessity, and turned from one objective to another on an extremely broad front. They occupied Trier, having first ravaged the elector's lands in order to punish him for opposing the French interest. Louis himself went to Nancy in Lorraine and then on to Alsace. Here, in July 1673, his forces entered the Imperial towns – whose liberties had been left intact by the Westphalian treaties – and in September broke down the Rhine bridge at Strasbourg. This was a far cry from Maastricht, besieged and taken by Condé in the same year, and it promptly strengthened the opposition in Germany. Leopold signed alliances with the United Provinces and Spain. He moved the Regensburg Diet to announce a declaration of war on France by the Estates of the Empire. His troops recovered Bonn. From Switzerland to the North Sea the world was now alight.

At this stage Louvois seems to have considered the Rhineland as no more than a suitable arena for campaigning. Farther west and in Alsace the government of Paris had something more constructive in view. Franche-Comté fell again to Louis in 1674, this time for good. The future of Lorraine would be more chequered, but the French grip on this duchy became tight enough to frustrate all the efforts of Duke Charles IV and Duke Charles V to recover it until the end of the century. At the same time the administrative arrangements by which Louis's chief ministers shared out between them responsibility for different regions of the monarchy were now altered.

Louvois took Alsace and lands on the upper Moselle from Pomponne, and from Colbert the fortifications of Breisach and Philippsburg. In 1679 he would also take over Metz, Toul and Verdun. The new intendant for Alsace was Jacques de la Grange, Louvois's man: he began to sweep away the tissue of Alsatian local liberties which had been more or less left intact between 1648 and 1672, in spite of Louis's title to sovereignty there. The further expansion of France was under way.

The birth of this new order west of the Rhine coincided with the first combination of powers hostile to France which deserves the title of a 'Grand Alliance'. Sweden's attempt to mediate petered out, while a bewildering set of bargains soon linked together the United Provinces, Spain and the emperor – and also exiled Charles IV of Lorraine. Even Brandenburg turned again, and joined in. The elector palatine and the rulers of Mainz and Trier were associated. Only Bavaria and Hanover remained loyal to France, but neutral. It was the turn of Louis's opponents to take the initiative. Their troops tried to re-enter Alsace, but the two last campaigns of Turenne drove them back across the Rhine. They advanced up the Moselle as far as Trier. They crossed the Spanish Netherlands in 1674 and replaced the French as oppressors of the civilian population south of Liège. At the same time, the collapse of Louis's alliance with England was another fatal blow to his original design against the Dutch. The fleets of Tromp and de Ruyter together drove off English warships from the Holland coast. Dutch convoys from the East and Levant reached port safely, in England men digested the sad news of the Dutch seizing St Helena or New York, and on top of this the entry of Spain into the war threatened English commerce in Spanish markets. News of the treaties which formed the great alliance disconcerted the English government and cheered its critics. When the Lords and Commons assembled at Westminster in October 1673 – determined to revoke the royal Declaration of Indulgence for Papists and Dissenters – a view gained ground that the alliance with Catholic, autocratic France threatened liberty and Protestantism in England. For some, this was a matter of conviction, for others a politically useful pose. Charles could not finance the war without fresh grants of money, and by the end of the year everyone realised that this was out of the question. The Anglo-Dutch treaty was completed early in 1674. It was a decisive defeat for Louis.

He reacted by intensifying his diplomacy elsewhere. It is noticeable that the new French offers of a subsidy to Charles II, if he would undertake to dismiss Parliament again, were very moderate in amount. Paris reserved money for use in more promising centres, above all in Stockholm. Here, although constitutional checks and balances weakened the administration as in England and Holland, the real problem was a growing threat to Swedish power overseas. Once France had to ease its pressure on the lower Rhineland, Brandenburg and the Brunswick princes (Hanover excepted) and Münster all cast longing looks at Sweden's German provinces. Once the allied armies, of which they formed a part, had been repulsed by Turenne and Condé on the Moselle and in Alsace, they positively preferred to look northwards. Denmark also signed agreements with the Dutch and with Leopold. Little by little, therefore, the French ambassador was able to convince the Swedes that they must ferry more men across the Baltic into Pomerania. Their policy of neutrality, like the neutrality of the Spaniards, was doomed because they had not the strength to stand apart from a major conflict. In December 1674 the fighting between Brandenburg and Sweden began, ultimately spreading from Pomerania to the lands round Bremen and Verden. After the unexpected victory of the Brandenburgers in the skirmish at Fehrbellin in 1675, the Danes joined in and fought desperately to win back Scania. Pomponne and Louis, if they could no longer hope to cripple the United Provinces with the weight of an English assault by sea, had at least managed to weaken the combined assault of German powers west of the Rhine by forcing a diversion along the North Sea and Baltic hinterlands.

Inside France

Admittedly, the strain of war on the French monarchy was considerable. Higher taxes were the greatest popular grievance. New duties caused an uproar in Bordeaux in 1675, and later in the same year at Rennes, Nantes and St. Malo. The fever of unrest became linked with widespread trouble already brewing in Lower Brittany.[6] Fresh burdens crystallised the expression of a general misery, in which manifold grievances and fantastic rumours of still more taxation combined to provoke violent protest. In Brittany, the poor attacked not only the bureaux of those who farmed the new taxes but also the nobility. The latter had recently been buying off Colbert's recent assault on seigneurial justice by offering the government larger grants which were then mainly collected from the peasants. The remedy was suitably repressive. Troops were brought back from the Pyrenean frontier to deal with Bordeaux. The governor of Brittany, the duke of Chaulnes, made pitiless use of the men whom Louis indignantly diverted from service against the Germans. The Dutch had some hopes of landing on the Biscay coast but never managed to make contact with the rioters; events in the Fronde of 1650–3, with foreign intervention at Bordeaux, were still recalled at the Hague during this war. The monarchy had grown strong enough to scotch the possibility, and thereafter the French Atlantic provinces remained submissive enough.

In spite of these hardships, for which the war was only partly responsible (see below, p. 260) their consequences must not be exaggerated. Fiscal pressure got much worse in the later years of Louis's reign, while by a stroke of good fortune the harvests never failed between 1672 and 1678, as they were to fail after 1692 with fearful results.

Some men prospered exceedingly. When Mme de Sévigné was in Brittany after the troubles, she coined a careless and terrible phrase – *à force d'avoir pendu, on ne pendra plus* – but her letters from Paris abound in pictures of splendour and luxury. At Versailles in July 1676 she breathlessly took in everything: the king's grand apartment, the furnishings, the jewelled coiffure of one lady, the huge winnings of another courtier at cards, the background music, the gondola rides

---

6   For a good account of the events in Brittany, see R. Mousnier, *Peasant Uprisings*, in *Seventeenth-Century France, Russia and China* (London 1971), pp. 114–49.

along the canal, and the comedy performed – with just a hint of the hard world outside when couriers arrived so that the king slipped away to read their despatches, before returning. It is true that Louis's expenditure on building dropped, but a serving soldier might have grudged the money spent on the stupendous *salle des bains* in Versailles before the war ended. Colbert could hardly complain. His estate at Sceaux testified to the impressive growth of his personal fortune during this period. Or, to take the example of Racine: in 1674 the office of a treasurer at Moulins, then vacant, was given to the tragedian who had finally outshone all his rivals. Racine never went to Moulins, but the appointment added to his income by a third and raised his social status. He could marry a lady of property in 1677, which doubled his assets. The author of *Iphigénie* (January 1675) and *Phèdre* (January 1677) no doubt deserved all this. The great war did not hamper him, nor check the interest of court and public in numerous revivals of Corneille's plays and in many new productions. The grand vogue for opera in Paris had also just begun.

During the war, pensions paid by the king to scholars and scientists were reduced. A severe cut affected at least one major project. The Academy of Science's double undertaking, to determine by Jean Picard's method of triangulation the true meridian through Paris 30 leagues north and south of the capital, and to survey this area with modern instruments, had been completed before the war began. Picard and Cassini, with Colbert's support, wished to extend their survey over the rest of France. They were largely held up until the war ended. But other members of the Academy persevered with a systematic dissection and description of animals; Mariotte progressed with his new study of the physiology of plants. Louis XIV may have been fighting the United Provinces while the king of Denmark invaded his ally Sweden; but the great Dutchman Huygens and the great Danish astronomer Roehmer remained in Paris, drew their pensions and continued their researches. Perhaps economies in official largesse at this time explain why one young man of genius failed to win royal patronage. Leibniz, employed by the elector of Mainz, was sent to the French court in 1672 on a curious political mission. The plan which he had to sponsor – that Louis XIV should substitute for his threatened attack on Germany a crusade to Egypt – was an intelligent fantasy which made better sense in the days of Napoleon and Pitt.[7] It had no chance of impressing Pomponne or Louis. He also came to Paris hoping to secure patronage, and to enter a more powerful intellectual circle than could be found in Mainz or Frankfurt. In fact,

---

7   Viz. in 1803 the British government inspired *A Summary Account of Leibnitz's Memoir...to Lewis the Fourteenth, recommending...the Conquest of Egypt, as conducive to the establishing a supreme authority over the Governments of Europe.*

he failed to get a place on Colbert's pension list but made friends with a host of scholars, and these years saw the flowering of his phenomenal talent in mathematics. He learnt much from Huygens, possibly even more from the manuscripts of Pascal's geometry, lent him by members of the Pascal family. He met Arnauld and Malebranche. In 1676 he left France, travelling to England and Holland, and sought out a lens-grinder at the Hague, Spinoza, and a draper of Delft, Leeuwenhoek. The extraordinary microscopic researches of Leeuwenhoek had first struck the learned world's attention during the Anglo-Dutch war, when in 1673 the Royal Society of London began to print his letters safely received from Holland. These exchanges were not disturbed by conditions of war.

Such intellectual giants lived relatively easy lives, because a highly stratified society made or left a niche for them. During the same period the French government had practical reasons for continuing with a scheme already begun. The buildings of the Invalides in Paris were complete enough in 1674 to house the first inmates, the ancient or broken soldiers for whom the state at length felt some responsibility. Discipline was harsh. It was a kind of honourable imprisonment, which met a need by keeping ex-soldiers from begging in the streets. But Louis XIV felt that what had been done was not enough, and he soon commissioned plans for a spectacular new chapel prolonging the unadorned 'Église des Soldats'. Fifteen years later the great dome of Saint-Louis-des-Invalides had settled on the skyline of Paris. The king's priorities, and those of his age, were quite clear.

Inside England and Holland

In 1675 the war spread to a new point on the map. Messina in Sicily was one of the few genuinely prosperous cities of the Spanish empire. A privileged minority enjoyed rights which enabled them simultaneously to disregard the viceroy, exploit the unprivileged and irritate an interesting group of intellectuals and lawyers. Friction increased in 1674 between two parties, known as Blackbirds and Sparrows; the oligarchs or Blackbirds appealed to France, and Colbert pressed on Louis XIV the case for using French naval strength. Ships, supplies and soldiers were sent to Messina, beleaguered by the Spaniards. The fleets led by two great Protestant admirals, Dutch and French, de Ruyter and Duquesne, fought on various occasions in the approaches to the island. De Ruyter died of wounds, and on the whole the advantage rested with Duquesne. But Louis was not Mazarin; his Mediterranean policy remained a sideshow. His army on the Catalonian frontier was a nuisance rather than a danger to the Madrid government. During this phase of the fighting Pomponne's diplomacy mattered more.

The need to stop England from joining the enemy alliance was paramount. Elements in Whitehall were now strongly anti-French, but friction and faction remained the chief traits of English public life and Louis's envoys manoeuvred accordingly. In June 1675 'country' critics, James Duke of York, and the French ambassador were all combined against Lord Treasurer Danby who wanted to help the Dutch. The ambassador turned to Charles: Parliament was prorogued in October 1675 for fifteen months – and the first instalment of a promised new French subsidy was paid in March 1676. In 1677 Louis's victories in Flanders and reports of increased French power at sea inevitably caused acute alarm. Danby responded to the pressure, wanted to satisfy the Commons by a policy designed to check France and, when the new parliamentary session began, secured a satisfactory vote of supply for the navy. He hoped in addition to raise extra troops, calculating that these would strengthen the king's hand both at home and abroad. He seemed to triumph by arranging the marriage of William of Orange and Princess Mary, James's elder daughter. William came to London. Charles sent to Paris their joint terms for peace. But parallel with these moves, the French envoys managed to restrain him by offering a larger subsidy; Danby could not counter this by maintaining a safe majority for the court in the Commons, so that Charles again adjourned Parliament. Louis then rejected the peace proposals of William and Charles. These delaying tactics depended on the ability of the French to exploit a political situation in England which Danby had failed to stabilise on the basis of effective parliamentary management and an anti-French policy. Under the surface there were domestic ferments which the European war simply intensified. France, provided that an active English alliance was not needed as in the spring of 1672, could profit from them with relative ease.

It could also profit from divisions in the United Provinces, provided that Louis asked for less than in the autumn of 1672. The Dutch had drawn together under the menace of invasion, but he could hope to play on the conflict of rival interests as in England, exploiting the smouldering feud between Orange and anti-Orange groups in different provinces and cities. The French did indeed try direct approaches to William. From the end of of 1674 until early in 1677, through the French governor at Maastricht, a secret negotiation was intermittently started and restarted in order to win over the Prince. On each occasion William drew back. Instead, the real task of French diplomats and soldiers was to detach the United Provinces from the hostile alliance, and from William himself. The right mixture of force and blandishment was by no means easily concocted, and the credit for finding it must probably go to Vauban as well as to Pomponne and Louvois. Vauban, in the winter of 1675–6, may have helped to persuade Louvois that French strength and French prospects depended not on sporadic conquests which ranged up to the Dutch frontier but on a serious effort to create an efficient frontier zone in the south; and the campaigning of 1676 and 1677 saw the capture of many places in this area. Vauban felt convinced that such outlying places as Maastricht weakened Louis by locking up valuable manpower in ineffective garrisons. As things turned out, William of Orange's failure to recover Maastricht in 1676 or to take Charleroi in 1677 accentuated the desire of the United Provinces to come to terms. In addition to this, the tireless French civilian administrators managed to put into the field a greatly improved army early in 1677. The regiments were in better shape than in the preceding years. Their victories in Flanders spread alarm everywhere and helped the French diplomats.

Charles II had earlier offered to mediate, in order to cover the risks of his isolated position. As usual, the pope wished to mediate between Catholic states. A congress of diplomats accordingly gathered in the Dutch city of Nijmegen in the course of 1676, and the French government calculated that one possible advantage to be gained by taking part might be a separate Franco-Dutch settlement – a lethal blow to the whole enemy alliance.

As the news of French victories early in 1677 rolled across Belgium to Nijmegen, Louis XIV's proposals sounded very sweet in Dutch ears. He offered to relinquish some of his Flemish conquests in return for compensation elsewhere, possibly in Catalonia and Sicily. He offered Maastricht and, above all, a new commercial agreement with the United Provinces. Bargaining continued while the fortunes of war fluctuated, and with them the demands of the Dutch and the stiffness of William. Every further French advance in Flanders, as we have seen, convinced Danby and other Englishmen that a revival of the Anglo-Dutch partnership of 1668 was required to protect English interests. Louis therefore gave way a little more on points in dispute with the Dutch. He would reduce Colbert's tariff of 1667 by 50, not $33\frac{1}{3}$ per cent; he was finally willing to revert to the tariff of 1664, a striking concession. As the peace interest in Holland grew stronger, the possibility that Charles would fall into line with militant opinion in England mattered less. News from Spain, of a palace revolution in Madrid favourable to Louis, was another useful straw in the wind.

News also came in from a different quarter. Ever since a truce had been arranged in October 1676 between the Poles and Turks, partly with French encouragement, the western courts eagerly canvassed King John Sobieski. His alliance of 1677 with Sweden foreshadowed a Polish attack on Brandenburg. The French tried to involve him in Hungary where there was a chance that the Turks would intervene as well – on the grand scale. In Paris it was a reasonable assumption that the situation in eastern Europe might develop in such a way that either Austria or Brandenburg would be driven to opt for a settlement in Germany.

It is not possible to prove that increasing pressure from the east reacted at once on the west; but whereas in September 1676 Leopold's troops took Philippsburg on the Rhine, in November 1677 they lost Freiburg. Louis and Louvois could balance this last success against the failures of their Swedish ally who lost Stettin a month later. With a keen eye for the interdependence – which their own policies encouraged – of events in all parts of Europe, the advisers of the French king prepared to use the same technique in the following year.

The Achievement of Peace

1678 is the *annus mirabilis* of Louis XIV's reign. His government never blended military strength and diplomatic skill with more remarkable results. The forces in the Netherlands moved early, taking Ypres and Ghent. They at once set the scene for a fresh initiative at Nijmegen. Louis now offered Maastricht to the Dutch, and a commercial treaty on the terms already agreed in 1677. He offered to return a fairly large number of towns, including Ghent, Limburg and Charleroi, to the Spanish Netherlands; either Freiburg or Phillipsburg, but not both, to the emperor; and Lorraine to Duke Charles V, either diminished in size, or with its original boundaries if the French could keep Nancy and the main roads radiating from it. In all other respects he demanded a restoration of the settlements of 1648, which meant that the Germans must recognise French sovereignty in Alsace as enforced by Louis, and that they must give back to Sweden what Sweden had lost during the war. A time limit of a few weeks was attached to the offers.

These were generous to the Dutch, of necessity, but to no one else. They tempted the peace party in Holland to come to terms in spite of the treaties which committed the United Provinces to a common cause. They came close enough to what the Dutch – taking into account the intricate internal balance of political power in the country, with William at odds with the municipalities of Amsterdam, Leiden, Haarlem and their friends elsewhere – would accept for the sake of peace. The issue was doubtful for several weeks but Louis allowed negotiations to continue after his original time limit, set for 10 May, had expired. From the French camp near Ghent, he put pressure on the Hague and Amsterdam, while the impossible situation in London influenced even William of Orange. The mood of the Dutch weighed with the Spanish viceroy in Brussels, who on 3 June declared himself willing to accept the French conditions. Louis had now come within an inch of splitting the opposing alliances. One week later the Austrian, Danish and Brandenburg envoys at Nijmegen publicly protested against Dutch policy as a breach of faith. Three weeks later, the Dutch and Spaniards were ready to sign treaties of peace.

Louis XIV had made the restoration of Sweden's possessions in Germany one of the conditions of his offer *cum* ultimatum to the Empire in April 1678. It did not feature in the clauses of his proposed treaty with the Dutch until a very late stage. His negotiators then abruptly revealed that he planned to hang on to Maastricht and the Flemish towns until Sweden received satisfaction. For the Dutch, this was to screw up the price of peace intolerably and they would not hear of it. William gained support again for continuing the war, on one side of the sea, and Danby on the other. A new Anglo-Dutch treaty was signed in July; but Charles simultaneously discussed another subsidy arrangement with Louis's ambassador in London, a move which was 'leaked' in Amsterdam and the Hague, and weakened the Dutch war-party. The French at Nijmegen meanwhile went to the limit of their instructions in making concessions and on 10 August the Franco-Dutch treaty was at last signed. The Dutch had made their separate peace; Louis had won it from them. The grand alliance of powers, and the new alliance of England and Holland, were both shattered. There was equally little left of Louis XIV's original design of 1672 against the United Provinces but his defeat was masked, his victory manifest.

Fighting continued in Flanders until Spain formally agreed to the surrender of Franche-Comté and of some fifteen towns in the southern Netherlands. France agreed to restore Ghent, Courtrai, Oudenarde and Louvain, as well as the duchy of Limburg and a fortress in Catalonia. It looked like Louis's triumph, but in the circumstances certain Dutch interests differed from William of Orange in thinking the terms satisfactory. They still seemed to leave a respectable barrier between the United Provinces and France, and the threat to the Scheldt estuary from Ghent had been lifted. For apologists of the treaty in Madrid, Spain had at least saved Sicily and Catalonia. Its old Mediterranean empire survived intact, even if the old Burgundian element of the Habsburg empire was shrivelling with melancholy speed before their eyes.

Louis could now have turned his main armament against the German states, but his advisers believed that victory was already within their grasp. Every scrap of evidence suggested that Emperor Leopold could not continue the struggle without Dutch support. After a fruitless summer campaign in the Black Forest area, a last despairing Habsburg attempt to assemble a new army broke down completely in October 1678. In the Rhineland war weariness was acute, and everywhere in Germany the civilian population hated the princes who raised troops and quartered them in countrysides or towns outside their own territories – invoking the emperor's authority to do so. Equally disliked were recent Imperial edicts which barred the import of French goods into the Empire. Farther east the Hungarian rebellion reached a fresh and dangerous climax. Yet the months of delay before Leopold's envoys signed their treaty with France in February 1679 are deeply significant in European history. All the cards seemed stacked in favour of Paris, and against Vienna; none the less delay occurred. For the war had seen the growth of a party at Leopold's court which was dedicated to the repulse of France. It was a creed as well as a policy. Franz Lisola was dead, but from 1673 this interest had a far tighter grip on Viennese political councils than in the 1660s. It inherited the old Habsburg hatred of the Bourbons, and the old obsession with the Spanish succession problem. It assumed in practice a hereditary Habsburg right to the elective Imperial title. It feared that Louis XIV aimed at this supreme title and at power in Germany. It wanted to save, while Louis continued to dismember, the Empire. It wanted to rescue Franche-Comté and Lorraine, and to protect the four electorates of the Rhineland. It was reinforced by the exiled Lorraine court, now headed by young Charles V who passionately wanted to recover his inheritance. Leopold sympathised deeply. He may have combined irresolution with obstinacy, but hated Louis XIV with absolute consistency for the last thirty years of his life. In general, French diplomats and statesmen did not underrate this element at the Viennese court, and they nearly always overestimated Vienna's practical ability to mount a sufficient armament in Germany. Their misjudgment on that crucial point influenced French policy in Europe until 1688.

The collapse of the alliance and Austrian military setbacks finally forced the Habsburg envoys at Nijmegen to come to terms. They exceeded their instructions to do so before a new French ultimatum expired. They surrendered on 3 February 1679, and Leopold had to acquiesce. The militants in Vienna protested in vain. This treaty confirmed the dominance of Louis XIV in western Germany. It left outstanding the question of the Swedish empire. The Danish invasion of Scania had petered out after 1676 but the struggle for Pomerania continued. Accordingly one body of French troops entered Cleves and Mark, directly threatening the elector of Brandenburg. Marshal Créqui left Sedan with another, and moved forward to the gates of Minden. This set the stage for treaties of peace which were practically dictated by Louis XIV at St Germain and Fontainebleau to the princes of northern Europe. They restored Pomerania and the lands of Bremen and Verden to Sweden, apart from a few small shavings of territory – tiny consolation prizes for Sweden's enemies. The position would have been still further consolidated if Pomponne had carried through his design for a triple alliance between France, Sweden and Denmark, but this broke down. It was replaced by Louis's new treaty with Brandenburg (of 25 October), promising the elector aid if he were attacked and a subsidy for ten years, putting the lands and fortresses of Brandenburg at the disposal of French troops when necessary, and assuring the king of the elector's support in the affairs of Germany and Poland. Similar agreements were made or renewed with Saxony and Bavaria. It was a marvellous diplomatic construction for the assertion of French interests in central Europe. It was also the masterpiece of Pomponne, who fell from power a few weeks later for a reason that had nothing to do with these matters. The arrangements were solidified by a cluster of royal or princely marriages: between the Dauphin and Elizabeth of Bavaria, between Philip of Orleans and 'Liselotte' of the Palatinate, and between Marie-Louise of Orleans and Carlos II of Spain. Dynastically, the survival of Carlos was a misfortune for Louis XIV, while at long last Leopold had a son and heir (born in July 1678, later Emperor Joseph I) who survived the first few months of infancy. All the same, this was the glittering climax of French influence in the framework of European politics.

'O Achilles!'

Twenty-five years earlier the ending of internal disorder in France had generated a mixture of submissiveness and gratitude to the monarchy in many circles. Catholic and Protestant clergy alike could plausibly expound the subject's necessary obedience to God's viceregent. Any theory of limited obedience, to them, involved total disharmony in the state. But contemporary education was classical as much as Christian. Artists and literary men visualised Louis as Apollo, driving his horses with the courage needed to crush the monsters – of the Fronde. The Most Christian King was equally Apollo; his emblem of the sun and its irresistible rays and his proud motto of *nec pluribus impar*, in association with the letter 'L', were placed on countless frontispieces and textiles, and on the walls or furnishings of royal buildings. It was the theme of innumerable entertainments. The literate classes in France matched this by an increasing tendency to refer to the king in language not only of submission; their formulae of adulation were wrought into a fixed habit of mind. Conceivably this might have been checked by real military set-backs in the 1670s, but instead the triumph of 1678 was exploited to place the person of the monarch above criticism. In a very real sense, God's viceregent was now deified. Louis's peculiar glory in the eyes of his subjects at that moment consisted in frustrating a powerful coalition, laying down terms for a peace, imposing them on one opponent after another without permitting any alteration, and in making sacrifices to defend an unfortunate ally; with the prospect of future advances still before him. The achievement, and the prestige of the achievement, were such that they tended to make the monarchy impervious to its own defects, and they confirmed the primacy of foreign wars and foreign policy over domestic problems in the outlook of French statesmen, which was another notable feature of the régime.

'O Achilles, how fortunate you were to be praised by Homer!' It was the duty of artists and literary men to eulogise the king. As Racine put it, referring to the Dictionary on which the *Académie Française* had been working for so many years: 'Every word in the language, every syllable, is precious to us, because we consider them as the instruments which must serve the glory of our august protector.' The truth is that the Academy wasted very valuable energy on a continuous series of panegyrics for the king its master. Significantly, two of the greatest men of letters in France were appointed Historiographers Royal in 1677 – Boileau and Racine, 'the farmers-general of Mount Helicon'. They regarded it as a step forward in their careers, pledged themselves to the task of recording the triumphs of Louis XIV for posterity, and assumed that this was the loftiest possible subject-matter for literature. Bossuet, the Dauphin's tutor, had been coming to a conclusion parallel with theirs. To a wide circle of friends and disciples, as well as to the young prince, a work later known as the *Politique tirée des propres paroles de l'Écriture Sainte* was distilled. His axioms were taken for granted by a majority in France around the year 1680.[8] 'The whole state is in the person of the prince.' 'In him is the will of the whole people.'

8   For an account stressing contemporary discontents, and discounting official propaganda, see *New Cambridge Modern History*, V, pp. 245–6. However, the monarchy's strength at this period – reinforced by the instruments of propaganda at its disposal – seems the point of greater importance.

The Ottoman Empire and its Impact on Europe, 1672–88

Poland and John Sobieski

In 1672 Louis XIV made his long-prepared attack on the United Provinces, but soon turned against Belgium and west Germany as well. In the same year the Ottoman government assaulted Poland, and then became involved on one front after another. Campaigns in southern Poland merged into campaigns against the tsar. Next the sultan intervened in Habsburg Hungary and finally struck at Vienna in 1683. In the east as in the west, particular objectives mattered less to the strongest power than the general activity of war.

There are few signs that a revival of Moslem religious fervour lay behind this Ottoman militancy. Instead, a series of powerful grand vezirs regarded the conduct of war as their natural responsibility. It won them the prestige which helped to maintain them in office. It employed gainfully, and controlled, the vast military apparatus of the state. It created a grand lottery which was the obvious avenue of promotion for rising men who stepped into the shoes of those killed or disgraced. It disciplined unruly marcher principalities and unstable frontiers. These were internal stresses in the Ottoman empire, but it was a matter of European significance that Ahmed Köprülü – after the long struggle with Venice over Crete had ended – should have decided in 1670 and 1671 not to intervene in Hungary on the side of the rebels against Leopold, and kept the sultan's forces east of the Carpathians. The Ottoman involvement in Ruthenia and the Ukraine left the Habsburg lands relatively unembarrassed on their Hungarian front for nearly ten years. Louis XIV was robbed of a potential ally strong enough to put terrible pressure on Louis's German opponents; Ottoman intervention against Austria at this date would have altered the course of German history. On the other hand, Ottoman intervention in the Ukraine possibly mattered less because by then the main trends in eastern Europe were irreversible.

After the truce of Andrusovo in 1667 with Russia, the Polish government was too weak to restore control over its share of the Ukraine. The Muscovites had already made strenuous efforts to build a fortified line between the middle Volga and the upper Donetz. The Austrians and Magyars maintained defences large and small from Croatia to the Danube below Pressburg, and in Upper Hungary. The Poles, by contrast, now failed to rebuild their ruined strong-points. When French engineers examined Kamieniec-Podolski in 1671, for example, they admired the marvellous natural advantages of the site but foresaw that the fortifications were too poor to resist the Turks for more than a week. Yet this town, in Podolia and a few miles from the Dniester, was an important commercial centre (particularly for Armenian traders) as well as the military gateway to Ruthenia. Even more serious, the Poles failed to devise any way of holding the Tartars in check. Some Cossacks still collaborated, but their hetman (now Peter Doroshenko) was more often friend than foe to the Crimean Tartars. And the Tartars, whether from the Crimean peninsula or from pastures farther west, had little difficulty in raiding across the Ukraine and into Polish Podolia and Volhynia.[1] Except in periods of heavy rain, they rode with their numerous remounts swiftly over the open country between palisaded townships, seized cattle and country-men, and retreated again. The Poles lacked strength to resist them, in spite of the energy shown by men like John Sobieski in leading occasional counter-expeditions. Their administration was unable to raise taxes and forces quickly enough so that reinforcements from Poland proper or Lithuania, if they came at all, came too late in each campaigning season to help the frontier lords.

The Muscovites, rather than the Poles, threatened Doroshenko's liberty of action. In June 1669 he imitated earlier hetmen by deciding to acknowledge Ottoman suzerainty. Ahmed Köprülü welcomed this approach, and also tried to tidy up local confusion in the Crimea by appointing a new Khan, Selim, one of the most talented of the ancient Ghiraj dynasty, a poet as well as a man of action. By 1671 Doroshenko and Selim were pushing raiding parties all over the Ukraine and deep into Poland. The Polish commander, Sobieski, retorted with a spectacular counter-attack in the late autumn, retaking points on the Dniester and the Bug, and harassing the raiders as they withdrew homewards with their haul. The Ottoman government at Adrianople began to prepare for an expedition on the grand scale in the following year, to be led by the sultan himself. From that moment until the end of the century the problem of resisting or

[1] See map 2, p. 25 above, and map 4, p. 232 below.

repulsing the Ottoman armament, with all its political complications, perplexed Christian Europe.

Some of the consequences of this are of great interest. The number of diplomatic missions sent out from Warsaw and Moscow to the courts of western Europe, bidding for aid, increased notably. They foreshadowed the alliance of Muscovy with Poland, Austria and Venice in 1686, the mission of Tsar Peter I to the west in 1697, and the closer association of the Russians with the European diplomatic system. The Turkish war gave John Sobieski his chance of winning the Polish crown and enabled him to impose the necessary minimum unity on the state for a few years. His achievement was significant, even if short-lived and carried through by only the narrowest of margins. The popes also, after a period of fading political influence, successfully revived the old idea of a crusade. For the last time they played a positive role in international politics. Their nuncios at the Polish and Austrian courts, using the funds which Catholic clergy were able to raise when Rome requested them to do so, helped in persuading at least some politicians in both countries to give priority to the idea that Islam must be beaten back. The clash of Moslem and Christian became sharper once more, at a moment when the ideological venom of Catholics and Protestants recovered some of its earlier potency in the last twenty years of the century.

A first-class domestic crisis in Poland and the Turkish war were completely entwined between 1671 and 1674, but one element in this confusion was the instinctive view of many Poles that the former mattered more than the latter. The Turkish assault in no way diminished the friction between the commander-in-chief, Sobieski, and the government which he had opposed since the election of Michael Wiśnowiecki as king in 1669. Sobieski's enemies were reluctant to rally behind him in order to strengthen both the country's armament and his personal power. Moreover, the enormous area of Poland and Lithuania made it impossible to focus attention on any one external danger, coming from one quarter only. In the north, men feared the Swedes' return across the Baltic to take advantage of Brandenburg's involvement in the western war. Or they dreaded another march by the tsar into Lithuania. The Turkish and Tartar pressure was not only seasonal, it was diffused and intermittent. It could be seen that the Ottoman government had difficulties in maintaining an immensely long line of communications, difficulties in controlling Wallachia and Moldavia, difficulties with the Crimean khan. A massive Turkish attack in 1672 was followed by their more lethargic effort in 1673, which ended with a Polish victory. In 1674 the Ukraine and Podolia suffered fire and sword, but not Poland proper. Whatever the losses of territory or manpower in the south, a man in Warsaw or Vilna might well think that the defence was sufficient for its purpose.

Early in the year 1672 a Diet at the capital broke up in confusion, unable to agree on any measures for the country's defence. The bitterness of a second assembly, in June, with Sobieski present, only died down with the arrival of grim news from the south. The Turks appeared on the Dniester, crossed it, and took Kamieniec-Podolski almost effortlessly; they and the Tartars reached Lvov in August. Sobieski launched an effective counter-raid conciding with the negotiation of a truce. The terms were grievous to the Poles, glorious for the sultan. He kept Podolia and Kamieniec-Podolski, insisted on the annual payment of a hefty tribute, and secured control of the Ukraine for Doroshenko. How long this truce would last was anybody's guess; both sides tended to see it as an insurance for a limited period. Immediately, new disorders broke out in Poland. Sobieski organised a 'confederation' to confront the forces which had delayed coming into contact with the Turks, and in Lithuania the chief officeholders also banded together. The pattern of these events was more or less repeated in 1673. Sobieski reached Warsaw in February. The threat of civil war was exploited with cliffhanging virtuosity to prevent actual violence from breaking out and the parleys were at white heat for a few weeks, until King Michael's party and Sobieski's reached an agreement which dissolved the 'confederation'. But the nuncio wrote very gloomily to Rome just then that God could only have permitted such a monstrous body politic to exist in order to reveal His omnipotence in preserving it. He believed that the Poles would do best to ratify their shameful peace with the Turks. Instead, the truce broke down and for the third year running Sobieski won victories in the autumn. His military triumph at Chotin on the Dniester coincided, almost to the day, with Michael's death in November.

As in 1648 and 1669 (and again in 1697) the election of a new Polish king was a European concern. While in Rome, when a pope died, the Catholic powers could at best mobilise 'French' or 'Spanish' parties of cardinals to propose an Italian candidate of whom they approved for the papacy, in Poland the chances of securing the election of a foreign prince always seemed higher. Every reigning house in Europe regarded this crown as a glittering speculation, given the surprising uncertainties of Polish politics. For Austria, France and Brandenburg the upshot of the struggle in 1674 was, of course, a deadly serious matter. It could weaken or strengthen their hands for the war in Germany.

As in 1669, Vienna championed Charles of Lorraine, and Paris a member of the Condé family. Berlin suggested one of the elector's sons, Moscow the tsar. The foreign envoys at Warsaw prepared to spend large sums of money, to offer large numbers of men for the struggle against the Turks, to use the flowers of their Latin rhetoric to orate before assemblies of Polish politicians, and to whisper to them privately with their hands in their purses. It was John Sobieski who carried the day. After the victory at Hotin he enjoyed the prestige of an indispensable war leader, and showed skill in wooing support while the elaborate procedure for an election got under way. The so-called Convocation Diet met; he pleaded the national emergency for his absence on the southern frontier. Before the final Election Diet began at Warsaw, he published an eloquent appeal in which his countrymen were warned against any candidate who might be tempted to buy peace with the Turks on shameful terms, in order to impose absolute authority over a truncated Poland. He asked for a ruler who aimed to keep the whole country intact under the sway of its ancient laws. In May 1674 he reached Warsaw to attend the Diet. Soon, as Lorraine and the Hohenzollern prince (and another prominent candidate, Philip William of Pfalz-Neuburg) lost ground, their supporters moved into the Sobieski camp. Tsar Alexei's envoy never had a chance to win his master a following. The other principal ambassadors were made to realise that Sobieski alone could block an election of the foreign candidate whom each of them most feared, whether French or German. Accordingly Sobieski, long known as a member of the 'French' party which had backed Condé princes for the Polish succession, at last became its candidate. There is some evidence that he persuaded Louis's ambassador of his ability to come to terms with the grand vezir. Poland, it was hinted, could then intervene in Germany or Hungary against the emperor. There is clearer evidence that he promised the ambassador, who was bishop of Marseilles, to support his nomination as a cardinal. This sort of bargaining continued behind the scenes while the Polish nobility at Warsaw, deputies from the many local assemblies, struggled towards their fateful decision. By a miracle, it seemed, doubts were resolved and John III Sobieski was elected on 12 June 1674. What many had feared, a double election of two rivals, did not occur.

For the next ten years Sobieski was powerful enough to subdue his Polish rivals and enemies, and therefore powerful enough to carry out a diplomacy which defended essential Polish interests. He steered most of the triennial assemblies of the Diet to a peaceful conclusion. He balanced prudently between the Habsburgs and the Bourbons, before allying with Leopold in the face of a Turkish onslaught in 1683. But he could not create a stronger royal authority in Poland with a firmer constitutional basis than his personal prestige. When he and his wife tried to gain a hereditary title by scheming for the election of their son Jacob as king in his father's lifetime, or by seizing the duchy of East Prussia, or by angling for the kingship of Hungary, the opposition quickly swelled. After 1683 the number of Diets ruptured by the *liberum veto* (see above, pp. 41–2) increased, and faction became uncontrollable. In the last years of his life the monarchy in the Polish commonwealth was a cipher again.

In 1674 this gloomy future was happily unforeseen. The king moved south in the autumn with larger forces than in the past, and spent the winter restoring Polish positions in parts of the Ukraine. Turkish-held Podolia was still firmly wedged between these strongholds and Ruthenia and it gradually became clear to Sobieski that he would never be able to manoeuvre freely in Poland, or deal with other European powers to any advantage, unless he gave way to the Turks. Great military activity in 1675 and 1676, with the Tartars moving up again as far as Lvov ('they went up and down scattered in little troops of twenty and thirty men', wrote Laurence Hyde, an English ambassador in the city 'whereby they did the more mischief, because the country did not in that manner know them from others'),[2] and with Sobieski engaged much farther down the Dniester valley, ended with a truce signed in October 1676. Poland ceded Podolia and surrendered all claims on land which lay east of it; the sultan did not hold out for the payment of an annual tribute. The Diet at Warsaw ratified the truce in 1677.

The Fate of the Ukraine

Among the reasons for this long span of five years which it took the sultan to bring Poland to terms were his concern for the Ukraine, and the tsar's entry into the war. One of the greatest themes of the century is Muscovy's advance southwards, and since 1667 the subjection of Ukrainian lands east the Dnieper had been pressed home. Officials appeared, taxes were imposed and the Peryslavl agreement of 1654 was reenacted in terms which accorded with Moscow interests, not with those of the various hetmen. Doroshenko's claims to dominance and his appeals to Istanbul led the tsar to protest to the sultan and to oppose Doroshenko. In the background a religious element counted for something here. The Turks were aware that Greeks, Romanians and Serbs occasionally visualised the tsar as a potential champion of Balkan Orthodox peoples. The numerous visits of Greek clergy to Moscow brought Alexei into contact with them. Rulers of the Danubian principalities, when deposed by the Ottoman government, also begged for help. More pressing was the initiative of Muscovite soldiers and officials in the Ukraine who regarded Doroshenko's destruction as a practical necessity. They had no intention of being dislodged from Kiev either by him or his Ottoman overlord. Accordingly, while Turkish forces fanned out farther east in 1674 to assist

2 *Correspondence of Clarendon and Rochester* (ed. S. W. Singer 1828), i, p. 600.

the hetman, Russian troops moved west over the Dnieper in order to besiege his headquarters in Chigirin. Two years later the place was taken, and the hetman captured. This set the scene for a direct encounter between the stronger powers, and while in one half of Europe men waited breathlessly to learn the fate of such besieged cities as Maastricht and Ghent, in the other the future seemed to hinge on the ability of a Muscovite garrison in Chigirin to resist the Turkish army under a new grand vezir, Kara Mustapha. In 1677 he was driven back. In 1678 he triumphantly entered what had become a shambles.

Both parties at length realised that they would gain little by continuing the struggle in remote and ruined regions, and bargaining began. It took a tortuous course but ended with an agreement reached in the Crimea in January 1681, and ratified in Adrianople by the Sultan in April 1682. The concessions were equally balanced. The Russians accepted the Dnieper as their frontier, except for Kiev, while the Turks lost their Ukrainian puppet ruler and undertook not to put garrisons in the wide area between the Dnieper and the river Bug. Moscow, therefore, could not hope to stretch out overland towards the Christian peoples of the lower Danube. The Sultan could not challenge Russian dominance in the Ukraine east of the Dnieper. The two great empires had met, and for the time accepted a stalemate at the expense of others.

Ukrainian historians have a phrase for this period: they call it 'the Ruin'. Their country had finally been partitioned and devastated. The continual movement of raiders and soldiers was matched by civilian migrations hither and thither. One of these crossed from west to east in 1674–6 ahead of the Turks. A little later there is evidence that poor conditions beyond the Dnieper brought people west again. Later still things slowly settled down at a low level; under Hetman Ivan Mazepa (1687–1706) there were churches built or reconstructed.

At the same time Polish Catholic culture still influenced Orthodox Kiev. Some of those educated here continued to play an important role in the Muscovy to which the city was joined in 1667. They could borrow from Roman authorities – in theology, ecclesiastical history and methods of exposition – in formulating judgments which remained essentially Orthodox. Their finest preachers imitated the style of Catholic orators. The sermons of Lazarus Baranovich, teacher at the Collegium and Metropolitan of Chernigov (northeast of Kiev) from 1657 to 1680, apparently deserve the epithet 'baroque'. One of his pupils was Simon of Polotsk, who moved from Lithuania to Moscow to become the most fashionable of progressive churchmen there, Alexei's favourite preacher and tutor of his children. For their part, some Orthodox clergy in the Ukraine deplored the Metropolitan of Kiev's recognition, in 1686, of the superior jurisdiction of the Moscow Patriarch. It was another sign of the growing Russian presence, like the Tsar's garrison in the city. Further west the general picture changes again. The Orthodox in surviving Polish lands, such as Volhynia and Galicia, lost touch with their co-religionaries elsewhere, and the Uniate bishops (pp. 27, 30 above) enjoyed John Sobieski's enthusiastic support in putting pressure on all clergy, brotherhoods and monasteries to obey them. Masterful Joseph Shumliansky, for thirty years Uniate Bishop of Lvov, led this movement. The Orthodox who were not Uniate disappeared.

The Prospects of Muscovy

When the Turks marched north in 1672, Grand Vezir Ahmed Köprülü had one reason for thinking that the empire of Muscovy was desperately weak and unsettled: the terrible upheaval of a great tract of country, Stenka Razin's rebellion of 1667–71. Comparable with developments in the Ukraine after 1648 this appears as another widespread protest against the forward movement of governmental power and the encroaching discipline of landlords over a subject population, Razin began as a successful outlaw who built a fortified settlement on the river Don. Taking his followers across to the Volga he reached the Caspian to prey on trade routes between Persia and Astrakhan. By 1670 he and his captains were strongly installed in Astrakhan itself. The tsar vainly issued pardons and warnings. The matter became serious when Razin brought his ships and men upstream again. He was here on the rim of more settled country, but the response to his appeal for support was a widespread and violent repudiation of all authority, a spasm which shook larger towns and tiny settlements in an area stretching up the Volga to Nijni Novgorod and westwards as far as the river Oka. Smaller outbreaks occurred beyond Moscow and even in the farthest north. In some places, Cossack bands arrived to raise the peasantry. Beyond them, rumours of the most varied kind were incitement enough for the inhabitants. Razin named his enemies, the enemies of all good men: they were government officers (but not the tsar personally), the clergy and the rich. And the good men everywhere rose up, slaughtering their local oppressors and the agents of oppressors. Action came first, ideas mattered less; but many people believed that the tsar's eldest son, who had died early in 1670, was really in hiding and would emerge to bring justice and sweetness to the land. A pretender conveniently appeared. After fearful losses weariness set in, and the disorders gradually died down. Government violence replaced and perhaps surpassed even that of the rebels. Razin was captured in

April 1671 and executed in June, while the Cossack captain at Astrakhan lost the town in September. For the rest of Europe, this was no doubt a remote convulsion, but the sheer scale of the rising nevertheless made it memorable. Stenka Razin, 'Little Stephen', passed into Russian mythology, and neither Peter the Great nor Catherine the Great could forget the imprint which he left on the popular mind in this part of their empire: they had to confront rebellions no less serious along the Volga.

All the same, Russia progressed under Tsars Alexei (1645–76) and Theodore (1676–82). If Stenka Razin declaimed against the government, the rich and the clergy, it was because they all pushed on with the work of settlement. Exploitation and subjection went hand in hand. To take an example from the Volga country: the old Tartar principality of Kazan had long been ruled by Russian governors who took orders from an office in Moscow – the 'prikaz of the palace of Kazan' – which remained the responsible administrative organ for this region until the days of Peter. The governors supervised the country side and its garrisons from their newly built stone citadel in the city of Kazan. The original Moslem communities, with their own local laws and jurisdiction, were permitted to survive. But between these and the unsettled land was placed a line of fortified points, linked by a strip of open ground cut through the forest. Gradually the barrier was advanced southwards. On the right bank of the Volga, below Kazan, new defences were constructed stage by stage, in 1645, 1664, 1667 and 1684. On the other side of the Volga work began in 1680 for another barrier, equally designed to protect new settlements. These were often founded by monasteries, indispensable agents of Russian economic expansion. For this very reason, no doubt, the tsar's government and the ecclesiastical authorities installed many new monasteries in the middle Volga region after 1650. Their business was not the contemplative life, but plantation.

Along parts of the moving frontier, military colonists were given dwellings and small pieces of ground in new townships. Unattached persons appeared with them. So, above all, did laymen and churchmen with assignments of land granted by the tsar. These were preceded, accompanied, or followed by a host of fugitive peasants, because the serf-laws' fierce discipline in older provinces was continually balanced by the lure of unsettled and allegedly fertile countryside to the south and east. Many found employment with the new planters. Their former lords failed to trace their whereabouts, the new ones harboured and exploited them, in due course invoking the severity of the regulations against fugitive labourers. Others accordingly fled farther on, into less governed country. But steadily the combined authority of tsar and landowner caught up with the tide of emigrants, while the failure of the great rising in 1670–1 went far to strengthen the social framework which the legal code of 1649 had formally sanctioned. The harshness of the régime, and its material achievement in enlarging the area of plantation, are both beyond dispute. Other vast areas remained unworked, but the islands of settlement became more numerous in a wide arc swinging round old Muscovy from the Dnieper to the Volga.

In this process the extent of the government's dominance over society marks a fundamental difference between Muscovy and Poland or Lithuania. The boyars and all the tsar's 'servants' had none of the 'rights' of Polish noblemen. For example, he could employ whom he wished; it was therefore easier for humble men of ability to become influential. The 700 or 800 officials of the Moscow *prikazy* resembled the jurists and lawyers of western Europe in the way they used their talents to win preferment. The seniors were given places in the Duma, a select assembly of nobles occasionally summoned by the tsar. Other officials of the same kind, and military commanders of varied origin, helped to govern the provinces. Such a personnel was lacking in Poland, where crown appointments always went to the territorial nobility, or to bishops who belonged to the same class. But in one respect, Russian and Polish developments converged. The distinction between *pomestiya* and *votchiny*, between revocable service grants of land assigned by the tsar, and inherited property, gradually dwindled in Russia. Land-holders more universally became landowners, with a hereditary right to what had earlier been allotted to them while serving the state. This signified the growth of a more firmly fixed interest which the government could no longer control or dislodge. The experiments of Ivan the Terrible in the sixteenth century in redistributing property would not be repeated. It also meant that the military drawbacks of the old system of land grants were recognised. What the state required instead was higher taxation in order to pay a standing army. The landowning interest grew stronger, the administration therefore held out for the fullest possible payment of state taxes by the subject population, and a long series of surveys and censuses proves that it got its way. This did not occur in Poland, where a far higher proportion of the various forms of tribute or tax paid by the unprivileged went to the land-lords. The predecessors of Peter I insisted on the subjection of the masses. They would leave it for him to insist once again on the service obligations of the more powerful elements in society.

Progress, or even change, in commerce and crafts was less evident at this date. The main provincial centres of the past retained pre-eminence as markets for corn, salt, leather and fur, towns like Vologda on the trade route between Moscow and Archangel, and Nijni Novgorod and Kazan. The fine churches of Jaroslavl, mostly built before 1650, are some measure of its citizens' wealth. Moscow, with a population of 200,000 ideally situated to profit from the waterways of the country, always produced and consumed on the grand scale. But foreign trade probably stood still. Between 1650 and 1690 the number of ships using the port of Archangel, and the amount of customs revenue raised there, did not alter. Ordyn Naschokin, the statesman advising Alexei between 1661–7, clearly aimed to increase the Russian share in trade passing through Sweden's Baltic possessions. His bargaining did not give his countrymen easier access to the sea, while his tariff of 1667 was more a hindrance than a help. It stifled business for all-comers. Similarly, it seems that Russian merchant interests persuaded the tsar to treat foreign traders and fortune-hunters more rigorously than earlier on, without being able to take their place. The English Muscovy Company lost its privilege in 1649. Englishmen complained that Dutchmen gained accordingly, but around 1670 the great foreign merchants in Moscow, men like Peter Marselis, John van Sweeden and David Backarach – importers of munitions, exporters of grain, founders of iron-forges, manufacturers of glass – all died, and their successors operated on a more modest scale. A promising development had faded out, and here too it would be necessary for Peter I to make a fresh start.

The government's preoccupation with war in the south after 1672 may be partly responsible for the hiatus. When Alexei died in 1676 foreign observers in Moscow feared that the old guard of boyars would return to power, that foreign soldiers would be dismissed and foreign merchants relegated to Archangel. Then in the autumn news of the Turkish-Polish treaty suggested that an Ottoman armament would soon directly threaten Russian interests in the Ukraine. (A young Genevan, François Lefort, later Tsar Peter's trusted adviser, had arrived in Russia some months earlier but despaired of finding employment; yet by the end of 1676 he was more hopeful of getting a post in the army – he would surely be needed.) It proved impossible to reverse Alexei's policy; the fateful Ukrainian campaigns continued. After the Turkish victory at Chigirin in 1678 men anticipated the fall of Kiev. They feared the worst. Against this background a major military reform was put in hand. There had been, ever since the 1630s, a tripartite division of the tsar's army between the old 'service' levies, the old *streltsy* or permanent guards, and troops organised on Swedish and German models with the hierarchy of officers familiar in western Europe. A fair proportion of these officers were foreign soldiers of fortune. The general appointed in 1678, Vasily Galitzin, tried to apply the western system of discipline and command to the *streltsy* and feudal levies. Early in 1682 this reform reached a further stage. The government decided to decree the formal abolition of *mestnichestvo*, originally a strict order of precedence for families in attendance on the tsar, which had come in course of time to have a much wider significance: it meant that too often men declined to serve under those whose fathers and forefathers had ranked below their own. The significance of this challenge to conservative instincts is not easy to measure, nor can one be certain of its bearing on the disorders and intrigues which followed Tsar Theodore's death a few months later. Certainly Galitzin triumphed. For the next seven years this progressive politician, with his ready sympathy for men and books hailing from the west, with his desire to advance Russian forces southward through the steppe to the Crimea, dominated the government. The failure of his Crimean expeditions of 1687 and 1689 led to his downfall, and Peter the Great's apprenticeship as a statesman would in turn be profoundly influenced by the long crisis of the Ottoman wars in Europe.

The Ottoman Empire

That crisis depended on the power of successive grand vezirs to mobilise enormous forces in the Ottoman empire, the oldest and most solidly based in Europe. The United Provinces, or the Swedish dominion, were parvenus by comparison with the Ottoman state. Reserves of manpower from Asia backed Turkish strength in Europe, manpower from Europe was available in Asia; but the sultans' own 'eastern problem' gave no trouble while the Persian empire declined rapidly in the later seventeenth century. Moreover, the feudal element in Ottoman society had always been reinforced by a large standing army. The fief-holders collected tithe or tribute of various sorts; the permanent forces, Janissaries and others, were maintained in Europe by heavy taxation of the non-Moslems, a great majority of the subject population. The army was too crushing a burden to allow economic resources to be developed which would have made it less of a burden, but had the prestige and strength which assured Ottoman dominance. The technological, economic and administrative superiority of certain western states already looks clear enough. All the same, the Turks were not more backward than their neighbours on the land frontier between Dalmatia and the Crimea. As military engineers or irrigators, they were probably more competent. They attracted useful 'renegades' from Italy and France, just as Scotsmen and Germans went to Poland and Russia. They enjoyed the advantages of a more effective autocratic power over a wider area than the individual governments opposed to them, while since 1660 the internal stability of Ottoman rule was maintained by Mehmed and Ahmed Köprülü. The mere tenure of office by Ahmed for fifteen years (minus one day) appears an extraordinary achievement, the reward of continued success at home and abroad, and the sign of administrative continuity. After the siege of Vienna in 1683 this index reads differently: there were twelve grand vezirs between that year and the treaty of Carlowitz in 1699. Ahmed had won Crete, parts of Hungary and Podolia. His successors lost the Morea, nearly all Hungary and Podolia. But the Ottoman repulse of the Russians in 1711 and of the Austrians in 1736–9 refutes the too simple assumption that some great transformation occurred in the Ottoman empire when Kara Mustapha followed Ahmed Köprülü as grand vezir. It is easier to count his blunders between 1676 and 1683 as a politician or soldier than to discover any deep-seated change in Ottoman government and society at the time. These remained a compound which hardly altered for decades.

The working of the Ottoman system of management can be illustrated at various points. When the emperor surrendered a small part of his Hungarian territory by the treaty of 1664 (see above, p. 129), officials at Istanbul duly filed a schedule which gives a blue-print for the new régime there. It is a faithful copy of the arrangements which long existed in Turkish Hungary. The old landowners were eliminated, and the land was parcelled out between Moslem fief-holders: they are entitled to take such and such tribute from the subject population, which in addition will pay to the state such and such taxes on goods and sales, plus a capitation. Or, to take a different element in the system. Mehmed Köprülü brought the principality of Transylvania to heel in 1660, and raised the annual tribute from 15,000 to 40,000 gold crowns. Accordingly, every year a special embassy made its way to Istanbul where a permanent legation resided in the 'Transylvanian House'. It wrestled with the often ticklish problem of exchange (because the Turks insisted on gold), handed over the money due, and received a receipt. Supplementary payments – like the 600 wagons and 1800 oxen required in 1678 for use in the Ukraine – and bribes for officials, completed the annual tax. At this heavy cost Transylvanians retained self-government, the Estates and nobility survived, while Calvinist Prince Michael Apafi ruled for over twenty-five years (1661–88). Although the Turks intervened much more frequently in Bucharest and Jasi to depose and appoint the princes, the Danubian principalities similarly made annual payments at Istanbul and kept their ancient class structure.

At the same time no one could fail to observe the heavy Moslem pressure on the whole Balkan empire, buttressing the Ottoman government. In some parts of Bulgaria, Serbia and Albania, Islam conquered whole districts. Turkish emigrants settled in eastern Bulgaria, Islamised Albanians moved into Macedonia, and many of the Moslems who appeared in the towns of Hungary came from Serbia. Along the great military route which led from Istanbul to Sofia,

Belgrade and Buda the mosques and baths and schools in the cities were the visible signs of this Moslem penetration, due in the first place to the sultan's dominance, but maintained also by preachers and teachers of the faith. No one, also, could fail to heed the lesson which this taught: that conversion was the gateway to a career in government service, as in Catholic Austria, Anglican England after 1660, and increasingly (for Huguenots) in France during the same period. It was, above all, in Albania and Serbia that the régime successfully recruited volunteers who left their homes, renounced the Christian faith of their fathers and aimed high. The once notorious Ottoman institution of *devshirme*, the conscription of Christian boys for the Janissaries and other bodies, counted for little after 1650; but the entry of Serbs, Bosnians and Albanians into the personnel of government still helped to broaden the base of Turkish dominance over their vast empire. One fairly well-documented example of this concerns a man named Papović,[3] a shepherd from the Bosnian-Montenegrin frontier, born about 1627, who went off to Sarajevo to serve the Turkish provincial governor. By 1672 he had secured a post at Istanbul and the patronage of the grand vezir. In 1675 he was farming the poll tax imposed on 12,000 Christian house-holders in Cyprus. In 1676 his duties involved impounding for the sultan the estates of wealthy deceased persons. 'Osman Pasha' now rose from one high post to another. He was governor in turn of Syria, Anatolia and Egypt. He married a daughter of the Grand Vezir Kara Mustapha. Like a number of other converts of this type, he is believed to have built both a mosque and an Orthodox church at his birthplace. Like almost every other high official he got into trouble on occasion, was moved at frequent intervals from place to place, and was sometimes down-graded. He died fighting in Hungary in 1686.

Osman's conversion, his collection of the poll tax in Cyprus, and his chapel in Bosnia, together symbolise the complex relation of Orthodox to Ottoman interests in the Turkish empire. The sultan is, on one hand, the grand oppressor of Greeks and other Christian peoples. He denies them freedom, he crushes them with his taxes and crude administration. Yet he also formally recognises by the issue of imperial patents the Greek Synod's election of successive patriarchs at Istanbul, and the choice of other patriarchs and metropolitans. He acknowledges the patriarch of Ipek's jurisdiction over the Serbian church, and the metropolitan of Bucharest's in the Danubian principalities. Ecclesiastical taxes were everywhere collected with the co-operation of Turkish officials and forces. Orthodox monasteries by and large kept their property. The patriarch of Istanbul remained a

3   F. Babinger, *Das Archiv des Bosniaken Osman Pascha* (Berlin, 1931).

post of outstanding influence, although the Ottoman government often encouraged members of the Synod – metropolitans and 'officials' – to complain against him. He might then be deposed, and rival candidates had to offer enormous bribes to win the government's support before an acceptable candidate was installed. Taxation of the poor footed the bill. The Moslem statesmen exploited the Orthodox church, but also defended it. The clergy lamented the dominance of Islam, while their own privileged position helped them to resist the ancient enemy at Rome, and Catholics were never permitted more than a precarious toe-hold in Ottoman Europe. The Franciscans, it is true, laboured courageously here and there. The Catholic archbishops of Sofia worked in Bulgaria throughout the century, and another mission survived in Moldavia. Young Greeks were attracted to the Roman college of St Athanasius at Rome, to be taught by Jesuits; and a convert like Leo Allatius, librarian of the Vatican, poured out propaganda literature. But just as most Greek students returned from Padua better qualified to rebut Catholic theology, so a solid nucleus of the Orthodox remained aware of and hostile to this threat from the west. Hence their concern to bring Muscovy firmly back into the world of Greek scholarship, and their hopes that the tsar had a part to play in rescuing Orthodoxy from the Turk.

The Greeks balanced one fearful loss and several gains in the second half of the seventeenth century. The surrender of Crete by Venice in 1669 closed a period of intellectual activity in which the island saw the successful fusion of Greek and Italian thought. Against a backcloth of splendid Venetian building in Cretan cities had appeared a new style of ikon-painting, a lively theatre and important romantic epics. *Erotokritos*, the work of Vicentios Kornaros, favourite reading or listening of many Greeks in the next few generations, depicting the struggles of the Hellenes against barbarians (or Turks), was written during the war. After the Turkish victory, intellectual society vanished and many emigrants fled to the Ionian Isles or Italy. The Greek communities of Venice and Corfu were strengthened by this retreat from the east. New Greek printing presses in Venice helped to keep up the flow of books into the Turkish empire.

At the same time, nothing could deprive the Greeks of their place in the Ottoman economy. Armenians dominated the commerce across Anatolia, traders from Dubrovnik had important settlements in Sofia and Belgrade, Jews were more prominent as financiers, but Greek business influence radiated right across the Balkans and into the principalities. They provided the marine which handled a great part of the trade between Egypt and Istanbul. This permanent economic influence was matched by the intellectual revival of their church. The controversial figure of the Patriarch Cyril Lukaris, executed by the Turks in 1638, had stimulated intense discussion. His followers were accused of crypto-Protestant doctrines. Other teachers, it was alleged, had shown too much sympathy for Catholic heresies, old and new. Gradually the Orthodox clergy settled down again, and out of this feverish phase there emerged a defensive movement which stood by the ancient faith. A little Aristotelian philosophy from Padua and a certain awareness of current specualtion in western Europe were added, but not much else. The conservative vigour, not the thinking, was the novelty. Lukaris had introduced some firstclass teachers to the old 'Academy', the school of the patriarchs in Istanbul, and those who studied or taught there emerged as leading figures in the next fifty years. They became associated with the coterie of rich merchants and men of affairs, who also acquired property by handling church finances. The patriarchs, the school, the select families, the teachers, mostly residing in the Fanar district of the capital, even if totally overshadowed by the Ottoman court and split by their own quarrels, had become a formidable grouping. Two Greek functionaries serving the sultan himself helped to consolidate its position: the chief dragomans or interpreters, Panajiotti Nikousios (1661–73) and Alexander Mavrocordato (1675–1700). Mavrocordato had defended at Bologna University Harvey's thesis on the circulation of the blood, before he became a teacher at the Academy and then secretary to Nikousios.

Closely linked with the Greeks of Istanbul was the spread of their influence in the Danubian principalities. Marriage ties with the greater Romanian families became more frequent. Princes Sherban Cantacuzeno and Constantine Brâncoveanu, in Bucharest between 1678 and 1714, were both generous patrons of Greek scholars. Greek printing presses were installed, Greek schools founded or reformed. The man who best represented Orthodoxy at this time, a student at the Istanbul Academy, a vehement champion of the truth against both Latins and Protestants, was Dositheus. Appointed patriarch of Jerusalem in 1671, he defeated Louis XIV's ambassador in a great diplomatic struggle and secured Greek guardianship of the Holy Places in 1672. His *Confession* and other work repudiated the Protestant arguments associated with Lukaris. With a number of monasteries in Moldavia and Wallachia under his direct control, he played a big part in confirming Greek influence in that area. He was Bossuet for the Orthodox church.

Grand Vezir Kara Mustapha, for whom statesmanship was the art of aggression carried on by various means in peace and war, had three practical choices before him when the Ukrainian campaigns ground to a halt. He could resume the attack on Venice in spite of the treaty of 1669. He could raise again the difficulties left by the recent pacification with Poland, and aim for Lvov and Cracow. He could

4 The Ottoman Advance and Retreat 1682–8

```
0        100       200       300 miles
```

- - - - - The Ottoman frontiers
1664–83

←——— The Ottoman army's
advance 1682–3

▓▓▓ The Habsburg Conquests
1684–8

•Lezno

•Breslau

SILESIA

Prague •

•Cracow

BOHEMIA

Kamienic-Podolski

•Passaú

•Trnava

•Kassa

R. Dniester

Linz •

Vienna •

Sopron •

Esztergom •

R. Tisza

Jaşi •

AUSTRIA

R. Drava

HUNGARY

•Buda

MOLDAVIA

Berg Harsan

TRANSYLVANIA

Venice •

Belgrade •

WALLACHIA

•Bucharest

Bologna •

BOSNIA

•Sarajevo

SERBIA

R. Danube

PAPAL
STATES

•Ipek

BULGARIA

Rome •

Dubrovnik •

•Sofia

Adrianople •

Istanbul •

Naples •

Salonika •

▲Athos

MOREA

Euboea

Smyrna •

Messina •

Palermo •

Corinth •

Athens •

GREECE

Candia

CRETE

Map 4

intervene in Habsburg Hungary, taking advantage of the fact that the sultan's treaty of 1664 with Leopold was due to lapse after twenty years unless renewed, and taking advantage also of the continued unrest in Hungary. The rebel Thököly (see above, p. 133), from his refuge in Transylvania, could be used by the Turks as they had used Hetman Doroshenko. It is not possible to say with any certainty whether Kara Mustapha ever seriously weighed the case for an assault on Dalmatia; the Venetian Republic feared the worst until the summer of 1683. Instead, he moved gradually to the conclusion that his presence in Hungary offered him the odds-on chance of a successful campaign. At best this promised the capture of Vienna, a prize which had eluded even Sultan Suleiman the Magnificent. More modestly, it could mean the annexation of Habsburg Hungary – leaving Thököli as a puppet ruler – or pave the way for a later attack on Poland from both sides of the Carpathians. With these ideas lodged in the grand vezir's mind, the Ottoman empire at once became the most volatile element in the whole continent.

The Impact on Central Europe

There were signs of intense strain in central Europe around 1680, due first to the plague which just then spread westwards from Hungary. Average monthly mortality in the town of Sopron was thirty-five between January and July 1679; it shot up to 800 in September and October. Graz would lose 3500 out of 15,000 inhabitants. The worst visitation of the century struck Vienna before fanning out through most of the Wiener Wald during the next two years; and the Turkish invasion of 1683 came too soon afterwards to allow the population of Lower Austria to recover until the eighteenth century. This epidemic (and others between 1650 and 1800) are commemorated in the votive pillars to be seen in many Austrian market-places. Men were vehemently urged by such contemporary preachers as Abraham a Sancta Clara to believe that the plague was God's judgment on sinners, and accordingly to express gratitude for His mercy when the infection vanished. Sculptors and designers responded with an idea in the idiom of the day, a representation in stone of clouds veiling the pillar and opening to reveal the Holy Trinity. Unfortunately the Augustinian friar Abraham, and court architect Luigi Burnacini who designed for Vienna the grandest of these pillars after the plague of 1679–80, enjoyed greater consideration than the city's medical officer who had spoken to the deaf, he said, in recommending preventive measures. His sensible sanitary precautions were taken in hand too late. As the poor died Emperor Leopold hastily left Vienna in the autumn of 1679, not to return for eighteen months.

He went to Prague, and the plague followed him. One of the alleged centres of infection in Prague was the Jewish quarter, so that movement into and out of this part of the city was for bidden; among the reasons given for steeply rising prices would be the effect of this restriction on Jewish traders who no longer supplied the retailers. Leopold, as the mortality figures ebbed and then rose again, left for Linz. More serious, the epidemic coincided with severe agrarian disorders in Bohemia. Acute friction between landlord and subject was added to other problems perplexing the government, and rumours quickly linked them all together. Some believed that Magyar raiders would come to help the Bohemian peasants, others that 'Hussites' and Protestant exiles were infiltrating to stir up the coun-try – and that they were French agents. In fact, the landlords' legal right to require forced labour from the unfree led to intolerable conditions on individual estates in bad times, and the impulse to stand the hardship no longer was erratically communicated from place to place. The court had little idea what to do, and its Patent of March 1680 preached docility to the subject and moderation to the lord. Unrest increased during the spring, so that troops were sent to restore order. A Patent of June 1680 altered the legal basis of tenures still further to the disadvantage of the peasants, but this probably mattered less than the harsh practical demonstration of the tight alliance between the Habsburgs and privileged Estates. Only sixty years later would Austrian statesmen begin to learn that a régime of this kind materially impoverished government as well as peasantry.

Six months afterwards a comet, with its long tail blazing, glittered in the winter sky. The wise men of the west had usually agreed for twenty years past that these belonged to the natural order of the universe, in spite of appearances. The Englishman Halley would prove – with particular reference to the comet of 1682, named after him – that they appeared and reappeared at intervals of time which could be calculated. A young Huguenot professor then at Sedan, Pierre Bayle, was content to demonstrate 'by various reasons taken from philosophy and religion that comets are not the presage of misfortune', in a notable book also published in 1682. But unlettered folk in Bohemia or Germany, and their clergy, knew of no reason why they should not believe that an apparition of this sort gave warning of catastrophes to come. Nor, for that matter, did pious and educated John Evelyn, FRS, the diarist in London.

Statesmen, in this depressing world of plague and peasant risings, felt impotent to deal constructively with them. Their thinking moved more easily down the old groove of diplomacy and warfare. By 1681 the main issue of the immediate future was becoming clear to most men with any concern for politics, the rulers, courtiers, office-holders, members of the privileged Estates, diplomats, merchants and all who could read the literature on current events which poured from Dutch and German presses. It was the prospect of renewed Ottoman pressure from the east, and of its interlock with the ever-increasing weight of French pressure on western Germany. Were further concessions called for in the Rhineland and the Empire to Louis XIV, and to what extent? How far did – or should – the right answer to this question depend on the actions of the sultan and his grand vezir, or on the policy of the emperor towards the Ottoman threats of conquest in Hungary?

In response to such a tangled problem statesmen groped their way forward as one emergency succeeded another. It is easier for us than for them to see the broad outline of what actually occurred between 1678 and 1688, and in particular to observe the diplomatic structure of Europe altering as the Turkish war approached, began, and continued.

Up till 1681 a majority of Leopold's advisers held that Louis XIV was their most dangerous opponent. The French seizure of Strasbourg convinced them (see below, p. 257). Accordingly, between 1680 and 1684 they tried to build up alliances strong enough to challenge France. These were designed to revoke the concessions made at Nijmegen, and to restore the settlement of 1648 in Germany – as Vienna interpreted it. Or the settlement of 1678–9, without allowing France an inch more than that, was the less ambitious proposal suggested. Some plans for an alliance or alliances embraced certain German states only; others involved Spain, the United Provinces, Sweden and, very tentatively, England. Most of the negotiations broke down although Habsburg envoys moved incessantly from court to court. The agreements actually signed did not promise help to Leopold unless Louis chose to send his troops across the Rhine.

Concurrently, between the winter of 1682–3 and the spring of 1684 a defensive-offensive coalition of powers against the Turks was formed piecemeal. While Kara Mustafa in 1683 marched from Adrianople to Vienna, and his Tartar auxiliaries raided into Moravia and passed the Wiener Wald, Leopold steadily won supporters: Bavaria in January, Poland in March, Saxony in July, together with the 'Circles' of smaller states in Bavaria, Saxony and Franconia. The crisis proved that a Turkish thrust up the Danube divided the Empire neatly into two. In the south the threat seemed direct; no one could deny that a disaster in Austria menaced all the lands immediately beyond it. Farther north a Turkish army at Vienna still seemed a long way off, while a new round in the old quarrels over Pomerania and the lands of Elbe and Weser – hotted up and then damped down by French diplomats – helped to deter Brandenburg and its rivals from taking part in the rescue of Vienna. A token troop of Hanoverians reached the Danube in September, 1200 Brandenburgers arrived in Hungary in October, but that was all. Kara Mustafa's defeat made its most positive mark elsewhere. The Venetians determined to join the struggle. The Holy League of the emperor, Poland and Venice under the aegis of the pope was negotiated during the winter, and signed in March 1684.

Victory at Vienna momentarily seemed to restore the position in Germany to what it had been in 1681, so that proposals for a 'Holy' league encountered some sharp criticism. The interest at Leopold's court which had always wanted to concentrate on checking French dominance again pleaded that active resistance to Louis XIV was the most urgent priority. They hoped for a disengagement in Hungary. They reacted indignantly while Louis continued to demand with menaces a formal recognition from the Diet at Regensburg of his recent gains in west Germany. They were supported by William of Orange, because French troops had once again – when the siege of Vienna reached its agonising climax – entered the Spanish Netherlands. But the pull of the prospect for a major advance into Hungary, of a thorough vanquishing of Islam and the Turks, now began to exert the more powerful pressure. Pope Innocent and his nuncios beat the big clerical drum. The futility of more warfare over Alsace seemed daily clearer, even to the waverers. The capture of Luxembourg by one French force, and the movement of another down the Moselle to Trier, convinced them. William of Orange was seen to be weaker than his opponents in the United Provinces who wanted to keep the peace with France. Spain, too clearly, was now a useless ally who always begged for help but never gave it. So, by August 1684, the die had been reluctantly cast by Leopold. At Regensburg the emperor and Empire agreed to recognise for a period of twenty years the *de facto* possession by France of Imperial territory – including Strasbourg – which Louis already occupied. For his part Louis was content not to insist on a final *de jure* settlement in his favour. At the time he had good reason to think that the Habsburg and allied forces would be trapped by the war in Hungary, unable either to withdraw or to advance, leaving him with a freer hand in the west. The campaign of 1684 indeed began badly for the Christian commanders, which was one reason why Leopold compromised with France at Regensburg.

The Ottoman advance and the ebb-tide of Ottoman retreat sucked the allied armaments back into Hungary. Vienna hoped for expansion, feared Polish empire-building south of the Carpathians, was susceptible to Catholic crusading impulses. It could not disengage on this front. In spite of a disappointing failure to take Buda in either 1684 or 1685 the allies generally pressed forward with the result that European history entered a new phase. In 1686 Leopold became the master of Buda, and of Belgrade in 1688. Before that date a Venetian conquest of the Morea was completed. Poland made a bid to overrun the Danubian principalities. In 1686 Muscovy joined the alliance of Leopold and Sobieski, after winning from Poland a final renunciation of Kiev and the eastern Ukraine; in the following year Galitizin launched his first assault on the Crimea. It seemed as if decades of Ottoman dominance in eastern Europe were coming rapidly to an end. From Habsburg Belgrade or Venetian Athens, even the Balkans looked vulnerable.

The German Standing Armies

The continued rivalries in north Germany, French pressure and the new danger of an Ottoman assault, made for the steady growth of standing armies in central Europe. Conflict looked inevitable so that the competitive need for armaments seemed obvious. Broadly, this was one response to encirclement, when another did not and could not occur: the Holy Roman empire itself remained as weak as ever.

After 1648 the standing forces maintained by the German rulers had at first been very small. They were primarily the garrisons of fortified places. War in 1672–9, of course, led to the raising of troops on a bigger scale. Both France and the Dutch paid over large subsidies, and what they paid was soon seen to be proportionate to the military potential of courts with which they bargained. A ruler like John George of Hanover learned to combine these foreign doles with the taxes levied on his own subjects, in order to create a bigger army than his revenue from taxes alone would have justified – and then to use his army as a lever in bargaining for further subsidies from the rival powers. And he could also exploit the lands of neighbouring unarmed states by quartering troops on them; this spared the resources of his subjects.

A further significant turn of the screw occurred shortly after the treaties of Nijmegen. In this period of nominal peace the standing forces in a number of German principalities did not diminish. Montecuccoli in Vienna saved from dissolution many Habsburg regiments which had fought in Germany during the recent war. Two new princes on the scene, John George III of Saxony and Max Emmanuel of Bavaria, eager to shine as warriors, raised regiments which inaugurated the continuous history of the Saxon and Bavarian armies. In the case of Saxony, this involved a fierce tussle with the Estates. Regiments were recruited, but the quarrel was still undecided in 1683. An abler man with the same military ambitions, Ernest Augustus the new ruler of Hanover, likewise substantially enlarged his army; the Hanoverian Estates were no longer in a position to protest.

Ernest Augustus, his Brunswick brothers or cousins, and Frederick William of Brandenburg, were all now maintaining forces bigger than their revenues could carry. But they were militarily strong enough, not only to keep up with aggressive neighbours but also to bid for foreign financial support. 'The structure of politics' may be an overworked phrase; but by 1688 this problem of the interrelation of military budgets, tax revenues, external subsidies, the relief to be gained by quartering or employing troops on foreign soil and the prestige of keeping up the largest possible armament, was built into the structure of German politics. It explains why German regiments would be available for service in Hungary and, with Venice as paymaster, in Greece during the coming years, and why the Dutch and English took over so many German troops after 1688, employing them in the Netherlands, Spain and elsewhere. The old days of the *condottieri*, of Mansfeld and Wallenstein and all the other independent colonel-contractors, were gone. The German princes were the new *condottieri* and contractors. The regiments were their own. Their soldiers, both officers and men, came from all parts of Germany.

In 1683 the Turks threatened Vienna, while John George of Saxony had raised an army for which his Estates tried to deny him the necessary funds. So he led his regiments into Bohemia and Austria where they lived off the country – and helped to rescue Vienna. When France and the emperor agreed to the truce of Regensburg in 1684, German rulers solved the difficulty of maintaining their forces as economically as possible in the obvious way. Max Emmanuel took his, over and over again, into Hungary. Württemberg and Saxony sent theirs to Greece. Ernest Augustus had offered Leopold 10,000 men in 1684, if peace with France was assured. At the same time he negotiated with Venice. His regiments in fact fought in both Hungary and Greece, one of his own sons died in Transylvania, another in Serbia and a third came back safely from the Morea. Frederick William of Brandenburg was more cautious as long as his treaties with France lasted. But in 1686 he sent 8000 men, a third of his whole army, to take part in the successful siege of Buda. Unexpectedly, the Turkish wars had given a strong new twist to the development of European military institutions.

Venice: The Last Imperial Adventure

Breaking historical developments arbitrarily into periods at least reduces hindsight. The Venetian republic and the Ottoman empire declined together in the eighteenth century, but if we close the account with a snap in 1688 it becomes easier to understand the contemporary view of some in Venice that a revival of their old empire was made possible by the Turkish disaster of 1683. The debate between Venetian politicians who advised sticking to neutrality at that moment, and others who voted for an aggressive partnership with Leopold and Sobieski, was a stiff one. The Venetian senate was still a real constitutional assembly, in which a decision depended on argument and oratory. Militancy won the day. Francesco Morosini, a hero of the last war in Crete, was appointed captain-general. For him, and for his friends, Venice was not merely 'the international drawing-room of Europe' where foreign princes rented palaces and opera houses flourished. For them it was, or deserved to be, the centre of an imperial power with naval and military resources to deploy. The Arsenal of the city mattered more than tourist attractions, carnival time, or the famous entertainment of the Doge's annual wedding with the sea.

Venetian successes for the first few years of a war which lasted down to 1699 were very remarkable. From his base in Corfu, Morosini won a footing on the Gulf of Arta in 1684. Ships of war scoured through the Cyclades. A few slight gains were made in Dalmatia. But by August 1687 he had conquered the Morea and dominated the Isthmus of Corinth. His colleague and rival, Girolamo Cornaro, forced an entrance to the Gulf of Cattaro. The Venetians, based on Corinth and the east coast of the Morea, were now apparently poised to push the Turks from their more important positions in Athens, Thebes and Euboea, and to throttle Istanbul itself from the Aegean. Cattaro was a promising springboard for the Bosnian hinterland. They were closer than the allies battling in Hungary to the heartlands of Ottoman power.

At the same time there were many reasons why this marked the limit of the Venetian recovery. The doubters of the winter of 1683–4 had in fact a strong case. First of all, the state had no standing army. There were irregulars in Dalmatia, militias on the Terra Firma and a few garrisons, but that was all. Venice depended on hiring troops from Germany or Switzerland, on small contingents sent by the grand duke of Tuscany and the duke of Modena, and a miscellany of volunteers. In Italy the independent rulers did not share the passion of German princes for army commands, and no longer sought to dispossess each other by competition in armament. Sons of noble families with a military tradition served by preference in the Imperial or Spanish forces. The poor did not have the long-ingrained custom of Swiss or Scots of seeking a livelihood by 'following the wars'. The Venetian struggle against the sultan roused Catholic enthusiasm, and the popes blessed it, but traces of any popular or patriotic concern in Italy for these campaigns are hard to find. If the Republic had been of the financial stature of Amsterdam, its army would of course have been larger. The government increased many taxes during the winter of 1684–5, but fell back – as during the Cretan war – on the principle of 'aggregation'. In other words, offices were sold to non-noble purchasers, and it was agreed to acknowledge as new members of the Venetian nobility those willing to pay for the privilege; thirty-eight families were added to the 'Golden Book', or schedule of nobles, in the course of the war. By these measures a certain amount of additional capital was raised for the state, but the small number of persons involved does not suggest that the unprivileged citizen class had any great desire to seek political power or that it had great surplus assets. Conservative objectors to 'aggregation' stressed that the purchase of office or status diminished the capital available for commerce and industry; revenue from taxes on goods would therefore sink, and the numbers in useful employment. Certainly, the war's economic consequences for Venice were unfavourable. The trade in Venetian silks with Istanbul declined again.

Morosini, and the Swedish general Königsmarck, found it extremely difficult to decide what to do next once they reached the Isthmus of Corinth in 1687. Turkish commanders had been quick to see that they ought at all costs to defend the island of Euboea, athwart mainland Greece. Accordingly Morosini and Königsmarck wanted to attack it, without feeling strong enough to do so. They ventured instead to Athens, bombarded and captured the Acropolis – where the Parthenon was a Turkish powder magazine as well as a mosque, so that one explosion on 26 September 1687 did more damage than the slow wear of centuries – and then found that the defence of so large a city some miles from the sea appeared impossible. It was exposed to enemy attacks from Euboea and Thebes. It would earmark an excessively numerous garrison. Its reserves of food and water were low. Plague began to decimate the army. The whole episode shows the Venetian leaders entangled in an undertaking utterly beyond their means. To ease the task of holding Athens, the whole Greek population of the town was ordered to leave and go elsewhere. A little later Morosini withdrew, allowing the Turks to return. Those antique marble lions which he took away with him as trophies, today guarding an entrance to the Arsenal in Venice, commemorate a defeat.

Much also depended on the attitude of subject peoples in the Turkish empire. Were the Venetians welcomed as liberators? To a very slight degree. We hear of secret missions sent across the mountains to Arsenius III, patriarch of the Serbs; and the patriarch appointed a new bishop at Cetinje on the coast, who became for some years a useful instrument of Venetian policy in seeking to win over the Orthodox in Montenegro and Herzogovina. But by 1689 Arsenius had decided to turn instead to the Habsburg commanders.

The republic of Dubrovnik recognised the emperor's suzerainty, to the chagrin of Venice. Much is obscure about these transactions but certainly there was no widespread conviction in this region that a Venetian conquest deserved popular support. The Greeks were divided and uncertain. The people of Epirus, and the Mainotes, encouraged Morosini when he first appeared. Some of the intelligentsia of Athens were welcoming enough, but the forced removal of the inhabitants to Venetian-controlled territory caused hardship and vexation. Soon the Turks found a Greek 'prince' to lead opposition in the Morea to the new government, and got the patriarch at Istanbul to anathematise those who had gone over to the Venetians. A shrewd mixture of threats and promises was to bring many Athenians back to Athens. In general, if Venetian administration in the Morea between 1700 and 1715 proved somewhat superior to that of the Turks before 1685, the difference between these two forms of alien control was never great enough to rally the Greeks to Venice.

Ottoman Reactions

The Ottoman government was meanwhile trying desperately to hold on to Hungary. A satisfying account of this effort, before the final sacrifice of a great area between Vienna and Belgrade, and of Transylvania, would need more accurate quantitative estimates of the total Turkish armament each year up to 1688 than can be given. One cannot say positively that the states of central Europe were technically superior in political management or in the science of warfare to the Ottoman countries, or benefited from a more lively economy. The balance of power between the Christian emperor and the Moslem sultan appears practically even, in 1683 and also in 1684. The divisive jealousies of Leopold's different commanders in the field, Charles of Lorraine, Max Emmanuel of Bavaria and Lewis of Baden, continually came near to wrecking their cause. But with the settlement in Germany, from August 1684, much new manpower was available on the eastern front and the odds gradually tilted against the sultan whose losses were cumulative. However, the Habsburg forces in consequence traversed longer distances as they moved forward. It was they, as much as the Turks, who then had to compete with the disadvantage of long lines of communication across difficult country: which tended to offset a superiority in armament. In any case that superiority vanished after 1688 when the emperor and German princes were compelled by Louis XIV to divide their resources between east and west.

The impact of defeat in September 1683 on the Ottoman high command was profound. Officers who died in the fighting were followed by others summarily executed. While in retreat from Vienna Kara Mustafa managed to destroy some of his harshest critics and rivals in the army. Sultan Mehmed simultaneously withdrew from Belgrade to Adrianople; there, other opponents of the grand vezir secured instructions which led to his own speedy death. But the system itself took the strain well. The sultan's authority remained intact and unchallenged. A new grand vezir and new heads of finance and the chancery, were appointed. Nor, according to Turkish memorialists, was there any lack of vigour in measures taken to raise men and money throughout the empire, and to improve the defences. The new commander at Buda soon showed that a great Turkish citadel was no less effective in standing a long siege (July–October 1684) than Vienna had been in the previous year. He repulsed Lorraine and Max Emmanuel without help from a relieving force. By the spring of 1685 orders had been given for the assembly of a powerful new army at Belgrade. Large stocks of timber and powder and corn were prepared. Money was distributed to many provincial governors in Asia as well as in Europe to find the men required. After a short period of anarchy in the Crimea order was restored, and the Tartars reappeared in Hungary.

All the same, the Turks continued to lose ground. Their opponents, unable to take Buda in 1684, occupied most of the Danube left bank as far as Pest. They began to push menacingly down the Drava from Styria. They re-entered Upper Hungary in spite of Thököli's attempt to stop them. Ottoman garrisons still held many useful strongholds but they became increasingly isolated, and for this reason – as more troops arrived from Germany – the failure of the main Ottoman force based on Belgrade was decisive. It no longer had that mass, or the same percentage of well-disciplined infantry units, which made the armies of Ahmed Köprülü and Kara Mustafa so formidable. In 1685 it moved north to recover lost ground but without success. Led by yet another grand vezir, Suleiman, it reappeared in 1686 in order to save Buda, but had not the strength to break through defence lines hurriedly built by the besiegers. In 1687, when the Imperialists advanced down the Danube, a serious error of judgment by Suleiman may have contributed most to the Christian victory of Berg Harsan (12 August 1687).[4] His defeat paralysed his army, shook the whole frame of government and led to further serious losses of territory.

One element in this general malaise stands out, the revolt of the army. To prepare for the campaign of 1686 the government had imposed special new taxes, embracing even the property of mosques. At the same time it tried to end certain abuses which allowed what

---

4 Berg Harsan (Nagyharsány) is a few miles south of Mohács, scene of the shattering Ottomon victory over the Magyars in 1526.

looked like surplus pay to the Janissaries and other standing troops. The reform incensed the Janissaries, who felt that their wages were often short and never punctual. The disaster of 12 August first affected military headquarters. Senior commanders would not obey the grand vezir's order to return northwards. They chose a grand vezir from their own number, while Suleiman fled to Istanbul. But the same mood of violent disgust had gripped highly placed persons at the court, while Moslem teachers of great official and popular influence supported them. News that part of the army was now marching south added to the uproar. Sultan Mehmed got rid of Suleiman, but frenzy increased and generated a demand to get rid of the sultan himself. It was an extreme demand, an extreme remedy; the attitude of certain politicians may not have been entirely destructive. They wanted to install a new government, strong enough to handle the problem of insurgent troops on the doorstep. Before the troops reached Istanbul the sultan was deposed. A brother, who had all his life been kept in comfortable detention at court (to strip him of any political influence) now became Suleiman II. But the life-cycle of an army rebellion ran its full course. From August 1687 to July 1688 the Ottoman empire reverted to a morbid condition familiar to those old enough to remember the years before 1656. The soldiers entered the city, disrupted the course of politics and business, appeared to settle down, broke out again, and were gradually brought under control by a government which removed some malcontent leaders by offering them tempting posts in the provinces – and crushed others. It had the backing of property owners in the city. Meanwhile Hungary, except for Temesvár, and Transylvania, were lost for good. The Morea had been taken by Venice. Yet the Ottoman government still proved strong enough to keep the rest of its empire in Europe.

After the death of Kara Mustafa in 1683 the treatment of foreign ambassadors by Ottoman ministers became less brusque and brutal. From 1685 successive grand vezirs tried to open a negotiation for peace with each of the signatory members of the Holy League. A friendship with France was actively courted. But these were tactics, enforced by political necessity. More profoundly, Islam on the defensive continued to give Turkish society a tough sense of self-sufficiency which repudiated any real dependence or borrowing. As far as a career in the Ottoman army or bureaucracy was concerned, the old principle that men of Christian origins had to accept Islam before they could be employed still applied. A stolid resistance political and cultural to the outside world was an emphatic element in Ottoman governing circles throughout this period. Mavrocordato the dragoman, before 1700, could never bring foreign influences to bear on the sultan's court or statecraft as Galitzin had done at the Kremlin. Greek churchmen won greater victories in Moscow than in Istanbul.

When the worthy Katib Chelebi (1609–57) settled down to compose his 'Geography' he turned for help to a former French priest converted to Islam, and was therefore able to borrow from a 1621 edition of Mercator's Atlas. When he wrote a biographical dictionary he included the lives of certain Greek scholars. These were timid innovations, the very slow dawn of a view that traditional teaching in the mosque-schools was too narrowly based.

By contrast, western Europe continued to build up a useful literature about many aspects of the region under Ottoman rule. Accompanying or following the ambassadors, consuls and merchants, were the scholars; ahead of them, Catholic missions forged through Syria to Persia and Georgia. The most famous of early English Arabists, Edward Pococke, had been chaplain to the Levant Company merchants at Aleppo before 1640, and the first Arabic books printed in Oxford appeared in 1648; Pococke's successors at Aleppo, and the English ambassadors' chaplains in Istanbul continued to associate Anglican clergy with the search for ancient texts in the Levant. Paul Rycaut, English consul at Smyrna, published a work on *The Present State of the Ottoman Empire* in 1668 which won European fame. Leibniz read it, Racine read it, many editions and translations appeared. He also wrote *The Present State of the Greek and Armenian Churches, anno Christi 1678*, dealing with a matter of great topical interest to western controversialists. Shortly after Rycaut left Smyrna, a young Italian called Luigi Marsigli arrived in Istanbul on the Venetian envoy's staff; the collection of oriental manuscripts and the study of Ottoman military institutions became two of his lifelong interests, and his work was of the greatest value. Most prominent of all were the French. Mazarin competed fiercely with Chancellor Séguier in employing agents to search for Greek and oriental books; many treasures from the monasteries of Mount Athos went to Moscow at this period, but others reached Paris. Colbert first bought for the king, and later for his own library. Trade or politics no doubt ranked uppermost in his mind when he thought of the Levant, and when he decided to send out selected young men to learn oriental languages on the spot at the state's expense. But his Academy of Inscriptions needed antique medals and pieces of sculpture, and he wanted books. A circular letter to all French consuls ordered them to co-operate, while between 1672 and 1689 the three French ambassadors at Istanbul were unwearied in attending to this attractive part of their duties. Nointel (1672–9) headed a real cultural mission. In accordance with instructions, he tried to defend the Catholic interest against the Greeks in everything that concerned 'guardianship' of the Holy Places in Palestine. A member of his staff, Galland, was the first scholar to translate into a western tongue the *Thousand and One Nights*. He himself toured the Greek islands,

Cyprus, Syria, Palestine and mainland Greece. He travelled in state. Scholars and artists accompanied him, and he set them to work. The printed and manuscript materials – including valuable drawings – arising from this expedition, many of them published within a few years, were voluminous. At almost the same time a Huguenot doctor from Lyon and an English gentleman, Jacob Spon and George Wheler, were the first to give a detailed account of the classical remains at Athens. Indeed, layer upon layer of history down to their own day interested the educated classes of Christian Europe in the lands under Ottoman control. The Moslem world, on the other hand, never reached out westwards with the same sort of alert curiosity. Occasional embassies sent abroad on short missions entirely lacked the importance of their counterparts in Istanbul. All that they did, perhaps, was to help in imprinting on the west a stock image of Turkish dress and manners. Would not an Aga sent by the sultan to Paris in 1668 find his immortality in *Le Bourgeois Gentilhomme?*

The Uneasy Calm of Western Europe, 1678–88

The Economy in Spain and England

This, surprisingly, was a decade of peace in western Europe. While along the Danube fighting overshadowed everything, governments here were almost always able to or preferred to bargain. A short war divided France and Spain in 1683–4, the Danes expelled the duke of Holstein-Gottorp from his lands, and in 1686 besieged Hamburg. These events caused great alarm but the case for restraint normally proved stronger, as if an impulse to keep the peace had at last gathered some momentum. Louis XIV's ascendancy enabled him to continue French expansion towards the Rhine by the mere threat of force, without having to use it. Peace also depended on the life-span of Carlos II, who had now survived both childhood and adolescence. Within the unsteady framework provided by recent treaties society was at least rid of the incubus of annual campaigning. Other problems, of the most varied kind, absorbed its energy and store of talent to the full.

In Spain a series of bad harvests and terrible epidemics combined to make the years 1677–88 a depressing ordeal. In Catalonia, the most resilient of the regional economies, many rural parishes were decimated by increases in the death-rate until the end of the century. Between 1677 and 1685 reports reaching the Council of Finance in Madrid described the impact of dearth and disease in widely separated provinces. Important towns abruptly lost a significant number of inhabitants, and therefore of workers and tax-payers. In 1678 the premium on silver and the better coins in circulation also rose to an unprecedented level. A staggering increase in the cost of living led to popular demands for deflation, which for once accorded with the government's own need. In 1680 a decree cut the premium on silver and demonetised coins with any silver content. The result was a drop in prices which caused even more hardship than the previous inflation. It coincided with the worst weather and the fiercest epidemics. After a phase of monetary chaos further decrees accepted higher premiums for silver, while climatic conditions improved. But during the early 1680s the severity of this 'crisis of Castile' can hardly be overpainted.

In dramatic contrast, England and Scotland moved towards a higher level of prosperity in one of the decisive economic advances of the century. Business profited enormously when Charles II withdrew from the war against Holland, leaving Dutch and French to fight it out. The English clothing trades revived. English shipping and commerce flourished. The English were neutrals in a world at war, and paid the lower taxes of a state at peace. This expansion slowed down after 1678, but a stimulus had been given at the most favourable moment possible. The domestic market was permanently enlarged, and in spite of reviving overseas competition the profits of foreign trade would in future be bigger than in the past. Signs of depression in the cloth industry were partially due to growing textile imports by the East India Company, which paid handsome dividends. The re-exports from West Indian and American colonies grew. Even during the political upheaval of 1678–81 there were big increases in the amount of bullion coined, credit was extended, prevalent rates of interest went down. And while the wealthier classes apparently spent more and saved more than in any earlier period, the government was the greatest beneficiary of this new prosperity.[1] Revenue from customs and excise grew automatically with the expansion of business and the debts of the crown were reduced.

The unrest in England after 1678 and England's role in Europe have both to be placed against this background of economic activity, with a ruler closer to solvency than before. The ink was scarcely dry on the Franco-Dutch treaty when revelations of a 'popish plot' to murder Charles, and of his brother's alleged intention to set up what Lord Shaftesbury called 'a military and arbitrary form of government', ignited passionate debate. Any hope vanished that Parliament would vote extra grants to maintain the new troops raised by Danby; peace in Europe removed the public pretext for increases in expenditure. On the other hand, Charles had just enough revenue and credit to rob Parliament of the power to coerce him on constitutional questions by cutting off supplies. Three general elections within two years returned majorities which voted for the exclusion of James from the succession. By proroguing or dissolving, the king confined the sessions to March–May 1679, October 1680–January

---

[1] At the same time, from 1685 the agricultural interest suffered considerably from lower corn-prices and lower rents. Cf. the position in France, p. 260 below.

1681 and a week in March of the same year. There were no more parliaments during his reign. From 1681 French subsidies added moderately to royal income, but increased normal revenue was decisive. Provided that Charles avoided expensive entanglements abroad, he could preserve the hereditary Stuart monarchy at home. His inactivity in turn helped to preserve general peace in Europe. It was much more difficult for anyone to begin planning a fresh challenge to Louis XIV if English support was not to be wooed at any price.

The frenzy in England clearly had other, deeper implications. At first the issue was whether the court's critics would triumph with their view that royal policy imperilled the whole constitution. From 1681 the tables were turned, and the issue was whether a sufficient interest in the country accepted the view that opposition to the court imperilled society itself by striking at the very principle of authority which safeguarded order and property. Many Englishmen came close to sharing the opinions of Frenchmen after the Fronde. They accepted a doctrine of necessary obedience to a sovereign who ought not to be challenged. By this time, also, he could not. Shaftesbury failed to keep his hold on London in 1682 and fled to Amsterdam to die. The Rye House plot failed in 1683, and such ineffective notables as Lord Russell and Algernon Sidney were executed along with the real conspirators – government at last dared to place its net over members of the Protestant nobility who dared to defy it. The risings led by Monmouth and Argyll failed in 1685, after James had succeeded Charles effortlessly. The royal authority rode higher, the standing of its critics seemed to be curving rapidly down. It was one sign of the times that Sir Robert Filmer's manuscripts, composed forty years earlier to defend absolute monarchy and unconditional obedience, were now printed; they won enormous popularity. It was another that John Locke did not venture to publish his own treatises against Filmer, even from his refuge in Holland. The censorship in England was restored, an instrument of control like the remodelling of municipal corporations, the purging of JPs and militia officers, and the packing of juries. Adding all this together, it seemed to some observers that England (with Scotland and Ireland) was now joining the European movement towards autocracy, imitating firmly established examples in France and Denmark, and keeping in step while another major power, Sweden, trod the same road at the same moment under King Charles XI.

Sovereignty in Sweden

In the autumn of 1680 the House of Lords in Westminster, encouraged by Charles in person, rejected an Exclusion bill sent up by the

House of Commons. A majority of the peers supported the monarch against the country's elected representatives. Just then, in Stockholm, the Riksdag entered the throes of a discussion which ended with a clear assertion of royal authority in the state. There was popular approval for this blow at powerful magnate interests. There was never a chance or hint of armed protest, as in England after 1680.

The shock of defeats by land and sea and the strain of war had completely discredited chancellor De la Gardie. The king's quarters in the field during the fighting became an effective centre of government, and gradually stripped the councils in Stockholm of their power. After the war his officers naturally wanted to strengthen Swedish defences. They had ambitious plans for a new fortified base at Landskrona to protect Scania, and a new naval base at Karlskrona to control the seaway to Pomerania. They argued that financial weakness accounted for much that was amiss with their troops and ships, and blamed the politicians in office, assuming that government resources had scandalously enriched men of influence ever since Charles X's death in 1660. They wanted to use a commission of enquiry in order to recover them. It was a device not very different from Louis XIV's tribunal of 1661 which sentenced Fouquet and reduced crown debts. Finally, those close to the king also decided to press for the radical solution of their problem, favoured by Charles X himself before 1655 (see above, p. 113), a wholesale resumption of the crown's lost revenues from land. They were supported by a number of great noblemen who had always opposed De la Gardie in the Council of State.

The Riksdag opened on 5 October, and Admiral Hans Wachtmeister soon threw down a challenge by suggesting that his Majesty's wish to improve the fleet depended on sound finance in future, and therefore on a strict enquiry into past mismanagement. Comments in the Nobles' House were very restrained, and thereupon Charles XI chose his 'Great Commission' of thirty-six nobles and officials. It laboured for two long years, scrutinising a sea of papers to calculate how much individual politicians had gained from excessive salaries, grants, alienations, and loans on easy terms, since 1660 – and to discover who had voted approval of these transactions in the Council of State. It was a political, not a judicial inquisition; some who still had influence, or relatives with influence, got off lightly. Its judgment that the crown was owed 4 million *daler*, improperly expended, was possibly a harsher blow to the 118 families affected, above all persons bearing the name of Brahe, Wrangel or De la Gardie, than the resumption of crown land.

This second policy also stemmed from the Riksdag of 1680. Many nobles had accepted the Great Commission as a kind of lightning-conductor to avert more radical measures. But the peasant deputies, strongly backed by clergy and burghers, wanted 'resumption' which they believed to be the one effective alternative to intolerably oppressive taxation in future. Their great petition of 23 October was undoubtedly welcomed by some men near the king. A bigger battle now began, while a flurry of speeches laid bare the clash of fundamental interests. In the Nobles' House, Wachtmeister weighed in with a demand for the resumption of all previous royal grants of land, except those which did not exceed 'a few hundred' *daler* in annual revenue. The opposition countered by a powerful memorandum of 2 November. This, and the petition of 23 October, are the clearest expressions of class antagonism in seventeenth-century Sweden. The reformers repeated what had been said in 1650. The wealth of the rich for the most part rightly belonged to the crown. The poor had grown poorer, and could not pay taxes because great men had taken the land from which substantial taxes were paid in earlier times. Against them, it was held that the crown surrendered crown lands and crown taxes to settle its debts; the creditors were entitled by law to this revenue. For nearly three weeks argument continued. The discredit of De la Gardie's régime must have counted for a great deal in the ranks of the lesser nobility, who could only hope for something better – above all, better and more punctual pay – under a stronger and wealthier government. These followed Wachtmeister and supported the unprivileged. Others knew that every radical policy lost its cutting edge as time went by: the corruption of administrators, passive resistance, difficulties of definition, loss of documents, sheer inertia, would all tend to safeguard individual interests. Still others declined to resist spokesmen who were royal servants, or feared agrarian unrest while their private fortunes stood at a low ebb after the long war. Accordingly, by a flatly phrased motion which in no way concealed the significance of the decision, the nobles acknowledged that all counties, baronies, former royal manors, together with all donations worth more than 600 *daler* in annual revenue, were once more at the crown's disposal. Soon, the persons appointed by Charles to his 'Resumption Commission' began their herculean labour to work this out in detail, and enforce it.

At the same time it was realised that a discussion of constitutional doctrine could not be avoided. Did the laws of the kingdom allow the king, or the Riksdag, to query the powers of the Council of State as these had been exercised since 1660? Some speakers in the Nobles' House evidently hoped to shackle the Great Commission by posing this question of principle. The militants therefore wanted a ruling which justified the crown's claim to govern and to make an unfettered choice of its advisers. A committee from the four Estates – nobles, clergy, burghers and peasants – worked out a declaration which in its final form vested sovereignty solely in the king, and which used phrasing partly borrowed from European theorists of absolutism. In a Swedish setting, the declaration meant that the king was not bound by earlier constitutional settlements, and that he alone determined the council's membership and powers. A formidable safeguard of the magnates' place in government had been dismantled by the time members of the Riksdag went home. The powers of the Riksdag itself were intact; but in practice, they too would increasingly give way to the royal will.

This was the curtain-raiser for what followed. When the Riksdag met again in 1682, more money was needed. Additional categories of landed property were brought within the king's right of resumption. The constitutional problem was better understood than in 1680, as the debates showed. If the king's powers were absolute, all rights of property seemed vulnerable. If they were limited, not only the security of the realm but also the interests of the unprivileged might be threatened. The cause of monarchy triumphed. Heavy new taxation was imposed on all classes. Burghers, peasants and clergy protested, but it was almost more significant that the nobles should be taxed afresh even while the crown took from them lands affected by the resumption. Moreover Charles, with his enduring concern for defence, had already raised the question of military manpower. He alarmed the Riksdag by proposing that each province should accept a definite liability to maintain a foot-regiment, manned by a new method of recruitment. Peasant deputies for areas remote from Stockholm must have been made uncomfortably aware of an increasingly rigorous central authority, even though the day was passing when landlords could shield their own employees from military service while others were conscripted.

The government's activity ranged over many fields in the next fifteen years, with varying success. Its methods were always and unsparingly autocratic. While the Riksdags of 1685, 1689 and 1693 tamely accepted royal demands, Charles and his officials displayed an administrative energy which is hard to parallel anywhere in Europe at the time. Commissions sat to reform the law. They issued a new book of psalms, and a new catechism. For the resumption of royal lands, roving officials with copies of all relevant documents made detailed enquiries in every province, so that bit by bit government revenue was increased by recovering the various types of property involved. In Sweden and Finland the total resumption was worth about 700,000 *daler* when Charles died in 1697, perhaps a third of the normal income from these countries. Economical management, with the punctual payment of salaries, became the hallmark of Swedish public finance. The final gains in Bremen, Pomerania and the Baltic lands were slightly larger, and maintained the military establishments overseas. Unlike Gustav Adolf or the German princes, unlike De la Gardie and the kings of Denmark, Charles XI did not depend on subsidies from the western powers for the pay of his troops; but his diplomacy was more cautious in consequence. Having recovered these old endowments, his bureaucracy then carried out further surveys in order to revise peasants' tax schedules, and to fix the figures for leasing out crown lands on profitable terms. In 1681 a new surveyor-general in Latvia employed thirty assistants (including students from Uppsala University) and thirty NCOs borrowed from the Riga garrison. They measured land-holdings and the size of crops in relation to sowings, estimated the numbers of cattle and of men. The astounding statistical richness of their labours in the Baltic provinces had its counterpart in the meticulous Swedish cartographic surveys of Pomerania in the last years of the century.

The authorities in Stockholm paid particular attention to Scania. The old conciliatory policy was in ruins, discredited by the recent war and by sharp-shooting bands of partly Danish sympathisers who fought on after the war. Charles wanted a complete subjection of this exposed country. He wanted to introduce Swedish law, Swedish clergy and the use of the Swedish language. He moved Scanian noblemen northwards, and cleared inhabitants away from the neighbourhoods of his fortresses. The new measures were enforced by the governor, von Ascherberg, and by Bishop Knut Hahn. In 1685 the possibility of another war with Denmark led to even greater pressure, and by the end of the reign a fusion of the new provinces of the south with old Sweden was reasonably complete. After 1700, during the next Northern War, they no longer proved a danger-spot as in the days of De la Gardie. The work of Ascherberg was in certain respects comparable with the labours of Louis XIV's intendant in Alsace, La Grange, during the same period. Charles had been less successful in the eastern Baltic. Swedish landowners were quickly expropriated but the native noblemen protested doggedly, and the Estates summoned to Riga in 1681 refused to give way. Ultimately, government officials carried out their instructions from Stockholm but bitterness caused by resumption proved an element of weakness in this part of the empire. John Patkul's rebellion, after 1700, arose partly from the sense of grievance felt by some Baltic Germans at what they considered the partial confiscation of their lands.

On the whole the economic trend in Sweden was upward. Government control remained rigid, but the Board of Mines understood clearly that foreign merchants could alone provide credit and capital which the mining districts needed to carry on business. Rising English imports of Swedish iron led to a growing favourable balance of trade with that country. Imports of colonial goods from England could be paid for, as well as the old staple necessities of salt and fish. An English colony flourished with official encouragement at

Narva, where the Swedish authorities carried out one of their finest exercises in the art of town-planning. The accusation that Charles XI starved his empire of capital, and halted economic development by continuing to reckon salaries in terms of land, and taxes in terms of goods, has not stuck. Internal grain prices were often kept artificially low by state-control, but trade and the marine recovered and began to enjoy real prosperity. A heavy mintage of Swedish silver coins reflected it, while Charles continued cautiously to draw back from the risks of any expensive commitment abroad.

Dutch Commerce

Against this Baltic background it is easy to discern with what vigour the United Provinces set about recovering from the commercial losses of recent warfare. A marked increase in the amounts of grain carried westwards through the Sound between 1680 and 1690, overwhelmingly in Dutch ships, was one favourable response to their hopes. The comparative failure of English shipowners and merchants in the Baltic to maintain their own advance of the war period was another. If the English import of iron increased, brought direct from Stockholm or Gothenburg, this had to be paid for by bills of exchange drawn on Amsterdam. English exports of coal also increased, but these provided the fuel needed by Dutch breweries, stills and sugar refineries; so that Rotterdam flourished on them as much as Newcastle.

Symptomatically, the total value of the Dutch East India Company's sales in Europe between 1680 and 1690 increased by a larger margin than in the previous decades; these would go on increasing until 1720. The Company always handled an enormous range of commodities in many areas, but at this date the 'Indian Craze' of western Europe for oriental textiles suddenly became a boom. The English Company and English interlopers were quick to take advantage of it, and of a developing sense of fashion which demanded novel designs and finishes every year, but there was a dizzy rise in the value of eastern piece-goods sold at Amsterdam in the 1680s. We can watch the Dutch directors keeping a very careful eye on prices: as soon as the war ended in 1678 the cost of spices shot up, while the profit on raw silk was low, and they let the stocks of silk run down. After a few years the market for spices weakened, while silk prices rose. Instruction duly went out to Batavia for the despatch to Europe of large consignments of silk, apparently larger than those which reached London. At the same time Jan Hodde, a mathematician, a burgomaster of Amsterdam and president of the Dutch company, sat down to solve an intellectual problem of great complexity: he wanted to draw up the accounts of this immense concern in such a way that a deeper analysis of its assets and liabilities would be possible. His appreciation that a balance sheet should value stocks distributed all over the world in terms of one currency only, that consistent principles must be applied to measure depreciation, and that such a balance needed to be struck with reference to a fixed date, showed a new insight into the theoretical and practical aspects of large-scale business undertakings. 'I remember,' Sir William Temple was to write, 'that walking in a long gallery of the Indian house at Amsterdam where vast quantities of mace, cloves and nutmegs were kept in open chests ranged all along one side of the room I found something so reviving by the perfumed air that I took notice of it...'[2] These eastern products were medicinal, romantic, profitable, as many like Temple realised, but their sale in Europe posed also the questions with which Hodde wrestled.

With its base in Zeeland a new West India Company had been founded in 1674. The wide ambitions of the old one were a thing of the past; the Portuguese crown held Brazil and England now commanded the whole American coastline from Maine to new settlements in Carolina. Accordingly, the slave trade remained the core of this second company's interest, which step by step came nearer to winning the Madrid government's contract for the supply of African labour to Spanish America. Its first agreement with the holder of the *assiento*, or contract, was signed in 1677; a useful partner was the long-established Amsterdam business house of Coymans; and the Dutch ambassador in Madrid strongly supported them both. By 1683 the *assiento* was in the hands of Balthazar Coymans. A few years later this Dutch contract was cancelled, but not before causing grave alarm in Paris. The scare may have been exaggerated, but French (and English) interests feared that the Dutch ships which ferried slaves from Curaçao to Cartagena or Vera Cruz, with a Spanish permit to do so, would speedily increase their trade in many other commodities. The *assiento* allowed Coymans special facilities in Seville, and it could be anticipated that the Dutch share in commerce between Spain and America would also increase, allowing them to take a still larger share of the precious metal brought from America to Andalusian ports.

European states and merchants continued to compete violently for the silver and gold from overseas. No one could be certain who was winning this critical struggle, and modern estimates are not much more helpful, but between 1678 and 1688 the balance of advantage appears to have rested with the Dutch. Treaties of 1648, 1659, 1667 and 1670 had placed the commerce with Spain of three leading powers, the United Provinces, France and England, on firmer foundations, and to each the Spaniards had to pay for a trading deficit with

2   *Works of Sir William Temple* (edn, 1740), i, p. 181.

bullion or coin. But our rather uncertain figures show that the French share in what the silver fleets of 1681, 1682, 1685–7 and 1689 brought to Europe was disappointingly small, while cloth exports from France to Spain declined. Louis XIV's repeated bullying of the Genoese republic may have had something to do with the large amounts of metal still shipped from Spain to Genoa, but without doubt Amsterdam remained Europe's financial capital. Although the Dutch excelled in developing various forms of credit, their huge commerce demanded maximum bullion resources and maximum flexibility in using them. They accordingly bid higher than anyone else in purchasing gold or silver, they allowed the unrestricted import and export of these metals, and insisted on a pure standard currency – the *rixdaler* was their king. They met, easily enough at this date, their own extra requirement of bullion in Asia, where Japanese exports of silver and gold had fallen away. American silver continued to reach Amsterdam via Cadiz – a little was also carried across the Pacific to be in part purchased by Batavia.

In 1682 Spain threatened foreign merchants who trespassed in the American trade with swingeing fines. So Colbert's new ships of war were sent to await the silver fleet's return, an English squadron hovered close to them, and the crisis ended with a compromise. In 1683–4 France and Spain were at war, while the fines imposed on persons caught handling French goods in Mexico were again extremely heavy. In 1686 Louis planned a naval demonstration before Cadiz and a possible attack on the galleons during their Atlantic crossing. There was a chance that Dutch warships would assist the Spaniards, but after an anxious phase of threat and counter-threat by the French commander patrolling outside Cadiz and by Spanish officials on land, a settlement was reached. Despite Louis's truculent defence of the French interest, these were years of solid success for Dutch trade in the Atlantic.

A more melancholy point may be added. While European shippers, and planters in Spanish, Portuguese, French and Dutch settlements regarded African slaves as so many 'pieces' – a 'piece' was a male of a certain size in good health while sub-standard males, and women and children, were valued as fractions of this unit – to be sold or brought at current prices, isolated Capucin friars and others expressed the idea that this was a shame and a scandal. They counted for nothing in their day.

The Consolidation of France

French naval pressure on Spain simply duplicated Louis XIV's policy on land. Having split the coalition of hostile states, he enjoyed so obvious a military superiority over each of its former members that he could afford to mix his diplomacy more openly with straightforward threats than in the past. It is sometimes said that his leading ministers of this period, Louvois and Colbert de Croissy, now debased the subtler approach of Mazarin or Lionne to the problems of Germany and the Netherlands. Their diplomacy looks cruder, but they could retort that except on one occasion the French armies and generals were not given the option of making war. Louis himself had lost his earlier enthusiasm for active campaigning. The famous definition of these years as a 'gnawing, aggressive peace' is apt, but it describes an armed truce which would not have satisfied Louis in his prime, nor Gustav Adolf nor Napoleon.

The Franco-Spanish treaty of Nijmegen called for the appointment of a joint commission to fix in detail the new frontier in Flanders, exchanging one enclave against another in order to devise a more sensible boundary than in the past. The envoys began meeting at Courtrai in December 1679. Louis not only demanded more than his fair share along the frontier, and permitted his troops to tax Spanish subjects. He claimed the dependencies of Ghent in the heart of the country. When this was refused, he requested compensation in Luxembourg. At the same time, instructed from Paris, the Parlement of Metz set up a special tribunal – the Chamber of Reunions – to enforce royal sovereignty over all former dependencies of the three bishoprics, Metz, Toul and Verdun, in accordance with what was laid down in the treaty of 1648. Ever since Richelieu founded this Parlement it had toyed intermittently with the policy, familiar enough in French legal tradition, of questioning the tax rights and other privileges of lords by a scrutiny of ancient charters, in order to extend the rights of the crown. Little was done for thirty years, but Louvois now spurred the Metz Chamber into action and in 1680 it produced many new claims in the Luxembourg duchy. Louis quartered troops on the country and soon blockaded the city and citadel of Luxembourg. He both coaxed and bullied the Spaniards, month after month. At one moment he called off the blockade, at another demanded Luxembourg itself in exchange for concessions elsewhere. His ministers waited for the moment when they could calculate that Spain had not the slightest chance of finding allies to remedy a hopeless military weakness. This occurred in 1683; the Dutch and Germans had to reckon with French threats in the Rhineland, the risk of a fresh explosion in the Baltic, and the Turkish assault on Vienna. Large French forces entered Belgium in September without a declaration of war. The court of Madrid's despairing obstinacy may have come as a surprise during the winter, but in other respects the assessment made in Paris was correct. No one intervened, and in April 1684 Vauban commenced the siege of Luxembourg, which fell in June. Spain, and other states, recognised French rights of possession over these new conquests for a period of twenty years. In the eyes of the world it was an important victory. Few men doubted that, in French hands, this strategic acquisition of Luxembourg would close or open the Moselle valley as it suited Louis XIV.

The treaty of 1679 with the emperor similarly provided for a special commission, in this case to arrange for French and Habsburg forces to withdraw from their quarters in the territory of German princes. Very slowly the French troops withdrew; but not long afterwards the Chamber at Metz began to publish its judgments, which declared Louis's sovereingty over a number of places in the Saarland and Rhenish Palatinate, the properties of various rulers or lords. Another French tribunal at Breisach annulled all the ancient liberties of towns and lords in Alsace. Taken separately, such annexations were small by comparison with gains of the recent war. Yet the creeping barrage of this penetration into the Empire in peace time naturally worried German patriots who protested in a vehement flurry of pamphlets, and German princes who confronted the suave French diplomats at their courts. Above all, the Imperial Diet in Regensburg became the focus of bargaining. By 1681 Louis was demanding a formal recognition of all French gains to date, in return for his renewed guarantee of the 1648 and 1679 treaties, these modifications apart. At this point Louvois seized Strasbourg. French troops entered the Imperial city on 30 September 1681. By one interpretation, the blow accorded with a judgment of the Breisach tribunal. By another, it flatly contravened the laws of the Empire. The French government continued manoeuvring to secure acceptance of its claims, including Strasbourg. For three years argument went on ceaselessly, while the state system of Europe buckled under the strains of an impending Ottoman invasion, of Vienna actually besieged and of an indecisive campaign in Hungary after the first Ottoman defeat. Louis exploited the emergency to increase his pressure, while new coalitions were planned to resist him but always fell apart. At length he triumphed, or seemed to triumph, at Regensburg in 1684. This settlement, and the one for Luxembourg, belong to the same complex of negotiations; the fall of Luxembourg allowed the French to threaten the Empire by moving an army down the Moselle to Trier. Emperor Leopold's ministers reluctantly accepted a formula which fell short of full satisfaction for France. In fact the occupation of Strasbourg was one of Louvois's enduring achievements, but at the time he had good reason to think that Louis XIV's dominance of the Rhineland would never be easy to defend, and would not go unchallenged.

These developments have a double interest. The consolidation of a new type of authority under the French king went hand in hand with his successful defiance of foreign rivals. In such a town as Besancon conquest meant the arrival of a French governor and a French intendant, the destruction of municipal liberties, a better administration but harsher taxes, a very large garrison, the building of barracks – and a towering new citadel designed by Vauban. Broadly the same may be said of Strasbourg after 1681, and of Luxembourg after 1684. The intendants of Metz for the three bishoprics, at Strasbourg for Alsace, and at Saarlouis (from 1685) for the new province of the Seurre, receiving their instructions from Paris and carrying them out with a technical competence and vigour new in those areas, signalled the transfer from one kind of régime to another. Bourbon rule may have been riddled with anomalies in the eyes of eighteenth-century reformers; nothing looks odder than its failure to shift the old customs barrier from the ancient frontiers of France to the new; but this royal power, exercised over a very wide region, had become the dominant element in local government. Under the Spanish crown or the Empire, local liberties and small-scale lordships would continue to hold their own. Under Louis XIV they did so no longer. We may find it hard to distinguish justly between these two neighbouring worlds, because personal hereditary privilege was written into the law of both, but contemporaries had little doubt that there was a profound difference between them. Paris asserted control over its conquests, from Dunkirk to the edge of Switzerland, without having to face serious internal resistance. The contrast of the periods 1635–60 and 1685–1700 in this great tract of Europe, between a phase of anarchy and a phase of increasingly effective royal control from the distant Bourbon court, is remarkable on all counts.

It depended partly on a new development in military science, and therefore on a new type of frontier. The decade after 1678 has rightly been called the classical age of French fortifications. This was an essential element in the government's policy. Vauban, who held the post of commissary-general for fortifications from 1677 convinced Louvois, in spite of the minister's often brusque treatment of him, that every stronghold which he built or redesigned, on sites of which he approved after a detailed survey, could contribute far more to the state's power for defence or aggression than the random clusters of old walled towns and their citadels. New works, which took account of recent theory and practice in siege warfare, offered the prospect of impregnable security; alternatively, they provided better bases for a future advance into neighbouring lands. It was a programme of economy, as well as of necessary expenditure: economy, because a lesson of the war just past had been that a multiplicity of garrisons robbed the field armies of manpower; expenditure, because Vauban's plans were often very elaborate. His concentric rings of fortification, designed to minimise the impact of enemy artillery for as long as possible during a siege, tended to cover a wide area. Intendants had the ticklish task of settling the terms on which to expropriate much valuable urban property before the contractors could begin work. However, Louvois for the land frontiers, Colbert and then Seignelay as ministers of marine for the ports, kept Vauban travelling almost continuously round and across France after 1678. The amount of building which he supervised was prodigious, but he tried to establish priorities which cut down waste. He wanted two distinct lines of fortifications along the Flanders frontier in order to demolish defence works in front or behind the lines. He insisted on the advantages of Luxembourg; when this was taken in 1684, neighbouring strong-holds which he had himself built earlier, together with many old forts in the duchy, were at once destroyed. He turned again and again to the problems of Lorraine and Alsace. Here was a moving frontier, as the 'reunions' proceeded, while the ultimate risk of a Habsburg counter-attack increased with every forward move which Louvois made to anticipate it. No sooner were the French in Stras-bourg, a step eagerly advocated by Vauban, than he arrived to pre-pare plans for refortifying the city. By 1688 four bridgeheads across the Rhine between Mainz and Basle, two of them new, were ready, and he was busily at work far down the Moselle. The names given to some of Vauban's creations in this forward area – Fort Louis, an island in the Rhine, Montroyal (Trarbach) on the Moselle, and Saarlouis – commemorate the Bourbon monarchy's expansion into German-speaking lands. Certain of these were lost later on, but Vauban gave Louis XIV the frontiers which helped to keep his enemies out of France between 1689 and 1714.

At the same moment the king reached the height of his public splendour with yet another transformation at Versailles. J. H. Man-sart, the civilian counterpart of Vauban, made enormous additions here after 1678, and the general aspect of the place today is Mansart's work of the 1680s. Apart from the Stables, the Orangery, or the long range of building attached at each end of the older palace, it is the *Galerie des Glaces* – flanked by the two beautiful saloons of War and Peace – which seems an apotheosis. Le Brun's ceiling depicted tri-umphal episodes of the recent war and, in the centre, the monarch who had charged himself with the burdens of government. Other decorations celebrate the glories of peace. They show the poor relieved, the marine restored and countrysides set under the plough again. Even the mirrors, it could be said, declare the superb quality of a new French manufacture and, by reflecting back to the onlooker this world of artifice, appear to give it greater substance. Indeed, if history outside the palace differed cruelly from the version created here by painters and craftsmen, the illusions of Louis as he moved through these halls, or in the smaller retreats of Trianon and Marly, were as important as any other single force in society. Courageous in the face of illness when he survived his first serious operation in 1686, increasingly devout after marriage with Mme de Maintenon, outliving all his old advisers one by one, his self-confidence was now complete.

While the wealthy few and court requirements were still a stimulus in or around Paris, and military expenditure on balance helped many frontier regions, the economy of France as a whole experienced mixed fortunes. The returns of foreign trade increased, so that a total of 411 ships left La Rochelle for Africa and America in the years 1680–9, against 273 in 1670–9, and the same buoyancy has been noted at other ports.[3] But Marseilles still languished, exports to Spain fell, and we cannot prove that German pamphleteers were right when they detected and denounced a heavier import of French luxury goods into the Empire. In any case, commercial expansion did not atone for growing rural impoverishment. During the war years down to 1678 it seems that signs of a general recession already became widespread: regional or local increases in the amount of corn, wine and olives produced, or cattle reared, which occurred here and there in the fifteen years before 1670, can no longer be found. Agricultural rents were stationary, or sank. After the war there was no reversal of this trend, for the unprivileged tax-payer or his landlord. Conditions were already very bad when a new phase of fearful hardships set in after 1688. Undoubtedly, Louis's failure to reduce government expenditure had much to do with this long continued depression. Colbert, still a politician in power, was now a powerless financier, and his great days were over. They were over because commercial activity, which he had encouraged with such vigour, did not match or counteract the decay of rural areas and rural classes. Popular joy greeted the news of his death in September 1683.

Louis simply shuffled the court cards in the pack. He permitted Louvois to take over the office in charge of buildings, gave the controllership of finance to Claude Le Pelletier who belonged to Louvois's interest, disgraced Colbert's gifted nephew Nicolas Desmaretz who deserved it, and left Colbert's son Seignelay with the consolation prize of responsibility for marine affairs and other miscellaneous duties attached to that post. More than ever before, Louvois became the great spender. Le Pelletier never came near to insisting on positive reforms. He did indeed talk about the case for them, and his administration is notable for fact-finding commissions, instructed to report on conditions in different parts of the country. They were voices, and nothing more. They stimulated criticism of

3 See J. Delumeau, Le commerce extérieur français an XVIIe siècle, in XVIIe Siècle, 70–1 (1966), pp. 81–105.

Colbert's tariff politics, and some pleas for freedom of trade. But commercial problems mattered less than the agricultural decay, and on this topic memoranda received by the controller-general (before he quitted his post in 1689) were damning and complete. Not in the short, nor in the long, but in the medium term Colbert's rescue operation had failed.

Louis XIV and Innocent XI

The fundamental civilised need to discuss and oppose, stiffly repressed in the municipalities, Parlements and Estates of Louis XIV's France, found an opening in ecclesiastical politics. For this reason an apparently trivial issue became serious after 1678, and helped to push the government into grave errors of judgment with far-reaching consequences. The Gallican Articles of 1682 and the revocation of the Edict of Nantes, inseparably entwined, may have had profound historical origins. But the case for not committing the monarchy to these two radical manifestoes was equally powerful, and it was open to the king to have proceeded differently. He and his ministers were impregnable; they misread the signs and blundered.

The famous affair of the *régale* was for several years no more than a tiny storm in a couple of Pyrenean tea-cups. In 1673 Louis summed up the decisions of the Paris Parlement and his council by formally extending this royal right – to collect revenues of a vacant see until the vacancy was filled, and during that period to appoint to empty benefices which did not involve a cure of souls – from some to all the bishoprics of France. Two bishops refused to accept the ruling, Pavillon of Alet and Caulet of Pamiers. They were hundreds of miles from Paris, but remembered at court for their obstructiveness in the debate over the Formulary condemning Jansenism. Royal measures against them gradually became harsher. It was not Louis's mistake to enforce the extended *régale* when bishops died and their sees became vacant, but to insist that bishops appointed many years earlier should explicitly recognise this new claim of his. He spoilt a good case by reviving memories of the government's old feud with opponents of the Formulary. Pavillon died in 1677 and Caulet in 1680, but the damage was done. For, at this point Pope Innocent XI allowed a momentous reversal of alliances within the Catholic church to occur. All the champions of rigour in spiritual matters were overjoyed by his election in 1676. In 1677 Jansenist emissaries began to appear in Rome. One of the Messieurs of Port-Royal made the journey there by way of Alet, in time to collect from Pavillon a bulky dossier on the whole subject of the *régale* and the sufferings of the clergy in the two bishoprics, together with an eloquent appeal to

Innocent for help. This referred first to the old crusade against the casuists but its main emphasis was placed on Louis's extension of the *régale*. An alliance of Jansenism with the Vatican, which would last for twenty years, now started to grow stronger; and Innocent XI's concern for the defence of church rights against the French monarchy grew with it. Louis was justified in June 1678 when he referred to Rome's abrupt change of position, in a conversation with the nuncio in Paris. The nuncio himself felt equally surprised. In fact, six months earlier Innocent had set up a new commission to study French affairs. Its secretary, Agostino Favoriti, was deeply influenced by the Jansenist agents, while its advice to the pope was responsible for a series of briefs to Louis in which Innocent advanced step by step to a direct assault on the French government's ecclesiastical policy. A brief of March 1680, in veiled terms, threatened the king with excommunication if he did not retract. The challenge was soon public news in Europe.

Step by step Louis matched this new policy with measures of his own. He turned to a new adviser who came rapidly to the fore: François de Harlay, archbishop of Paris since 1671, must be ranked with members of the Le Tellier and Colbert families as a leading politician in this middle period of the reign. Louis now dismissed Pomponne, whose Jansenist affiliations disqualified him as a reliable minister, and Colbert de Croissy took his place as secretary for foreign affairs. A sequence of clerical assemblies – with a membership determined by fierce official pressure – met under the archbishop's direction in 1680, 1681 and 1682. On each occasion the meeting was intended either to warn or to constrain the Pope. A climax was reached early in 1682 when Innocent sent a brief denouncing the assembly and all those who attended it. They were cowardly, unworthy, and he grimly declared null and void the proceedings of a body which had no authority except the royal summons and sought to legislate for the church in France without his sanction. It was a violent counter-claim to the government's view that the king, with his council, his Parlement and his churchmen could legislate on such a matter as the *régale*. In any case, already before Innocent's brief arrived in Paris, a new declaration had been published by the assembly which added immeasurably to the friction. It contained the four famous Gallican Articles (19 March 1682); apparently Colbert, more than anyone else in the council of ministers, advised Louis to make this daring and dangerous move.

The first Article drafted by Bossuet and others in the archbishop's committee of experts states that, in conformity with the word of God, sovereigns cannot submit in temporal matters to any ecclesiastical power. Subjects cannot be released by such a power from their due obedience sovereigns. The second and third limit the pope's plenitude of power by the authority of General Councils and the constitution of the Gallican church. The fourth concedes the pope's primacy in questions of faith, but made it depend in the last resort on the consensus of the church. For centuries these issues had been debated in France. Now, clearly, the immense recent growth of royal authority and the heat of this fresh battle with Rome brought the Gallican interest to the point of insisting on a decisive victory. The crown proposed to assert dominance over the church in France by claiming independence for it within the framework of the whole church, in accordance with law and custom which had 'subsisted invariably'. It was the crown which required all Frenchmen to assent to the four Articles.

From the spring of 1682 the problem of the *régale* was therefore merged into a discussion over fundamentals which aroused a much wider circle of clerics and laity than before. Apart from the Jansenists, the faculty of theology at Paris refused to acknowledge the royal ordinance and some of its members were banished to the provinces. Individual courtiers, led by the dukes of Créqui and Villeroi, protested openly. Villeroi's brother, the Archbishop of Lyon, encouraged other clergy to remonstrate. Pope Innocent, although differences of opinion in Rome persuaded him not to condemn the Gallican Articles formally, adopted a tactic which added to the disarray in France. By the end of 1682 he was simply refusing to confirm the appointment as bishop of anyone who had been a member of the assemblies of 1681–2. He employed this sanction over a long period, so that by 1688 there were thirty-five empty bishoprics in France. A cathedral chapter might be cajoled into choosing the royal nominee for a bishopric as its 'vicar', but it was impossible to mask this restraint on royal authority so long as the government dared not break with Rome completely. The archbishop of Paris might go serenely on his way, confident of the king's trust, and Colbert de Croissy rarely muted the thunder of his despatches to Rome where the French ambassador behaved with extraordinary truculence. But this deadlock between the Most Christian King and the pope cast its shadow for years on the conduct of affairs in Europe, and also on the fate of Protestantism in France.

The Edict of Fontainebleau

Catholic Frenchmen were divided far less by their final assault on the Huguenot churches. Jesuits, Jansenists or Gallicans were not too busy rending each other to forget the opponent in their midst who differed from them all. To struggle with him, as he weakened, was both a stimulus and a duty. They held the initiative at court, in the

Estates and Parlements, and at every level of society in most areas. A general Catholic revival in France still gathered impetus in spite of its internal stresses, long after the old Calvinist dynamism had disappeared. By 1672 the legal safeguards protecting the Huguenots had been largely whittled away, leaving very little of the original Edict of Nantes intact. What remained was the guarantee, seventy-five years old and several times solemnly confirmed, of religious tolerance for a still significant minority.

Louis XIV had strength enough in 1680 to set limits to the Catholic monopoly of influence. He could have left the Huguenots little, but something. Yet he himself, in virtue of his position, was perhaps more susceptible than anyone else in France to the notion that uniformity of faith was a necessary objective of sound policy. While he insisted on the purity of his doctrine during the quarrel with Rome, the more intolerable seemed a refusal to conform to his example. Protestants, by maintaining a different faith, appeared as the insubordinate subjects of a Catholic king, their conversion would testify what he could do for the church. This was a matter of principle. Louis and his advisers never set out to prove, as might have been expected, that the Huguenots imperilled state security between 1672 and 1678. The loyalty of Admiral Duquesne and of Huguenot army officers could not be impeached during years of war against the Protestant Dutch. Instead, events in England and Ireland in 1678-81 whipped up indignation in France. They showed that Protestant disloyalty paralysed a monarchy, that the 'popish plot' was a Protestant one which destroyed Catholic martyrs like Lord Stafford and Bishop Plunket. The French government could feel all the stronger by comparison. Its overriding impulse at this favourable moment in the reign was for continued progress towards the ideal of Catholic unity untainted by heresy.

The king may have wished to prove his piety while defying the pope. A vast body of Catholics in France quite simply hated their Protestant neighbours. They responded eagerly to measures which broke up Huguenot congregations one by one, or closed an increasing number of professions to those who would not abjure. Offices and jobs became available, rivals in business were disposed of, while – very important – Protestant charitable endowments fell into Catholic hands. Two other views of the problem deserve emphasis. In the mind of so fervent a defender of the Gallican Articles as Bossuet, a real link existed between a Catholic standpoint which allowed the pope less sweeping powers than Rome claimed, and the wish to bring Protestants back into the fold. Differences of substance between the protagonists had been narrowed after a century of strenuous debate, he felt. As his own *Exposition of the Catholic Faith* implied, the theology of moderate Protestants was such that in doctrine they were not far removed from orthodoxy. Their opposition to all papal authority remained a cardinal error; but now they could learn, from the Gallican Articles, that in the church of France the pope's functions were balanced by the rightful status of king and clergy. The moment was therefore at hand when the Huguenots both could and must accept reunion with this church of their forefathers, unassailable and central in its teaching, under the king to whom all Frenchmen owed absolute obedience.

The second view depended on administrative convenience. Every locality in the country had its feuds and friction. Confessional strife intensified them, and made more difficult the task of royal bureaucrats required to keep the peace and to collect taxes. The intendants accepted privilege in some spheres but, authoritarian to the core, they had strong levelling and streamlining instincts in others. Always Catholics, educated by Jesuits and Jansenists, they disliked the special status which the Edict of Nantes gave to the Protestants in France. It was grit in the machine of good provincial administration. It was an extra problem among many others. How desirable to get rid of it, by getting rid of this inconvenient distinction between most of the population and a troublesome minority! What looked like a marvellous simplification of their job of course turned out to be a mirage after 1685, when intendants would stagger under the burden of handling the Protestants, now merely 'new Catholics' in the eye of the law. This was not foreseen, either by statesmen at court or by provincial officials – to judge from their correspondence – as they pushed forward with a promising reform. Equally, one finds no firm evidence that Colbert, before he died in 1683, ever paused to consider whether the general policy towards the Protestants had far-reaching economic drawbacks, nor that Louvois anticipated difficulties with Protestants in the army which would weaken it. On balance, they both approved of the course which they themselves helped to set. Their families remained rivals, always eager to put the other at a disadvantage, but they did not differ over this point of policy and did not simply acquiesce because the king willed the policy. The underlying common bias of the French monarchy, statesmen, churchmen and administrators against the Protestant interest inside the country was a cement of the state in later seventeenth-century France. Louis XIV failed to see that he should have applied it with greater prudence.

The puzzle is to explain why the government did not rest content with the complete subjection of the Huguenots, or with methods short of outright violence to continue the process of attrition. Quite evidently, many persons assumed that this would be a reasonable programme to follow when the long war ended. Henri Daguessau, intendant in Lower Languedoc, with its large and compact population of Protestants, had been unwearied in using every administrative and legal device to weaken them. He welcomed the legislation of the years 1679–80, which destroyed the last mixed tribunals (staffed by men of both creeds), and excluded Huguenots from all judicial and financial offices. But when the time came, he deplored the use of troops and the abandonment of the bare principle of toleration. Likewise Paul Pellisson, administrator of the *caisse des conversions* (a fund based originally on the revenues of vacant benefices), at first hoped that missionary work in the provinces combined with the offer of doles to converts, would reap a harvest of souls for the church. Mme de Maintenon was not alone among Catholics in disliking the viciousness of making converts by force. When in 1681 the intendant Marillac in Poitou, with Louvois's consent, took a fresh initiative and employed troops, the government was still cautious enough to repudiate him.

The *dragonnades* of Marillac immediately won a notoriety which they deserve. There was nothing new in France about using troops to crush disorder or even to enforce tax collection, but his novelties were real enough. First he discriminated against Huguenots in the administration of the *taille* – in assessments, the appointments of collectors and chasing up the arrears. He then brought in troops, and turned the screw tighter by billeting most of them on the Huguenots, while offering special concessions to converts; all this he did with Louvois's consent. And he encouraged brutality in order to compel the Protestants to abjure. He claimed over 30,000 converts within a few months. The results were far-reaching. He proved that such strong-arm methods brought heretics into the church more effortlessly than mere restrictive regulations and the old blend of mission work and doles. Just as important, he unintentionally stimulated emigration on a much larger scale than before. The trickle, already increasing, became a flood; and the Huguenots were soon to prove that the government could not effectively check the flight of either men or money abroad. The *dragonnades* of Poitou were startling enough to raise a ferment everywhere. Reports spread quickly to other districts, where Huguenots mentally prepared themselves to give way to the demand for uniformity or to leave the country. Gazettes in Paris enthused over the details of this triumph of king and church. Those printed in Dutch cities preached Protestantism in danger, and the refugees reaching London or Rotterdam added to the alarm by their physical presence and by their writings. This repercussion outside France was one reason why Louvois rebuked Marillac and removed the troops from Poitou.

All the same, the arguments against a policy of haste or of violence were listened to less and less. Each new measure increased the momentum. The interest of many Catholics in legislation which placed the Protestants at a disadvantage, by excluding them from offices and professions, was overshadowed by a confessional and political interest which aimed to make Protestants Catholic. The laws of 1681–3, which allowed the conversion of children from the age of seven, ordered the closing of a church if such a convert relapsed and took his place once more in the congregation, and then finally – for the same misdemeanour – authorised a sentence of exile on the minister responsible: these pierced the basic defences of Protestantism in France. The internal unity and discipline of families, the very existence of congregations for public worship and of a Protestant clergy, were all threatened. Any further menace of compulsion, of the *dragonnades* renewed and extended, would cause hysteria to develop, with a momentary sense of complete hopelessness on one side and of complete triumph on the other.

In 1683 the Protestant communities of the south staged a protest. Inspired by Claude Brousson, a lawyer who had spent many years opposing the militant Catholic interest in the Parlement of Toulouse, congregations in the Cevennes and Vivarais districts braved authority by meeting for worship where this had been forbidden. It was a demonstration, not a rising, but led to local disorder which justified the use of troops. Once they were called in, the impotence of the minority was again proved to Catholic and Protestant alike.

Early in 1685 an intendant in the Pyrenees suggested to Paris that the troops in his area would have no difficulty in overawing its Huguenot population. He asked for authority to attempt this and a similar request again reached Louvois from Poitou. Louvois and the court hesitated, but for the last time and not for long. The merit of such a policy now outweighed its defects. The government saw less reason to draw back. Outside France the Truce of 1684 consolidated recent French gains in the Rhineland, while Leopold had still to win in Hungary. The Spaniards were beaten, the Dutch government was pacific. With Monmouth's rebellion crushed, Catholic James II sat safely on his throne. Inside France, the Huguenots appeared so weak and the Catholic interest so strong that only Louis's firm veto would have halted the general trend. But at court Louvois was egged on by his old father, now chancellor. The minister in charge of ecclesiastical matters was a cipher. Seignelay, responsible for the navy and much else besides, and the new controller-general, refrained from any sort of protest. The king's confessor had never raised scruples in the royal conscience (see below, p. 278), and did not do so now. All the stiffer Gallicans wished to humble the pope, and bent to the labour of conversion in the provinces by one means or another: theirs would be the glory of the church in destroying its ancient enemy, his the shame of seeking to cripple it by a misguided denial of right over the *régale* and the appointment of bishops. In the assembly of the clergy which met at Paris in June 1685, Daniel de Cosnac bishop of Valence thundered against heresy – his eloquence had been no less fervid against Rome, in the assembly of 1682.

Louis XIV and his ministers therefore saw no objection, if intendants employed regiments to assist churchmen to close Protestant places of worship, and to secure as many converts as possible. They wanted compulsion without indiscipline, if necessary sparing the rich and privileged. Their instructions on this point are not always consistent but in general the tactic of 1681, when Marillac soaked the most substantial families first, was reversed. But like Marillac before them, Foucault in Pyrenean Béarn and Bâville in Poitou were utterly ruthless, and their schedules of abjuration listed converts by hundreds and thousands. Other intendants and bishops copied them, and asked for the same kind of military backing. A majority of the Protestants everywhere prepared to make the same gesture of obedience to the king, of surrender to the Catholic church. Some elements in that majority certainly planned to leave the country if they could. Most were simply dazed, just like the courtiers at Versailles, who judged that France had been transformed since the year began with the Catholic monarchy's greatest victory since Calvin's day. In this feverish atmosphere, in October 1685, the ruler and his ministers decided on a grandiose declaration revoking the Edict of Nantes. What has occurred, runs this manifesto, has gloriously enabled the king to decree that the old edict is obsolete and useless, and to cancel it. The anxiety of Henri IV and his successors to end the necessary evil of schism, as soon as possible, was known to all and the decades of patient evangelism were now happily concluded. The most important practical decision was to distinguish between ministers, who were expelled from France forthwith unless they abjured, and the laity who under heavy penalties were forbidden to go: they were all 'new Catholics' henceforward, to be watched by the intendants and proseletyzed by missionaries.

The Edict of Fontainebleau can be regarded as the culmination of a movement with distant and profound origins, but the events which led up to it were not anticipated by the French government. Occurring as they did, they tempted Louis XIV to a gesture which satisfied his highly developed sense of the dramatic in kingship. It was a *coup*, a stroke, intended to amaze and confound. Observers like the prince of Orange, for whom the measure seemed inspired by the calculation that it would bind to France all other Catholic interests in Europe, and so destroy any chance of organising a new coalition against Louis, were almost certainly wrong. The calculation was that France could now afford the assertion of an accepted principle of government without the need to compromise. The state could move a stage nearer the perfection of monarchy, Catholic and autocratic, despite the pope.

The Huguenots in Europe

Historians have tried hard to measure the consequences of this attack on Protestantism. Emigration was on a far bigger scale than Louis anticipated, but less than is commonly imagined. According to one recent enquiry, the proportion of emigrants to the number of Huguenots in different regions varied sizeably. Nearly half the Protestants of Picardie, and a third in Dauphiné and Orange, left France. In the broad area stretching from Normandy to Bordeaux – excluding Brittany – a quarter joined the emigration. On the other hand, less than a tenth escaped or chose to leave the south and southwest – Upper and Lower Languedoc, Cevennes, the Vivarais and Velay. Almost all the Protestants of Béarn remained behind. The total emigration between 1680 and 1700 is tentatively given as 175,000, a fifth of the Protestants but less than a hundredth of the whole population of France.[4]

As to effects on the economy, there are many uncertainties. It was not the prime reason for appalling conditions inside France in the 1690s; it was one among multiple causes of depopulation and depression. In the Atlantic and Channel ports, business remained vigorous; this depended partly on foreign shippers, partly on that share of the trade which had always been in Catholic hands (and which now increased), but partly on the 'new Catholics' who conformed. The minister for marine affairs, Seignelay, used his influence to temper bureaucratic or clerical zeal, and was responsible for a relatively mild régime in Paris. Some textile manufactures certainly decayed, but it is easier to prove that the city of Lyon gained because so many Huguenots had left the silk-works of Tours and Nîmes, and that these towns declined, than that this always volatile industry suffered as a whole from the persecution. The number of skilled artisans who left the country and could not be replaced – in textiles, jewellery, watch- and clock-making, shipbuilding, metal working – is the crucial figure which eludes us. The refugees' fixed assets, including their land, were available for other men to exploit. One novelty was a complex web of trustee-ownership by which new Catholics took responsibility for the property of exiles, sending the income abroad to relatives or friends. The flight of currency and manpower were the government's greatest worries, and the second was easier to check than the first. Not even

4 Cf. S. Mours, *Essai sommaire de géographie du protestantisme réformé français au XVIIᵉ Siècle* (1966).

Louis XIV at the height of his power could control the mechanism of exchange by letters of credit; the funds needed by importers, foreign merchants or travellers inside France were met by payments made outside, and at discounts of greater or lesser severity the assets of Frenchmen could be transferred in the same way. It is not possible to say how far the Huguenots contributed to, or merely took advantage of, an unfavourable balance of payments. A marked increase in the deposits and reserves of the Bank at Amsterdam occurred in 1687, while normal rates of interest fell to 2 per cent; Huguenot cash balances were given as one explanation for a state of affairs which irritated many Dutch investors. It seems that wealthy Huguenots, like wealthy Catholics, were normally great hoarders at this period; the crisis of their lives compelled then to move, and then to exploit, their capital. And like other Frenchmen, they had always bought offices. Forced to sell out by Louis's decrees before 1685, they had more capital to spare. It is these funds, rather than former investment in French industry and trade, which reappear as the apparently plentiful resources of a few Huguenots in their countries of exile. All the same, the activity of Huguenot financiers outside France in the next century was matched by the influence of their relatives or associates who continued to reside in Lyon or Paris. Samuel Bernard, greatest of Louis XIV's bankers during the War of the Spanish Succession, had punctually abjured his Protestantism on 17 December 1685.

Public opinion in Protestant Europe, before and after 1685, appreciated more clearly the straits of the majority who left France than the wealth of a few. They were poor men who taxed the generosity of their hosts. They were a liability, not an asset. They arrived in Geneva, Rotterdam or London empty-handed, with a desperate need for assistance and employment. This was particularly clear in Switzerland. The escape routes to Geneva or Neuchâtel or through the Vaudois valleys of Piedmont, poured out a flood of refugees from Dauphiné, Orange and Provence. The movement became marked in 1682, reached a climax in 1686–7, and then diminished. It was soon obvious that this could only be a temporary halt – they would have to move on. The critical problem for individual pastors and gentry who took an initiative in discussions with cities, cantons and the rulers of other states, was to find additional places of settlement for a growing multitude who lived on charity. More than half the refugees who reached Switzerland (35,000 out of 60,000) went next into Germany. One notable Huguenot leader was Brousson, who had organised the demonstration of 1683 in Languedoc – he would soon wish to return to France, whatever the risks. Another was Henri de Mirmand, also from Languedoc – he belonged to the minority, receiving enough money from his father-in-law at home to live comfortably abroad.

A more difficult question is the impact of this persecution on the 'Protestant interest' in Europe. At some levels the response was quite straightforward. In England Anglican sermons overflowed with sympathy, collections made in Anglican churches from 1681 gradually became more generous. Amsterdam, Rotterdam and other Dutch towns were soon promising the fresh arrivals from France burgher status, freedom to follow their trades and exemptions from most taxes for periods of years. The older Huguenot families already long settled in England, like the Papillons and Houblons, came to the fore in trying to find employment for some of the refugees – and in using their skills. In the United Provinces it was the Walloon or French-speaking churches which were obvious rallying-points for the refugees, and were themselves rejuvenated as a result. They had been declining in numbers; within a few years their congregations grew larger and their old buildings proved too small. Their pastors baptised more infants, their deacons paid out more in poor relief. They appointed additional clergy in order to find employment for preachers and teachers coming from France; and one celebrated example of this was the invitation from the Walloon congregation of Rotterdam to Pierre Jurieu, professor of theology at the Academy of Sedan, closed by Louis XIV in 1681. The municipality of Rotterdam also created a new College, conferring on another Sedan professor the chair of philosophy and history – Pierre Bayle began his long exile under the happiest auspices. In their different ways, which were indeed irreconcilable, Jurieu and Bayle were both to stiffen the interest opposed to the king of France.

Protestant fervour, for the most part, aligned easily with Protestant economic interests. The Dutch conviction that religious tolerance multiplied the number of workers, consumers and skills was strongly rooted, and on this occasion it fused with Calvinist hatred of Roman oppression. In addition, Louis's measures alarmed the many alien merchants and mariners in France. His officials too often assumed that all Protestants came equally within the scope of the royal decrees. Naturalised Protestants were treated like native Huguenots. Many Dutch and English, long resident in France packed up and came home. The gigantic interest of the Dutch in the wine and salt of France, two staples of their commercial system, appeared in jeopardy. It looked as if Colbert's aggressive economic policies, chiefly aimed against the Dutch share of French trade, were being revived in a new form. On the whole, tension over these points gradually died down. The 'new Catholics' held their ground. The administration learnt to apply the new rules without causing too much uproar in the business world.

The refugees posed one very difficult problem. It was all very well for the patricians of Protestant cities to offer needy foreigners charity, but the grant of tax exemption for periods of years or of the right to practise any trade affected the ordinary labouring poor. *They* paid taxes, and *their* wages could be forced down by the presence of desperate immigrants willing to work for the next meal on any terms. Disturbances in London, and in various Dutch towns, suggest that the populace might regard the French king as a villain, but loved the Frenchman on its doorstep even less. Here again, the difficulty gradually became less irksome. The families coming out of France had at first been concentrated in a few major centres, Geneva, Lausanne, Zürich, Rotterdam, Amsterdam and London. Then they began to fan out, moving into other Dutch and English towns, as well as into Germany. They reached Ireland and America. They both scattered and settled. They merged slowly into their countries of adoption, and enriched them.

The political consequences of Louis XIV's persecution are just as finely balanced. On a broad view it might appear that the Edict of Fontainebleau, with the general policy behind it, knocked away one by one valuable Protestant wedges in the French diplomatic system: Brandenburg, certain Dutch interests and, after a short interval, England. Frederick William promptly published his famous Edict of Potsdam in October 1685, deploring the oppression of fellow-Calvinists and inviting refugees to settle in his lands. Thereafter the French could never rely on him. In the United Provinces, the sense of Protestantism in danger and the threat to Dutch trade in France were calculated to bring William of Orange and the cities of Holland closer together at last. Above all, it might be thought, events in France cast a long shadow over English politics. James II said that he wanted a standing army which included some Catholic officers, and a church settlement which included toleration for Catholics and Dissenters. The Edict of Fontainebleau seemed to expose the fraudulence of this. His rule was proved a sham, a prelude to despotism which would be maintained by a Catholic army with French assistance. His policy was Louis XIV's, thinly disguised. It was one thing to accept with relief the destruction of Monmouth's rebellion in June 1685. It was another to agree to James's ostensible programme, when he unfolded part of it to his Lords and Commons in November, a few weeks after Louis's Edict – and the Lords and Commons did not agree. A new anti-French alliance in Europe, and a weakening of the recent English bias towards a stronger monarchy, were therefore made more likely by the decision taken at Paris. Victor Amadeus II of Piedmont, it has also been held, was angered by Louis's peremptory instructions. Under pressure, he took action against his Protestant subjects in the Vaudois valleys. But his resentment foreshadowed the end of the long French dominance at Turin.

There is a measure of truth in this view but all sorts of intricacies must be allowed for, which undoubtedly modify it.

The Huguenot exiles were not conscious agents of a change in the political climate. Few were militant. Particularly in northern France, their leading ministers had for decades preached a doctrine of loyalty and obedience to the monarchy, Catholic and hereditary. The earlier career of Elie Benoît, who wrote in exile his great history of the Huguenots, reveals a persevering but exceedingly docile pastor at Alençon. Even more prominent, Jean Claude, who ministered to the Parisian Huguenots in their church at Charenton for twenty years, had been responsible for holding the Protestant congregations to an attitude of dignified protest, of due obedience to royal commands, combined with loyalty to the Calvinist faith. Expelled from France immediately after the revocation, his stirring *Lamentations of the Protestants Cruelly Oppressed in the Kingdom of France* (English trans., 1686) gave a version of recent history which justified opinions more radical than those held by the author. Benoît and Claude always considered themselves loyal subjects of Louis XIV and pinned their hopes for the future on a change of heart at Versailles. Either the king would turn to better advisers, or his death – and his operation in 1686 was an item of news for all the new coffee-houses of Europe – promised the chance of a new era. The first generation of Huguenot exiles never appreciated the finality of the revocation, and their political conservatism subjected them to severe intellectual and moral strains. Ministers who had left France in conformity with the Edict of Fontainebleau felt uneasily that they had no moral right to beg the laity left behind to defy the law, by refusing to conform or by taking the unlawful and dangerous pathway to exile. In time a few radicals emerged, of whom the most notable was Pierre Jurieu. Jurieu began as a strong defender of monarchy, developed as a passionate exponent of biblical prophecies which in the normal fashion linked the accomplishment of these prophecies with a date – 1688, and finally argued for liberty against despotism. But in 1686 the prophecy to which he leaned was a miraculous conversion of Louis XIV to Protestantism. Other extremists, in a more practical fashion, felt that the great need of the day was to venture back into France in order to maintain the faith. From Switzerland a handful reached the Cevennes, and helped to water the seeds of a radical protest against church and state in the next generation.

Protestant statesmen on whom the Huguenots depended manoeuvred with the utmost caution. The sheer multiplicity of their concerns was bewildering, as the case of Brandenburg shows. Frederick William had many grievances against Louis XIV in the twelve months before the revocation. French Baltic policy aggravated him, by again rebuffing his secret plans for an attack on Sweden. He saw no justification for Louis's bombardment of independent Genoa on a trivial pretext. He was worried by the accession of Catholic James II in England, and still more by the death of the Calvinist Elector Palatine, to whom a Catholic succeeded. Not long afterwards came the news from Fontainebleau, to which he retorted with his Potsdam edict. The elector's intense indignation cannot be doubted, and the Brandenburg ambassador at Paris acted in the spirit of his master by sheltering such men as Jean Claude and organising the flight of many Huguenots from France. Yet politically this was a minor move in the game. The crucial problem was viewed from a different angle. The *ratio status* of German rulers, like the *raison d'état* of Louis himself, referred to a complex of governments and alliances in which the politicians continually sought to adjust the balance to their advantage. These politicians normally believed in the merits of religious uniformity within the state; they did not normally believe that alliances between states required a common religious basis. This was an ideal or a mask, not an essential.

Louis XIV brought his internal policy to its ideological climax when the international situation favoured him, in eastern as in western Europe. His more prudent opponents realised that, for the moment, there was little to be done. The period of uneasy calm continued.

Newton – and the Counter-Reformation

While a majority of mankind had always to get and spend, and smaller numbers keenly observed the course of public events, the gifted few confronted deeper problems.

In the short period November 1679-January 1680 two men who disliked each other intensely, Robert Hooke – acting as a secretary of the Royal Society in London – and Isaac Newton in Cambridge, exchanged a handful of letters. Hooke asked Newton to forget their past disputes, and to begin again contributing to the researches of the Society. He put up a query about falling bodies, and Newton replied with a 'fancy' or suggestion of his own. Hooke pointed out an error in the professor's argument; Newton worked for a short while on the topic, then dropped it, and broke off the correspondence. In 1684 Edmond Halley, in his turn a Royal Society secretary, once more approached Newton, explaining that neither he, nor Hooke, nor Sir Christopher Wren, could find a satisfactory basis for their suspicion that the movement of the planets must depend on a certain relationship of centrifugal and centripetal forces. Halley's tactful enthusiasm at last lured Newton to focus the full power of his extraordinary mind on a problem which had moved into and out of it erratically during the past twenty years. As a result, the whole intellectual history of the next century owed a debt to his intense labour in Trinity College Cambridge, between 1684 and 1687, when generous Halley had the satisfaction of publishing the *Mathematical Principles of Natural Philosophy*. As the work drew to a close, Newton took some part in opposing James II's attempt to plant Catholic monks on the Anglican universities, but this was an isolated incident in his career before 1688. The greatest offshoot of the English 'lesser gentry' lived in a society which had left him free enough to disregard society; he was a professor, but was never compelled to take holy orders, and laboured in the solitude he needed.

Almost twenty years earlier Newton had worked out that the centrifugal forces affecting the planets would be inversely proportional to the square of their distances from the sun. He had also seen that the same statement could be true of the moon's path round the earth and, further, that a counter-force 'requisite to keep the moon in her orb' corresponded with 'the force of gravity' at the earth's surface. Maybe hindsight tells us, as it told Newton later, that the outlines of a universal balance between centrifugal and gravitational forces were then already visible, but why he abandoned the subject at this promising stage has never been clear. Optical problems absorbed him, no doubt, but he did not apparently take it up again because his mathematical techniques in maturity were able to produce results which would have been too difficult before 1670 or 1675. When Halley persuaded him to resume work on an enquiry which he at first visualised as a treatise on the Laws of Motion, Newton rarely used the calculus which he had himself devised in the intervening years. His proofs, of superlative importance, that the inverse-square law applied to elliptical orbits (as of the planets) and that the gravitational force of a spherical body (though composed of infinitely numerous particles) was concentrated at its centre, relied on a geometry which would very soon become outmoded.

On the other hand, because he waited Newton gained enormously for a different reason. The impact of his argument was all the more persuasive in the long run because he used much recently gathered astronomical data to apply and illustrate his laws of motion, a theme epitomised in the title of Book III of the *Principia*, 'On the System of the World'. His was indeed a new world-picture, and educated minorities were better prepared to consider it, having become accustomed to reports from learned societies and their correspondents, to the use of clocks and telescopes and micrometers, and to an awareness of the more exact measurement which went with improved instrument-making. If this public failed to understand Newton's mathematics, it followed him more easily as he proceeded in this third book to survey the orbits of heavenly bodies, and to find that all known phenomena confirmed his theoretical predictions. He quoted observations taken from Greenwich, Cambridge, Rome, Venice, La Flèche in Anjou, Boston in New England, from points in Maryland and Jamaica to bear him out with respect to the orbits of comets, a matter on which his debt to Halley, Flamsteed and others was as great as their debt to him. In later editions it proved possible to bring together further detailed contemporary evidence for the comets of 1664 and 1680–3 to complete this aspect of the enquiry. But the data and – *pace* Newton's later objections to the term – the hypotheses were marvellously interlocked. If 'the force of gravity' could once be accepted by the reader it seemed that the solar system was above all one of force and motion obeying inherent mathematical principles. The whole structure was exact and complete. Implicitly, in this first edition of 1687, Newton's underlying notion was that God had made and God still tended the Newtonian universe. Explicitly, he declared that fashionable Cartesian physics were utterly irreconcilable with astronomical phenomena. The 'vortices' of Descartes did not fill up every inch of space, whirling the heavenly bodies round with them. Such bodies moved instead through a void, acting on each other from a distance. Theory and data were linked to prove it.

Conservative instincts, and progressive scientists of the last forty years, had alike been challenged from London and Cambridge. Both would struggle in the next forty, in their own fashion, to resist Newtonian attitudes.

In the *Principia* Newton also acknowledged that Leibniz had ten years earlier hit on a new method not very different from his own for determining curves and areas, and for drawing tangents. Both men indeed were leaning heavily on the work of other contemporaries, but in the periodical *Acta Eruditorum* of Leipzig (his birthplace) Leibniz first published in October 1684 his own account of the differential calculus, and he and his disciples did much to give the world of learning this fundamentally important intellectual tool, with a notation employed by mathematicians for generations to come. True, critics of Newton's teaching on gravity felt uneasily that the Englishman had posited an almost occult force working mysteriously across empty space, while others saw Leibniz inserting into mathematics an indefinite symbolism which obscured strict calculation. These new mysteries were no less than those of revealed religion, and they were harder to accept; but in the end the critics of Newton, with Leibniz among them, and Newtonian opponents of the differential calculus, would alike have to give way.

These specialised advances were appreciated later. At the time readers of such journals as the *Acta Eruditorum*, the *Journal des Savans* of Paris, or the 'News of the Republic of Letters' which Pierre

Bayle had just started to edit in Rotterdam (1684), moved quickly from topic to topic. They followed in the wake of intellectual leaders like Leibniz or Malebranche who still took most of the major branches of knowledge for their province, and they benefited because writers were locked together by this discussion of differences between them. The ink flowed copiously in large treatises, smaller pamphlets, contributions to journals or personal correspondence, and the zest for controversy in Germany, France, Holland and England counterbalanced the other bias towards censorship and uniformity. Huguenots in Holland and England maintained their contacts with many French Catholic scholars. Copies of the French journals in Holland were eagerly sought for in France, although Louis XIV tried to ban the import of Bayle's News from January 1685. English material was especially plentiful in the 'Universal and Historical Library', edited by the Swiss Jean Le Clerc, a friend of John Locke, with 100 or 120 pages of reading matter a month. The great publishing houses in Holland – Elzevir, Leers, Marteau – cashed in on an unprecedented demand. It was a reflex of all these conditions that Leibniz, having described his calculus in the *Acta Eruditorum* of October 1684, in the November number entered a controversy just then unravelling for the umpteenth time some favourite themes of the age. Malebranche from Paris had issued in 1680 his work on the doctrines of Nature and Grace. Jansenist Arnauld, now an exile in Belgium, retorted with a tract which distinguished between what he called 'true and false ideas', blaming the false ones of Malebranche on Descartes. Leibniz from Hanover sent his contributions to Leipzig and to Rotterdam. Through intermediaries he wrote privately to Arnauld and Malebranche, proposing a metaphysical system of his own. He held to the absolute perfection of the Creator's work, a pre-established harmony in all things. Miracles could be regarded as in conformity with the general order of the universe, and there were 'final causes'. There was a Grace freely given to man, who ascended to the City of God to enjoy immortality. The old scholastic theologians were often right. Clear ideas were no guarantee of their truth and the mathematics or physics of the great Descartes bristled with error, just as Arnauld was wrong about Grace. In fact, nearly all the points were raised which thoughtful persons, with a sufficient stock of contemporary learning, loved to debate. The number of items in the major European journals between 1680 and 1690, arising from this controversy alone, is simply amazing. They epitomise the intellectual climate of the decade.

One concept continued to tantalise in the background, Christian unity. Shortly before the Turks knocked on the gates at Vienna in 1683, and Saxon Protestant troops joined with Bavarians and Poles to save it, a conference of Catholic and Protestant representatives met in Hanover. They hoped to define the terms on which an ecclesiastical union might be possible. It was in part an assembly of idealists like Leibniz, and they did not see as clearly as we can that the main trends of recent history were against them in spite of the current crisis. Earlier, there had been German Catholic rulers, conciliatory by temperament, who welcomed discussion of the doctrinal impediments to union. There had been a school of Lutheran theologians, who emphasised that they shared with the Catholics certain fundamental beliefs. There had been the promising model of Calvinist churches tolerated in Catholic France. But although Louis XIV's defiance of Innocent XI seemed to loosen the Roman moorings of the Gallican church, the success of his anti-Protestant policy gradually overshadowed his Gallicanism and darkened the whole European scene for would-be conciliators. In any case the cardinal dilemma, between a reunion of all with Rome and a union by way of compromise on the part of all, stood no chance of being resolved. The Hanover conference petered out. Emperor Leopold's victories in Hungary fortified a militant Catholic advance in the southeast. The Protestant interest continued to decay in Poland. The accession of a Catholic ruler in England, the first since 1553, sounded alarms from another quarter, and the Edict of Fontainebleau dealt the harshest possible blow at a gallant but feeble ecumenical movement. The Catholics, both inside and outside France, could not and did not condemn the revocation. The anti-Catholic bias of Protestant opinion everywhere grew sharper. It was a midpoint, and no more than a mid-point, in the long phase of religious intolerance in Europe which continued deep into the eighteenth century. Without allowing for the tremendous weight of the Counter-Reformation at its climax – reached in these years, and not earlier – enlightenment and revolution later on remain incomprehensible.

There were signposts pointing ahead, like the new Biblical criticism in works by Spinoza and the Oratorian Richard Simon or the slow decay of belief in witches and demons. Suspicious governments, churches and peoples still overshadowed almost everywhere the true pioneers. Widespread persecution, autocracies and oligarchies unenlightened by comparison with those of a later period, and poverty for the masses, all continued throughout the age of Louis XIV. Its marvellous vitality and variety have to be set in this austere frame.

The Jesuits and the China Mission

The authorities in Rome were often worried by the apparent pliancy of Father La Chaize, Louis's Jesuit confessor, who seemed not even to try to moderate his master's Gallicanism. Yet the confessor could have argued that his career coincided with the apogee of Jesuit influence in France. Their colleges were predominant in secondary education, their affiliated fraternities spread right through the social structure in many areas, and their pastoral activity was incessant. This ascendancy was nowhere more noticeable than in Paris, where thanks to La Chaize himself the greatest of all French schools now basked in royal favour: in 1682 the old Jesuit college, with new endowments given by the king, was renamed the *Collège Louis-le-Grand*, a formidable complex of grammar classes and university faculties, of day-boys and boarders, of teachers and researchers. Although the curriculum remained very conservative, wedded to the old combination of Latin grammar, logic and classical texts which were all taught in Latin,[5] together with the familiar scenario of periodic theatrical performances and prize-givings, the French Jesuits were progressive in certain respects. As mathematicians and astronomers – above all those who trained their telescopes from the roof of the College in Paris – they attracted the attention of Colbert no less than of de la Chaize, and took their place in the schemes of both.

Colbert had found that he could use clergy who were mathematicians. He needed teachers of hydrography, and also naval chaplains. After 1681 a number of Jesuits were detailed to give the necessary technical instruction at various places, while they supervised new seminaries at Toulon and Brest. Other such plans had a touch of the fantastic, but finally they merged into what proved one of the great imaginative ventures of the age.

At a far end of the world the Jesuits had kept their station in Pekin for almost a century. They supplied Chinese emperors with the mathematical expertise needed to solve those complex problems of the calendar which determined the sequence of Chinese official ceremonies – and in 1678 the head of this mission, the Belgian Ferdinand Verbiest, sent a renewed and urgent appeal to Europe for fresh recruits. This was published, while a Jesuit from China reached Holland in October 1683 by a ship from Batavia. He was armed with copious material for propaganda, and began to move from country to country in order to beat up support. When he reached Paris, scientists at the Observatory were quick to see that there might be an opportunity here for properly trained and equipped observers to survey more accurately than before the geography of the east, collecting samples and specimens which European researchers in various fields required. Colbert took a lively interest in these suggestions during the last few months of his life. At the same time a

---

5   By a coincidence, in 1682 J. B. de La Salle began to place education for the poor in the towns of Rheims, Guise and Laon on a much improved basis, thanks to his new brotherhood of teachers, later the widespread 'Institut des frères des écoles chrétiennes'. He insisted that French should be the language of instruction. See W. J. Battersby, *De La Salle* (London, 1949).

handful of French missionaries, sent out by the Society of Foreign Missions (see above, p. 146), had continued to labour in Indo-China. The king of Siam, resenting Dutch commercial hegemony in that region, had despatched his ambassadors to Paris in 1683. La Chaize now continued where Colbert left off. Mission work, the advancement of science, the unfolding of Louis XIV's glory everywhere, the chance of political or economic gain at a cost to the Dutch – all these ideas were mixed up in the discussions at Paris and Versailles in 1684. Father Fontaney, senior mathematician at the Paris College, was deeply involved with La Chaize. The plan of a mission of mathematicians to China, going by way of Siam, was accepted by Louis. A new phase in Europe's relations with the extra-European world began early in 1685 when one set of missionaries, with the title of 'royal mathematicians', left France for the east. Another left early in 1687. The problem of how to harmonise Christian doctrine with Chinese words and rites, the brave guess of Leibniz and a few others that Confucian ideas and Chinese institutions had a useful message for the west would, within fifteen years, receive much excited attention. In the 1680s the educated public in western Europe already had a glimpse of new worlds coming nearer – as it gazed at the printed editions of Verbiest's letters, or at the glazes of Chinese porcelain before the experts of Dresden learnt to copy them.[6] But perhaps such messages from outer space will always have to compete, then as now, with more dismal and more threatening intelligence nearer home.

6 Strictly speaking, Chinese influence on the ware made at Delft, Rouen and other places was very noticeable from 1650 onwards; but in 1682 a new era began in the history of Chinese porcelain, with the appointment of an extremely talented director to the Imperial factory in the province of Fukien. New styles and standards of work in China then gradually made their influence felt in Europe. Cf. W. B. Honey, *European Ceramic Art* (edn. 1963), pp. 32, 36.

Epilogue:
The Interlock of 1688

The International Structure, 1685–7

In 1685 no one doubted the clear ascendancy of Louis XIV's government in the west. His recent victories were both cause and consequence of this, the balance of power was tilted high in his favour. But the complex of political conditions was such that the restoration of a more equal balance, feared by the French and desired by their opponents, depended on four great issues. Each was a regional affair. Each had implications which spread far and wide. The first was the new French dominance, secured in 1678 and advanced in 1684, in the area between old France and the Rhine: was it permanent? The second was the Turkish war; how long would it last? The third was the new Catholic monarchy, but without a Catholic heir, in England, Scotland and Ireland: how long would James II live, and would he break the Anglican establishment before he died? The fourth was an intense struggle for power in north Germany: would the Danes compensate for recent losses by an advance in Germany, and how would their restlessness react on Brandenburg, Sweden and the Brunswick princes? Emergencies, like the death of Louis or Carlos or Leopold, might of course deflect attention to other quarters. Barring such accidents, all statesmen with any width of vision realised that the future depended principally on the interplay of these four sets of questions. They knew that they would neglect any one of them at their peril.

Although the French envoy in Adrianople never thought much of the Ottoman army, and reported home accordingly, it seemed to his masters that the Turks were strong enough to pin down the Holy Alliance. Even if the Turks drew back, it was still possible to visualise the allies being sucked forward into the Romanian principalities or the Balkans. While this continued, the Rhine frontier from Mainz to Basle would remain exposed to a devastating French attack, and therefore to the threat of such an attack. If the Dutch held aloof because they did not regard the fate of Strasbourg as one of their vital interests or because they feared James II, if the manpower of the bigger north German states was either hired out for use in the Turkish wars or diverted by a continuous crisis on the lower Elbe, if French threats and assurances were adjusted with sufficient skill – the day would dawn when the Empire and the Habsburg emperor willy-nilly converted the Truce of 1684 into a final settlement, once again enhancing Louis's prestige while adding to his strength. There is little doubt that, at least for Louvois, this policy of pressure-with-out-war depended on the continuation of war in the east. He feared a truce or treaty between sultan and emperor as the worst imaginable misfortune for France, but already had difficulty in advising Louis when the campaigning in Hungary turned in Leopold's favour. The fall of Buda in 1686, the destruction of the Ottoman field army in 1687, and the occupation of Belgrade in 1688, as we can see in retrospect, struck at the foundation of recent French foreign policy. Earlier, Louis could afford to wait and watch while he tightened the pressure on Germany, especially during the period in each year when Habsburg forces were safely committed in Hungary. Now, time was running out faster and faster. Reports came in that the Austrian regiments were getting more efficient, or that the Turks seriously intended to negotiate. The French ministers justifiably believed that their opponents in Germany and Austria did not want the settlements of 1679 and 1684 to last; victors in Hungary they were unlikely to accept the permanent sacrifice of Lorraine, Alsace, Strasbourg, Breisgau or possibly even Luxembourg. The crisis of 1688 in the west may look curiously delayed, but it turned more than anything else on the chronology of the Turkish war.

A year after the agreement of 1684 the Elector Palatine died child-less, and Philip William of Cleves-Jülich (and of Neuburg on the Danube) inherited his title and lands; he was Leopold's father-in-law. Through the duchess of Orleans, who had certain rights in this inheritance, the French government challenged the new ruler and claimed that at least compensation was due to her. This meant that, to the 'reunited' lordships and towns in Germany already occupied by France, a new category of properties in dispute was now added – in the territory north of Alsace. It hinted at the possibility of further French expansion into Germany, and at a new piece of blackmail which would have to be bought off at a price not yet determined. The Orleans claim was a pretty specious concoction, but gave Louis a bargaining counter which caused great alarm. It was an extra instrument in the war of nerves. Louis also decided to involve Pope

Innocent by inviting him to settle the dispute. This was a bid for papal support, without giving way on the points about which Paris and Rome already differed. As a result, from December 1685 onwards the 'Orleans inheritance' in the Palatinate was a forbiddingly technical piece of litigation handled at Rome, with correspondence flowing back and forth between the Roman court and Paris, Heidelberg and Vienna. Only one thing seems clear: the French government was content to let the affair simmer and crackle without going to the length of a direct collision with Philip William until 1688. It was an auxiliary in the main battle.

Another matter came to the fore in 1686. The League of Augsburg, joined by the Emperor, Bavaria, Spain – representing the old Burgundian Circle of the Empire – Sweden, and other German states and Circles, was designed to protect the agreements of 1678-9 and 1684. But when the more cautious Dutch and German politicians came to scrutinise the clauses of this treaty, they found that most of the troops scheduled to defend the Empire were in fact fighting in Hungary. The rest were forces which existed on paper, but nowhere else. Many powers declined to join so useless a coalition. France protested loudly all the same, and retorted by planning new bridgeheads on the Rhine; in 1687 Vauban's building programme was further extended. Louvois and his subordinates were not responding to a threat posed by the Augsburg alliance. They had in mind the struggle for supremacy in Germany looming ahead of them, when the Turks stopped fighting. They wanted a military supremacy with such manifest powers of defence and attack that the enemy would have no sensible choice other than to accept the situation permanently.

In July 1686 Christian of Denmark assaulted Hamburg. For the next few months the elector of Brandenburg gave his whole attention to this problem. The French were delighted, and they learnt with equal pleasure of his new quarrel with Vienna over the alleged maltreatment of Brandenburg troops serving in Hungary. In 1687 the Danes again threatened Hamburg, while family feuds helped to paralyse the court at Berlin. In fact, Louis could count on the unwillingness of Frederick William to move against France. In Hanover other negotiations were binding to the French interest Duke Ernest Augustus – now returned home from a last glorious spell of junketing in Venice. At the end of 1687 Louis's advisers thought that the diplomatic ascendancy of France in north Germany was secure, more secure than twelve months earlier.

They were right as to the past, wrong about the future. The old elector was dying, and his son Frederick would be much easier game for anti-French councillors in Berlin and anti-French interests in Europe. He was less of a shrewd, balancing statesman than his father, whose death in 1688 brought a whole phase of European diplomatic history to a close. A second misfortune for Louis at this stage was the weakness of the Danes. Hamburg was Christian V's Strasbourg – and a much greater prize – but he could not take it in spite of repeated efforts, and always drew back when Brandenburg, the Brunswick rulers and Sweden drew sufficiently together to menace Denmark with a counter-stroke. In 1686 and 1687, Christian looked dangerous enough to absorb all the vigilance of the neighbouring powers. In 1688 they had begun to take his measure. With Dutch diplomatic support, they felt more confident that they could hold him. If they had to, they were willing to look to the defence of the Rhineland.

The caution of the Dutch at first matched theirs. William of Orange's resounding political defeat in 1684 was an epoch in his own career and in the evolution of the United Provinces. He went to extremes in standing out for a bold policy of giving armed assistance to the Spanish Netherlands, after Louis XIV's army invaded them in 1683. William's domestic critics in turn almost ruptured the union of the provinces in order to thwart him. It may well be that their judgment on the military question was sounder than his, but the French ambassador momentarily exerted as much influence in the Hague and Amsterdam as any French ambassador had ever done in Warsaw, Regensburg, London or Madrid. This was the most violent upheaval in Dutch internal affairs since 1672. Thereafter both sides drew back, so that an important novelty in Europe was soon the relative harmony of the Dutch, with noticeable side-effects in William's coolness when possible alliances were suggested, and in the fading political influence of the Amsterdam municipality. In particular, Pensionary Fagel and the prince believed that an Austrian treaty with the Turks was an essential preliminary to any useful discussion for a new anti-French partnership. They were unimpressed by the Augsburg alliance. They also objected to any undue emphasis on the defence of the Protestant interest, a theme which hummed round them in and after 1685. Half the potential for any future stand against France would have to come from the Catholic princes, and the prickly Catholic zeal of Leopold's ambassador at the Hague warned them not to beat the Protestant drum too loudly. Above all, they had on their hands the problem of how to handle James II while they waited for him to die; and during this waiting period it seemed best to cut entanglements to a minimum. Their position only changed at the end of 1687 when they first seriously considered a new policy towards England, while the overwhelming Austrian victories in Hungary seemed to bring nearer a treaty with the Turks. An agreement with Leopold was now worth more, and mattered more. In May 1688 an envoy sent to Vienna began trying to convince the Habsburg court that James II had committed himself to the French interest in Europe against the wishes of most English Catholics, that William's policy towards England did not and would not harm the Catholic interest. He also offered full Dutch support for Austrian claims on the whole Spanish inheritance, while urging the case for peace with the Turks and the gentle treatment of Hungarian Protestants. The discussions were both intricate and tentative, but proved the preliminary to a new Austro-Dutch agreement.

In England meanwhile the notion of resistance was discredited. Hopes for a Protestant succession in the near future encouraged moderates to stay their hand while James, as hastily as he dared, altered the establishment. Many of the new men were Catholics. Sunderland and Jeffries and Godolphin were not, but they welcomed changes which gave them greater power. The remodelling reached a new stage when Sir Edward Petre, SJ, joined the Council in November 1687. It was an extraordinary occurrence that in England, of all places, a Jesuit should acquire a formal political status denied to La Chaize in Versailles or (after 1691) to Father Menegatti in Vienna. But it was no odder than James's long friendship with the Quaker William Penn. The eccentricities of the king make one hesitate before associating him too neatly with the onward march of the Catholic interest in Europe, or with the trend to absolutism on the French model. Admittedly, many good Protestants compared the Declarations of Indulgence with the Edict of Fontainebleau: both set aside the laws of a country in the name of a personal prerogative. They saw James's standing army as a new instrument of government resembling Louvois's, preparing to enforce the collection of taxes or to dragoon Protestants. They saw Parliament going the way of Estates and Parlements. Indeed, such developments were possible, and the past twenty-five years had shown that the court attracted Englishmen willing to serve it under almost any colours. Clifford, Arlington, Jeffries, Sunderland or the soldier John Churchill would all willingly have bettered themselves in a régime less tied to constitutional forms than the Stuart monarchy of 1660–85. But James was not a shrewd enough captain for this ship and this crew. He cared too narrowly for his personal image as a Catholic ruler to see that wider issues were involved.

What he most wanted, he got: a Catholic ambience at court, a Catholic Chapel, a Catholic nuncio, diplomatic representation at the Holy See, Catholic schools and friaries in London and the universities. He failed to understand that this obsession with ecclesiastical trimmings made it more difficult for him to attain and maintain what was probably within his grasp, given the political frustration of recent years in England, a stronger government and a diminished role for Parliament. The strengthening of the executive, the remodelling of municipal corporations and local government, and a deliberate attempt to prepare the ground for the election of submissive MPs were policies which had a chance of success if carried on not too blatantly; but James lacked flair for the manoeuvring required. Nor did he compensate for this by an awareness of international problems. He could not see that England belonged to Europe as well as to the Catholic church. The most insular of rulers, he converted England into an island open to invasion whereas it was normally protected by alliances based on the European balance of power. The issue here was not ideological. The courts of Vienna and Madrid appealed insistently to James. The pope never ceased to quarrel with Louis XIV. William of Orange understood as clearly as anybody the case for a combination of anti-French powers which included Catholic and Protestant interests. Yet James failed to substitute for this possible alignment a serious approach to Louis. He made no offers to France and, except for a cash payment in 1685, got little or nothing in return. The English government's utter weightlessness in continental affairs helped to keep the peace for several years after James's accession, because it enfeebled the chances of building up a new coalition against France. It also left England open to a Dutch invasion, and contributed to the orientation of French policy. The ministers in Paris convinced themselves, perhaps too easily, that English isolation suited them while they dealt with their fundamental concern, the relations of France and Germany.

The Year 1688

Towards the end of 1687 the outlines of a new European crisis began to appear. They were not very distinct at first, and those best informed saw only parts of the whole picture. As before, the force or threat of arms seemed to matter most, in Hungary between Buda and Belgrade, in the Rhineland between Mainz and Basle, and in Holstein between Hamburg and Kiel. As before, statesmen wrestled with the problem of fixing the priorities between these widely separated areas, and it was grafted on to the normal struggle of individuals or factions for political power in each of the courts. In spite of other uncertainties one point now looked beyond dispute. The old Ottoman empire, north of a line not far up the Danube from Belgrade, appeared to have vanished beyond recall. What no man contemplated five years earlier replaced it: an enlarged Habsburg dominion east of Vienna, with Emperor Leopold no longer compelled as in 1684 to defer to French threats in Germany. Louis XIV had waited, even after the fall of Buda in 1686, for a possible Turkish recovery. After some hesitation, he decided to wait again in the spring of 1687. Now he was compelled to reckon with a speedy pacification in southeast Europe, and therefore with a stronger challenge to his own position. On Louvois's estimate, the improved French defences were nearly complete but the future of the Twenty Years Truce was at stake.

During the winter of 1687–8 Elector Max Henry of Cologne, frail and fading, took thought for the future of his archbishopric and persuaded his Chapter to choose the stoutly francophile William Egon von Fürstenberg as his 'coadjutor' – if the pope confirmed this, Fürstenberg had an overwhelmingly good chance of becoming the next elector of Cologne, and of succeeding Max Henry in Liège, Münster and Hildesheim. This was a useful French diplomatic victory. It was a setback for the courts of Vienna and Munich whose envoys had argued in vain with the canons of Cologne, as well as for the Dutch. After a few weeks the excitement died down because no serious change was likely at this sensitive point so long as Max Henry lived, but the indirect consequences were important. Negotiations over the future of Cologne drew together the states which, for one reason or another, had an interest in this part of the Rhineland. They involved the pope, and Innocent duly refused to confirm the choice of Fürstenberg as coadjutor. Cologne also influenced the thinking of the court in London. A very noticeable element in international affairs, in 1688, was Sunderland's assumption that nervousness over the lower Rhineland would automatically pin down the Dutch, and deter them from attempting anything elsewhere. After months of close discussion during the summer of 1688, William and his adviser Bentinck showed themselves far more perceptive on this critical problem than James and Sunderland. They saw that Louis's championing of Fürstenberg made it easier for them to rally the German princes, while Louis's overriding interest in the disputed lands farther south reduced the chances of a French campaign against the United Provinces on the pattern of 1672.

During the autumn of 1687, also, the king of England's queen became pregnant – for the first time in five years. For William, this threat to his own wife's otherwise certain precedence in the succession[1] was now added to what he had learnt of James's plans for bringing a pliant House of Commons to Westminster. It was the worst possible news. It pushed him towards a determination to intervene in England if necessary. Earlier, he had disliked the principle of the Exclusion bills; now he came near to accepting it, to listening with real attention to English plotters against James whom he had rebuffed before. James, for his part, failed to see that a prudent policy of insurance abroad was needed if he intended far-reaching measures at home. He should have wooed the Dutch, tried to break up the fragile harmony of their cities, Estates, States-General and the

1 For the English succession, see the dynastic tables, no. 4, p. 295 below.

Stadhouder. Instead, he alarmed them. He refused to compromise on matters in dispute between the rival East India companies. He did not collaborate in policing the sea against Algerian pirates. He had already raised the difficult question of the English and Scots regiments in the Dutch army, a long-established institution of common interest to the three countries. After an abrasive correspondence with William he now recalled the troops to England; it looked like a vicious attempt to weaken the defences of Holland. A new Anglo-French alliance was also discussed: by this tactic Colbert de Croissy got what he wanted, maximum friction between London and the Hague, without giving any important French commitment to James. Rumours spread, and Dutch political circles were alarmed. William to some extent shared these fears, and took the opportunity to win generous votes from the provinces for a heavy programme of naval and military expenditure. James gained much less but felt little disquiet, although he sensibly enlarged his navy to match the old national rival at sea. He did not realise that his ambitious schemes at home were provoking other schemes, still bolder, but much more carefully weighed.

William firmly told the English malcontents that he would not 'meddle' unless 'invited' to do so, by men of substance in the country. All the same, the Dutch leaders nerved themselves to anticipate any repetition of what had occurred in 1672. If they could secure their land frontiers and raise enough support in England, they wanted to strike first, in order to reverse Stuart policies at home and abroad before it was too late. They wanted to strike a blow all the more telling because it could be welcomed by Englishmen as an act of liberation. They wanted to forestall any radical movement, as hostile to Mary and the Dutch as to James, with designs for a new commonwealth or republic. Abetting one conspiracy and crushing another, invading the country and rescuing it, restraining James or supplanting him, continuing to wait for James's death or waiting no longer: William, between May and July 1688, must have pondered these dangerous alternatives ceaselessly. The course of events, which he himself influenced but could not control, then settled his line of action. James, unconscious of the danger, relied on a phenomenal record of past success: the stricken ghosts of Monmouth and Argyll, the loyalty of his subjects and members of his own family, his navy and large standing army, all defended him. He was to be proved wrong at every point. He failed to recognise the great administrative capacity of the Dutch for preparing, concealing and mounting an expeditionary force of troops and ships. He took too little notice of the ideological vehemence which increasingly coloured the personal ambition of his adversary. In 1688 William's Protestantism clinched his dynastic claim, just as it abhorred the recent blotting out of

Calvinist churches in his ancient inheritance of Orange, in France. His hatred of the French king had developed, conveniently but with passion, into a belief in the excellence of princely authority which accepted a constitutional framework. He chose to see James – who had not been in France for thirty years and rarely heeded Louis XIV's wishes – as the reflection of French influence and French methods of rule in England.

At this moment, a particular strand in James's policy had fatal results. An order that his Declaration of Indulgence for Catholics and Dissenters should be read out in all the churches girded seven loyal and conservative bishops to petition the king in protest; friends more radical in temper immediately printed the petition which therefore became a public manifesto. James took up the challenge. The bishops were committed to the Tower. Two days later his son and heir was born; amid rising agitation their trial began. On 30 June a London jury returned its verdict in favour of the bishops, and the king's enemies at last despatched an appeal begging William to intervene in England. But while William had been anxiously waiting for the opposition's firm commitment, other news reached him. Elector Frederick William had died in Berlin, Elector Max Henry in Cologne. Only ten days after an uproar of popular applause in Westminster Hall signified James's setback in the case of the seven bishops, the Chapter House of Cologne cathedral filled with canons, who met to choose their new archbishop. The birth of a Stuart prince, the deaths of Max Henry (who was a Wittelsbach) and of the Hohenzollern elector, together opened the next round in the struggle for supremacy in western Europe.

The coadjutor Fürstenberg presided over a body bombarded by every conceivable pro-and anti-French interest in Germany. It was a perfect small-scale model of the aristocratic and political structures of the age.[2] It contained Fürstenberg himself, three nephews and two cousins of his, the core of a party which intended to satisfy France and vote the coadjutor into office. They were opposed by two sons of the Elector Palatine, a Baden prince who had spent a lifetime as one of the emperor's leading anti-French statesmen, and a son of the Imperial vice-chancellor in Vienna. Promises of preferment to the less well-born canons had multiplied recently, but a number of them now turned against Fürstenberg. Encouraged by the siren voices of Munich, Heidelberg and Vienna, they held firm at this crucial meeting; and the result was that the French candidate secured thirteen votes, a Wittelsbach candidate nine, and two others one each. Fürstenberg declared his majority sufficient. The rest declared that the technical disabilities which had debarred the pope from

2   M. Braubach, *Kurköln* (Münster, 1949), pp. 81–109.

confirming his appointment as coadjutor, six months earlier, meant that he needed a two-thirds majority. They held that the Wittelsbach candidate, the elector of Bavaria's brother – against whom these objections did not lie – only needed one more than a third of the votes; and he had them. In effect, it was a double election. It produced a deadlock, during which legal argument gave way to military pressure. If Fürstenberg had won an unqualified victory in the election there would have been no need for him to call French troops into the Cologne lands. There would have been somewhat less anxiety in north Germany about the future of the Rhineland territories surrounding the see of Cologne, which belonged to Brandenburg and the Elector Palatine. Louis XIV would not have seen his influence in the archbishop's government threatened with extinction, would not have had an extra grudge against the Elector Palatine for encouraging the opposition to Fürstenberg. His advisers might have paid more attention to what was going on in England. As it was, the Rhineland absorbed the attention of every power; William finally considered the position there just sufficiently safeguarded by his new allies to let him risk the daring attack on James II. A mission of Bentinck's had led to a whole cluster of agreements by which different German princes hired out some 13,000 men to the Dutch. By no means all of them reached Holland, but on paper they were a replacement for an expeditionary force of the same strength destined for England. Other German soldiers reinforced the municipal garrison in the city of Cologne at the end of September.

A month earlier Louis, Louvois and Colbert de Croissy had already made up their mind. They observed the unexpected consequences of Max Henry's death, linked them with the expected consequence of Leopold's triumphs in Hungary and decided to stop tinkering. The truce of 1684 and the future of Strasbourg, the Orleans claim in the Palatinate, the defiance to their man Fürstenberg over Cologne: they prepared to solve all these problems by combining them in a single enterprise. France and the United Provinces were now moving in opposite directions along roughly parallel lines. Neither intended to meet the other. Both governments felt, for different reasons, that there was no time to lose. Louis showed his hand first, and this enabled William to show his. In September French armies occupied almost the entire Rhineland. A clear statement of Louis's terms on every point in dispute was published, with a time-limit (1 January 1689) attached to the offer. In November William's army mastered England. The emperor's army had already taken Belgrade, Ottoman envoys had reached Vienna to discuss peace. By the narrowest of margins the king of Denmark was again persuaded not to start fighting in the country east of Hamburg. By another narrow margin, and with his usual hesitation, Leopold was verging towards the view that Protestant William, not Catholic James, should have his support and friendship. Troops formerly in Hungary were back in Germany, where more troops were being raised to drive out the French. Later, the elector of Bavaria would be tempted by offers of dominion in the Spanish Netherlands, and the duke of Piedmont-Savoy successfully detached from France, but the outlines of a new alliance of powers against Louis XIV were already drawn by his formidable enemies. Another period of general war in the west, with the setting arranged in this way, was at hand.

Perhaps the Marquis Halifax should have the last word: 'Our affairs here,' he had written from England to William of Orange in May 1687, 'depend so much upon what may be done abroad that our thoughts, though never so reasonable, may change by what we may hear by the next post.' The future would show that the converse of this, the impact on the Continent of English affairs, assets, and ideas, mattered no less during the next two centuries; but the truth is that, both before and after 1688, changes of apparently local or regional importance in widely scattered areas interacted to produce complex results. In this lies the perennial fascination of *European history*.

The Ruling Dynasties
Further Reading
Index

The Ruling Dynasties

Note: in order to show clearly the network of family alliances, many of the female names given here are in italic. The italicised names always occur twice: to indicate descent, and also marriage into another family. (1), (2) and (3) refer to a first, second or third marriage, and to the offspring of these marriages.

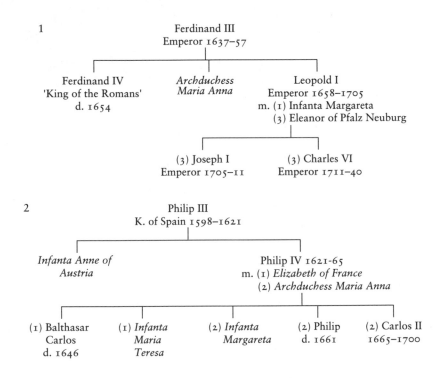

1

Ferdinand III
Emperor 1637–57

Ferdinand IV
'King of the Romans'
d. 1654

*Archduchess
Maria Anna*

Leopold I
Emperor 1658–1705
m. (1) Infanta Margareta
(3) Eleanor of Pfalz Neuburg

(3) Joseph I
Emperor 1705–11

(3) Charles VI
Emperor 1711–40

2

Philip III
K. of Spain 1598–1621

*Infanta Anne of
Austria*

Philip IV 1621-65
m. (1) *Elizabeth of France*
(2) *Archduchess Maria Anna*

(1) Balthasar
Carlos
d. 1646

(1) *Infanta
Maria
Teresa*

(2) *Infanta
Margareta*

(2) Philip
d. 1661

(2) Carlos II
1665–1700

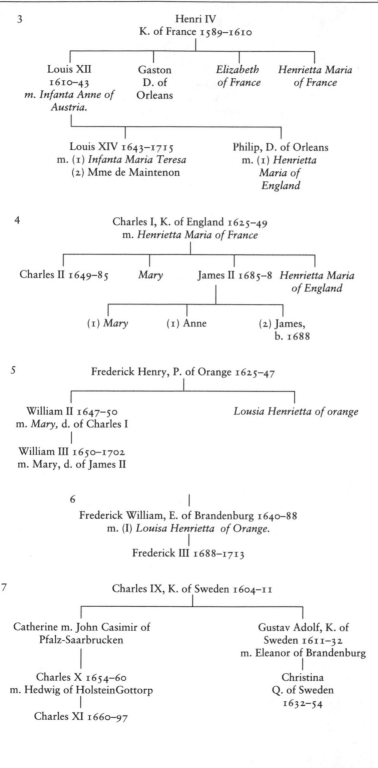

3

Henri IV
K. of France 1589–1610

Louis XII
1610–43
m. Infanta Anne of
Austria.

Gaston
D. of
Orleans

Elizabeth
of France

Henrietta Maria
of France

Louis XIV 1643–1715
m. (1) *Infanta Maria Teresa*
(2) Mme de Maintenon

Philip, D. of Orleans
m. (1) *Henrietta*
Maria of
England

4

Charles I, K. of England 1625–49
m. *Henrietta Maria of France*

Charles II 1649–85   *Mary*   James II 1685–8   *Henrietta Maria*
of England

(1) *Mary*   (1) Anne   (2) James,
b. 1688

5

Frederick Henry, P. of Orange 1625–47

William II 1647–50
m. *Mary,* d. of Charles I

Lousia Henrietta of orange

William III 1650–1702
m. Mary, d. of James II

6

Frederick William, E. of Brandenburg 1640–88
m. (I) *Louisa Henrietta of Orange.*

Frederick III 1688–1713

7

Charles IX, K. of Sweden 1604–11

Catherine m. John Casimir of
Pfalz-Saarbrucken

Gustav Adolf, K. of
Sweden 1611–32
m. Eleanor of Brandenburg

Charles X 1654–60
m. Hedwig of HolsteinGottorp

Christina
Q. of Sweden
1632–54

Charles XI 1660–97

8   Alexei, Tsar 1645–76
                                     m. (1) Maria Miloslavski
                                         (2) Natalia Naryyshkin

(1) Sophia	(1) Theodore	(1) Ivan	(2) Peter I
Regent	Tsar	Tsar	Tsar
1682–9	1676–82	1682–9	1682–1725

Further Reading

I have tried to show what happened in Europe within a span of forty years. Historians nowadays often prefer longer phases for study, for example 1500–1650, or 1648–1789; while what is called 'early modern Europe' usually covers c.1500–c.1800. This enables them to view the more gradual contours of social, economic, intellectual or technological change. Since 1945 they have been wonderfully successful, and their work – in many countries – has produced a veritable cascade of history books. One must now choose, and prefer, and omit, in order to survive.

To fit my account into the broader framework a number of guides can be used: H. G. Koenigsberger, *Early Modern Europe 1500–1789* (London, 1987) which is simple and clear or the more complex Companion Volume (XIII) of the *New Cambridge Modern History* (1979); P. Chaunu, *La civilisation de l'Europe classique* (Paris, 1966), with many diagrams and illustrations, which is concerned with the years 1620–1760; and W. Doyle, *The Old European Order 1660–1800* (Oxford, 1978), or G. Treasure, *The Making of Modern Europe 1648–1780* (London, 1985), or R. J. Bonney, *The European Dynastic States 1494–1660* (Oxford, 1991). There is always more to find in I. Wallerstein, *The modern World-System II: Mercantilism and the Consolidation of the European World-economy 1600–1750* (New York, 1980). Set in a smaller frame are T. Munck, *Seventeenth Century Europe ... 1598–1700* (Basingstoke, 1990); D. H. Pennington, *Seventeenth-century Europe* (London, 1970), plus the venerable but valuable G. N. Clark, *The Seventeenth Century* (Oxford, ed. 1945)

Using the longer time-span historians have therefore been able to study various topics which, in passing, help to illumine the years 1648–88: for example T. K. Rabb, *The Struggle for Stability in Early Modern Europe* (Oxford, 1975); *Royal and Republican Sovereignty in Early Modern Europe*, ed. R. Oresko (Cambridge, 1997); P. Burke, *Popular Culture in Early Modern Europe*, (London, 1978); P. Musgrave, *The Early Modern European Economy* (London, 1999); B. P. Levack, *The Witch Hunt in Early Modern Europe* (London, 1987); W. Monter, *Ritual, Myth and Magic in Early Modern Europe* (Brighton, 1983; or A. Maczak, *Travel in Early Modern Europe* (Oxford, 1995).

Equally relevant are J. U. Nef, *War and Human Progress* (Harvard, 1950) and B. M. Downing, *The Military Revolution and Political Change* (Princeton, 1992); *Absolutism in Seventeenth-century Europe*, ed. J. Miller (London, 1990); J. de Vries, *The Economy of Europe in an Age of Crises 1600–1750* (Cambridge, 1976); J. Adamson, *The Princely Courts of Europe, 1500–1750* (London, 1999); *European Jewry in the Age of Mercantilism 1550–1750*, ed. J. I. Israel (London, 1998); and *A History of Technology*, vol. III. (*c.*1500–*c.*1750), ed C. Singer (Oxford, 1957). For a general study of the churches: W. R. Ward, *Christianity under the Ancien Regime* (Cambridge, 1999); *The Church in the Age of Absolutism and Enlightenment*, ed H. Jedin and J. Dolan (London, 1981) together with J. Delumeau, *Catholicism between Luther and Voltaire* (London, 1977); and R. S. Dunn, *The Age of Religious Wars 1559–1689* (London, 1970). For the arts: first H. Wolfflin, *Renaissance and Baroque* (ed. London, 1964); then M. Kitson, *The Age of the Baroque* (London, 1966); V.–L. Tapié, *The Age of Grandeur* (London, 1960); relevant volumes in the *Pelican History of Art* (Yale, 1998); and also *The New Oxford History of Music*, vols V and VI (1998). For the sciences see chapter 8 below.

Alongside modern learning it is rewarding to approach old Europe through the eyes of contemporary travellers: the Netherlands, France and Italy are vividly revealed in the early years of John Evelyn's *Diary*, ed. E. S. de Beer (Oxford, 1955) and earlier editions; Russia in *The Travels of Olearius* ed. S. H. Baron (Stanford, 1979); and Germany in (if you can find it) *Master Johann Deutz*, tr. B. Miall (London, 1923).

Chapter 1 The Empire

The attraction of German history in this period depends partly on the complexity of its political landscape. Perhaps regional studies are worth consulting first: F. L. Carsten, *The origins of Prussia* (Oxford, 1947 and G. Benecke, *Society and Politics in Germany 1500–1750* (London, 1974) on Lippe, and J. A. Vann, *The Making of a state*: *Württemberg 1593–1793* (Cornell, 1984), or G. L. Soliday, *A Community in Conflict* (Brandeis, 1974) on Frankfurt, or C. R. Friedrichs, *Urban Society in an Age of War: Nördlingen 1580–1720* (London, 1995)). Then look at the broader scene: R. Vierhaus, *Germany in the Age of Absolutism* (Cambridge, 1988) may be compared with J. G. Gagliardo, *Germany under the Old Regime 1600–1790* (London, 1991), J. A. Vann and S. W. Rowan, *The Old Reich ... 1495–1806* (Brussels, 1974) and F. L. Carsten, *Princes and Parliaments in Germany* (Oxford, 1959). A brief, illuminating account of the political tangle and of an important statesman is G. Menk, *Friedrich von Waldeck 1620–1692* (Arolsen, 1992).

For the Lutheran church consult the opening chapters of N. Hope, *German and Scandinavian Protestantism 1700–1918* (Oxford, 1995), and also M. Fulbrook, *Piety and Politics in England, Württemberg and Prussia*, (Cambridge, 1983). P. H. Wilson, *German Armies ... 1648–1806* (London, 1998) introduces another crucial topic. More light-hearted, *The Letterbook of Sir George Etherege*, ed. S. Rosenfeld (Oxford, 1928) gives an impression of higher German society in the 1680s, observed by an Englishman at Regensburg.

Chapter 2 Eastern Europe, 1648–60

(1) The issues in the Ukraine emerge in W. H. McNeil, *Europe's Steppe Frontier 1500–1800* (Chicago, 1964), F. G. Sysyn, *Between Poland and the Ukraine: The Dilemma of Adam Kysil 1600–1653* (Harvard, 1985), and in the two last chapters of I. Ševčenko, *Ukraine between East and West* (Edmonton, Alberta, 1996). W. E. D. Allen, *The Ukraine* (Cambridge, 1940) remains valuable; also useful is N. L. Chirovsky, *An Introduction to Ukrainian History*, vol. II (New York, 1984). *La Description d'Ukranie de Guillaume Le Vasseur de Beauplan*, ed. D. F. Essar and A. B. Pernal (Ottawa, 1990) – with maps – is remarkable; it was first published in Rouen in 1657/60.

(2) For Muscovy (and indeed for the Ukraine) G. V. Vernadsky, *The Tsardom of Moscow 1547–1682*, pts 1 and 2 (New Haven, 1969), is a comprehensive guide. The person and powers of the Tsar become clearer in P. Longworth, *Alexis* (London, 1984). Outside the Kremlin the following all dig deeply: R. Hellie, *Enserfment and Military Change in Muscovy* (Chicago, 1971), R. O. Crummey, *Aristocrats and Servitors. The Boyar Elite in Russia 1613–1689* (Princeton, 1983), and J. M. Hittle, *The Service City* (Harvard, 1979). General readers can become more intimately acquainted with Tsar Alexei's capital city in A. Voyce, *Moscow and the Roots of Russian Culture* (Newton Abbot, 1972) nor should they overlook J. H. Billington, *The Icon and the Axe: An Interpretive History of Russian Culture* (New York, 1970) on this period.

(3) The whole cluster of histories which become Polish-Lithuanian history is visible in N. Davies, *God's Playground. A History of Poland*, vol. I (Oxford, 1981) but R. I. Frost, *After the Deluge: Poland-Lithuania and the Second Northern War 1655–1660* (Cambridge, 1993) takes a closer look at this crisis. In *A Republic of Nobles*, ed. J. K. Fedorowicz (Cambridge, 1982) and in *East-Central Europe in Transition*, ed. P. Burke (Cambridge-Paris, 1985), several contributors discuss matters of interest here. A diverting source, used with due caution by historians, are the *Memoirs of J. C. Z. G Pasek* (New York, 1978); in a different translation they become *Memoirs of the Polish Baroque*, ed. C. S. Leach (Berkeley, 1976).

(4) The simplest introduction to events in the Ottoman empire at this time is D. M. Vaughan, *England and the Turk* (Liverpool, 1954). The best general surveys can be found in Stanford J. Shaw, *History of the Ottoman Empire and Modern Turkey*, vol. I (Cambridge, 1976) and *A History of the Ottoman Empire to 1730*, ed. M. Cook (Cambridge, 1976). Important for the background is I. Metin Kunt, *The Sultan's Servants: The Transformation of*

Ottoman Provincial Government, 1550–1650 (New York, 1983). The long
war with Venice is described at length in K. M. Setton, *Venice, Austria and
the Turks in the Seventeenth Century* (Philadelphia, 1991). At home, the
inner apartments of the Ottoman Sultans' palace are now visible thanks to
L. P. Peirce, *The Imperial Harem* (Oxford, 1993). R. Mantran, *Istanbul dans
la seconde moitié du 17e siècle* (Paris, 1962) is a study of the city on a grand
scale, while A. Pallis, *In the Days of the Janissaries* (London, 1951), from a
contemporary source, is singularly good reading.

  The Ottoman provinces in Europe can be studied in B. A. Cvetkova, *Les
institutions ottomanes en Europe* (Wiesbaden, 1978), P. F. Sugar, *South-
eastern Europe under Ottoman Rule 1354–1804* (Seattle, 1977), A. E.
Vacalopoulos, *The Greek Nation 1453–1669* (New Brunswick, 1976),
D. P. Hupchick, *The Bulgarians in the Seventeenth Century* (Jefferson,
North Carolina, 1993), L. Hadrovics, *Le peuple serbe et son église sous la
domination turque* (Paris, 1947) and B. McGowan, *Economic Life in Ottoman Europe* (Cambridge, 1981) More distant were the border principalities:
for these *A History of Romania*, ed. K. W. Treptow (Iai, 1996); L. Makkai,
Histoire de Transylvanie (Paris, 1946) or S. Pascu, *A History of Transylvania* (Detroit, 1982); and the papers in *Historians and the History of Transylvania*, ed. L. Peter (Boulder, 1992), are all worth a search. To these may be
added F. C. Carter, *Dubrovnik* (London, 1972).

Chapter 3   France and the Fronde

Convenient surveys of a broad span of French history include R. Briggs,
Early Modern France 1550–1715 (Oxford, 1977) and J. B. Collins, *The
State in Early Modern France* (Cambridge, 1995). To confront this half-
century more directly P. Goubert, *Louis XIV and Twenty Million Frenchmen*
(London, 1978), combined with the chapters by R. Mousnier and G. Livet in
the *New CMH*, vol. iv (1970), and with O. Ranum, *Paris in the Age of
Absolutism* (New York, 1970), make a good start. Le Roy Ladurie, *The
Ancien Regime 1610–1774* (Oxford, 1996) is both broader and more
detailed; other large surveys are R. Mandrou, *Louis XIV en son temps
1661–1715* (Paris, 1973), E. Labrousse, *Histoire economique et sociale de
la France*, vol. ii (Paris, 1970) and the handsomely illustrated panorama of P.
Goubert and D. Roche, *Les Français de l'ancien régime* (Paris, 1984) For a
large-scale view of one region, a study of both E. Le Roy Ladurie, *Les
Paysans de Languedoc* (Paris, 1966), and W. Beik, *Absolutism and Society
in Seventeenth Century France: State Power and Provincial Aristocracy in
Languedoc* (Cambridge, 1985), is rewarding. An earlier regional study
deserves notice: R. Roupnel, *La Ville et la campagne du 17e siècle: étude
sur les populations du pays Dijonnais* (edn Paris, 1960).

  On the Fronde: R. J. Bonney, *Political change in France... 1624–1661*
(Oxford, 1978), and then O. Ranum, *The Fronde: A French Revolution
1648–1652* (New York, 1993) and E. H. Kossmann, *La Fronde* (Leyden,
1964), G. Treasure *Mazarin: The Crisis of Absolutism in France*
(London, 1995), A. Lloyd Moote, *The Revolt of the Judges 1643–1652*

(Princeton, 1971) and R. M. Golden, *The Godly Rebellion, Parisians, Curés and the Religious Fronde, 1652–1662* (Chapel Hill, 1981). Events in Bordeaux, and the links between this city and the English radicals, are described in the final chapter of H. N. Brailsford, *The Levellers and the English Revolution* (London, 1961); cf. S. A. Westrich, *The Ormée of Bordeaux* (Baltimore, 1972). There are two modern studies of de Retz by English authors, J. H. M. Salmon, *Cardinal de Retz, The Anatomy of a Conspirator* (London, 1969) and D. A. Watts, *Cardinal de Retz: The Ambiguities of a 17th century Mind* (Oxford, 1980). Sec also G. Dethan, *La vie de Gaston d'Orléans* (Paris, 1992).

Chapter 4   The Spanish Empire in Europe

(1) Good introductions to Spanish Habsburg history are now J. Lynch, *The Hispanic World in Crisis and Change: 1598–1700* (Oxford, 1992); and, in the inter-state context, R. A. Stradling, *Europe and the Decline of Spain 1580–1720* (London, 1980). For a closer look at 1650–1700, R. A. Stradling, *Philip IV and the Government of Spain 1621–1665* (Cambridge, 1988) is followed by H. Kamen, *Spain in the later Seventeenth Century, 1665–1700* (London, 1980); these should be compared with the older work of E. J. Hamilton, *War and Prices in Spain 1651–1800* (Harvard, 1947) A. Domingo Ortiz, *La societad española en el siglo XVII* (Madrid, 1963, 1970) presents a fine general survey of both secular and ecclesiastical groupings in Spanish society; and another book with a broad context is D. R. Ringrose, *Madrid and the Spanish Economy* (Berkeley, 1983). For regional studies there are P. Vilar, *La Catalogne dans l'Espagne moderne* (Paris, 1963), vol. I, pp. 587–710, J. Casey, *The Kingdom of Valencia in the Seventeenth Century* (Cambridge, 1979), C. R. Phillips, *Ciudad Real 1500–1750* (Harvard, 1979), and R. L. Kagan, *Lawsuits and Litigants in Castile 1500–1700* (Chapel Hill, 1979). But some readers may prefer, to the admirable works of modern research, old M. de Villars, *Mémoires de la cour d'Espagne de 1679–1681*, ed. A. Morel-Fatio (Paris, 1893), and his wife who was with him and wrote the *Lettres de Madame de Villars…*ed. A. de Courtois (Paris, 1868). Different again, and giving useful clues to the ecclesiastical atmosphere in this period are T. D. Kendrick, *Saint James in Spain* (London, 1960) and S. N. Orso, *Art and Death at the Spanish Habsburg Court: The Royal Exequies for Philip IV* (Missouri, 1989).

(2) R. Villari, *The Revolt of Naples,* (ed. Cambridge, 1993) explains the background to the revolution of 1648: his approach may be compared with Benedetto Croce's *History of the kingdom of Naples* (edn. Chicago, 1970), G. Coniglio, *Il viceregno di Napoli nel sec. XVII* (Rome, 1955, pp. 274–322 and G. Galasso, *Il Mezzogiorno nella storia d'Italia* (Florence, 1977). For a topic of great importance see J. A. Marino, *Pastoral Economics in the Kingdom of Naples* (Baltimore, 1988). In contrast, A. Reumont, *The Carafas of Maddaloni* (London, 1854) is an old curiosity shop, though a valuable one; another family's history can be found in T. Astarita, *The*

Continuity of Feudal Power: The Caracciolo di Brienza in Spanish Naples (Cambridge, 1992). Two good studies in biography are M. Schipa, *Masaniello* (Bari, 1925), and F. Nicolini, *La giovinezza di Giambattista Vico (1668–1700)* (Bari, 1932).

For comparisons with the northern half of Habsburg Italy see D. Sella, *Crisis and Continuity: The Economy of Spanish Lombardy in the Seventeenth Century* (Harvard, 1979), and the same author's general survey, *Italy in the Seventeenth Century* (London, 1997).

Chapter 5   The United Provinces and Sweden, 1648–72

(1) Everyone should read Sir William Temple, *Some Observations upon the United Provinces of the Netherlands*, ed. G. N. Clark (Oxford, 1972). Of modern writers perhaps J. H. Huizinga, *Dutch Civilisation in the 17th Century* (London, 1968) and A. T. V. Deursen, *Plain Lives in a Golden Age: Popular Culture...in Seventeenth Century Holland* (Cambridge, 1991) best convey the quality of Dutch life in this period. For general politics: J. L. Price, *The Dutch Republic in the Seventeenth Century* (London, 1998), J. I. Israel, *The Dutch Republic: Its Rise, Greatness and Fall, 1477–1806* (Oxford, 1995), P. Geyl, *Orange and Stuart 1641–72* (London, 1969), H. H. Rowen, *John de Witt: Statesman of the 'True Freedom'* (Cambridge, 1986) and also his *The Stadholders in the Dutch Republic* (Cambridge, 1988). A number of important topics are explored by A. M. Lambert, *The Making of the Dutch Landscape* (ed. London, 1985); J. de Vries, *The Dutch Rural Economy in the Golden Age 1500–1700* (Yale, 1974); V. Barbour, *Capitalism in Amsterdam in the Seventeenth-century* (Michigan, 1963) and P. Burke, *Venice and Amsterdam* (London, 1974); S. D. Muller, *Charity in the Dutch Republic* (Ann Arbor, 1985); R. W. Unger, *Dutch Shipbuilding before 1800* (Amsterdam, 1978) and J. R. Bruijn, *The Dutch Navy of the Seventeenth and Eighteenth Centuries* (Columbia, South Carolina, 1993); J. M. Postma, *The Dutch in the Atlantic Slave Trade 1600–1815* (Cambridge, 1990); and B. Haak, *The Golden Age: Dutch Painters of the Seventeenth Century* (New York, 1984).

From a European point of view the study of Anglo-Dutch relations is rewarding: they can be looked at in C. Wilson, *Power and Profit* (London, 1957); R. L. Colie, *Light and Enlightenment, a Study of the Cambridge Platonists and the Dutch Arminians* (Cambridge, 1957); and above all in many papers in the series *Britain and the Netherlands*, ed. J. Bromley and others (1964–). Remarkable in various ways are the brief W. R. Valentiner, *Rembrandt and Spinoza* (London 1957); the itinerant M. Bowen, *The Netherlands Display'd* (London, 1926), and the bountiful S. Schama, *The Embarrassment of Riches: An Interpretation of Dutch Culture in the Golden Age* (London, 1987); without forgetting *The Anglo-Dutch Garden in the Age of William and Mary*, ed. J. D. Hunt (London, 1988)

(2)   For an introduction to Sweden after 1648: J. Lisk, *The Struggle for Supremacy in the Baltic* (London, 1967), A. Andersson, *A History of*

Sweden (London, 1955), E. F. Heckscher, *An Economic History of Sweden*, (London, 1967), D. Kirby, *Northern Europe in the Early Modern Period 1492–1772* (London, 1990) or S. P. Oakley, *War and Peace in the Baltic, 1560–1790* (London, 1992). But indispensable in this context are the shorter works of Michael Roberts, especially his *Essays in Swedish History* (London, 1967), *The Swedish Imperial Experience* (Cambridge, 1979) or *From Oxenstierna to Charles XII: Four Studies* (Cambridge, 1991). C. Weibull, *Christina of Sweden* (Gothenburg, 1966) is a translation from the Swedish; S. Åkermann, *Queen Christina of Sweden and her Circle* (Leyden, 1991) describes her more esoteric and millenarian interests. B. Whitelocke, *Journal of the Swedish Embassy...in 1653 and 1654* (London, 1772 and 1855) gives the observations of a contemporary witness.

Chapter 6   Denmark, the Austrian Lands, Piedmont

1)   For Danish history, in addition to the general works mentioned above see T. Munck, *The Peasantry and the Early Absolute Monarchy in Denmark 1660–1708* (Copenhagen 1979); and T. Kjaergaart, *The Danish Revolution 1500–1800: An Ecohistorical Interpretation* (Cambridge, 1994); and A Friis and K. Glamann, *History of Wages and Prices in Denmark 1660–1800* (London, 1958). In the *Scandinavian Economic History Review* can be found A. Lassen, 'The population of Denmark in 1660', vol. 13 (1965), and J. Jorgensen, 'Denmark's relations with Lübeck and Hamburg in the 17th century', vol. 11 (1963). A moving and once famous autobiography is the *Memoirs of Leonora Christina, 1663–85*, tr. F. E. Bunnett (London, 1872 and 1929).

(2)   On the Austrian Habsburg lands there is much to explore, first in R. J. Evans, *The Making of the Habsburg Monarchy 1550–1700* (Oxford, 1979) or in J. Bérenger, *Finances et absolutisme autrichien dans la seconde moitié du XVIIe siècle* (Paris, 1975) and P. F. Sugar, *A History of Hungary* (London, 1990). A swifter introduction is C. Ingrao, *The Habsburg Monarchy, 1618–1815* (Cambridge, 1994)). Following them J. P. Spielman, in *Leopold I of Austria* (London, 1977) and his *The Crown and the City: Vienna and the Imperial Court, 1600–1740* (West Lafayette, Indiana, 1993), gives a good account of the ruler and his capital; while two contrasting spokesmen of the age, both active in Vienna, are depicted in S. J. T. Miller and J. P. Spielman, *Christobal Rojas y Spinola, Cameralist and Irenecist 1626–1695* (Philadelphia, 1965) and R. A. Kann, *A Study in Austrian Intellectual History: From Late Baroque to Romanticism* (London, 1960), of which part deals with the preacher Abraham a Sancta Clara.

(3)   For the developments in Piedmont: M. D. Pollak, *Turin 1564–1680* (Chicago, 1991), and G. Symcox, *Victor Amadeus II* (London, 1983); and *Royal and Republican Sovereignty in Early Modern Europe*, ed. R. Oresko (Cambridge, 1997).

Chapter 7   France after 1652

Clearly, many – probably most – of the works already mentioned for chapter 3 also belong here. In addition the old learning of E. Lavisse, *Histoire de France*, vol. vii (Paris, 1907), now reissued as *Louis XIV* (Paris, 1983), has much to offer; while there are many stimulating pieces in *Louis XIV and Absolutism*, ed. R. Hatton (London, 1976) and in *Louis XIV and the Craft of Kingship*, ed. J. C. Rule (Ohio, 1969). A very good discussion of important issues is A. Lossky's *Louis XIV and the French Monarchy* (New Brunswick, NJ, 1994) The work of C. W. Cole, *Colbert and a Century of French Mercantilism* (New York, 1939) and his *French Mercantilism 1683–1700* (New York 1943, which are spacious, can be compared with the more compact J. Meyer, *Colbert* (Paris, 1984) and A. P. Trout, *Colbert* (Boston, 1978). E. Esmonin, *La taille en Normandie ... 1661–1683* (Paris, 1913), J. Dent, *Crisis in Finance: Crown, Financiers and Society in Seventeenth-Century France* (Newton Abbot, 1973), S. Kettering, *Patrons, Brokers and Clients in Seventeenth Century France* (Oxford, 1986), J. E. King, *Science and Rationalism in the Government of Louis XIV 1661–1683* (Baltimore, 1949), Harcourt Brown, *Scientific Organisation in 17th Century France* (New York, ed. 1967) and E. L. Asher, *The Resistance of the Maritime Classes ... in the France of Colbert* (Berkeley, 1960) are relevant to these Colbert studies. For decor, propaganda and opposition: Norbert Elias, *The Court Society* (Oxford, 1983), J. Klaits, *Printed Propaganda under Louis XIV* (Princeton, 1976), P. Burke, *The Fabrication of Louis XIV* (Yale, 1992), R. Mettam, *Power and Faction in Louis XIV's France* (Oxford, 1988), L. Rothkrug, *Opposition to Louis XIV* (Princeton, 1964) and W. Beik, *Urban Protest in Seveenth Century France* (Cambridge, 1997). For the army: A. Courvoisier, *Louvois* (Paris, 1983), J. A. Lynn, *Giant of the Grand Siècle: The French Army, 1610–1715* (Cambridge, 1997) and J. Bérenger, *Turenne* (Paris, 1987). One excellent contemporary observer of the scene may be found in *Locke's Travels in France 1675–9*, ed. J. Lough (Cambridge, 1953. For two important topics, not discussed in my text, see G. de Vaumas, *L'éveil missionaire de la France au xviie siècle* (Paris, 1950), and L. W. B. Brockliss, *French Higher Education in the Seventeenth and Eighteenth Centuries* (Oxford, 1987).

Chapter 8   Religion and Science

(1)   An introduction to the wider world of popular and intellectual thinking in France, of which Jansenism was one element, is R. Briggs, *Communities of Belief: Cultural and Social Tensions in Early Modern France* (Oxford, 1989). A clear, brief account of the Jansenist controversy can be found in the *New CMH*, vol. v chap 6, or in L. Cognet, *Le Jansénisme* (Paris, 1961) and R. Tavenaux, *Jansénisme et politique* (Paris, 1965), while there is much to be learnt from the varied standpoints of L. Goldmann, *The Hidden God* (London, 1964), N. Abercrombie, *The Origins of Jansenism* (Oxford,

1936), J. Mesnard, *Pascal* (London, 1952) and R. Knox, *Enthusiasm* (Oxford, 1950, chapters 9 and 10).

(2) For religion in Russia P. Pascal, *Avvakum et les débuts de Raskol* (Paris, 1963) is a masterpiece on a big scale, to be compared with Avvakum's own short autobiography, *The Life of the Archpriest...by himself* (London, 1963), and with P. Miliukov, *Outlines of Russian Culture: Religion and the Church in Russia* (New York, 1960), N. Lupinin, *Religious Revolt in the Seventeenth Century: the Schism of the Russian Church* (Princeton, 1984) and with P. Bushkovitch, *Religion and Society in Russia: The Sixteenth and Seventeenth Centuries* (Oxford, 1992).

(3) The literature on seventeenth-century philosophy and science grows continuously, but E. Bréhier, *The History of Philosophy: The Seventeenth-Century* (trans. Chicago, 1966) and A. R. Hall, *From Galileo to Newton* (ed. 1981, New York) are outstandingly useful. E. J. Dijsterhuis, *The Mechanisation of the World Picture* (Oxford, 1961) is more demanding, H. Kearney, *Science and Change* (London, 1971) less so. On particular facets and personalities, J. L. Heilbron, *Elements of Early Modern Physics* (Berkeley, 1982), *The Western Medical Tradition 800 BC–AD 1800* (chapter 6) ed. R. Porter (Cambridge, 1995), *The Scientific Revolution in National Context*, ed. R. Porter and M. Teich (Cambridge, 1992), A. E. Bell, *Christian Huygens and the Development of Science in the Seventeenth Century* (London, 1947), M. Boas, *Robert Boyle and Seventeenth-century Chemistry* (Cambridge, 1958, and H. C. King, *The History of the Telescope* (London, 1955), are all helpful.

Chapter 9   Diplomacy and War, 1661–78

An outline of this intricate topic is L. André, *Louis XIV et l'Europe* (Paris, 1950) while there are good detailed discussions in H. H. Rowen, *The Ambassador Prepares for War: The Dutch Embassy of Arnauld de Pomponne 1669–71* (The Hague, 1957), C. J. Ekberg, *The Failure of Louis XIV's Dutch War* (Chapel Hill, 1979) and C.-G. Picavet, *La diplomatie française au temps de Louis XIV, 1661–1715* (Paris, 1930). A short and helpful study is C. Badalo-Dulong, *Trente ans de diplomatie française en Allemagne – Louis XIV et l'Electeur de Mayence, 1648–1678* (Paris, 1956). From other and non-French points of view, D. Ogg, *England under Charles II* (edn, Oxford, 1963–4), chapters 8–10, 15–16, H. Pirenne, *Histoire de Belgique*, vol. v (edn., Brussels, 1926), pp. 1–39, and O. Redlich, *Weltmacht des Barock. Österreich in der Zeit Kaiser Leopolds I.* (edn. Vienna, 1961), pp. 77–157, complicate but improve the perspective. For the whole period down to 1688 a good biography of William of Orange in English is S. B. Baxter, *William III* (London, 1966), although its natural bias against Louis XIV occasionally seems overemphatic. A German study, F. Textor, *Entfestigungen und Zerstörungen im Rheingebiet während des*

17. Fahrhunderts . . . (Bonn, 1937), has valuable suggestions about the warfare and military thinking of these years. It should be compared with P. Lazard, *Vauban, 1633–1707* (Paris, 1934). On French expansion eastwards M. Roux, *Louis XIV et les provinces conquises* (Paris, 1938), gives a swift survey; G. Livet, *L'intendance d'Alsace sous Louis XIV, 1648–1715* (Strasbourg, 1956), pp. 381–434, is masterly and detailed on one area.

For the delimitation of the Belgian frontier following the treaty of Nijmegen the work of N. G. d'Albissin (*Genèse de la frontière franco-belge* . . . *1659–1789* (Paris, 1978) is important. Finally, *The Peace of Nijmegen 1676–1678/79* (Amsterdam, 1980), ed. J. A. H. Bots, is a collection of papers describing many issues raised during the 1670s; while *À la gloire du Roi. Van der Meulen peintre des conquêtes de Louis XIV* (Musée des Beaux-Arts de Dijon, 1988) is both beautiful and informative.

Chapter 10   Eastern Europe, the Venetian Empire, and Italy, *c.*1672–*c.*1688

(1)   For Polish difficulties in the borderlands and elsewhere both O. Subtelny, *Domination of Eastern Europe and Foreign Absolutism 1500–1715* (McGill and Gloucester GB, 1986) and A. S. Kamiński, *Republic vs. Autocracy: Poland-Lithuania and Russia, 1686–1697* (Harvard, 1993), supplement the authorities already noted for Chap 2. There are also two biographies, O. Laskowski, *Sobieski King of Poland* (Glasgow, 1944) and Forst de Battaglia, *Jan Sobieski* (Graz/Warsaw, ed. 1982, in German and Polish versions), which describe the remarkable career of a Polish nobleman and king.

(2)   Meanwhile in Muscovy, for the later part of Alexei's reign and those of his successors, Vernadsky and Longworth (above, chapter 2) can be compared with C. Bickford O'Brien, *Russia under Two Tsars* (Berkeley, 1952) and Lindsay Hughes, *Sophia Regent of Russia 1657–1704* (London, 1990). There are some interesting details of a Scotsman's career in Russian service at this date in B. Buxhoeveden, *A Cavalier in Muscovy* (London, 1932).

(3)   The struggle for supremacy in southeast Europe between 1664 and 1700 is surveyed by D. M. Barker *Double Eagle and Crescent* (New York, 1967), by I. Parvev, *Habsburgs and Ottomans between Vienna and Belgrade* (Boulder, 1995), J. Stoye, *Marsigli's Europe 1680–1730* (Yale, 1995) and Z. Zlatar, *Between the Double Eagle and the Crescent* (Boulder, 1992). For the year 1683, see J. Stoye, *The Siege of Vienna* (edn. Edinburgh, 2000) and, looking further north, A. Lossky, *Louis XIV, William III and the Baltic Crisis of 1683,* (Berkeley, 1954).

(4)   The general background in Ottoman Istanbul/Constantinople and Edirne/Adrianople at this period can be viewed in G. F. Abbott, *Under the Turk in Constantinople* . . . *1674–1681* (London, 1920), in A. Vandal, *Les voyages du marquis de Nointel, 1670–1680* (Paris, 1900), and meticulously in Mantran (above, chapter 2). For Christians and Jews in the empire, see S.

Runciman, *The Great Church in Captivity* (Cambridge, 1968) and G. Scholem, *Sabbatai Sevi the Mystical Messiah 1626–1676* (London, 1973).

(4) For the Venetian war-efforts Setton (above, chapter 2) is a sure guide. On this topic there is something of interest in G. Hanlon, *The Twilight of a Military Tradition: Italian Aristocrats and European Conflicts 1560–1800* (London, 1998); J. M. Paton, *The Venetians in Athens 1687–1688* (Harvard, 1940), is an intriguing miscellany of texts and notes. For the Republic itself, and the varied elements of stagnation and resilience, J. C. Davis, *The Decline of the Venetian Aristocracy as a Ruling Class* (Baltimore, 1962); R. T. Rapp, *Industry and Economic Decline in Seventeenth-century Venice* (Cambridge, Mass. 1976); P. Burke, *Venice and Amsterdam* (London, 1974); P. Musgrave, *Land and Economy in Baroque Italy: Valpolicella 1630–1797* (Leicester, 1992); and B. Pullan, *The Jews of Europe and the Inquisition of Venice 1550–1670* (Oxford, 1983). For comparisons between Venetia and the regime elsewhere in Italy: G. P. Brizzi, *La formazione della classe dirigente nel sei-settecento* (Bologna, 1976), and R. B. Litchfield, *Emergence of a Bureaucracy: The Florentine Patricians, 1530–1790)* (Princeton, 1986) or E. W. Cochrane, *Florence in the Forgotten Centuries 1527–1800* (Chicago, 1973).

Reading about the arts in Italy at this time could begin with J. Lees-Milne, *Baroque in Italy* (London, 1959, E. Waterhouse, *Italian Baroque Painting* (London, 1962), or A. Blunt, *Sicilian Baroque* (London, 1968); and go further with R. Krautheimer, *The Rome of Alexander VII, 1655–1667* (Princeton, 1985), F. Haskell, *Patrons and Painters* (London, 1963), and R. Wittkower, *Gian Lorenzo Bernini* (London, 1955).

Chapter 11   After 1680

(1) Economic conditions before and after 1680 are examined in: H. Kamen, *Spain in the later Seventeenth Century, 1665–1700* (London, 1969); C. Wilson, *England's Apprenticeship 1603–1763* (London, 1965); T. C. Smout, *Scottish Trade on the Eve of the Union, 1660–1707* (Edinburgh, 1963; S.-E. Aström, *From Stockholm to St Petersburg…1675–1700* (Helsinki, 1962); J. Israel, *The Dutch Republic* (see p. 302 above); and K. Glamann, *Dutch-Asiatic Trade 1620–1730* (Copenhagen, 1958). For the political changes in Sweden, see A. F. Upton, *Charles XI and Swedish Absolutism* (Cambridge, 1998). For the impact of warfare on a single region in this period cf. M. P. Gutmann, *War and Rural Life in the Early Modern Low Countries* (Princeton, 1980).

(2) The causes and consequences of the Revocation of the Edict of Nantes have produced an immense literature, and continue to tantalise historians. Two good, short works are P. Deyon, *Du loyalisme au refus* (Lille, 1976) and J. Quéniart, *La révocation de l'édit de Nantes* (Paris, 1985). The papers entitled 'Les protestants en France au 17e siècle', *XVIIe Siècle*, nos. 76–7 (1967) offer further material, while references to the Huguenots in Le Roy

Ladurie's book on Languedoc, and in John Locke's notes (see p. 304 above) are of great interest. *The Huguenot Connection... and Early French Migration to South Carolina*, ed. R. M. Golden (Dordrecht, 1988) goes still further afield.

For different aspects, see G. H. Dodge, *The Political Theory of the Huguenots of the Dispersion... Pierre furieu* (New York, 1947), W. C. Scoville, *The Persecution of the Huguenots and French economic Development* (Berkeley, 1960), and H. Lüthy, *La banque protestante...* (Paris, 1959), especially vol. 1, pp. 35–77. As a quarry of tacts and ideas the first volume of E. Labrousse, *Pierre Bayle* (The Hague, 1963), is admirable. M. de Chambrier, *Henri de Mirmand* (Neuchâtel, 1910), although hard to find, is a wonderful old book on the exile in Switzerland and Germany, while D. F. Poujol, *Histoire et influence des églises wallonnes dans les Pays-Bas* (Paris, 1902), is good on the Huguenot side of its subject. E. de Beer, 'The Revocation of the Edict of Nantes and English public opinion', in *Proceedings ...Huguenot Society of London*, vol. 18 (1947–52) describes some of the results in England.

(3)   For the intellectual scene the following are valuable: I. B. Cohen, *The Newtonian Revolution* (Cambridge, 1980), G. E. Christianson, *In the Presence of the Creator: Isaac Newton and his Times* (New York, 1984) and *Archives of the Scientific Revolution*, ed. M. Hunter (Woodbridge, 1998); R. W. Meyer, *Leibniz and the Seventeenth-Century Revolution* (Cambridge, 1952); A. M. Barnes, *Jean Le Clerc... et la république des lettres* (Paris, 1938); P. Dudon, *Michel Molinos* (Paris, 1921); P. D. Walker, *The Decline of Hell* (London, 1964); W. I. Hull, *Benjamin Furley and Quakerism in Rotterdam* (Swartmore, 1941); and R. Mandrou, *Magistrats et sorciers en France au XVIIe siècle* (Paris, 1968). Finally P. Hazard, *The European Mind 1680–1715* (edn London, 1953) is a rightly famous work, although one must beware of antedating the developments which it traces with verve and sympathy.

Chapter 12   Epilogue

The Anglo-Dutch Moment (Cambridge, 1991), ed. J. I. Israel; *The Revolutions of 1688*, ed. R. Beddard (Oxford, 1991); J. Orcibal, *Louis XIV contre Innocent XI* (Paris, 1949); M. Braubach, *Wilhelm von Fürstenberg 1629–1704* (Bonn, 1972) all give an idea of the Continental background to the British revolutions.

Index